Confucius Now

Contemporary Encounters with the *Analects*

Edited by

David Jones

OPEN COURT

Chicago and La Salle, Illinois

To order books from Open Court, call 1-800-815-2280 or visit
www.opencourtbooks.com.

Open Court Publishing Company is a division of Carus Publishing Company.

Printed and bound in the United States of America.

Library of Congress Cataloging-in-Publication Data

Confucius now : contemporary encounters with the analects / edited by David
Jones.
    p. cm.
    Summary: "A collection of essays on the teachings of the ancient Chinese
philosopher Confucius as collected in the Analects, focusing on the relevance
of Confucius's project for contemporary life and scholarship"—Provided by
publisher.
  Includes bibliographical references and index.
    ISBN-13: 978-0-8126-9610-3 (trade paper : alk. paper)
    ISBN-10: 0-8126-9610-7 (trade paper : alk. paper) 1. Philosophy,
Confucian. 2. Confucius. Lun yu. I. Jones, David Edward.
    B127.C65C67 2007
    181'.112—dc22
                                2007040710

Contents

PART 3
SELF-CULTIVATION IN CONFUCIUS

PART 4
SPIRITUAL CULTIVATION IN CONFUCIUS

PART 5
MORAL CULTIVATION IN CONFUCIUS

Introduction

Confucius Now: Contemporary Encounters with the Analects provides a foundational narrative of resonating voices that articulate the contemporary importance of Kongzi, or Confucius, one of the world's greatest teachers and philosophical thinkers. Confucius is China's first great teacher and the life's blood of what it means to be Chinese today, even after the Cultural Revolution that attempted to eradicate all that was religious in China. But the religion of China never really accustomed itself to the views of transcendence embraced by the Abrahamic traditions of Judaism, Christianity, and Islam or those found in pre-Buddhist India. The Chinese religious sensibility emerged as an immanent practice that sought harmony over freedom, consensus over choice, intimacy over integrity, and communitarianism over individualism. These religious sensibilities find their clearest and fullest expressions in the philosophies of China, especially in the philosophy of its first master, Kongzi.

This book is in many ways a religious book. Its religiosity is akin to the human spirituality found in Confucius's own thinking, in his own words compiled into the "ordered sayings" (*Lunyu*, or *Analects*) by his students, and in the spirituality of the Chinese people that these ordered sayings reflect. For Confucius, this spirituality is irrevocably social, as Henry Rosemont, Jr., and Roger T. Ames, two of our contributors, often say, and there is nothing more natural than human sociability. And as Edward Slingerland, another contributor, has written in his translation of the *Analects*, "the social world should function in the same effortless, wu-wei fashion as the natural world."[1] To learn to be natural and effortless, to be *wu-wei*, with our fellow human beings is a philosophical and religious challenge that is clearly and insightfully articulated by the writers in this volume.

One goal of *Confucius Now* is to celebrate the revival of Master Kong's teachings. The contributors of this book have all contributed to putting Confucius back on the radar screens of academic philosophers and the thoughtful general public. This is especially so of Herbert Fingarette, Roger Ames, Henry Rosemont, Jr., Philip J. Ivanhoe, Edward Slingerland, and Kwong-loi Shun. In his landmark book *Confucius: The Secular as Sacred*, Herbert Fingarette, who came out of retirement for this project, was looking for an alternative to Western philosophizing, especially the way Westerners approached their ethical lives. He turned to Confucius and initially found him to be "a prosaic and parochial moralizer" and "his collected sayings, the *Analects*, seemed . . . an archaic irrelevance." As a young student, my impression of the Master was similar to Professor Fingarette's, but over the years through a generation of translations of the *Analects* such as Arthur Waley's, D. C. Lau's, Roger Ames and Henry Rosemont's, and Edward Slingerland's (and there are other fine ones) I overcame that original reaction and came to the same conclusion as Herbert Fingarette: "Later, and with increasing force, I found him a thinker with profound insight and with an imaginative vision of man equal in its grandeur to any I know."[2] The profound insight and imaginative vision of Confucius and its reach into the future is not expressed in any volume better than this current one.

Another reason for compiling this book is to put into some form of practice what Confucius taught—the intergenerelationality of teacher and student. The distinguished Confucian scholars present in this volume—Herbert Fingarette, Roger Ames, P. J. Ivanhoe, Henry Rosemont, Jr., and Kwong-loi Shun—bring some of their best students, themselves now rising in the ranks, with them: Jim Behuniak, Sor-hoon Tan, Ni Peimin, Mary I. Bockover, Amy Olberding, Hui-chieh Loy, Jeffrey Richey, and Edward Slingerland. This book celebrates the relationship between teachers and students by bringing them together, often for the very first time, by providing a forum for their voices to resonate with each other and sometimes even to disagree. Being irreducibly social, the relationship between student and teacher is one of the most important we have.

Confucius Now represents a historic occasion because it not only brings together some of the rising stars in Confucian scholarship with their teachers, but also brings together scholars never appearing in the same book before. The Confucian table is a large one with room for varying interpretations of the great master, and it is a place for conversation, for it is through conversation that families flourish and robust relationships ensue, and the family is central to Confucianism.

We begin our encounter with the *Analects* through the recreation of a portion of the book that inaugurated Western philosophical interest to the philosophy of Confucius. In "Discovering the *Analects*," Herbert Fingarette reworks his ideas from *Confucius: The Secular as Sacred*. He begins by saying, "There is no doubt that the world of the *Analects* is profoundly different in its quality from that of Moses, Aeschylus, Jesus, Gautama Buddha, Laozi, or the Upanishadic teachers. In most respects the *Analects* represents the world of a humanist and a traditionalist. He is, however, sufficiently traditional to render a kind of pragmatic homage, when necessary, to the spirits." Fingarette proceeds to his main concern, *li*, the rites or ritual propriety. The importance of *li* can never be underestimated, and we owe a debt to Herbert Fingarette for bringing attention to its supreme significance with the publication of *Confucius: The Secular as Sacred*. As we recall, Yan Hui, Confucius's most exemplary student and beloved disciple, inquires about *ren*, authoritative conduct or benevolence, and is told how to become *ren* in the following way: "Do not look at anything that violates the observance of ritual propriety; do not listen to anything that violates the observance of ritual propriety; do not speak about anything that violates the observance of ritual propriety; do not do anything that violates the observance of ritual propriety" (12.1). As Fingarette says,

> Holy rite [*li*] is thus a luminous point of concentration, concrete symbol, and expression of the ideally all-inclusive human harmony, the *dao* or ideal Way, the perfectly humane civilization. Human life in its entirety finally appears as one vast, spontaneous and holy rite: the community of humans. This, for Confucius, was indeed an ultimate concern. It was, he said, again and again, the only thing that mattered, mattered more than the individual's life itself.

To find this "luminous point of concentration," this holographic entry point into the "all-inclusive harmony" is the natural way for Confucius. This way is the way of heaven, or *tian*.

Having set the stage for a more direct encounter with the *Lunyu*, David Jones ushers readers through parts of the text in "Walking the Way In-Between with Confucius: *Tianwen* and Emerging Patterns of Human Heavens." In this chapter, he introduces readers to a theme that emerges from or underwrites all the chapters in the book—the nature of the self and how this conception promotes a new ground of in-betweenness for our ethical and religious lives. Following Fingarette's lead, Jones argues that Confucius defines the self relationally, that is, as a being in context. Self-cultivation will then entail reflecting upon those relationships and roles that constitute the self and developing an enthusiasm for the engagement of perfecting those ever-changing relationships and roles.

The challenge to find meaning in this world of dynamic human relationships is taken up in the next section of the book, "Thinking Through Confucius." In "Paronomasia: A Confucian Way of Making Meaning," Roger Ames concerns himself with the problem of meaning in the *Lunyu*. He suggests that the pervasive concern throughout the text is a sensitivity to the proper use of language. To become authoritative in one's conduct, to engage in the requisite practice of self-cultivation, is to get language right and be sensitive to its nuance because "for Confucius, 'saying' and 'doing' are inseparable." Hence, according to Ames, "the expectation is that we are not just 'discovering' definitions about an existing world, but actively delineating a world and bringing it into being." Semantic and phonetic associations will explain terms in the *Analects* metaphorically or paronomastically. Such a paronomastic process mirrors the content of Confucius's teaching. In a world constituted by conditioning relations and roles, meaning cannot be traced to any singular source. Rather, meaning arises through the cultivation of relations in particular contexts as co-creative acts. For Ames, paronomasia is the way of making meaning in a communicating community.

The issue of meaning is also addressed in "Confucius on Form and Uniqueness" by James Behuniak, Jr., who examines formalism in the *Analects*. He argues that Confucian formalism is more than just congruity to form. Forms, for Confucius and subsequent Confucians, serve greater functions than the preservation of formal details. Behuniak submits that Confucius adheres to form not simply to accord with the past, but rather to promote a unique present. The production of a unique present is seen in the roles of the self, which is the focus of the chapter. For Confucius, the teacher/student relationship, where roles are clearly demarcated, is one of the best examples of co-creating a unique present. Consequently, the ability to "realize the new" is the most desirable trait to be found in Confucius's students; this is especially seen in Yan Hui, who Confucius recognizes for his ability to take what is given and extend his learning into new terrain. It is Yan Hui, Confucius's favorite pupil, who "being told one thing, realizes ten" (5.9). Confucius expects his students to make new connections with what he initially gives them. When giving students one corner of the square, Confucius expects them to "return with the other three" (7.8).

Sor-hoon Tan picks up this theme of co-creativity of a meaningful unique present in her "Three Corners for One: Tradition and Creativity in the *Analects*." By looking at the meaning of *chuan tong* (tradition) in Confucianism, Tan opts for an understanding of the transmission of a high-order tradition. High-order tradition is "the intellectual and spiritual crystallization from low-order tradition," which includes the customs and habits of the people. High-order tradition promotes "the creation of founders of religions, sages, artists, and thinkers." As such, high-order tradition links the past to the future by being dynamic and constantly evolving. It represents the transmission of Confucius into contemporary times since it is "a very selective part of the past that has been deliberately cultivated, preserved, and transmitted because it is considered valuable." In other words, what is transmitted is meant to be put to use because it is worth transmitting through learning and teaching, and there is a necessary freedom in what one chooses to transmit. According to Tan, "freedom in the Confucian context *emerges* in experience—freedom is the product of self-cultivation." The creativity found in the *Analects* is always situational and interpretative and uses past experiences to create new unique experiences and fashion a better future.

The next section focuses more specifically on self-cultivation. In "The 'Golden Rule' in the *Analects*," P. J. Ivanhoe organizes his discussion around three prominent questions concerning the "Golden Rule" in the *Analects*: Why does Kongzi employ two terms, *zhong* and *shu*, to describe the "one thread" of his Way? Second, does a given interpretation explain the apparent order and relative degree of difficulty that Kongzi seems to attribute to *zhong* and *shu*? And, what role does the interpretation of the Golden Rule play in a larger account of Kongzi's ethical philosophy? In addressing these questions, Ivanhoe suggests *zhong* is dispositional in its concern with moral self-discipline and that it keeps one attentive to the performance of role-specific duties vis-à-vis how one wishes to be served by others. In other words, "Those who are *zhong* are 'conscientious' about their obligations and seek to understand and fulfill them by imagining." By imagining how one would like to be treated if in another's place allows practitioners to realize what appropriate (*yi*) behavior is. *Zhong* then is prior to *shu* "for one must first steep oneself in the Way in order to understand and appreciate the goods internal to this distinctive form of life." *Shu* complements *zhong*, for it refines and enhances the practice of *zhong*. In practical terms, *shu* comes into play once one has started to master the *li*, or rites. According to Ivanhoe, "We need to understand what it is to perform our duties to others before we come to appreciate how to fulfill our obligations in a caring and sensitive manner." Hence, "the goal of self-cultivation is to take on a good second nature through a protracted course of study, practice, and reflection rather than to develop and express any innate inclination to follow and enjoy moral action."

Developing a "good second nature" is further investigated by Edward Slingerland in his "Crafts and Virtues: The Paradox of *Wu-wei* in the *Analects*." Slingerland refers to *wu-wei*, or "effortless action," as a spiritual ideal that is "a kind of unselfconscious, effortless mastery of ritual and other Confucian practices attained through a lifetime of rigorous training in traditional cultural forms." In his essay, he addresses the "paradox of *wu-wei*"—how can one be trained to unconsciously and spontaneously love *dao*, the way, if one does not already love it? To put the paradox in another way, "If such a feeling needs to be instilled through training . . . we have the problem of how one can try not to try. . . ." Following the work of George Lakoff and Mark Johnson, who are the most prominent advocates of the view that conceptual metaphor plays a central role in human cognition and serves as a primary tool for reasoning about ourselves and the world, Slingerland analyzes *wu-wei* as sharing its conceptual schema structure with two main "families" of metaphoric expressions, that fall under the rubric of "effortlessness," but differ slightly from each other in their conceptual structure. The first family is "following" (following, *cong* 從; following/adapting to, *yin* 因; leaning on, *yi* 依; and flowing along with, *shun* 順) and the second family of metaphors is the "at ease" family that expresses the same concept of effortlessness but in slightly different form (at ease/at rest, *an* 安; relaxed, *jian* 簡, *shu* 舒; still, *jing* 靜; at rest, *xi* 息, *she* 舍, *xiu* 休; wandering/rambling, *xiaoyao* 逍遙, *fanghuang* 彷徨; and playing/wandering, *you* 遊). In the "following" family the subject surrenders control and physical impetus to the Self, and in the "at ease" family the focus is on a unitary Subject portrayed as simply resting or not exerting force, with no mention of the Self. Conceptually, the difference in structure between these two families is rather slight, which leads to the two types of metaphors being used together in an interchangeable manner. These two families of metaphors form the core of the *wu-wei* constellation and determine its basic conceptual structure. Further, this basic structure motivates other sets of conceptually related metaphors such as the "losing/forgetting" family. Once again, as we saw in Ames's analysis of semantic and phonetic associations of how terms are explained metaphorically and paronomastically in the *Analects*, Slingerland further shows how the process of language mirrors the content of Confucius's teaching.

In "Slowing Death Down: Mourning in the *Analects*," Amy Olberding reorients us back to the practice of self-cultivation. The practice of cultivating the self will invariably lead us to the question of how to manage death. By closely looking at the issue of mourning throughout the *Analects*, she focuses on what might best be considered Confucius's failure of mourning, that is, the arrangements made for the funeral and burial of Yan Hui, Confucius's most beloved student. Attending to the passages concerning Yan Hui's death and burial, she examines Confucius's claims about the efficacy and meaning of mourning *in situ*, in a circumstance in which Confucius struggles to apply his own strategies for handling grief. By distinguishing mourning from grief, she concludes that mourning is culturally constructed and has its home in the public space; it is in this public space where the meanings of its various signs and ritualized behaviors reside. Hence, mourning is wholly artifice that formalizes and regulates the expression of sorrow. Grief, on the other hand, may be wholly private. The question becomes, how does one engage in robust mourning? Olberding shows that Confucius's therapy for loss is predicated on the view that there are a variety of "reasons" or antecedent beliefs, which do not all have equal merit, that may create the conditions for grief. She concludes that "while it is important to recognize the way in which grief comes unbidden at the moment of loss, its origins in the ways we choose to formulate value must not be neglected." This formulation of value appreciates and affirms the death of the other as a "frantic clawing at a spur of rock, the rock of a hoped for self, an achieved self. Yet death denies this achievement. To slow down and prolong this experience is to forego retreat, to spurn any saving numbness, and to remain, suspended in a place where nothing can block a lonely thought." Foregoing this retreat reveals to oneself how fragile one's own life is and allows one to "see the vista opened by death." Through mourning, grief becomes present as the appreciation of the pain that one realizes at the moment of loss that is "also that instance in which I am most exquisitely human."

Learning to be exquisitely human is the subject of the next section, "Spiritual Cultivation in Confucius." In his "An Unintegrated Life Is Not Worth Living," Henry Rosemont, Jr., writes, "For myself, a signal criterion for measuring our understanding of the text is an increasing desire to follow the Master's pedagogic practices and share the text with others whom we believe also share our basic concerns about how best to lead our all-too-human lives." Not only does the text of the *Analects* have intrinsic historical value, but also it speaks clearly about the problems of the present. This present, according to Rosemont, is a present that is "becoming ever more fragmented aesthetically, morally, and politically, and barren spiritually—with violence more the rule than the exception today." Perhaps unlike most other of the world's religions or spiritual traditions, classical Confucianism, without monks, nuns, anchorites, or hermits, contemplates only doing what is appropriate in the human's manifold relational roles as child, parent, neighbor, sibling, friend, student, spouse, and so forth. This is the *ren dao*, the human way. These roles are what constitute a self. Hence, our "moral and political lives are not and cannot be distinct from our spiritual development, but are essential to it." Such an emphasis places Confucianism in a unique position among the world's religions and refocuses human beings to live a uniquely authentic and authoritative life among others. Some will be more adept at it than others, but the Confucian project encourages all to move along the way. Some will be *sheng* (sages), others *junzi* (exemplary persons), and there will be *shi* (apprentices). "All *sheng* are *junzi*, and all *junzi* were formerly *shi*, but the converse does not hold. These are, in other words, ranked types of persons, and the ranking is based on a progression from scholarly apprenticeship to sagehood: *shi* are, relatively speaking, fairly numerous; *junzi* are scarcer, and *sheng* are very few and very far between, owing to 'the heaviness of the burden, and the distance of the journey'" (*Analects* 8.7). In the final analysis, the *sheng* are at the highest end of the continuum of what constitutes a human being because not only do they possess the qualities of the *junzi*, they "feel customs, rituals, and tradition—the *li*—holistically, as defining and integrating the whole of human society, and as defining and integrating as well the human societies of the past, and of the future." This seeing and feeling is a union of self and all others, and as Rosemont says, an "at-one-ment."

To feel "at-one-ment" means at some level to be embodied. It is to this embodiment that Peimin Ni directs his attention. In "*Gongfu*—A Vital Dimension of Confucian Teaching," Ni reminds his readers that unlike in the West, where the term *gongfu* is used narrowly to refer to martial arts (*kungfu*), in China its most common meaning is the time spent, and by extension, the effort spent on something. Additional meanings refer to the proper and effective ways of making an effort or spending time, instructions on how to make such efforts, and the function, effect, or manifestation of the abilities. As seen in other essays, these meanings cluster with each other, are mutually connected, and promote polysemy: the words have multiple meanings in varying contexts. Having embodied abilities is to be the sage, to act with *wu-wei*, to feel the *li*, and to enact the *li* appropriately without effort. Ni's reading of Confucianism as a *gongfu* system means to take Confucian teachings as instructions or prescriptions about how to conduct one's life; it means to take Confucianism as a system of knowledge about "how," rather than a system of knowledge about "what." By attending to knowledge of how, understanding Confucianism as a *gongfu* system involves addressing a complex of mental habits, social values, functions of language, and social institutions as foci of praxiology. Such an orientation not only helps us gain insight into Confucian teachings and corrects an excessive intellectualizing of Confucian texts, but also adds a significant dimension to living an examined life, that is, to also live a cultivated one.

Mary Bockover sees Confucianism in the West as too often treated as an exclusively ethical teaching in her "The *Ren Dao* of Confucius: A Spiritual Account of Humanity" where she argues that the spiritual framework embedding Confucian principles must be understood to do justice to the teaching. She maintains that Confucian ethics simultaneously evokes a deep respect for spirits and spiritual agency, as well as recognition that the human way (*ren dao*) is essentially entailed by and coextensive with the way of heaven (*tian dao*). She begins by deliberating on *li*, the rites or ritual propriety, and concludes that *li* are twofold in nature. First, *li* serve "the central social purpose of allowing us to recognize and respond to each other in a meaningful and civilized way" and are "the 'vessel' for cultivating human relations." The second nature of *li* is religious, because the sacred dimension of *li* links humanity to the Confucian conception of an immanent heaven and are the vehicles for its expression. For Bockover, the spiritual function of *li* is often overlooked in discussions on Confucian philosophy. It is through *li* that humanity fine-tunes its relation with the natural reality it encounters. Such a fine-tuning depends on humanity's ability to discern the past so it can move into the future through the secular and contemporary expression of *li*'s spiritual dimension. The human way (*ren dao*) is an expression of the great way of *tian*. The human way of benevolent conduct (*ren*) is ritualized in particular normative forms of *li*. *Li* provide opportunities for goodness (*ren*) to be transmitted and for personal authority and power (*de*) to be established and reciprocally expressed through roles that are relevant to one's culture. These roles have political as well as ethical dimensions. Bockover concludes by posing the questions, how might the US invasion and occupation of Iraq be judged by Confucian ethical and religious principles, and how might our leadership at this time be judged?

The final section takes up the question of moral cultivation. In "Zhu Xi and the *Lunyu*," Kwong-loi Shun looks to the legacy left by Confucius in the work of both Mengzi (Mencius) and Zhu Xi. Shun focuses on *ren* (humaneness, benevolence) as one of the most prominent concepts in the *Analects*. He reconciles the two different ways in which the neo-Confucian philosopher Zhu Xi (1130–1200) uses *ren* with Mengzi's use of *ren* (as one among the four ethical attributes of *ren, yi, li*, and *zhi*): on the one hand with Han thought, which adds the attribute of *xin* (trustworthiness), and on the other hand with his own sense of an all-encompassing ethical ideal. Zhu Xi, regarding Heaven and Earth and the ten thousand things (the totality of all that is) as originally forming one body with oneself, characterizes *ren* in the same terms. Although deviation from this all-encompassing ethical ideal is a constant challenge, the task of self-cultivation is to enlarge one's heart/mind (*xin*) until one sees everything as connected to oneself. In consort with other writers in this book, Shun shows how Zhu Xi endorses the idea that *xin*, the heart/mind of Heaven and Earth, gives life to all things. Hence, *ren* refers to a ceaseless life-giving force that runs throughout the four more specific attributes in the way that it runs through the life cycle of a plant throughout the four seasons. Shun adds, "Just as Heaven and Earth have this life-giving force as their heart/mind, human beings also have this life-giving force, namely *ren*, as their heart/mind. And just as the life-giving force of Heaven and Earth goes through the four phases . . . , *ren* in human beings also manifests itself in the four attributes of *ren*, *yi*, *li*, and *zhi*." This view of *ren* enables Zhu Xi to observe how the life-giving force manifests itself in different ethical attributes. Following the lead of Mengzi, human nature is fundamentally good and ethical failure is a deviation from the original state of being human. This original state is characterized by *ren*, "which involves one's forming one body with all things, and ethical failure is due to one's focusing inappropriately on oneself in a way that separates one from other people and things." Confucius's focus on the more practical manifestation of *ren* rather than on the nature of *ren* itself moves the Confucian discourse beyond practical considerations to a "more explicit discussion of the fundamental characteristics of the original nature of human beings."

If the self is constituted by an innate goodness, it becomes imperative to get our language correct to express that goodness as fully as possible. The *zheng-ming* doctrine (correcting names) is taken up by an analysis of passage 13.3 of the *Lunyu* by Hui-chieh Loy. His analysis resonates with much of what our other authors have written about the importance and vitality of language in the *Analects*. For Loy, Confucius's attention to language use has political as well as ethical dimensions, for it "seems that there are forms of incorrect naming and speaking that can lead to sociopolitical disorder" and that "any attempt to reinstate order in the sociopolitical realm must begin with the imposition of order on the linguistic realm." In 13.3, the conversation is between the Master and his pupil Zilu. The conversation is *in situ*; it takes place within some particular context. Loy reminds his readers that Zilu is a particular character, and that Confucius is not speaking to some unnamed audience. In addition, there is a specific point of reference to a prince who desires his services. As Loy says, "The entire conversation is presented as taking place within a fairly specific set of circumstances. That is, some occasion where it makes sense for the disciple to ask such a question." Further, Confucius's answer to Zilu is not about general politics or governance, but about "the particular policy for a particular state in a particular point in time." The conclusion Loy draws from the teaching of 13.3 is that the linguistic order is a necessary condition of sociopolitical order; and where such linguistic order is lacking, it needs to be imposed in order that sociopolitical order can be restored. He concludes by asserting that such a claim is not self-evident and posses a series of questions for further contemplation: How is the imposition of a linguistic order possible or even plausible? How is it that correct speaking can be a *necessary* condition of social-political order? How is it that correcting the way people speak can be cast in the role of an urgent policy? Is there a need to posit a belief that language possesses a magical power that has unfailing influence on affairs both human and natural? Answering these questions, he suggests, requires that we "look more broadly at the larger *Analects* teaching on language and politics" through the lens of the specific concerns of 13.3.

As one reads this excellent collection of essays, it should come as no surprise that there are clusters of resonance between teachers and students contained within, and further resonance that extends from cluster to cluster. Distinguished scholars and thinkers such as Herbert Fingarette, Henry Rosemont, Kwong-loi Shun, Roger Ames, and P. J. Ivanhoe and some of the best upcoming scholars have written essays with relevant contemporary content that are also organized around Confucius's teachings and his seminal text, the *Analects*. From the outset, the major focus has been to aim at the relevance of Confucius's project for contemporary living and philosophizing by providing clusters of papers that display the contemporary relevance of one of the world's greatest teachers, social thinkers, and spiritual leaders. The contemporary presence of this dynamic model comes through themes and topics vis-à-vis each other. It is appropriate then for readers to be exposed to the archetypal relationship of teacher-student found in the *Analects*, that of Kongzi and his most beloved student, Yan Hui.

Jeffrey L. Richey takes up this task in his "Master and Disciple in the *Analects*," where he addresses the fundamental question of "whether and how particular figures are understood by the text (which is to say, its editors and redactors) as masters or disciples." Are these words to be used interchangeably within the Confucian context or do they specify very different aspects of this particular kind of relationship? To answer this question, Richey investigates the relevant passages of Yan Hui as a student and as a disciple. It is clear there are passages in the *Analects* that present Yan Hui and Confucius as sharing common interests in particular skills and bodies of knowledge; this common interest is one of student and teacher. Yan Hui, of course, excels in particular areas of Confucius's curriculum. Not only is he a student, he is an excellent student. Richey is quick to point out that Yan Hui is "depicted as eagerly, even childishly or simple-mindedly attentive to all that Confucius has to say, sometime to the point of arousing frustration on the master's part." Yan Hui is unflinching in what comes his way from Confucius. Richey further points out that "while these episodes generally portray Yan Hui as a capable and hard-working student of Confucius, they do not hint at the intimacy between Confucius and Yan Hui that is documented in other portions of the text"; "nor do they present Yan Hui as peerless among Confucius's students." However, in other passages, Yan Hui is seen more of a disciple than student. This is an entirely different type of relationship, yet not one that excludes the other. It is the relationship of the disciple to the master that the sacred person, the *sheng*, of Confucius is seen. For Confucius, Yan Hui becomes less of an exemplary student and becomes profoundly unique. In a cluster of passages in books 6 and 11, Yan Hui is said to have truly loved learning, be consistent in his moral stamina, is irreplaceable, and causes Confucius such suffering by his untimely death. "Yan Hui! You looked on me as a father, and yet I have not been able to treat you as a son. This was none of my doing—it was your fellow students who did it" (11.11). The teaching relationship, when performed appropriately and with the appropriate disposition, is fundamentally familial.

The significance of Confucius's teaching can perhaps be best seen in its unconscious manifestation in Chinese society today. Ronald Suleski turns readers' eyes to the magnitude of Confucius's influence on the organization of contemporary Chinese society. At the outset, he poses the question: "Is it possible to understand Chinese people without knowing something about Confucius and his influence on Chinese society?" Although Confucius may appear to be irrelevant as one looks at or experiences life in the fast-moving and action-packed cities of contemporary China, the opposite is most true. By providing the necessary historical background to Confucius's long reach into the future, Suleski presents a concrete foundation for discovering the *Analects*, our connection to Confucius, and to Chinese people. A look to the past and the present is to look to the China of the future.

The intent of *Confucius Now: Contemporary Encounters with the* Analects is to celebrate the family of those of us who hold the Master dear, who put his words into practice, who strive to leave the world and our communities better than we found them, who argue over interpretation and translation, who at the end of the day return home and sit at the same table, who eat the same meal, who discuss the particular events of the day, and who slowly mourn the loss of our dead teachers.

—David Jones

Notes

1. Edward Slingerland, trans., *Confucius: Analects* (Indianapolis: Hackett, 2003), xxi.

2. Herbert Fingarette, *Confucius: The Secular as Sacred* (New York: Harper & Row, 1972), vii.

PART I

The Text and Its Spirituality

Discovering the *Analects*

Herbert Fingarette

1

When I began to read Confucius, I found him to be prosaic, parochial, a moralizer. His collected sayings, the *Analects*, seemed to me an archaic irrelevance. Then I found that because of my interest in Daoism and Buddhism, I would be teaching a course in early Chinese philosophy. How could I do this without including Confucius? And how could I in good conscience teach Confucius if he bored me? Confronting this dilemma, and the stress it engendered, I challenged myself. I could not overlook the fact that hundreds of generations of highly intelligent scholars and teachers have valued Confucius's teachings as central to their great civilization. I must be missing something, I told myself. In order to pursue the question I learned to read the *Analects* in its own language rather than secondary sources. I was rewarded far beyond my expectations.

Once on the track, I relatively quickly and with increasing force found Confucius a thinker with profound insight and an imaginative vision of human nature equal in its grandeur to any I know. Increasingly, I have become convinced that Confucius can be a teacher to us today—a major teacher, not one who merely gives us a slightly exotic perspective. He tells us things not being said elsewhere, things needing to be said. He has a new lesson to teach.

I also saw that there are distinctive insights in the *Analects* that are close in substance and spirit to various recent philosophical developments. In these respects, then, he was "ahead of our times" until recently, and this is an important reason for his having been pretty much neglected in the West for several centuries. We had not yet caught up. Now, however, we can profit from the parallels in his thinking to the new strands of Western thought, for here his way of putting the issues places them in a fresh perspective. In coming to such conclusions, I tried to avoid the natural tendency to read into a text the ideas with which one is familiar. This, I realized, was what so many Western translators and commentators had failed to avoid in spite of their impressive achievements otherwise. The tendency to find one's own ideas in an alien text is understandable and powerful. Thus, for example, Christian scholars found, and translated accordingly, the distinctive concepts in the *Analects* as foreshadowings of Christian concepts. The relatively recent Western interest in Daoism and Buddhism has, not surprisingly, generated a tendency to find Daoist or pre-Buddhist concepts in the *Analects*.

I will only say here that my primary aim — and joy, when successful — has been to discover what I believe is distinctive in Confucius, to learn what he can teach me, not to seek ideas I already have, or what others have said. Another bias that I found pervasive in modern translations of the *Analects* was the psychologizing of Confucius, particularly its subjective orientation. We in the West take the subjective, "inner" life so much for granted that reading Confucius this way is quite unselfconscious, and hence all the more prejudicial. It is my thesis that, with respect to this fundamental bias, all the extant translations have misled. If I am right, they have introduced a way of seeing human nature that loses a major, distinctive feature of Confucius's thought.

In making these claims, one of my principal resources has been the original text. I have tried to see what it says, no matter how puzzling initially, rather than to find a ready-to-hand English term that roughly fits. Such a procedure gives us, so to speak, a Western tract that happens to have been written in Chinese.

I have tried to be faithful to Confucius's images and metaphors, rather than substituting familiar Western ones that would presumably make the text easier for Western readers to understand. On the other hand, when I found, as I did, some concepts that I initially derived from Confucius, but that subsequently suggested some modern Western philosophical concepts, I profited from this.

One further thing: I have tried to stay as strictly as possible within the confines of the earlier and purportedly more authentic passages of the *Analects*, mainly the first fifteen books out of the total of twenty; and even here I have been cautious about what scholars have taken to be later interpolations into these earliest passages. After eliminating certain passages in this spirit, and on this basis, I felt that I was now dealing with a text that has unity in terms of historical-social context, in linguistic style, and in philosophical content. It is this text, and this one only, that I have tried to interpret here. I assume it is faithful to the words of the historical personage we call Confucius. In any case, it is the text that has historically been a classic ur-text in the forming of Chinese culture.

As my remarks suggest, it is consistent with my purposes and method that, not being a Sinologist myself, I have relied heavily on secondary materials and commentary by Western scholars, including, of course, their often excellent summaries of the vast lore of Chinese scholarship. But my aim throughout is philosophical. I have done my own reading in the original text. Where relevant philosophical problems were rooted in textual problems, I have tried to find how Confucius meant his words through internal textual analysis rather than by assuming that sources external to the text could settle matters.

I must therefore bear responsibility for the translations of passages offered here. They are based, however, upon wide consultation, heavy borrowing, and in a number of cases, simple quotation from leading translations and scholarly articles. My main object has been to select translations or to retranslate with an eye toward bringing out the philosophical nuances of the text. I believe I have avoided what would be considered eccentric renderings designed to force the meaning in order to support my theses.

With these methodological remarks, I turn now to results of the method. In particular I shall present an account of the first major insight I achieved, an insight I saw, and still see, as central to an appreciation of what the Teacher taught.

*   *   *   *   *

There is no doubt that the world of the *Analects* is profoundly different in its quality from that of Moses, Aeschylus, Jesus, Gautama Buddha, Laozi, or the Upanishadic teachers. In most respects the *Analects* represents the world of a humanist and a traditionalist.[1] He is, however, sufficiently traditional to render a kind of pragmatic homage, when necessary, to the spirits.

"Devote yourself to man's duties," says the Master; "respect spiritual beings but keep distance" (6.20). He suited the deed to the precept and he "never talked of prodigies, feats of strength, disorders, or spirits" (7.20). In response to direct questions about the transcendental and supernatural he said: "Until you are able to serve men, how can you serve spiritual beings? Until you know about life, how can you know about death?" (11.11).

The topics and the chief concepts in the *Analects* pertain primarily to our human nature, our comportment, and our social relationships. Some of the constantly recurring themes are rite (*li*), true humanity (*ren*), reciprocity (*shu*), loyalty (*zhong*), learning (*xue*), music (*yue*), and such social relationships as prince, father, and son.

Writers who disagree in many other ways almost all tend to agree on the secular, humanist, and rationalist orientation of Confucius. Waley says the turn toward the this-worldly was characteristic of tendencies of the age not peculiar to Confucius.[2] The this-worldly, practical humanism of the *Analects* is further deepened by the teaching that humankind's moral and spiritual achievements do not depend on tricks or luck or on esoteric spells or on any purely external agency. One's spiritual condition depends on the "stuff" one has to begin with, on the amount and quality of study and good hard work one puts into "shaping" it. Spiritual nobility calls for persistence and effort. "First the difficult . . ." (6.20). "His burden is heavy and his course is long. He has taken *ren* as his burden—is that not heavy?" (8.7). What disquieted Confucius was "leaving virtue untended and learning unperfected, hearing about what is right but not managing either to turn toward it or to reform what is evil" (7.3). The disciple of Confucius was surely all too aware that his task was one calling not for amazement and miracle but for constant "cutting, filing, carving, polishing" (1.15) in order to become a fully and truly human being, a worthy participant in society. All this seems the very essence of the antimagical in outlook. Nor does it have the aura of the Divine.

Yet, in spite of this dedicated and apparently secular prosaic moralism, we also find occasional comments in the *Analects* which seem to reveal a belief in magical powers of profound importance.[3] By "magic" I mean the power of a specific person to accomplish his will directly and effortlessly through ritual, gesture, and incantation. The user of magic does not work by strategies and devices as a means toward an end; he does not use coercion or physical forces. He simply wills the end in the proper ritual setting and with the proper ritual gesture and word. Without further effort on his part, the deed is accomplished. Confucius's words at times strongly suggest some fundamental magical power as central to this way.

"Is *ren* (true humanity) far away? As soon as I want it, it is here" (7.29). "Self-disciplined and ever turning to *li* (ritual, ceremony) — everyone in the world will respond to his *ren*" (12.1). Shun, the great sage-ruler, "merely placed himself gravely and reverently with his face due South (the ruler's ritual posture); that was all" (i.e., and the affairs of his reign proceeded without flaw) (15.4). The magical element always involves great effects produced effortlessly, marvelously, with an irresistible power that is itself intangible, invisible, unmanifest. "With correct comportment, no commands are necessary, yet affairs proceed" (13.6). "The character of a noble man is like wind, that of ordinary men like grass; when the wind blows the grass must bend" (12.19). "To govern by *de* (the 'magical' power) is to be like the North Polar Star; it remains in place while all the other stars revolve in homage about it" (2.1).

Such comments can be taken in various ways. Duyvendak remarks that the "original magical meaning" of 2.1 is "unmistakable," or that the ritual posture of Shun in 15.4 is "a state of the highest magical potency."[4] In short, one may admit that these are genuine residues of "superstition" in the *Analects*.

However, many modern interpreters of the *Analects* have wished to read Confucius more "sympathetically," that is, as one whose philosophic claims would have maximum validity for us in our own familiar and accepted terms. To do this, these commentators have generally tried to minimize to the irreducible the magical claims in the *Analects*. For it is accepted as an axiom in our times that the goal of direct action by incantation and ritual gesture cannot be taken as a serious possibility. (The important exception to this generalization will be discussed below.)

The suggestion of magic and marvel so uncongenial to the contemporary taste may be dissipated in various ways. Only one of the sayings I have quoted comes from the portion of the *Analects* — books 3 to 8 — in which most of the text has widely been accepted as "authentic." The other sayings might be among the many interpolations, often alien in spirit to Confucius, which are known to be in the received text of the *Analects*. Or one might hold that the magical element is quite restricted in scope, tacitly meant to apply only to the ruler or even only to the perfect ruler. Still another possible method of "interpreting away" the "magical" statements is to suppose that Confucius was merely emphasizing and dramatizing the otherwise familiar power of setting a good example.[5] In short, on this view we must take the "magical" sayings as being poetic statements of a prosaic truth. Finally, one might simply argue that Confucius was not consistent on the issue—perhaps that he was mainly and characteristically antimagic, but, as might well be expected, he had not entirely freed himself of deep-rooted traditional beliefs.

Rather than engage in polemics regarding these other interpretations, I shall devote the remainder of my remarks to a positive exposition of what I take to be the genuine and sound magical view of humans in Confucius's teaching. I do not hold that my interpretation is correct to the exclusion of all others. There is no reason to suppose that an innovator such as Confucius distinguishes all possible meanings of what he says and consciously intends only one of these meanings to the exclusion of all others. One should assume the contrary. Of the various meanings of the Confucian magical teaching, I believe the one to be elaborated in the following remarks is authentic and central.

Confucius saw, and tried to call to our attention, that the truly, distinctively human powers have, characteristically, a magical quality. His task, therefore, required that he reveal what is already so familiar and universal as to be unnoticed. What is necessary in such cases is that one comes upon this "obvious" dimension of our existence in a new way, in the right way.

One has to labor long and hard to learn *li*. Although the word in its root meaning is close to "holy ritual," "sacred ceremony," Confucius places it in a larger context. He uses it as a conceptual framework within which to talk about the entire body of the mores, or more precisely, of the authentic tradition and reasonable conventions of society.[6] Confucius taught that the ability to act according to *li* and the will to submit to *li* are essential to the exercise of *de*. *De* is the perfect and peculiarly human power. Confucius thus does three things here: he calls our attention to the entire body of tradition and convention, ascribes a distinctive "magical" power to one who follows these, and calls upon us to see all this by means of a metaphor, through the imagery of sacred ceremony, holy rite.

The true noble man (*junzi*) is one who has labored at the alchemy of fusing social forms (*li*) and raw personal capacities in such a way that they are transmuted into a way of being which realizes *ren* and the power of *de*. *De* is realized in concrete acts of human intercourse. These have certain general features. They are all expressive of "true humanity" (*ren*), and hence of reciprocal loyalty and respect (*zhong*; *shu*). But the patterns are also specific: they differentiate and they define in detail the ritual performance-repertoires which constitute civilized, that is, truly human patterns of mourning, marrying, and fighting, of being a prince, a father, a son, and so on.

However, men are by no means conceived as being mere standardized units mechanically carrying out prescribed routines in the service of some cosmic or social law. On the other hand, neither are human beings self-sufficient, individual souls who happen to consent to a social contract. We become truly human when *li* is authentic, the civilized, living expression of it. *Li* is not a formalistic dehumanization. It is the specifically humanizing form of the dynamic relation of human-to-human.

The novel and creative insight of Confucius was to see this aspect of human existence, its form as learned tradition and convention, in terms of a particular revelatory image: *li*, that is, "holy rite," "sacred ceremony," in the usual meaning of the term prior to Confucius.

In well-learned ceremony, each person does what he is supposed to do according to a pattern. My gestures are coordinated harmoniously with yours—though neither of us has to force, push, demand, compel, or otherwise "make" this happen. Our gestures are in turn smoothly followed by those of the other participants, all effortlessly. If all are "self-disciplined, ever turning to *li*," then all that is needed—quite literally—is an initial ritual gesture in the proper ceremonial context; from there onward everything "happens." What action did Shun (the Sage-ruler) take? "He merely placed himself gravely and reverently with his face due south; that was all" (15.4). Let us consider in at least a little detail the distinctive features of action emphasized by this revelatory image of holy rite.

It is important that we do not think of this effortlessness as "mechanical" or "automatic." If that is so, then, as Confucius repeatedly indicates, the ceremony is dead, sterile, and empty: there is no spirit in it. The truly ceremonial "takes place"; there is a kind of spontaneity. It happens "of itself." There is life in it because the individuals involved do it with seriousness and sincerity. For ceremony to be authentic one must "participate in the sacrifice;" otherwise it is as if one "did not sacrifice at all" (3.12). To put it another way, there are two contrasting kinds of failure in carrying out *li*: the ceremony may be awkwardly performed for lack of learning and skill; or the ceremony may have a surface slickness but yet be dull, mechanical for lack of serious purpose and commitment. Beautiful and effective ceremony requires the personal "presence" to be fused with learned ceremonial skill. This ideal fusion is true *li* as sacred rite.

Confucius characteristically and sharply contrasts the ruler who uses *li* with the ruler who seeks to attain his ends by means of commands, threats, regulations, punishments, and force (2.3). The force of coercion is manifest and tangible, whereas the vast (and sacred) forces at work in *li* are invisible and intangible. *Li* works through spontaneous coordination rooted in reverent dignity. The perfection in holy rite is esthetic as well as spiritual.

Having considered *li* as holy ceremony in a broad Confucian sense of the concept, we are now prepared to consider its relevance to more everyday aspects of life. This is in effect what Confucius invites us to do; it is the foundation for his perspective on humankind.

I see you on the street; I smile, walk toward you, and put out my hand to shake yours. And behold—without any command, stratagem, force, special tricks or tools, without any effort on my part to make you do so, you spontaneously turn toward me, return my smile, raise your hand toward mine. We shake hands—not by my pulling your hand up and down or your pulling mine, but by spontaneous and perfect cooperative action. Normally we do not notice the subtlety and amazing complexity of this coordinated "ritual" act. This subtlety and complexity become very evident, however, if one has to learn the ceremony only from a book of instructions, or if one is a foreigner from a non-handshaking culture. The smile must be there if the act is one of friendly greeting, the handclasp strength, the duration, the eye contact, the tone of voice—all this and more must be within a certain range for each. Yet within this framework there is room for individual style and meaning. It is not rote behavior if it is genuine *li*. The "ritual" has "life" in it; we are "present" to each other, at least to some minimal extent.

As Confucius said, there are always the general and fundamental requirements of reciprocal good faith and respect. This mutual respect is present in the act but usually not as a conscious feeling. If I am too aware of a respect for you, I am much more likely to be piously fatuous or perhaps self-consciously embarrassed; and no doubt our little "ceremony" will reveal this in certain awkwardness. I may put out my hand too soon, and be left with it hanging in midair. The authenticity of the mutual respect is fully expressed in the correct "live" and spontaneous performance of the act. Just as an aerial acrobat must possess (but not think about his) complete trust in his partner if the trick is to come off, so we who shake hands, though the stakes are less, must have (but not think about) respect and trust. Otherwise we find ourselves fumbling awkwardly or performing in a lifeless fashion, which easily conveys its meaninglessness to the other.

Clearly it is not necessary that our reciprocal respect and good faith go very far in order for us to accomplish a reasonably successful handshake and greeting. Yet even here, the sensitive person can often plumb the depths of another's attitude from a handshake. This depth of human relationship expressible in a "ceremonial" gesture is in good part possible because of the remarkable specificity of the ceremony. For example, if I am your former teacher, you will spontaneously be rather obvious in walking toward me rather than waiting for me to walk toward you. You will allow a certain subtle reserve in your handshake, even though it will be warm. You will not slap me on the back, though conceivably I might grasp you by the shoulder with my free hand. There are indescribably many subtleties in the distinctions, nuances, and minute but meaningful variations in gesture. If we do try to describe these subtle variations and their rules, we immediately sound like book 10 of the *Analects*, whose ceremonial recipes initially seem to the modern American reader the quintessence of quaint and extreme traditionalism. It is in just such ways that social activity is coordinated in civilized society, without effort or planning, but simply by spontaneously initiating the appropriate ritual gesture in an appropriate setting. This power of *li*, Confucius says, depends upon prior learning. It is not inborn. What we learn is enormously complex, sometimes difficult to achieve.

The effortless power of *li* can also be used to accomplish physical ends, though we usually do not think of it this way. Let us suppose I wish to transfer a book from my office to my classroom. If I have no magic powers, I must literally take steps—walk to my office, push the door open, lift the book with my own muscles, and physically carry it back.

Instead I may use the magic of *li*. With no such effort on my part I turn politely, that is, ceremonially, to one of my students in class and merely express in an appropriate and polite (ritual) formula my wish that she bring me the book. This proper ceremonial expression of my wish is all; I do not need to force her, threaten her, or trick her. I do not need to do anything more myself. In almost no time the book is in my hands, as I wished! This is a uniquely human way of getting things done, far more complicated things than this simple achievement.

The examples of handshaking and of making a request are humble; the moral is profound. These complex but familiar gestures are characteristic of human relationships at their most human: we are least like anything else in the world when we do not treat each other as physical objects, as animals, or even as subhuman creatures to be driven, threatened, forced, maneuvered. Looking at these "ceremonies" through the image of *li*, we realize how rite that is literally sacred can be seen as an emphatic, intensified, and sharply elaborated extension of everyday civilized intercourse.

The notion that we can use speech only to talk about action or indirectly to evoke action has dominated modern Western thought. Yet modern philosophical analyses of everyday speech have shown how much the ritual word can also be a critical act rather than a report of, or stimulus to, action. The late Professor J. L. Austin was one of those who brought the reality and pervasiveness of this phenomenon into a focus in his analyses of what he called the "performative utterance."[7] These are the innumerable statements we make which function somewhat like the "operative" clause in a legal instrument. They are statements, but they are not statements *about* some act; they are the very execution of the act itself.

"I give and bequeath my watch to my brother," duly said or written is not a report of what I have already done but is the very act of bequeathal itself. In a marriage ceremony, the "I do" is not a report of an inner mental act of acceptance; it is itself the act which seals my part of the bargain. "I promise . . ." is not a report of what I have done a moment before inside my head, nor is it indeed a report of anything at all; the uttering of the words is itself the act of promising. It is by words, and by the ceremony of which the words form a part, that I bind myself in a way which, for a man "ever turning to *li*," is more powerful, more inescapable, than strategies or force. Confucius truly tells us that those who use *li* can influence those who are stronger, but this is not so for those who have only physical force at their command. Physical force, unlike the power of *de*, is limited by space and time and quantity.

There is no power of *li* if there is no learned and accepted convention, or if we utter the words and invoke the power of the convention in an inappropriate setting, or if the ceremony is not fully carried out, or if the persons carrying out the ceremonial roles are not those properly authorized ("authorization"—again a ceremony). In short, the peculiarly moral yet binding power of ceremonial gesture and word cannot be abstracted from or used in isolation from the totality of the ceremony. It is not a distinct power we bring to the ceremony; it is the power of ceremony. I can bequeath some of my property to someone only if in my community there is an accepted convention for bequeathal. I cannot bet two dollars if no one completes the bet by accepting. I cannot legally plead guilty to a crime while eating dinner at home.

There are myriad formulae for performing actions. Many words and phrases do not obviously express action, though that is what they are. "I'd like the Cobb salad," said to the waiter is not a psychological report but the act of giving one's order.[8]

*   *   *   *   *

The power of *li* cannot be used except as the *li* is fully respected. This, too, is Confucius's constant refrain. "The Three Families used the Yung Song . . . what possible application can such words have in the Hall of the Three Families?" (who were not entitled, according to *li*, to use this song) (3.2).

Professor Austin came to the conclusion that ultimately all utterances may in some essential way be performative. It was a basic thesis of Pragmatist philosophies that we use words to do things, profoundly important and amazingly varied things. Although not fully appreciated, the central lesson of these philosophical insights is not so much a lesson about language as it is about ceremony, which includes both gesture and words. What we have come to see as a result of this line of thought is how vast the area of human existence is in which the substance of that existence is the ceremony. Promises, commitments, excuses, pleas, compliments, and pacts—these and so much more are ceremonies or they are nothing. It is thus in the medium of ceremony that the peculiarly human part of our life is lived.

The ceremonial act is the primary, irreducible interpersonal event.[9] Language and gesture cannot be understood in isolation from the conventional practice in which they are rooted. No purely physical motion is a promise; no word alone, independent of ceremonial context, circumstances, and roles can be a promise. Word and motion are only abstractions from the concrete ceremonial act.

From this standpoint, it is easy to see that not only motor skills must be learned but also correct use of language. For correct use of language is constitutive of effective action as gesture is. Correct language is not merely a useful adjunct; it is part of the essence of executing the ceremony.

*   *   *   *   *

From this perspective we see that the famous Confucian doctrine of *zhengming*, the "rectification of terms" or "correct use of terminology," is not merely an erroneous belief in word-magic or a pedantic elaboration of Confucius's concern with teaching tradition. Nor do I see any reason to read into it a doctrine of "essences" or Platonic Ideas, or analogous medieval-age neo-Confucian notions.[10] The *Analects* provides no other hint of any such doctrines.

Of course we must be leery of reading our own contemporary philosophical doctrines into an ancient teaching. Yet I think that the text of the *Analects*, in letter and spirit, supports, but, more importantly, vastly broadens and enriches our own more recent linguistic analyses.

In general, what Confucius brings out in connection with the workings of ceremony is not only its distinctively human character, its linguistic and magical character, but also its moral and religious character. Here, finally, we must recall and place at the focus of our analysis the fact that for Confucius it is the imagery of Holy Ceremony that unifies and infuses all these dimensions of human existence. Perhaps a modern Westerner would be tempted to speak of the "intelligent practice of learned conventions and language." This has a fashionably value-free, "scientific" ring. But this quite fails to accomplish what Confucius's central image did.

The image of holy rite as a metaphor of human existence brings foremost to our attention the dimension of the holy in man's existence. There are several dimensions of holy rite that culminate in its holiness. Rite brings out forcefully the harmony and beauty of social forms and the inherent and ultimate dignity of human intercourse. It brings out also the moral perfection implicit in achieving one's ends by dealing with others as beings of equal dignity, as free coparticipants in *li*. Furthermore, to act by ceremony is to be completely open to the other for ceremony is public, shared, and transparent. It is in this beautiful and dignified, shared and open, participation with others who are ultimately like ourselves (12.2) that we realize—make fully real—our humanity. Thus perfect community is the Confucian analogue to Christian brotherhood.

Confucius wanted to teach us, as a corollary, that sacred ceremony in its narrower, root meaning is not a totally mysterious appeasement of spirits external to human and earthly life. Spirit is no longer an external being influenced by the ceremony; it is that which is expressed and comes most alive in the ceremony. Instead of being a diversion of attention from the human realm to another transcendent realm, the holy ceremony is to be seen as the central symbol manifesting the holy as a dimension of all truly human existence.

Holy rite is thus a luminous point of concentration, concrete symbol, and expression of the ideally all-inclusive human harmony, the *dao* or ideal Way, the perfectly humane civilization. Human life in its entirety finally appears as one vast, spontaneous, and holy rite: the community of humans. This, for Confucius, was indeed an ultimate concern. It was, he said, again and again, the only thing that mattered, mattered more than the individual's life itself (3.17, 4.5, 6, 8).

Notes

This article consists of edited and revised excerpts from the preface and chapter 1 of my book *Confucius: The Secular as Sacred*, New York: HarperCollins, 1972; Prospect Heights, IL: Waveland Press, 1998.

1. Cf. A. Waley, *The Analects of Confucius* (New York: Random House Modern Library, 1938), no. P66, 64–66.

2. See ibid., 32–33.

3. Cf. ibid., 66. "I do not think Confucius attributed this magic power to any rites save those practiced by the divinely appointed ruler." See also J. L. Duyvendak, "The Philosophy of *Wu Wei*," *Études Asiatiques* 3, no. 4 (1947): 94: "the original magical meaning" of such a passage as 2.4 is "unmistakable."

4. Duyvendak, "Philosophy of *Wu Wei*," 84.

5. See, for example, Waley, *Analects*, 66.

6. See, for example, H. G. Creel, *Confucius and the Chinese Way* (New York: Harper, 1949), 83. See also Waley, *Analects*, 9.3.

7. J. L. Austin, "Performative Utterances," in *Philosophical Papers* (London: Oxford University Press, 1961), 220–39; *How to Do Things with Words* (London: Oxford University Press, 1962); "Performatif-Constatif," in *La Philosophie Analytique*, Cahiers de Royaumont, Phil. no. 5 (Editions de Mincit, Paris, 1962), 271–305. See Herbert Fingarette, "Performatives," *American Philosophical Quarterly* 4 (1967).

8. Though the list could go on interminably, I mention here just a few more terms which commonly enter into formulas having an obvious performative function: "I christen you," "I appoint you," "I pick this (or him)," "I congratulate you," "I welcome you," "I authorize you," "I challenge you," "I order you," "I request you."

9. For characteristic examples of the trend to treat as a special, crucial category these and other first-person present-tense expressions using "mental" or "action" verbs, see S. Hampshire, *Thought and Action* (London: Chatto & Windus, 1959). See Waley, *Analects*, 32.33. See also Austin, "Performative Utterances," 220–39; *How to Do Things with Words*; and "Performatif-Constatif." I have offered a systematic analysis of the concept of the performative, which I believe concords with and amplifies the points I am making

here in connection with Confucius, though it was developed in a more general context. See Fingarette, "Performatives."

10. This position is taken more or less explicitly in the various works of Fung Yu-lan. The *Analects* passage that is most explicit—indeed the only fully explicit passage on *zhengming*, is *Analects* (13.3). See Waley, *Analects*, 172. Even so, the passage does not itself say that names must "correspond" to "actualities." Fung Yu-lan, *A History of Chinese Philosophy*, vol. 1 (Princeton: Princeton University Press, 1952), 60.

Walking the Way In-Between with Confucius: *Tianwen* and Emerging Patterns of Human Heavens

2

David Jones

The *Lunyu*, or the "ordered sayings," is commonly known in the West as the *Analects*. The *Analects* were eventually written down and compiled into twenty books by disciples of Kongzi (or as he is known in the West, Confucius) shortly after his death in 479 BCE. Contemporary scholarship puts the recording of what the Master said, or intended to say, as the *Analects* into tiers of three hundred years of editorial activity.[1] In this regard, the received *Analects* appropriately mirrors the form of the intergenerational philosophical disposition of Confucius and the text's content. Disciples of disciples edited the text we now read as the words of Confucius himself. The content of the received *Analects* also presents challenges concerning what the Master said, since different disciples ask the same questions and yet receive different answers. The problem of consistent intended meaning is further compounded because Confucius himself seems to have intended to offer different responses to different students' question. For instance, in 11.23, Zilu inquires of the Master, "On learning something, should one act upon it?" The Master said, "While your father and elder brothers are still alive, how could you, on learning something, act upon it?" Then Ranyou asked the same question. The Master replied, "On learning something, act upon it." Confucius is furthered queried by Gongxi Hua. "When Zilu asked the question, you observed that his father and elder brothers are still alive, but when Ranyou asked the same question, you told him to act on what he learns. I am confused—could you explain this to me?" Logic forbids contradiction and demands consistency so that it may retain objectivity, and Gongxi Hua, being of logical mind, gets something of a *koan*-like response from Confucius: "Ranyou is diffident, and so I urged him on. But Zilu has the energy of two, so I sought to rein him in."[2] What Confucius establishes in his response is not only an explanation of his apparent contradiction. While he aims to put a subjective spin on the life-world of his disciples, who experience the same things in their lives completely differently depending upon what they are bringing to their experiences, he also is informing Gongxi Hua that while logic has its place, feelings, perceptions, and perspectives also play prominent roles in constituting a self. Likewise, individual selves need to realize the primacy of the other in moving toward a more harmonious future with each other.

Such a conception flies in the face of what constitutes a self in the West, where society is seen as a derived arrangement of autonomous individuals vying for recognition, success, and assertion of their rights, including rights to privacy and ownership. The philosophical question of personal identity and its essentialist focus on individual-over-time and survival is a remnant of a religious past with its commitment to a conception of soul, which finds its apotheosis in the hard-core rationalism of Descartes, a profoundly religious thinker in his own right. My soul, that essential part of me that is the most real, or substantial, to me and to others, is the construction of a particular kind of self that is at once a candidate for death or abduction once I close my eyes and drift off to sleep. We tell those most innocent among us, "Now I lay me down to sleep, I pray the Lord my soul to keep. If I should die before I wake, I pray the Lord my soul to take" (perhaps this is not the best of ways to promote restful sleep in children). If we think about this nighttime meditation, we soon begin to realize this is a traumatic experience to put a child through before she gives up her consciousness of the Waking Realm. Who is this lord that pilfers a child's psyche and robs her body of its soul, its animation, and its life? This particular lord is a transcendent god, unfathomable to the human mind and residing in an inexplicable eternal realm where nothing emerges but everything just is, and is forever. This realm is called heaven, at least in the confines of the Western, Abrahamic religious tradition.

This is not the god of Confucius, nor is this heaven's realm for Confucius. In their introduction to the *Analects*, Roger Ames and Henry Rosemont suggest, "Confucius is probably the most influential thinker in human history, if influence is determined by the sheer number of people who have lived their lives, and died, in accordance with the thinker's vision of how people ought to live, and die" (1). In the West, we tend not to appreciate this significant point because we overestimate the importance of our vision of the world. Our vision needs to see itself vis-à-vis other visions of humanity that recognize a different place for humans in the natural and social world, and in the heavens. It needs a little alterity, or betweenness, to see itself for what it truly is. As Erin McCarthy so astutely puts it, "this betweenness encompasses the social, individual *and* embodied aspects of self. In betweenness, a new space of relationship, an ethical space, is founded."[3] Casting our gaze toward ancient China, to Confucius, gives us this alterior reflection and promotes a new ground of in-betweenness for our ethical and religious lives.

The Betweenness with the Other

By lifting ideas from the Chinese tradition vis-à-vis our own, we can gain a greater understanding of ourselves by looking at this "other." What does this encounter with the other ultimately mean to us? Let me suggest that the encounter with the other is the encounter with ourselves, because it breaks through the silence of our solipsistic being and shows us our own face; the encounter with the other reveals our true face, reveals this face of ours in its face, the face of the other. The face of the other is the *elementum*, the *arche*, the first principle of the other, which is the ground of interpersonal contact. This ground of the other indicates an immediacy with other persons that Levinas calls "proximity." Levinas writes, "the proximity of the Other is not simply close to me in space, or close like a parent, but he approaches me essentially insofar as I feel myself—insofar as I am—responsible for him."[4] For Levinas, proximity is felt as immediate contact because proximity demands a response from us, a "respond-ability," that is, the possibility, and ability, to respond. This proximity is a weight, a consignment, that comes from the outside; the self is the subject that is subjected to the other and the subject of the other, the other who comes upon us to engage us in self-conversation, a conversation that interrupts the solipsistic egoistic silences of our dialogues that we can now know, through this encounter, as monologues. These monologues are what we have been calling our lives, and whose accustomed silent utterances have grown to comfort us.

Facing this other can be a joyous event for those daring enough to give up their heroic egos—those brave souls who want their solipsistic monologues interrupted. And we all ultimately desire the interruption of this solipsistic monologue. We are tired of ourselves being just our-selves. We want the other so we can have a conversation, a dialogue, a going through language to discover ourselves. Language is inexplicably communal, as is our spirituality. More than likely, we initially appropriate the other of Asia as the self of ourselves in a spiritual way. We have come home, we have arrived at the doorstep of the other, or so we think.

This type of appropriation that we experience, try out, and put on trial just doesn't seem to fit or get us very far except in deceiving ourselves. And as Sartre warns us, the worst of all kinds of deceptions is to live in bad faith. We need to go beyond this test, this trial, this experience. The proximity of the other demands a more authentic response; the response with the other demands that we be responsible. Levinas, *contra* Sartre who proclaims, "hell is other people," finds the possibility of responsibility, even the possibility of ethics, in the moment of the encounter with the other; we must allow the other to enter our horizon. The self takes on a new dimension in this encounter; this new dimension is a new subjectivity; this new dimension is the self discovering itself to be a self: a Westerner who is not pretending to be non-Western, but a Westerner who realizes the meaning of what Confucius says when he proclaims "in wanting to establish himself, he establishes others; in wanting to succeed himself, he helps others to succeed" (6:30). When we encounter the other, we find a new subjectivity. For Confucius, this subjectivity will not, however, be too subjective and suffer from the egological tendencies found in such phenomenological thinkers as Husserl.

For those of us who wish to extend the conversation to include the others of the other, to move ourselves to the social level more specifically, we can ask: When we study other cultures, when we attempt to understand the otherness of others and their culture, does this raise the question of "understanding" itself? Whose understanding, whose categories of understanding, or whose categories of knowing are we employing when we try to understand another's culture? Once we are able to ask these types of questions, we are ready for the first time to reflect meaningfully on our own cultural assumptions and predilections. Kant would have these categories as universal, but as Stephen Goldberg enjoins, "to reflect on our own cultural assumptions [is] a way of opening up a space within which to consider a very different set of assumptions in-forming another's culture."⁵ In the face of the other, we see the original face of our own assumptions and our own tendencies of experiencing, or trying out our reality, as is suggested by the Latin roots of "experience" (*ex* + *per*; in Latin *experientia* is a test or a trying out). Our experience in the world is a trying out, a testing, of our understanding that is knotted by the very experience of knowing itself. When we encounter the face of the other, we open a space within and see ourselves. As we open this space, we allow for the possibility of finding ourselves in the in-between ground of authentic experiencing and responsibility to others. Goldberg adds: "The rest is commentary."

So far, I have suggested that we have difficulty finding ourselves because we are too comfortable with our solipsistic lives, that we cannot find ourselves until we encounter the other. And perhaps we can give a different spin to the earlier quote of Confucius, "In experiencing the other, we experience ourselves; in knowing ourselves, we can know others." The philosophy of Confucius is central to the project of understanding Chinese thought and culture, and offers novel ways of thinking about our individual lives and our relation to the communities in which we participate. But even more significantly, the philosophy of Confucius is central to making a more inclusive democracy here at home, and to living the good life that was heralded as the primary concern of those wise Greek philosophers who started us on our current course.

When we first approach the text of the *Analects* of Confucius, we are confronted with what appears to be an assortment of unrelated sayings. Navigating through the *Analects* can be a daunting task for the initiate of Confucius's philosophy. There are ways, however, to make sense of this intergenerational text that includes three hundred years of editing by his philosophical offspring. One of the most straightforward ways of gaining some purchase on the *Analects* is to organize topically the text around such key terms as: *li* (禮 the rites or observing ritual propriety), *ren* (仁 benevolence, goodness, or authoritative conduct), *shu* (恕 understanding or putting oneself in the other's place), *zhong* (忠 dutifulness or doing one's utmost), *tian* (天 heaven), *dao* (道 way), *xin* (心, heart-mind), *yi* (義 rightness or appropriateness), *zhi* (知 wisdom or to realize), *he* (和 harmony), *de* (德 virtue, power, or excellence), *shan* (善 good or truly adept), *wen* (文 culture), *xiao* (孝 filial piety or filial conduct), *junzi* (君子 gentleman, exemplary person, or consummate person). This kind of approach reveals the conceptual structure and unity of Confucius's thought. Thinking through the *Analects* in this kind of way promotes an enhanced understanding of Confucius's thinking. In what follows, I discuss some of the key terms listed above and their relevant passages, especially *li* (the rites or observing ritual propriety) and *ren* (human-heartedness or authoritative conduct). I will mention also two other important terms: *junzi* (exemplary person), and *yi* (rightness, morality, or appropriateness). I discuss all of these terms in the revealing light of *tianwen*, or the patterns of the heavens.

The *wen* of *tianwen* means "to inscribe," "to embellish," and by extension comes to mean "culture."[6] *Wen* pertains, as Slingerland notes, "to the sort of acculturation—training in ritual, the classics, music, etc.—acquired by someone following the Confucian Way,"[7] for "Exemplary persons (*junzi* 君子) learn broadly of culture (*wen* 文), discipline this learning through observing ritual propriety (*li* 禮), and moreover, in so doing, can remain on course without straying from it" (6.27). It is interesting to note the inference made with *wen*: those who can write and embellish are those with culture. In other words, humans are beings with culture because they have a language that embellishes and inscribes. When we place *wen* with *tian* something of note happens. *Tian*, usually translated as "Heaven," immediately conjures up those culturally rich images from the Abrahamic tradition, which most Westerners seem to somehow share lurking in the depths of their souls. However, these conjured images are culturally specific and are foreign to the Chinese sensibility. Such images are far from universal. To translate *tian* as "nature" is also problematic because *tian* is often used alone to render *tiandi* (the heavens and the earth) more economically. What this economical move suggests is that *tian* is not independent from this world and that *tian*, in a profound sense, *is* the world. As Ames and Rosemont suggest, "*Tian* is both *what* our world is and *how* it is." Furthermore, there can be no creator god that is metonymically referred to as "Heaven," one who is absent from, and who is often seen as otiose in, His relation to His creation since "*Tian* is both the creator and the field of creatures. There is no apparent distinction between the order itself, and what orders it."[8]

Although the Chinese did have an anthropomorphic deity in Shangdi (上帝 often translated as Lord on High), this god is not seen as the creator of the universe *ex nihilo*. Rather, Shangdi was viewed as the ancient human ancestor of the Shang people, and then was appropriated by the Zhou as Tian, another anthropomorphic deity. This anthropomorphism suggests, according to Ames and Rosemont, "an intimate relationship with the process of euhemerization—historical human beings becoming gods—that grounds Chinese ancestor reverence."[9] This anthropomorphism without the original bequeathed upon humans by some creator God further points to the special relationship rulers will have with heaven, and its mandate (命 *ming*), and the intergenerational character of Confucian thought. Rulers must be in concert with *tian*, have its power (德 *de*), or lose its favor. These dead ancestors are the gods Confucius inherits. In both regards, *li*, observing ritual propriety, becomes of paramount concern for through *li* one is grounded to the authentic heritage of the past, extends oneself into the future, and consecrates the present.

Li

To understand Confucius is to understand his central thinking on *li*. For Westerners, the first encounter with *li*, the rites or observing ritual propriety, seems a bit odd, but the centrality of *li* in Confucius's thought cannot be emphasized enough. We begin to understand the centrality of *li* when Confucius says in a passage on *ren*: "Do not look at anything that violates the observance of ritual propriety; do not listen to anything that violates the observance of ritual propriety; do not speak about anything that violates the observance of ritual propriety; do not do anything that violates the observance of ritual propriety" (12.1). Why would Confucius accord such central prominence to *li*?

Chinese philosophy often appears far less abstract than its European counterparts and has been rejected by Western philosophers as not even being philosophical. Such a bias displays a philosophical disposition against the affective and somatic components of the human experience. Even the rationalistic tendencies in Chinese philosophy seem less abstract. Much of this tendency is a consequence of language. The focus, especially in Confucius's thought and the subsequent Confucian tradition, is on humans and their relation to "the other," whether that other is other human beings, other creatures that constitute the ten thousand things (萬物 *wanwu*), or everything that makes up the dynamically changing world. Confucius's overwhelming concern is the relation of the human being with other human beings engendered through the process of self-cultivation. While the Western philosophical tradition displays a strong abstract rationalistic disposition beginning with Plato and finding its apotheosis in Descartes's philosophy, Chinese philosophy is rationalistic in more concrete ways. It is worth repeating that Western thought sees society as a derived arrangement: an abstraction of atomic individuals constitutes society (Confucius would even see the individual as an abstraction), and each individual bears certain inalienable rights. The Chinese, on the other hand, traditionally have viewed society as being the source for the circumscribing characteristics of the individual. Consequently, society becomes a repository of values of the dead ancestors and gods, and is not seen as an arena for actualizing human potential as it is in the West. For the Chinese, individuals become concrete exemplars of value, and ought to be emulated as instantiations of reasonableness. The *junzi* (君子) for Confucius is just such a being.

This idea is not so uncommon in the West, however, for it is more a matter of foregrounding and backgrounding. Typically, Westerners will foreground individuality and background their belonging to communities, that is, the more social aspects of being human. The Chinese, on the other hand, are more inclined to reverse this process. Although these generalities may have exceptions in each respective tradition, I think it is important to orient ourselves in this direction and see what this distinction will yield as we think about a worldview that privileges "rites" over "rights," or as Randy Peerenboom has suggested, "right thinking" over "the right to think."[10]

This focus on humanity and the tendency for a concrete rationality lets us understand the central importance of *li* in the philosophy of Confucius. Once the human being as an integrally circumscribed participant in the social context becomes the focus of inquiry, we can more easily appreciate the centrality of *li* in Confucius's thinking. The word *li* seems to have the root feature of a holy ritual or sacred ceremony, as Herbert Fingarette has pointed out, and this provides its historical dimension, which is crucial for understanding Confucius's philosophy. The individual self, through the proper practice of *li*, extends its self into the matrix of tradition. This extension into tradition has a magical quality to it that extends far beyond the original meaning of *li* as holy rite. As Fingarette puts it, "the magical element always involves great effects produced effortlessly, marvelously, with an irresistible power that is itself intangible, invisible, unmanifest."[11] If we think about *li* in the context of the *junzi*, or the exemplar of social value and virtue, we find support for this claim of *li* having a magical, mysterious, and even heavenly power. If we read 2.1 and 2.3 with 12.15, 12.17, and 12.19, we can see that the *junzi*'s behavior should and will prompt emulation and that there is indeed a "heavenly" or divine aspect to it:

> The Master said: "Governing with excellence (德 *de*) can be compared to being the North Star: the North Star dwells in its place, and the multitude of stars pay it tribute." (2.1)

> The Master said, "Lead the people with administrative injunctions and keep them orderly with penal law, and they will avoid punishments but will be without a sense of shame. Lead them with excellence (德 *de*) and keep them orderly through observing ritual propriety (禮 *li*) and they will develop a sense of shame, and moreover, will order themselves." (2.3)

> The Master said, "Learn broadly of culture (文 *wen*), discipline this learning through observing ritual propriety (禮 *li*), and moreover, in so doing, remain on course without straying from it." (12.15)

> Ji Kangzi asked Confucius about governing effectively (政 *zheng*), and Confucius replied to him, "Governing effectively is doing what is proper (正 *zheng*). If you, sir, lead by doing what is proper, who would dare do otherwise?" (12.17)

Ji Kangzi Tzu asked Confucius about governing effectively (政 *zheng*), saying, "What if I kill those who have abandoned the way (道 *dao*) to attract those who are on it?"

"If you govern effectively, " Confucius replied, "what need is there for killing? If you want to be truly adept (善 *shan*), the people will also be adept. The excellence (德 *de*) of the exemplary person (君子 *junzi*) is the wind, while that of the petty person is the grass. As the wind blows, the grass is sure to bend." (12.19)

As the *junzi* looks, listens, speaks, and moves in accordance with *li*, others, as the above quotes suggest, follow his or her example without coercion or force. An exemplary person, a *junzi*, is given a divine posture. In 15.5, we see this divine posture and magical power that Fingarette speaks of: "The Master said, 'If anyone could be said to have effected proper order while remaining nonassertive, surely it was Shun. What did he do? He simply assumed an air of deference and faced due south.'" If the *junzi* acts in accordance with *li*, effects of his or her actions follow in natural ways. Shun has nothing to do except be his excellent and virtuous self, to be himself as an exemplar for others. This is the Confucian counterpart to the Daoist notion of *wu-wei*, or nondirected action, where the sage does nothing and nothing is left undone.[12] The emanating appropriateness and goodness of the *junzi* is contagious and has an amplifying effect. This kind of ability to effect meaningful change throughout the systemic flow of society is indeed godly.

Both the sacred and magical dimensions of *li* lead ultimately to harmony and order, which are Confucius's goals. The emergence and development of *li* are not consciously driven or ordered by some external transcendent source such as God, the Platonic Idea of the Good, or even compliance with some abstract moral principle such as the categorical imperative. *Li* are immanent and emerge from their social context; *li* govern the patterns of social intercourse.[13] What makes *li* so magical is the "intangible," "invisible," "unmanifest" power of human interactions, and *li*'s inherent emergent quality. The other side of the magic of *li* is its continuity. The continuity and reauthorization of *li* are necessary for "maintaining institutional and cultural continuity with a minimum of conscious intervention."[14] Our social conventions and customs are complex systems that comprise connections of many interacting units. These *li* are the manifestations of our in-betweenness with others, the basis of being-ethical-in-the-world, and constitute our intersubjectivity as subjects with other subjects. *Jian*, the word for the human world in Chinese, is 間. Its modern form indicates sunlight through a door (門 *men*). This sunlight reveals the space between the threshold of the door of humanity and the entrance into the lived space, the place of the family, behind the door. This is the threshold through which the human self crosses to meet the other. It is only through this encounter with the other that we discover our intersubjectivity as a self; it is only in the realization of this space in-between self and others that light is shed on what in means to be human. *Ren dao* 人道 is humanity, the way of humans as they enter the life-world of others.

Each person in a society has her own individual needs, desires, aspirations, ideas, and so on. Unlike democratic systems of government and social organization that base their development and structure on serving those needs of the atomic individual, Confucian society ordered itself on the principle of the community being greater than any individual part or the sum of its parts. Therefore, society is an organic community emerging from the interaction of all its parts. The community is a complex system that is not so much created by any individual—even Confucius himself—but that emerges as a result of individual transactions. These constitutive elements of society give rise to the society; there is no society without these transactions.

Confucius did not invent *li*, nor did he actually design a society based on the principles of *li* (although he did try to convince rulers that his philosophy was a means of gaining social and political order). What makes Confucius such an important social thinker is that he affirms and articulates a natural development of the emergence of order from the possibility of chaos, and the possible slip of society over the precipice of that very chaos. Arising spontaneously, *li*, as Tony Cua states, define "the conventionally accepted *style* of actions, i.e. the form and possibility of moral achievement within the cultural setting."[15] Historically, no social group consciously chooses its conventions—there is never any convening. For example, decisions to be either a bowing culture or a handshaking culture are never made consciously. These decisions emerge unconsciously and make manifest the inherent values within the shared context of interactions. Depending upon the inherent interactions of the participants in any given social system, certain forms of customs, mores, conventions, and so forth emerge as natural consequences from those interactions and transactions within the system. This emergent *li* is an expression and manifestation of the inherent values of the social system and its participants. And from Confucius's perspective, there can be nothing more divine. And how could there be, since the magic from proper execution of *li* is sublime and visible to the adept eye and trained executor of *li*?

Confucius merely looks at the interactions and the resulting manifestations of *li* and affirms the process as essential to the establishment of human social order. In fact, for Confucius nothing is more important than *li*, because any participant in society should "not look unless it was in accordance with the rites; . . . not listen unless it is accordance to the rites; . . . not speak unless it is in accordance to the rites; . . . [and] not move unless it is accordance with the rites."[16] In Confucius's world there is a profound awareness that *li* has an organic aspect; it has the inherent ability for growth or diminution over time. The structure, sustainability, and orderly flow of information within the system can and will change. Confucius suggests that observance and affirmation of this orderly flow is crucial to the preservation of society. If the social system's *li* are not responsive (responsible for the other) to the changing needs of society, stability is lost. Once lost, society's fragile fabric comes one step closer to losing its pattern of order, that is, its cultural patterns to inscribe and embellish the articulated aspect of what it means to be human in a particular context at a particular time in history's unfolding. Confucius knew that this step was a movement either toward the extinction of the social system or toward drastic and possibly undesirable change. Therefore, it is in the system's best interest to be adaptive; the alternative is chaotic extinction, or authoritarianism. Confucius thus allows for variation in *li* over time, but this variation must be in harmony with the emergent order of the system. Tu Wei-ming makes this point when he addresses the problem of *li* as a process of humanization and "an authentic way of establishing human-relatedness" and therefore "*li* is understood as movement instead of form." According to Tu, *li* had evolved from a "proper act of sacrifice to an authentic way of establishing human-relatedness" and "the emphasis is on its dynamic process rather than its static structure."[17] As Confucius himself says:

> The use of a hemp cap is prescribed in the observance of ritual propriety. Nowadays, that a silk cap is used instead is a matter of frugality. I would follow accepted practice on this. A subject kowtowing on entering the hall is prescribed in the observance of ritual propriety. Nowadays that one kowtows only after ascending the hall is a matter of hubris [that is, it's casual]. Although it goes contrary to accepted practice, I still kowtow on entering the hall. (9.3)

Frugality is a natural consequence (H. G. Kreel calls it a "reasonable convention"[18]) of the context at hand, and adapting to context is appropriate (*yi*), but laziness or haughtiness (not framing an everyday experience with human sanctity) is a fortuitous or forced change. Fortuitous or forced changes—those changes that do not affirm the sustainability of the social system or genuinely appropriate the emergent spontaneity inherent within the system—will cast the system into unforeseen consequences, into a chaos similar to Confucius's day. Similarly, neither following the "party line" nor consistently rebelling against it without appropriate reason are acceptable. These are reasons why Confucius "had nothing to say about strange happenings [prodigies], the use of force, disorder, or the spirits" (7.21). Confucius's heaven is to be found elsewhere. *Tian* is found in the emerging immanent patterns of human social behavior that are continually presenting themselves. Changes that do not promote continuance, sustainability, and subsequent growth in Confucius's idea of a social system will pollute the system. Its orderly flow of information could be disrupted, with destructive change, extinction, and the emergence of a new order as results. As Fingarette has noted, "The Confucian commitment to a single, definite order is also evident when we note that Confucius sees as the alternative to rightly treading the true Path: it is to walk crookedly, to get lost or to abandon the Path [*Dao*]. That is, the only "alternative" to the one Order is disorder, chaos."[19]

This commitment to a single, definite order is an appropriation of the emergent spontaneity that is immanent in the process of the *li*'s becoming, which will mutate at the proper time for its—and the social organism's—health and survival. Ultimately, the survival of *li* is dependent on the continued life of its interacting cells, of cultured human beings, and the continuous life of human beings depends on the progression of *li*. I use biological analogies for a reason. Biologists necessarily focus their attention on what is around them, to what is immediate, and Confucius has a profound sensitivity to the natural-ness of human interaction. Finding ourselves in the betweenness with others is constitutive of who and what we are in the contexts at hand. The realm of the immediate becomes the ideal for both Confucius and biologists; they see the ideal in the real because they are utterly amazed by the inherent order that defines the possibility of life. This order to which Fingarette refers is not a singular transcendent independent order that is to be followed blindly, but is rather a participatory and emergent order that is immanent and dynamic. Any system, biological or social, seeks one constant goal: to perpetuate itself in the face of extinction. And Confucius is acutely aware of this challenge. But there are, however, forces at work in the system that are more self-promoting, self-ishly motivated, and chaos driven.

Many of these forces arise from orientations where egos become more important than the health and well-being of the community. Such authoritari-anism is divisive and ultimately destructive. One virtue of Confucius's thought is his realization of the unknown immanent force that seeks emergence. This immanent force makes all life, not just human life (both biological and social), possible. As Ames and Hall have remarked, "order is realized, not instantiated."[20] Frequently, the Western approach instantiates order, that is, imposes overlays of order onto things either through the application of universal principles, contracts, or through laws, but Confucius's more intimate approach will seek out the way of things. Confucius (as other potential exemplars should strive to become) is an artificer of *dao*, that is, as one who skillfully crafts the way of natural phenomena, of which the human is seen as an intimate part, into human propriety. Confucius looks at the weakly interactive connectivity of his fellow beings, some of whom probably appeared arbitrarily impulsive to him, and designs his philosophy of *li*. When he views the emergent social order he sees a conditioned maximal information exchange, or the potential for that change, in the form of *li*. Through the interactions and transactions of those human beings who made up the dissolved Zhou Empire, Confucius comes to under-stand the need for social harmony. Confucius is the first thinker to realize that human harmony can be achieved only when there is an appropriate vehicle to give it expression. This vehicle, as Hall and Ames say, is the "repertory of those formal roles, practices, actions, and institutions that continue the living culture.

[*Li*] are meaning-invested behaviors that, when properly enacted, conduce to communal harmony."[21] *Li* is both the emergent and creative force within the social system.

A convergence of Confucius and Daoism would realize this emergent sense of order vis-à-vis the chaos-driven forces, but in fundamentally different ways. Daoists would affirm the natural order because of the interplay of *yin* and *yang* where polarity is requisite for emergence. Neither Confucius and most subsequent Confucians nor the Daoists impose any outside transcendent power in their respective approaches. Their virtue was in the realization of the unknown immanent force that seeks emergence, and it is, to borrow a phrase from the theoretical biologist Stuart Kauffman, "order for free."[22] This immanent force makes all life, not just human life (both biological and social), possible. From this context, this immanent force must be considered divine. For the Daoists, this immanent force necessarily creates order from all the intersecting interactions of chaotic reactions, and if this approach is applied to Confucius, we find that "order is realized, not instantiated."

Ren Dao and *Li*

I invoke the Daoists here with reason because Confucian and Daoist notions of *dao* are often seen in opposition. The term *dao* existed in Chinese thought well before Confucius's time and has a variety of meanings. Because of their reverence for natural cycles, the Daoists used the term to embody the way of the natural world and the patterns created by the continual ellipses of the sun, the waxing and waning of the moon, the seasonal changes, and so forth into an intelligible unity, a complex natural system. However, Confucius and the Daoists look at the world and its interactions from different perspectives. For Confucius, *dao* means the way of being human (*ren dao*) where a human being can become "consummately and authoritatively human,"[23] and the way of government. As an artificer of *dao*, Confucius skillfully crafts human propriety in ways that mirror natural phenomena. The crafting of human propriety takes place in and through *li*, which is the locus of creative self-cultivation.

Confucius was an astute observer of the interactions of his fellow beings. The exchanges he witnessed were very subtle. The flow of communication was not obvious, but it was present in very distinct and profound ways. Any resulting harmony from acting through *li* had nothing much to do with the content of the act itself, but through the action of the act. In other words, the vehicle for expression had been unconsciously convened already as the meaning of the interaction, and any failure to respond appropriately within the context of *li* would violate the natural order of social relations. The act of *li* gives presence to the betweenness of subjects. This is the region of being and ethical-being-in-the-world where one's subjectivity is overcome for an intersubjectivity of self. As Erin McCarthy says, "The goal in fully being human . . . is to stay in the between, more than one stays at either of the opposites ends, for it is in the between, where subject and object, self and other collapse, that ethics happen."[24] Excesses, either of authoritarian control or of freewheeling impulsivity, would pull the interaction back from the edge of the creatively human or push it over the edge into social chaos. To Confucius, *li* occupies a narrow zone between failing to perceive appropriately the boundary and pressing one's own advantage. Hence, Confucius was very concerned that *li* should be performed appropriately and with discipline. As an exemplar, Confucius "would not eat food that was improperly prepared, or that was lacking the appropriate condiments and sauces. Even when meat was abundant, he would not eat it in disproportionate amount to staple foods. Only in his wine did he not limit himself, although he never got drunk" (10.8). Hence, Confucius's *dao* is *ren dao*.

Perturbations to complex systems, including social systems, need not be large to have an immense impact; potentially the addition or loss of a grain of sand may bring a mountain down. Similarly, casual, nonchalant, awkward, and inauthentic performances or denials of *li* can have devastating effects. One needs only to look at contemporary society for examples of how chaos is rising in contemporary culture. We have forgotten how to apologize, express our gratitude, and show respect for our fellow beings—negative results of the emergent values of individuality present in our *li*. Also, we need only look at our arbitrary, contemporary sense of community—planned retirement apartments, condominiums, "communities" with swimming pools, golf courses, handy mini-marts, and so forth—to realize we are being brought together in soulless, unnatural, and artificial ways. Even our cities, the regions that maximize human interaction, are now beyond human scale. Any number of possibilities existed for the development of *li* in China, but the various constituent parts of Chinese society interacted in such a way that ordered the apparent chaos to express itself in the way gleaned by Confucius.

Cultures consciously do not convene and decide what types of cultures they wish to be; nor do they decide what customs and mores are preferable to others. *Li* are the emerging principles that give coherence and order to societies and any collective human endeavor; *li* are self-organizing evolutionary processes that are manifested through interaction and develop into networks of interdependence. These manifested and evolved networks of interdependence are the systemic basis of humanity. If harmony and order are primary goals, as they are in the traditional Chinese social and political context, then one must affirm authentic tradition as necessarily having a sacred dimension. By extending oneself beyond the immediacy of one's life, one extends oneself back into the authentic tradition of the past where the emergent *li* express the manifest values of culture. For Confucius, what and who we are in the most profound sense is a product of this authentic tradition that separates us from the nonhuman, which in turn, gives us a place for "ethics to happen."

Ren

The adage attributed to the Chinese that a picture is worth a thousand words is a good place to begin when discussing *ren* because it affords us some purchase on Confucius's social philosophy. The everyday term *ren* 人 simply means person. Although the major Confucian virtue of *ren* is written differently 仁, it is derived by adding the number two, *er* 二, to *ren* 人.[25] What this "picture" suggests is that the highest virtue in Confucius's thought is the equation of one person plus two. In other words, the highest virtue of *ren* is achievable in relationships of three or more, that is to say, only in the family, which is the Confucian model for societal relationships. In relationships where a "third" is introduced, or in relationships of three or more, we realize the difficulty of attaining the life of excellence and virtue (*de*) because of the continuous attention needed for harmonious negotiations. As Ames and Hall have remarked: "The cultivation of *ren* is . . . irreducibly other-entailing. One cannot become *ren* in Descartes' closet."[26]

Arthur Waley points out that *ren* "in the earliest Chinese means freeman, men of the tribe, as opposed to *min*, 'subjects,' 'the common people,'" and "the same word, written with a slight modification, means 'good' in the most general sense of the word, that is to say, 'possessing qualities of one's tribe.'" The extended meaning of this term according to Waley comes to be an accolade of kindness, gentleness, and humanity that ultimately distinguishes the "'human' as opposed to 'animal,' and [comes] to be applied to conduct worthy of a man, as distinct from the behaviour of mere beast."[27] A. C. Graham connects the commendation of *ren* more specifically to culture when he writes that "the noble, civilized, fully human, pride themselves on their manners and conventions [*li*], but above all on the virtues which give these meaning and which distinguish themselves from the boors and savages who do not know how to behave."[28] In the *Analects, ren* means good in the most general sense.[29] Although there are good reasons for his rendering of *ren*, Waley's translation of "Goodness" or "Good," or D. C. Lau's translation of *ren* as "benevolence," are somewhat unfortunate for Westerners who have been weaned on Platonic understandings of universals and the universal transcendent Good. Likewise, the word "benevolence" means very little to contemporary Americans. Even rendering *ren* as "authoritative conduct," the choice of Ames and Rosemont, requires overcoming certain undesirable connotations for those who distrust or dislike authority. Such a translation necessitates qualifying *ren* conduct as the type of authority commanded by the mere presence of an accomplished individual in the appropriate context, such as Tiger Woods in the context of a golf match. *Ren* is always about accomplished individuals who find themselves in some context, and who respond to others appropriately. This appropriateness arises only in the in-between state of ethical intersubjectivity.

Although *ren* has the sense of goodness that Waley focuses on, it is clear from the *Analects* that there is nothing common about its attainment. Confucius's sense of *ren* resonates with earlier meanings used by aristocratic clans during the Zhou to distinguish themselves from common people,[30] but there is something more profound operating here. Confucius's students are constantly asking him whether rulers or contemporary political figures have attained *ren*. His answer is always no. He ascribes *ren* only to figures of China's mythic past. Confucius does so not only to root individuals more firmly in their authentic tradition, but also to create a goal as elusive as approaching and reaching the horizon. Confucius places emphasis on the self-cultivation of individuals emerging from their authentic tradition in light of their present social context and it is, as P. J. Ivanhoe notes, "one of the most thoroughly and regularly discussed topics among Chinese ethical philosophers."[31] As Hall and Ames suggest, "one is born into and constituted by an incipient nexus of relationships that then must be cultivated and extended. Although these inchoate relationships, and the ritual structures through which they are extended, are immediately interpersonal, their greater significance lies in their character of locating and integrating the particular human being in the larger world most broadly construed."[32] Even when Confucius's disciples entreat him in 7.34 to acknowledge his own achievement of *ren*, he self-consciously replies: "How would I dare to consider myself a sage (*sheng*) or an authoritative person? What can be said about me is simply that I continue my studies without respite and instruct others without growing weary." This modest refusal and the ascription of *ren* to only quasi-mythical figures who modeled themselves after Shangdi and Tian emphasize the ongoing process of becoming human, not its ultimate achievement.

Becoming a *ren* person, or becoming fully human, is a difficult attainment according to Confucius. Nevertheless, this task is not impossible. In 4.6, Confucius seems to open the possibility of becoming *ren* regardless of rank when he asks and answers his own question: "Are there people who, for the space of a single day, have given their full strength to authoritative conduct? I have yet to meet them. As for lacking the strength to do so, I doubt there are such people—at least I have yet to meet them." The possibility of achieving, becoming, or being *ren* is a real option for everyone. In other words, becoming a *junzi*, an exemplary person, is a live option for everyone, no matter what class or rank.

Confucius's idea of *ren* can be analyzed by relating *ren* to two other important ideas. In 4.15, we come to learn of the "one continuous strand" that binds together Confucius's way: "The way of the Master is doing one's utmost (*zhong* 忠) and putting oneself in the other's place (*shu* 恕), nothing more."[33] One can look at *shu*, putting oneself in the other's place (also see 5.27) and *zhong*, doing one's best, as two fundamental ingredients of *ren*. When asked in 15.24 if there is "one expression that can be acted upon until the end of one's days," Confucius replies: "There is *shu*: do not impose on others what you yourself do not want." In 12.2, this same point is emphasized: "Zhong-gong inquired about authoritative conduct (*ren*). The Master replied, 'In your public life, behave as though you are receiving important visitors; employ the common people as though you are overseeing a great sacrifice. Do not impose upon others what you yourself do not want, and you will not incur personal or political ill will.'" Analects 6.30 makes the same point: "Authoritative persons [*ren* persons] establish others in seeking to establish themselves and promote others in seeking to get there themselves. Correlating one's conduct with those near at hand can be said to be the method of becoming an authoritative person [*ren* person]." Those familiar with depth psychology's ideas of projection can easily see Confucius is recommending that we should not project our personal needs and desires onto others, which is part of correlating our conduct with those in our immediate context. If we read 12.2 and 6.30 above with 7.22 and 4.17, we can see that Confucius even suggests we have a natural tendency to project our desires and needs onto others.[34]

> The Master said, "In strolling in the company of just two other persons, I am bound to find a teacher. Identifying their strengths, I follow them, and identifying their weaknesses, I reform myself accordingly." (7.22)

> "When you meet persons of exceptional character think to stand shoulder to shoulder with them; meeting persons of little character, look inward and examine yourself." (4.17)

When we examine ourselves, we realize the human tendency to project our in-adequacies onto others. Confucius enjoins us to redress this tendency; rectifying this tendency is a prerequisite for becoming *ren*. In other words, encountering the other is to become *ren*, to become more fully human; this encounter is to realize our in-betweenness with others, the open region of intersubjectivity where ethics is born. *Shu*, putting oneself in the other's place, is the method of moving ourselves closer to the ongoing goal of *ren*. The movement towards becoming *ren* requires a substantial amount of energy. This energy is "doing one's utmost," or *zhong*.[35] Marshalling *zhong* leads to the appropriate attitude for performing *li*.

This discussion started with 12.1 where Yan Hui asks Confucius what *ren* entails. He gets this response: "Do not look at anything that violates the observance of ritual propriety; do not listen to anything that violates the observance of ritual propriety; do not speak about anything that violates the observance of ritual propriety; do not do anything that violates the observance of ritual propriety." Proceeding Yan Hui's question is his more general inquiry about *ren* (authoritative conduct 仁) to which Confucius responds, "Through self-discipline and observing ritual propriety (*li* 禮) one becomes authoritative (*ren* 仁) in one's conduct. If for the space of a day one were able to accomplish this, the whole empire would defer to this authoritative model. Becoming authoritative in one's conduct is self-originating—how could it originate with others?" To discipline the self is to eschew profit or personal gain, that is, self-interest, as a motive for our actions and to embrace *yi*, or appropriateness, as a moral guide. If *li* are the coherent emergent order of our humanity, *ren* is the spirit, the authentic heart-mind (*xin* 心), the human-heartedness (*ren* 仁) and the authoritative conduct (*ren* 仁) that we must bring to our ever-present *li*. *Ren* means to become an authentic human being. To be authentic in actions through the social mechanism of *li* is to become a *junzi*.[36]

Junzi

The conventional way of translating *junzi* is "gentleman." Waley, Lau, Graham, and Slingerland translate the term this way. Other translations include Tu Wei-ming's "profound person" and Roger Ames's and Henry Rosemont's "exemplary person." In one way or another, all of these translations give sense to what Confucius means by the term. "Gentleman" is often the most misleading for Westerners, especially for Americans, and probably was chosen by Waley and Lau because of the relation between a gentleman, being gentle, and the Latin root *gens* and the Greek root *genus* where the clan gives rise to the gentleman. Unfortunately, this etymology is often lost on us. Slingerland chooses "gentle-man" because it is clear Confucius uses the term only in reference to men and to translate otherwise is to treat the term anachronistically. Tu's translation, "profound person," does not carry the practical and ethical connotations that seem necessary to grasp Confucius's thinking. For these reasons, "consummate person" or "exemplary person" may bring us closer to Confucius's meaning (given the caveat of not excluding women), but both are still without the connotations of civility found in "gentleman" and each lack the philosophical strength of "profound person." In addition, for a contemporary encounter with Confucius, that is, how he speaks to us today, "gentleman" raises further issues of gender equality in social and political spheres and gender neutrality in language use. To "rectify names" is a vitally significant Confucian project for a just and ethical society.

To understand the task of perfecting our natures by becoming *junzi* and moving toward the ever-withdrawing horizon of *ren*, we can begin with 7.33, where Confucius says that "as far as personally succeeding in living the life of the exemplary person (*junzi*), I have accomplished little." This passage resonates with 7.34 discussed earlier: "How would I dare to consider myself a sage (*sheng*) or an authoritative person? What can be said about me is simply that I continue my studies without respite and instruct others without growing weary." These passages and many others reinforce the nonteleological character and process orientation of the *Analects*. There is simply no divine realm beyond the magic of our social intercourse. Confucius makes a correlation between *ren* and the *junzi* in 4.5: "Wherein do the exemplary persons (*junzi*) who would abandon their authoritative conduct (*ren*) warrant that name? Exemplary persons [*junzi*] do not take leave of their authoritative conduct even for the space of a meal." Even our most mundane experiences such as eating a meal are infused with the magical power of *li*—we saw earlier Confucius's attention toward eating. If one approaches *li* in the right way (in the spirit of *ren*), our apparently mundane (or apparently profane) ways of acting transform themselves into divine manifestations of our *li*.

The *junzi* is one who through disciplined practice sets in motion a sympathetic vibration for others to follow. The path others will follow will be the way of *yi*, appropriateness, rightness, or morality.[37] The way of *yi* naturally will conflict with the mindless acquisition of wealth and power. In 4.16, the Master said, "Exemplary persons (*junzi*) understand what is appropriate (*yi*); petty persons [*xiaoren*] understand what is of personal advantage." *Analects* 4.2 reinforces this point: "Those persons who are not authoritative (*ren*) are neither able to endure hardship for long, nor to enjoy happy circumstances for any period of time. Authoritative persons are content in being authoritative; wise persons (*zhi*) flourish in it." Further support for the conflict between personal advantage and appropriateness is found in 6.19, "The life of a person lies in being true; as for the life of someone who is crooked, they will need good fortune to avoid losing it," and in 7.12, where the Master says, "if wealth were an acceptable goal, even though I would have to serve as a groom holding a whip in the marketplace, I would gladly do it. But if not an acceptable goal, I will follow my own devices." And even more specifically: "To act with an eye to personal profit will incur a lot of resentment" (4.12) and "to eat coarse food, drink plain water, and pillow oneself on a bent arm—there is pleasure to be found in these things. But wealth and position gained through inappropriate means—these are to me like floating clouds" (7.16).[38]

The *junzi*, much in the spirit of Socrates, prefers death to the acquisition of wealth and power and to evildoing: "For the resolute scholar-apprentice (*shi* [one who is striving to be a *junzi*]) and the authoritative person (*renren*), while they would not compromise their authoritative conduct to save their lives, they might well give up their lives in order to achieve it" (15.9; see also 8.7). Achieving *ren* is not selfishly rewarded by a better incarnation in a future life, a mystical union with the Idea of the Good (Plato), or a place in heaven, such as promised by the Abrahamic traditions. For Confucius, the reward is simply one of connection, of fitting in, of finding one's place in society and the tradition from which one emerges. This harmony of finding one's place is just not some ritualized form of hollow agreement that promotes the *staus quo*. It is a creative act, as Hall and Ames say, a "'making' of society that requires the investment of oneself, one's judgment, and one's own sense of cultural importances."[39] As Confucius says in 13.23: "The exemplary person (*junzi*) seeks harmony (*he* 和)

rather than agreement (*tong* 同); the small person does the opposite." The exemplary person must have the proprietorship of *yi*: "Having a sense of appropriate conduct (*yi* 義) as one's basic disposition (*zhi* 質), developing it in observing ritual propriety (*li* 禮), expressing it with modesty, and consummating it in making good on one's word (*xin* 信): this then is an exemplary person (*junzi* 君子)" (15.18). Exemplary persons integrate all of these attributes into their being, and integrate themselves appropriately into the matrix of social relations and authentic tradition, and locate the ethical space of being-in-between.

Finding Heaven on Earth is much more difficult than finding it elsewhere. Finding emerging heavens that are immanent manifestations of unfolding human values through *li* is even harder still. And for the exemplary person, finding ways of consummating oneself in between others is the most heavenly role one can possibly live, "for in wanting to establish themselves they establish others; in wanting to succeed themselves they help others to succeed. Being able to take as one's correlations those near at hand can be said to be the method of realizing *ren*" (6.30).

Notes

Portions of this paper are taken, but with significant changes, from "Teaching/Learning Through Confucius: Navigating our Way Through the *Analects*," *Education About Asia* 5, no. 2 (Fall 2000); and, both with John L. Culliney, "The Fractal Self and the Organization of Nature: The Daoist Sage and Chaos Theory," *Zygon: The Journal of Science and Religion* 34, no. 4 (1999), and "Confucian Order at the Edge of Chaos: The Science of Complexity and Ancient Wisdom," *Zygon: The Journal of Science and Religion* 33, no. 3 (1998). In "Teaching/Learning Through Confucius: Navigating our Way Through the *Analects*," I acknowledge my debt to Roger Ames and Graham Parkes.

1. For good introductions to their respective translations of the *Analects* see Edward Slingerland's *Confucius: Analects* (Hackett: Indianpolis, 2003) and Roger T. Ames and Henry Rosemont's *The Analects of Confucius: A Philosophical Translation* (Ballantine Books: New York, 1998).

2. Translations of the *Analects* are from Ames and Rosemont, *Analects of Confucius*.

3. See Erin McCarthy, "Ethics in Between," *Philosophy, Culture, Traditions* 2 (2003): 63–77.

4. Emmanuel Levinas, *Ethics and Infinity: Conversations with Phillipe Nemo*, trans. Richard Cohen (Pittsburgh: Duquesne University Press, 1985), 97.

5. From Stephen Goldberg, "Oh Father Where Art Thou? Globalization, Identity, and Chinese Visual Culture," unpublished manuscript.

6. Ames and Rosemont, *Analects of Confucius*, 58.

7. Slingerland, *Confucius: Analects*, 237.

8. Ames and Rosemont, *Analects of Confucius*, 46, 47.

9. Ames and Rosemont, *Analects of Confucius*, 47.

10. See R. Peerenboom, "Let One Hundred Flowers Bloom, One Hundred Schools Contend: Debating Rule of Law in China," *Perspectives* 3, no. 5, http://www.oycf.org/Perspectives/17_063002/One_Hundred_Flower_Bloom.htm.

11. Herbert Fingarette, *Confucius: The Secular as Sacred* (New York: Harper & Row, 1972), 6, 4.

12. See Edward Slingerland's chapter in this volume for a full development of *wu-wei* in the *Analects*.

13. For a more developed discussion of this aspect of Confucius's thinking see David Jones and John L. Culliney, "Confucian Order at the Edge of Chaos: The Science of Complexity and Ancient Wisdom," in *Zygon: Journal of Religion and Science* 33, no. 3 (September 1998): 395–404.

14. David L. Hall and Roger T. Ames, *Thinking Through Confucius* (New York: State University of New York Press, 1987), 22.

15. Antonio S. Cua, "Concept of Paradigmatic Individuals in the Ethics of Confucius," *Inquiry* 14 (1971): 44–55.

16. D. C. Lau, *Confucius: The Analects* (New York: Penguin Books, 1979), 112, 12.1.

17. Tu Weiming, "Li: A Process of Humanization," *Philosophy East and West* 22, no. 2 (1972): 194.

18. H. G. Creel, *Confucius and the Chinese Way* (New York: Harper, 1960), 83.

19. Fingarette, *Confucius*, 20.

20. Hall and Ames, *Thinking Through Confucius*, 16.

21. David L., Hall and Roger T. Ames, *Thinking from the Han: Self, Truth, and Transcendence in Chinese and Western Culture* (Albany: State University of New York Press, 1998), 259.

22. Stuart Kauffman, *At Home in the Universe: The Search for the Laws of Self-Organization and Complexity* (New York: Oxford University Press, 1996).

23. Ames and Rosemont, *Analects of Confucius*, 46.

24. McCarthy, "Ethics in Between," 71.

25. See Ames and Rosemont, *Analects of Confucius*, 48, for a discussion on two possible etymologies of *ren*.

26. Hall and Ames, *Thinking from the Han*, 259.

27. Arthur Waley, *The Analects of Confucius* (New York: Vintage Books, 1938), 27.

28. A. C. Graham, *Disputers of the Tao: Philosophical Argument in Ancient China* (La Salle, IL: Open Court, 1989), 19.

29. Waley, *Analects of Confucius*, 28.

30. Graham, *Disputers*, 19.

31. Philip J. Ivanhoe, *Confucian Moral Self Cultivation* (Indianapolis: Hackett Publishing, 2000), ix.

32. Hall and Ames, *Thinking from the Han*, 171.

33. See P. J. Ivanhoe's chapter in this volume, "The 'Golden Rule' in the *Analects*," where he discusses in detail this continuous strand of *shu* and *zhong*.

34. I am indebted especially to Graham Parkes for these ideas.

35. D. C. Lau suggests this type of reading when he says, "*Chung* [*Zhong*] is the doing of one's best and it is through *chung* that one puts into effect what one had found out by the method of *shu*" (*Confucius*, 16). See also *Analects* 1.4.

36. I have intentionally left out the various degrees or levels of *ren* achievement such as *daren* (persons in high station), *shanren* (truly adept persons), *chengren* (consummate persons), *renzhe* or *renren* (authoritative persons), *shi* (scholar-apprentices), *junzi* (exemplary persons), and *shen* or *shengren* (sages) for purposes of simplification. See Ames and Rosemont, *Analects of Confucius*, 60, for further discussion of the last three categories of *ren* listed above.

37. *Yi* is often considered a central term for the ethical dimension of Confucius's thought in the following ways: (1) When applied to a particular act, *yi* will usually mean "right" as in "that was the right action to take" or "that was the right thing to do." (2) In discussions about kinds of actions, *yi* means duty, the act that one ought to perform in a given particular situation. (3) When *yi* is applied to agents who perform a right act, *yi* means righteous, dutiful, or moral person. Further, given the Confucius's relational sense of self, *yi* is usually used in reference to acts while *ren* is used to characterize persons. See Lau, *Confucius*, 26. These distinctions of *yi*, however, fall under the governance of *yi* as appropriateness or fittingness and harmony (*he*) — one ought to find his or her proper place within a broader context. *Li* always provides this wider context. See Ames and Rosemont, *Analects of Confucius*, 53, for demarcating *yi* from a Western ethical understanding. See the following passages in the *Analects* for *yi*: 1.13, 2.24, 4.5, 4.10, 4.12, 7.3, 7.16, 12.10, 12.20, 13.4, 14.12, 14.13, 15.17, 15.18 16.10 16.11, 17.23, 18.7, 19.1

38. See also 14.1, 1.15, and 4.9.

39. Hall and Ames, *Thinking from the Han*, 271. See also 1.12, 2.14, and 15.22.

PART 2

THINKING THROUGH CONFUCIUS

Paronomasia: A Confucian Way of Making Meaning

3

Roger T. Ames

In reading the *Analects of Confucius*, we find that a pervasive concern throughout this most seminal of the Confucian texts is sensitivity to the proper use of language. In the *Analects*, for example, we are told explicitly:

> The Master said, "Someone who does not understand the propensity of circumstances (*ming* 命) has no way of becoming an exemplary person (*junzi* 君子); someone who does not understand the observance of ritual propriety (*li* 禮) has no way of knowing where to stand; a person who does not understand words (*yan* 言) has no way of knowing others (*ren* 人)."[1]

In fact, according to the *Analects*, not only do we need to understand how to use language in general, we are exhorted to realize what is at risk in the choice of each and every word: "Exemplary persons must be ever so careful about what they say. On the strength of a single word others can deem them either wise (*zhi* 知) or foolish."[2] While Confucius allows that one word can be a person's ruin, he also says that another word, "deference (*shu* 恕)," captures everything that he has been trying to convey to his protégés and can be practiced with profit until the end of one's days.[3] Indeed, the central Confucian moral sensibility of becoming consummate in one's conduct (*ren* 仁) is defined unambiguously as *ren* 訒: "speaking with caution and modesty":

> Sima Niu inquired about consummate conduct (*ren* 仁). The Master replied, "Consummate persons are cautious in what they say (*ren* 訒)."
> "Does just being cautious in what one says make one consummate?" he asked.
> The Master replied, "When something is difficult to do, how can one but be cautious in what they say?"[4]

In what follows, I make much of the claim in this passage that, for Confucius, "saying" and "doing" are inseparable. And I think that it is no accident that *ren* 仁 "consummate conduct" is defined in this passage with a term that sounds almost the same, *ren* 訒 "speaking with caution and modesty." On scrutiny, we find that defining terms by invoking a combination of the semantic and phonetic associations they bring to mind is a familiar characteristic of the *Analects* specifically, and of the early philosophical literature broadly. For example, we read in *Analects*: "Ji Kangzi asked Confucius about governing effectively (*zheng* 政), and Confucius replied to him, 'Governing effectively (*zheng*) is doing what is proper (*zheng* 正). If you, Sir, lead by doing what is proper, who would dare do otherwise?'"[5]

If one were to look in the English language for comparable examples of this strategy for extending meaning, one might point to the way that playing on the several variations of the sound "so," as "sew" and "sow," might expand the meaning of each. Or one might point to the way that playing off of the many senses of "light" such as "to set fire to," "levity," "illumination," and "to dismount" (alight) might stimulate unexpected images and meaning. The technical term for defining, and in fact redefining, expressions by using words that sound alike or that have a similar meaning is "paronomasia." Significantly, in this paronomastic process, the expectation is that we are not just "discovering" definitions about an existing world, but actively delineating a world and bringing it into being.

Paronomastic definition is to be found everywhere in classical Chinese literature. When we consult traditional dictionaries that themselves chronicle the cultural associations of this world—the second-century *Shuowenjiezi*, for example—we discover that terms are not as much defined analytically and etymologically by appeal to essential, literal, putatively "root" meanings, as they are generally explained metaphorically or paronomastically by semantic and phonetic associations. "Exemplary person (*jun* 君)," for example, is defined by its cognate and phonetically similar term, "gathering (群)," an association that arises between two words because of the underlying assumption that people will gather round and defer to exemplary persons. After all, the *Analects* insists, "Excellent persons do not dwell alone; they are sure to have neighbors."[6] "Mirror (*jing* 鏡 or *jian* 鑒)" is defined as "shining radiantly (*jing* 景)" or "looking into, overseeing (*jian* 監)": a mirror is a source of illumination. "Battle formation (*zhen* 陣)" is defined as "displaying (*chen* 陳)": a battle formation's most important service is to a display strength that will deter an enemy. A "ghost or spirit (*gui* 鬼)" is defined as "returning (*gui* 歸)": presumably the *qi* of the deceased disperses and finds its way back to some more primordial condition. "The way (*dao* 道)" is defined as "treading (*dao* 蹈)": as the *Zhuangzi* says so eloquently, "The way is made in the walking 道行之而成."[7] "King (*wang* 王)" is defined as "going to (*wang* 往)": the people repair to the true king. Such examples are legion.

We can perhaps appreciate this paronomastic strategy for defining and thus knowing things better by drawing a contrast with the way Aristotle goes about the business of knowing a world. Aristotle employs the methods of logic as the basic means of articulating the patterns of discourse for all of the sciences that provide us with knowledge. For Aristotle, logic is not one among the various ways of knowing, but is the tool employed by all who would come to know. In addition to his attempts to classify the various disciplinary means of coming to know—theoretically, practically, and productively—there were the more "encyclopedic" efforts associated with the organization of the body of the known. The focus in classifying things in such a way is upon articulating the objective description of the "knowable" in relation to the "known." Mary Tiles offers us a summary of this Aristotelian genera/species mode of classification:

> The kind of rational structure which is given prominence in Aristotle's works is the structure of a classificatory system—a hierarchy of kinds of things organised successively by kinds (or genera) and forms of those kinds (or species). (In turn species become in effect genera to be divided into [sub]species and genera grouped into more comprehensive genera.) Definitions were not in the first instance thought to be accounts of words but of the "what-it-is-to-be" a thing of that kind, in other words accounts of essence. To define an object—give its name a precise or correct use—was to locate it in a classificatory system.[8]

For Aristotle, the most fundamental question of philosophy is ontological: "what is *'on'* or being?" And since being is most basically substance (*ousia*), what is the substance of something? Substance in its most primary sense describes a thing as an individual (*tode ti*), and then by extension as a species (*eidos*) and as a genus (*genos*). The species tells us more about the substance of a thing than its genus because it is closer to the individual primary substance: the fact that Socrates is a human being tells us more about him than the fact that he is a mammal.

Tiles provides a further account of how the application of Aristotle's classificatory system is thought to lead to new knowledge:

> This is a hierarchical order based on qualitative similarities and differences. A key assumption underlying such an order is that a thing cannot both have and lack a given quality—the requirement of non-contradiction. Non-contradiction is therefore fundamental to this kind of rational order. . . . Knowledge of definitions (or essences) coupled with the principle of non-contradiction can serve as the foundation for further, rationally demonstrable, knowledge.[9]

Returning to our theme of paronomasia, it depends upon neither the identification of essences nor on the principle of noncontradiction. Such ontological and logical assumptions have little relevance for the classical Confucian worldview. In fact, we can make a case that the principle of noncontradiction is challenged fundamentally by examining and understanding a familiar grammatical structure we find in the ancient Chinese texts. The value of the grammatical particle *ye* 也 is usually translated as "is," as in the passages from the *Analects*, "the life of a person is in being true 人知生也直" or "to know what you know and know what you do not know—this then is wisdom 知之為知之不知為不知是知也."[10] Although students of the classical Chinese language have been told expressly that *ye* in its usual role of marking noun predication is not the copula verb "to be,"[11] it is often schematized this way: AB也: 'A is B.'[12] I would argue that *ye* 也 as it is appears in the classical language is not divorced from its usage in modern Chinese, where it is a "paronomastic" particle that marks an association between one thing and some other thing, attribute, or quality— sometimes only a loose association at that. *Ye* does not entail strict identity, but rather introduces a comment on a topic: an additional bit of information that we might glean about the subject by extending its range of associations.

Below we will see that A. N. Whitehead's ontological principle asserting that all particular things and their unique qualities have an equal claim on reality applies also to Confucian processual thinking and to the cosmological assumptions that give it context. This principle of parity among things rules out Aristotle's fundamental ontological question: "what is the 'being' of something?" and the corollary notion of natural kinds that would follow from things having a common essence. Confucius's world will not yield up an Aristotelian classificatory system.

What is remarkable about this Chinese paronomastic way of generating meaning is that a word is defined nonreferentially by mining relevant and even seemingly random associations implicated phonetically or semantically in the term itself. The success of the association and the quantum of meaning derived from it, then, is dictated by the degree of relevance, with some protean associations being more thought-provoking and productive than others. As we have seen above, Confucius is able to make much out of the association between the cultivation of human excellence (*ren* 仁) and careful attention to what we say (*ren* 訒). Another discernible pattern in this mode of definition is that erstwhile "nouns" default to "verbal nouns" or "gerunds"—"things" are defined as "doings"—underscoring perhaps the primacy of process over form as a grounding presupposition in this "eventful" cosmology. Indeed, the classical Chinese counterpart to the substance ontology and essentialism that provides the basis for the Aristotelian method of defining and knowing recounted above is an appreciation of the changing relations among "events" in the flux and flow of a processual cosmology.

Tropes similar to paronomasia are not unheard of in our own cultural narrative, particularly as a device in literary counterculture. Certainly for the likes of the antinomian maverick, William Blake, wit *is* indeed wisdom, and rhyme *is* reason. And in the pre-Latinized and heroic Anglo-Saxon language, "kenning" is used to "name and make things known" by compounding terms and creating memorable images: a dictionary is a "word-hoard" or "word-pantry;" an ocean is "the whales' bath," "the foaming fields," "the sea-street;" the king is "the keeper of rings," and so on. In conjuring forth such metaphors, kenning generates associations that expand the horizon of our knowledge.

A closer look at "paronomasia" as "knowing better by tracing out relevant associations" provides us with a key for unlocking an understanding of how

Confucius would propose that we lead significant lives. After all, in Chinese the vocabulary of "knowing," far from suggesting the analytical recovery of the real substance behind appearances ("getting," "grasping," "comprehending," "understanding"), is a language of mapping out one's way in the world: "knowing the way (*zhidao* 知道)," "advancing, passing through (*tongda* 通達)," and "unraveling patterns (*lijie* 理解)." I want to explore how in the Confucian sensibility this paronomastic strategy for defining and redefining our terms of discourse serves as a device for knowledge production. In doing so, I argue that paronomasia, far from being merely a literary trope, is corollary to the analogical or correlative thinking that is a defining feature of the Confucian project in which one makes this particular life meaningful by achieving relational virtuosity.

We perhaps need to say a bit more about the *qi* 氣 processual cosmology that is a broadly shared worldview in classical China to determine why it is that this interplay of homophones and synonyms is so central to the way in which Confucians realize their world. The distinguished French Sinologist Marcel Granet observes rather starkly that "Chinese wisdom has no need of the idea of God."[13] This characterization of classical Chinese philosophy has had many iterations, albeit in different formulations, by many of our most prominent Sinologists both Chinese and Western alike. Indeed, our best interpreters of classical Chinese philosophy are explicit in rejecting the idea that Chinese cosmology begins from and is informed by some independent, transcendent principle, and as such, entails Plato and Aristotle's reality/appearance distinction and the plethora of dualistic categories that arise in the wake of such a worldview: God/world, good/evil, objective/subjective, mind/body, self/other, reason/emotion, and so on.[14]

One implication of the irrelevance of our familiar reality/appearance distinction—and there are many—is the absence of a clear difference between literal and metaphorical language. In the dualistic opposition established when reality is distinguished from appearance, the first term stands independent of the second and effectively negates it by having a superior claim on reality: reason negates emotion, for example, and is an engine that can find truth without reference to emotion. In fact, sentiment obstructs rather than reveals truth. In Chinese cosmology, by contrast, both of any dyadic pair of terms—*yin* and *yang*, for example—describe some aspect of a real world, and are thus correlative and interdependent. Indeed, reason and emotion as thinking and feeling are both equally real functions of the Confucian "heart-mind" (*xin* 心), and both of them are necessary in our search for true relations.

As mentioned above, classical Chinese cosmology begins from what Whitehead has called "the ontological principle":—the notion of an ontological parity of finitude that gives all such things an equal claim on being real—what we might alternatively term "a realistic pluralism."[15] This ontological principle is an affirmation of the reality of any thing as it is constituted by the harmony of its constitutive relations, whether it be each and every thing, each and every kind of thing, or the unsummed totality of things. In the *Zhongyong* we read: "The way of the world can be captured in one phrase: since events are never duplicated, their proliferation is unfathomable."[16] Such a world of unique particulars is a *kosmoi* rather than a *kosmos* in the sense that construals of order are many, and the totality is not dominated by any one thing. There is no "God" in this "pluriverse." Rather, order is the emergent harmony achieved in the contingent relationships among everything—"the myriad things and events (*wanwu* 萬物 or *wanyou* 萬有)"—with the closest thing to God being the spirituality attained by a thriving community living inspired lives. With no assumed "One-behind-the-many" as the ultimate source of meaning, there is no single-ordered world, no "*uni*-verse," only the ongoing evolving harmony expressed as the quality of life achieved by the insistent, co-creating particulars.

In this world in which things are constituted by their conditioning relations, meaning, instead of coming from a single source, is situational. Meaning arises *in situ* through the cultivation of deepening relations that we have called "the art of contextualization (*ars contextualis*)." This collateral, relational nature of personal and cosmic creativity—indeed, "co-creativity"—is what Hellmut Wilhelm is remarking upon when he observes "the division of the creative process into two aspects is an idea frequently found in early Chinese writings."[17]

Wilhelm's insight is borne out by the *Analects* in its description of how we create ourselves as persons: "Consummate persons establish others in seeking to establish themselves, and promote others in seeking to get there themselves."[18] When we say that such consummate persons "appreciate" others, we are allowing that they recognize the magnitude and complexity of another human being, and that in so doing, they strive to be responsive to the needs and aspirations of one of their fellows. But there is another important sense of "appreciate" that we need to register. In achieving this kind of concerned intimacy, both persons in the relationship quite literally "appreciate" each other in the sense that they accrue a dividend of meaning from their meaningful relationship, and in so doing, make each other a more valuable human being. Thick and robust relations are a source of growth in the world, enriching the family, the community, and the cosmos. It is thus that the vocabulary of personal realization in Confucian philosophy is described in the language of growth and extension: "personal excellence (*de* 德)," for example, is defined again paronomastically as "getting (*de* 得)," "spirituality (*shen* 神)" is "stretching and extending (*shen* 伸)," "becoming human (*ren* 人)" is a "becoming relationally virtuosic (*ren* 仁)," and so on. Indeed, the cosmos is bigger and better because contemporary encounters with Confucius continue to produce meaningful people.

In such a cosmos, ordering the world is always local and analogical: it begins here and goes there in a search for appropriately shared relationality. This is what Confucius means when he says: "I study what is near at hand and aspire to what is lofty 下學而上達"[19] and "correlating one's conduct with those near at hand can be said to be the method of becoming a consummate person 能近取譬可謂仁之方也已."[20] But not all relations are equally productive. In this Confucian tradition in which meaning arises in qualitatively increasingly robust relations, we quite literally "make" friends. Friendship is a relationship that is constituted by the characters of the two persons involved, where the continuity of a real meaningful friendship is a matter of vibrant disclosure in which two persons "change each other's minds" in the most concrete transformative sense of this expression. In fact, the two persons are "individuals" only as an abstraction from such concrete relationships. Importantly, the realization of this vital relationship is not at the expense of their personal uniqueness and integrity, but indeed a consequence of it. Integrity means both the persistent particularity of each friend, and the "becoming one together" that is both the substance of real friendship and a source of cosmic meaning. This understanding of relationality as intrinsic, constitutive, and productive is an "aesthetic order" in the sense that any aesthetic achievement aspires to the fullest disclosure of the particular details in the totality of the achieved effect—the "connectivity" of the friendship itself.

People have often puzzled over what Confucius means when he says, "do not befriend anyone who is not as good as you are."[21] The point he is making here is that through a regimen of self-cultivation, one has the opportunity to grow from an inchoate to a distinguished (*daren* 大人) and efficacious person (*shanren* 善人). This project of personal cultivation is pursued by developing fertile relations within the everyday roles of family and community. Such growth starts here and goes there: it "is self-originating—how could it originate with others?"[22] But relations with other people are not always benign. Indeed, they can be a source of growth or of diminution—they can either make you larger or smaller:

> Having three kinds of friends will be a source of personal growth; having three other kinds of "friends" will be a source of personal diminution. One stands to be improved by friends who are true, who make good on their word (*xin* 信), and who are broadly informed; one stands to be injured by "friends" who are ingratiating, who feign compliance, and who are glib talkers.[23]

In the contrast between "small persons (*xiaoren* 小人)" and "exemplary persons (*junzi* 君子)" that is brought into sharp focus by the many references to it in the *Analects*, small persons are not only socially and morally retarded individuals, but in their selfish conduct, they are also a continuing source of communal disintegration. By contrast, in most of the passages that describe the process of becoming friends, the text repeatedly invokes "making good on one's word (*xin* 信)" as the activity out of which rewarding friendships develop. Good friends are "made" through effective communication.[24] It ought not to be surprising that the character for the Confucian sages, *sheng* 聖, is composed of the characters for "ear (*er* 耳)" and "mouth (*kou* 口)," suggesting that the members of this highest order of humanity in their hearing and saying are virtuosic communicators.[25]

It is this centrality of communication that returns us to "paronomasia" as the ground of meaning. After all, we need to ask: what exactly is a relationship? What is the actual "content" of personal relations, and how do relations themselves produce meaning? The primary verbal meaning of "relate" is "to recite, to rehearse, to tell, to give a detailed account of a situation or series of events." I want to suggest that such "relatings" are not only discursive, but also constitutive. Beginning from the wholeness of experience, we are inextricably embedded in a pattern of relationships. Our inchoate relations then grow in value through various modes of associative discourse: language, music, ritualized conduct, body, food, and so on. Individuals are constituted as distinguished persons through the expanding patterns of deference that locate them in a communicating community, and community itself is produced through effective "relatings" and the consociation of its members. There is a vital difference between individuals "having" relationships and persons achieving their individuality through the cultivation of the shared relationships that constitute them. Associated living and the personal collaboration such individuality entails do not bring discrete people together in relationships, but rather make increasingly productive what is already constitutively related.

Confucius is himself keenly aware of the "ontology" of language—the power of this language (*ming* 名) to command (*ming* 命) this world into being. To know a world is to realize it in the sense of "making it real." Confucius is making precisely this point when he explains to his protégé Zilu[26] what he means by the central Confucian precept, *zhengming* 正名:

> "Were the Lord of Wey to turn the administration of his state over to you, what would be your first priority?" asked Zilu.
>
> "Without question it would be to insure that names are used properly (*zhengming*)." replied the Master.
>
> "Would you be as impractical as that?" responded Zilu. "What is it for names to be used properly anyway?"
>
> "How can you be so dense!" replied Confucius. "An exemplary person would defer on matters he does not understand. When names are not used properly, language will not be used effectively; when language is not used effectively, matters will not be taken care of; when matters are not taken care of, the observance of ritual propriety and the playing of music will not flourish; when the observance of ritual propriety and the playing of music do not flourish, the application of laws and punishments will not be on the mark; when the application of laws and punishments is not on the mark, the people will not know what to do with themselves. Thus, when the

exemplary person puts a name to something, it can certainly be spoken, and when spoken it can certainly be acted upon. There is nothing careless in the attitude of the exemplary person toward what is said."[27]

Zhengming has been translated conventionally, and indeed unfortunately, as "the rectification of names." In fact, for Confucius, proper discourse is not merely using language according to received, stipulated definitions, but simply put, is the engine that produces appropriate relations. *Zhengming* as it is explained here should in fact be understood as paronomasia —as the ongoing search for productive associations that will ultimately constitute the necessarily meaningful relations of a thriving community. Paronomasia is a redefining of our terms of understanding, explanation, and performance through semantic and phonetic associations in the ongoing reauthoring of our world.

Confucius is trying to make several points in this passage cited above that in degree confound our commonsense. Following Aristotle, we are inclined to respect fundamental distinctions between "to make (*poiein*)" and "to act (*prattein*)," and between an efficient cause or agent (*kinoun*) that initiates change, and the material, formal, and final causes that define the outcome of change.

Confucius on the other hand does not begin from such assumptions about discrete agency and productive activity. Rather, he starts situationally from the wholeness of experience, and from the premise that we articulate ourselves in our relations as persons and build character through what we say and do in our associated living. Taking our understanding of experience one step further, we are nothing more or less than the ongoing and sedimenting aggregate of these various levels of discourse: what we say and hear, what our countenances express and how it affects others, what our formal behaviors communicate and what they precipitate, what our body language and gestures indicate and how they are interpreted, and what our voices and songs convey and how others are prompted to respond to them. As such, we are the organisms that in our doings and undergoings emerge discursively out of these performances of ourselves in community.

A way to perhaps bring this Confucian sensibility into clearer focus is to invoke a cosmological distinction made by the contemporary Sinologist Pang Pu. Pang Pu in explaining the "birthing, life, and growth (*sheng* 生)" of the cosmos makes a crucial distinction between "*paisheng* 派生" in the sense of one thing giving birth to an independent existent, like a hen producing an egg, and "*huasheng* 化生" as one thing transforming into something else, like summer becoming autumn. When we apply this distinction to the birth, life, and growth of relational persons in community, such persons are discursively articulating themselves and transforming themselves as a continuing pattern of relationships within the communal manifold. In this process of *creatio in situ*, there is no product independent of the producer. Discourse is simply the outside of an inside in one's relationship to others. Cosmologically there is no progenitor independent of the progeny, but rather a proliferating and living on of the progenitor in the progeny. Analogously, in community, there is no speaker independent of the speech, but rather a living on of the speaker in the speech.

In this Confucian model of constitutive relations, then, we are not individuals who associate in community, but rather because we associate effectively in community we become distinguished as individuals; we do not have minds and therefore we speak with one another, but rather because we speak effectively with one another we become like-minded; we do not have hearts and therefore are empathetic with one another, but rather because we feel effective empathy with one another we become whole-hearted as a community.[28] Indeed, paronomasia—defining a world by associated living—is the Confucian way of making meaning in a communicating community.

Notes

1. *Analects* 20.3. Most translations of the *Analects* are taken directly from Roger T. Ames and Henry Rosemont, Jr., *The Analects of Confucius: A Philosophical Translation* (New York: Ballantine, 1998).

2. *Analects* 19.25. See also 1.6, 1.14, and 2.18.

3. *Analects* 15.24.

4. *Analects* 12.3. According to the Sima Qian, Sima Niu was garrulous and impulsive. Sima Qian 司馬遷, *Shiji* 史記 [Records of the grand historian] (Beijing: Zhonghua shuju, 1959), 2214–15. Confucius is speaking specifically to this condition, thereby criticizing those who do not treat their words as having the force of action.

5. *Analects* 12.7.

6. *Analects* 4.25.

7. *Zhuangzi* 4/2/33.

8. Mary Tiles, "Idols of the Market Place—Knowledge and Language" (unpublished manuscript), 5–6. A revised version is available in "Images of Reason in Western Culture," in *Alternative Rationalities*, ed. Eliot Deutsch (Honolulu: Society for Asian and Comparative Philosophy, 1992).

9. Tiles, "Images of Reason," 7–8.

10. *Analects* 6.19 and 2.17.

11. Edwin G. Pulleyblank, *Outline of Classical Chinese Grammar* (Vancouver: UBC Press, 1995), 20.

12. Pulleyblank, *Outline*, 16.

13. Marcel Granet, *La pensee chinoise* (Paris: Editions Albin Michel, 1934), 478.

14. See Tang Junyi 唐君毅, "Zhongguo zhexuezhong ziranyuzhouguan zhi tezhi" 中國哲學中自然宇宙觀之特質 [The distinctive features of natural cosmology in Chinese philosophy], in *Zhongxi zhexue sixiang zhi bijiao lunwenji* 中西哲學思想之比較論

文集 [Collected essays on the comparison between Chinese and Western philosophical thought] (Taipei: Xuesheng shuju, 1988), 100–103; Xiong Shili 熊十力, *Mingxinpian* 明心篇 (Taibei: Xuesheng shuju, 1977), 180–91; Zhang Dongsun 張東蓀, *Zhishi yu wenhua: Zhang Dongsun wenhua lunzhu jiyao* 知識與文化：張東蓀文化論著輯要, ed. Zhang Yaonan 張耀南 (Beijing: Zhongguo guangbo dianshi chubanshe, 1995), 271–72; Angus C. Graham, *Disputers of the Tao* (Chicago: Open Court, 1989), 22; Joseph Needham, *Science and Civilisation*, vol. 2 (Cambridge: Cambridge University Press, 1956), 290; Nathan Sivin, *Medicine, Philosophy and Religion in Ancient China: Researches and Reflections* (Aldershot, Hants.: Variorum, 1995), 3; Chad Hansen, *A Daoist Theory of Chinese Thought* (Oxford: Oxford University Press, 1992), 215; Norman J. Girardot, *Myth and Meaning in Early Taoism: The Theme of Chaos (Hun-tun)* (Berkeley: University of California Press, 1983), 64.

15. A. N. Whitehead, *Adventures of Ideas* (New York: Macmillan, 1933), 356.

16. *Zhongyong* 26.

17. Hellmut Wilhelm, *Heaven, Earth, and Man in the Book of Changes* (Seattle: University of Washington Press, 1977), 37.

18. *Analects* 6.30.

19. *Analects* 14.35.

20. *Analects* 6.30.

21. *Analects* 9.25.

22. *Analects* 12.1.

23. *Analects* 16.4.

24. See David L. Hall and Roger T. Ames, *Thinking from the Han: Self, Truth, and Transcendence in Chinese and Western Culture* (Albany: State University of New York Press, 1998), 254–69, for a fuller discussion of Confucian friendship.

25. On the recently recovered bamboo strip texts we often find an abbreviated version of the character for sage composed solely of these two elements.

26. Zilu was one of Confucius's best-known and favorite protégés. He was a person of courage and action who was sometimes upbraided by Confucius for being too bold and impetuous. When he asked Confucius if courage was indeed the highest virtue, Confucius tried to rein him in by replying that a person who has courage without a sense of appropriateness will be a troublemaker, and a lesser person will be a thief. Confucius's feelings for Zilu were mixed. On the one hand, he was constantly critical of Zilu's rashness and immodesty, and impatient with his seeming indifference to book learning. On the other hand, Confucius appreciated Zilu's unswerving loyalty and directness—he never delayed on fulfilling his commitments. But being nearer Confucius in age, Zilu with his military temper was not one to take criticism without giving it back. On several occasions, especially in the apocryphal literature, Zilu challenges Confucius's judgment in associating with political figures of questionable character and immodest reputation—the wife of Duke Ling of Wei, for example, where Confucius is left defending himself. At the end of the day, enormous affection for the irrepressible Zilu comes through the text.

27. *Analects* 13.3.

28. The *Analects* 2.3 contains the gist of this Confucian philosophy as a shame or "face" culture: "The Master said: 'Lead the people with administrative injunctions (*zheng* 政) and keep them orderly with penal law (*xing* 刑), and they will avoid punishments but will be without a sense of shame. Lead them with excellence (*de* 德) and keep them orderly through observing ritual propriety (*li* 禮) and they will develop a sense of shame, and moreover, will order themselves.'"

Confucius on Form and Uniqueness

4

James Behuniak, Jr.

It is recorded that the son of Confucius, Boyu, was once asked if he had received any special instruction from his father. Boyu replied that he had not. He reports that his father expected of him what he expected of all his students: mastery of the *Rites* (*li* 禮) and the *Songs* (*shi* 詩). These texts are at the heart of the Confucian curriculum: an integral part of cultural form (*wen* 文), listed first among the categories under which Confucius taught (7.25). Boyu admits to being lax in his studies of the classics. Confucius's response speaks to their importance in his curriculum. He says: "If you do not study the *Songs* you will be at a loss as to what to say" and "if you do not study the *Rites*, you be at a loss as to where to stand" (16.13). Confucius elsewhere instructs his son that trying to become a person without mastering the *Songs* is like "trying to take your stand with your face to the wall" (17.10).

Throughout the *Analects*, Confucius's attitude towards mastering the classics and maintaining proper form is clear: he claims not to be an innovator, reveres antiquity, dreams of the ancients, and identifies himself as heir to the values and institutions of the past.[1] In the words of Edward Slingerland, Confucius exhibits a "profound conservatism."[2] Along with mastery of the classics, Confucius attends to formal details in areas as diverse as oral pronunciation, garment color, hunting and fishing, the timbre of court music, and the seasoning of meat.[3] In this regard, Confucius understands himself to be the custodian of tradition. With King Wen no longer among the living, Confucius maintains that the entire cultural heritage (*wen* 文) resides with him (9.5).

Among readers today, the formalism of Confucius is not always well received. The average undergraduate is more likely to identify with Boyu's laxity with regard to the classics than with Confucius's stern admonishment to master them. The philosophical reasons for Confucian formalism, however, are actually quite profound, and when teaching Confucius, it is possible to generate sympathy for these reasons. Confucius desires that his audience understand his deference to form, and he fears being misunderstood. As he says: "In referring time and again to observing ritual propriety, how could I just be talking about gifts of jade and silk? And in referring time and again to making music, how could I just be talking about bells and drums?" (17.11). There is more to Confucian formalism than mere adherence to form. These forms serve a function that Confucius considers of greater importance than the formal details themselves.

I submit that Confucius adheres to form not intending simply to accord with the past; rather, he adheres to form intending to promote uniqueness in the present. Deficiency in form, according to Confucius, excludes one from participation in modes of social intercourse through which one's unique qualities register as significant. In other words, Boyu is admonished to study the classics in the interests of his own uniqueness, for it is only through education in the classics that he acquires the means to embark on a project of self-cultivation that culminates in the appreciation of his singular quality. Confucius summarizes this project as follows: "Arouse sensibility (*xing* 興) with the *Songs*; become established (*li* 立) through the *Rites*; and consummate yourself (*cheng* 成) through music" (8.8). It is orthodoxy with respect to song, ritual, and music that enables these institutions to serve the function that Confucius envisions. By adhering to form, Confucius does not mean to stifle personal uniqueness; to the contrary, Confucius understands form to be necessary to the preservation and promotion of that uniqueness.

Arousing Sensibility through Song

The *Songs* illustrate well the manner in which adherence to form promotes uniqueness in the *Analects*. Confucius cites the *Songs* more often than any other ancient source. Wondering aloud why students neglect the *Songs*, he presents the following to be the advantages of mastering them: "An apt quotation from the *Songs* can arouse sensibilities, provide insight, bring people together, and help voice complaints. It enables one to serve one's father when close to home, and to serve one's lord when far away. And through them one acquires a broad vocabulary to distinguish animals and plants" (17.9).

The *Songs* provide the semiotic foundation for a variety of sophisticated conversations. The prerequisite for participation in these conversations is indeed rote memorization; this, however, is not the sole requirement. Confucius maintains that one must register what is important in a concrete situation in order to use the songs effectively. As he says: "If one can recite all three hundred songs by heart and yet, when given responsibility to govern, fails to move things forward; or when sent as an envoy to distant quarters, is unable to engage one's counterpart, then even if one has mastered so many, of what use are they?" (13.5). The songs are not simply memorized for the sake of posterity. The songs are memorized in order to maintain a common fund of images that help foreground what is important in the present. This focus on the present illustrates one of the hallmarks of Confucian education: "reviewing the old in order to realize the new" (2.11). Confucius regards the ability to "realize the new" (*zhixin* 知新) as the most desirable trait in his students. Confucius's favorite student, Yan Hui, is recognized for this ability: "being told one thing," we learn, "he realizes ten" (5.9).

In the *Analects*, canonical songs play an important role in generating opportunities to realize the new. In conversation with Confucius, Zixia asks:

"What does the song mean when it says,

> *Her smiling cheeks—so radiant. Her dazzling eyes—so sharp and clear. It is the unadorned that is colored?"*

The Master replied: "Color is applied to what is originally unadorned."
Zixia then inquired: "Does ritual form (*li* 禮) itself come after?"
The Master replied: "Zixia, you have stimulated my thoughts. It is only with people like you that one can discuss the *Songs*." (3.8)

In this exchange, Zixia draws on his familiarity with the *Songs* to guide the discussion in a new direction. He transforms an image into a moment of insight: a commentary on the relationship between refinement through ritual form (*li* 禮) and the unique, unadorned qualities (*zhi* 質) native to a person. We will return to this relationship.

In a similar exchange, Confucius and Zigong discuss the relationship between wealth and virtue. Model sayings are traded until Zigong introduces a verse: "*'Like bone carved and polished; like jade cut and ground.'* Is this not what you have in mind?" (1.15). Confucius recognizes Zigong's ability to deploy a song to inspire reflection and carry the conversation forward. He says, "Zigong, it is only with people like you that I can discuss the *Songs*. From what is established you realize what comes next" (1.15). In realizing what comes next (*zhilai* 知來), a philosophical connection is made rather than found. Zigong's insight is original: he introduces an image into the discussion and thus broadens the scope of the conversation. Confucius appreciates such ingenuity. Zigong "realizes" what comes next by "making it real" (*zhi* 知) in a particular context.[4] He exploits the fact that the songs are, as David Schaberg says, "intrinsically interpretable."[5] They open themselves to novel disambiguation in each unique context.

Confucius is said to have personally edited the *Songs*, assembling 305 canonical songs from a repository of three thousand. This original repository was collected from all corners of China in order to register the raw feeling and sentiments of the people.[6] Confucius recognizes that the songs convey raw emotive force, unassailable veracity, and the "uncontrolled genuineness" of a rustic purity.[7] In the repertoire of the creative student, the *Songs* facilitate the transmission of those qualities into the present. As Confucius sees the matter, to memorize the *Songs* is to have a broad range of qualitatively human experience at one's disposal. When one draws from this experience in articulating one's own unique sentiments, one can be assured that what one says will fall within the compass of what is communicable. In other words, so long as one's sentiment remains consonant with the fund of recognizable human sentiments, one can be vigorous in one's uniqueness without swerving into perversity or insignificance. As Confucius says: "Although the songs are three hundred in number, they can be covered in one expression: *'Go vigorously without swerving'*" (2.2).

Becoming Established through Ritual

Confucius's conservatism towards form is most plainly evident in his attitude towards ritual propriety (*li* 禮). In responding to Yan Hui's inquiry into becoming a person of associated humanity (*ren* 仁), Confucius relates the following: "Do not look at anything that violates ritual (*li* 禮). Do not listen to anything that violates ritual. Do not say anything that violates ritual. Do not move in any way that violates ritual" (12.1). It is difficult to see how such a scrupulous adherence to form could promote the unique qualities of a person. Confucius, however, appears not to see any conflict. In the same passage he says: "Becoming a person of associated humanity is self-originating (*youji* 由己). How could it originate from another?"(12.1). Along with the deference to ritual form, there is clearly some critical element of self-cultivation that Confucius identifies as wholly unique to the person.

One way of understanding the relationship between form and uniqueness in the *Analects* is to pursue the connection between cultural form (*wen* 文) and the unique qualities (*zhi* 質) of a person, a connection alluded to by Zixia above and discussed throughout the *Analects*. As do the *Songs*, ritual forms (*li* 禮) also serve to render unique expressions fitting and appropriate. Confucius says: "Exemplary persons learn broadly of cultural forms (*wen* 文), discipline this learning through observing ritual (*li* 禮), and moreover, in so doing, can remain on course without straying from it" (6.27 and 12.15). Confucius insists, however, that such formal refinement must be balanced with one's unique qualities, and that becoming an exemplary person (*junzi* 君子) is an ideal integration of the two. As he says: "When quality (*zhi* 質) overwhelms form (*wen* 文), one is a rustic (*ye* 野). When form overwhelms quality, one is a pedant. Only when form and quality are combined is one an exemplary person" (6.18).

Despite this ideal of balance, however, Confucius is so weary of pedantry and hollow formalism that, if pressed, he sides with the rustic. As he says: "The first to initiate ritual and music were the rustic folk (*yeren* 野人). The exemplary persons (*junzi* 君子) came to them later. When it comes to putting ritual and music to use, I accord with those who came to them first" (11.1). Perhaps following this cue, there are those around Confucius who propose that the rustic qualities (*zhi* 質) of one's person alone dictate whether or not one becomes an exemplary person. Ji Zicheng suggests as much: "Exemplary persons are determined by nothing other than their quality (*zhi* 質); what need is there for form (*wen* 文)?" (12.8). Zigong, representing Confucius's preference for a balance between form and uniqueness, delivers the rebuke: "Form (*wen* 文) is no different from quality (*zhi* 質), and quality no different from form. The skin of a tiger or leopard, shorn of its coat, is no different from the dog or sheep" (12.8). Form and quality, once blended, are one. The concluding trope suggests again that formal refinement (*wen* 文) in fact *promotes* the appreciation of unique qualities. Without formal refinement, real difference goes underappreciated: tigers and leopards are importantly different from dogs and sheep; however, shorn of the patterns (*wen* 文) that emerge on their coats, these differences might go undetected.

Here, the rationale for form is that, in the absence of structure for promotion and reinforcement, genuine qualities depreciate—and at worst, they fail to be differentiated from counterfeits. The balance, however, is very delicate: in order to be recognized as genuine, a quality must find its integral fulfillment through the operation of form, but form alone is not enough. For example, Confucius is once asked to comment on a boy from a neighboring village who comes carrying a message, a task that was complex in ritual form and normally executed by adults.[8] Asked if he thought the boy was making progress, Confucius responds, "I have seen him sitting in places reserved for his seniors, and walking side by side with his elders. This is someone intent on growing up fast rather than on making progress" (14.44). In sending messages, the boy was not becoming established (*li* 立) through ritual form; rather, he was simply usurping the places (*wei* 位) reserved for those better qualified than himself. The boy was all form and no quality. Confucius would no doubt encourage the boy to make progress, but he would remind such an upstart, "Do not worry about not having a place (*wei* 位); worry about what it takes to become established (*li* 立)" (4.14).

Ritual serves to establish excellence by maintaining the forms and institutions that enable its development. Such forms are not coercive; rather, they generate the positive freedom to achieve the cultivation of one's unique abilities. The world of sports provides useful illustrations of how form operates in the Confucian framework. To paraphrase William James: "The aim of a football team is not merely to get the ball to a certain goal. If that were so, they would simply get up on some dark night and place it there. Rather, the aim is to get it there under a set of conditions: the game's rules and the other players."[9] Formal regulations in a football game do not stifle creativity and personal expression; quite the opposite, these constraints furnish the conditions under which these and other qualities can be developed and recognized. Without regulation and form (*wen* 文), there would be no way to showcase the raw quality (*zhi* 質) of the athlete. He or she can only excel within the constraints posed by the form of the sport. The most excellent professional athletes so exemplify the form of a sport that their unique contributions become indistinguishable from the sport itself. In a very real sense, Pete Sampras *is* lawn tennis and Michael Jordan *is* basketball. Confucius would immediately recognize such excellence.

In the Confucian framework, form and uniqueness work together. However much a conservative he is, Confucius does not consider one aspect more important than the other. In fact, on occasion we find him privileging the more rustic, unrefined qualities unique to one's native disposition. Recall the discussion with Zixia: "Color is applied to what is originally unadorned" (3.8). The unique qualities of a person are never out of sight or out of mind for Confucius.

This reading of the form/quality (*wen/zhi* 文質) relation is in keeping with the aesthetic measure of harmony (*he* 和), the paramount value that informs early Confucian thinking. No account of Confucian "conservatism" is adequate without an account of the normative measure of harmony. We learn in the *Rites* that the unique taste of raw sugar and the unique texture of an unpainted surface possess their uniqueness prior to becoming ingredients in the aesthetic wholes that subsequently showcase those respective qualities. The same holds true for the person who studies ritual. The *Rites* reads: "What is sweet can be brought into harmony (*he* 和), and what is bare can be brought into vibrant color. And likewise, persons who are genuine and sincere (*zhongxin* 忠信) are capable of studying ritual (*li* 禮)."[10] To understand the function of ritual form, this conceptual link to the aesthetics of harmony (*he* 和) must be recovered. Just as raw sweetness is preserved in a dish and bare surface quality is preserved in a painting, what is unique to and most genuine about a person is ideally preserved through ritual form.

As Master You reminds us: "Achieving harmony (*he* 和) is the most important function of ritual (*li* 禮)" (1.12). The notion of harmony is best illustrated through its association with the culinary arts, and particularly with making soup. The *Zuozhuan* expresses this most clearly: "Harmony (*he* 和) is similar to soup. Soup is made by adding various kinds of seasoning to water and then cooking fish and meat in it. One mixes them all together and adjusts the flavor by adding whatever is deficient and reducing whatever is in excess. It is only by mixing together ingredients of different flavors that one is able to create a balanced, harmonized taste."[11] Flavorful soup is constituted by the ratio of its unique ingredients. Its harmony (*he* 和) is measured by the degree to which it succeeds in incorporating those unique ingredients in a productive way.

Onion, for instance, is wonderful in soup; but one does not therefore add all the onion at one's disposal. This would disrupt the unique contributions of other ingredients and would result in disharmony. The most harmonious soup effectively showcases the unique quality (*zhi* 質) of the onion: it balances its flavor with other ingredients, thereby tempering its otherwise strong taste. A more contemporary example of this ancient value is the popular Japanese television program *Iron Chef*. Here master chefs are challenged to prepare five dishes that showcase a single "theme" ingredient that is announced only at the moment of taping. Contestants have one hour to bring the uniqueness of the theme ingredient into harmony with whatever else is at hand, and they are judged in three categories: taste, creativity, and presentation. In order to win, a chef must succeed in bringing out the best in an ingredient in a variety of culinary combinations.[12]

There is something similar at work in the Confucian tradition; ritual (*li* 禮) showcases what is most unique about a person by harmonizing that uniqueness in a variety of social arrangements. Here too, taste, creativity, and presentation are considerations. Just as the Iron Chef brings out what is best in an onion, Confucius understands that "the exemplary person brings out what is aesthetically best (*mei* 美) in others" (12.16). While the unique features of an onion are rendered delicious in a well-harmonized soup, the strongest feelings and desires of a person are rendered social and communicable in a well-harmonized ritual. Soup and ritual each function as forms (*wen* 文) to temper an idiosyncrasy or excess that might persist in the absence of adequate expression. Both soup and ritual promote the expression of a unique quality (*zhi* 質); both give it outlet and render its expression palatable and aesthetically fitting.

It is evident that, in the refinement and expression of uniqueness through ritual, Confucius prioritizes the genuine expression of the uniqueness over the formalism of the ritual. When asked about what is fundamental (*ben* 本) to ritual in reference to the mourning rituals, Confucius says: "It is better to express real grief than to worry over formal details" (3.4). Rituals are designed to facilitate the public expression of feelings that are unique and personal. In performing the function of harmony (he 和), ritual operates in refining the transmission of those feelings. Like the canonical song, ritual form renders sentiment appropriate and communicable, while aiming at adequate expression. As Ziyou remarks, "In mourning one expresses one's grief fully, and stops at that" (19.14). The underlying idea is that optimal expression is fully achieved when a proper balance is struck between form and uniqueness. This is what harmony (*he* 和) means in the early Confucian tradition. The idea also informs Confucius's appreciation of the musical arts.

Consummation through Music

As we have seen, in insisting that his students study the canonical songs and not violate the rules of ritual propriety, Confucius displays his "conservative" deference to form. He exhibits a similar deference when it comes to music: "When the master was with others who were singing and they sang well, he would invariably ask them to sing the piece again before joining in the harmony (*he* 和)" (7.32). To contribute one's unique voice to a harmony requires deference to the chorus of others. To contribute deferentially results in a feeling of satisfaction: one's unique voice is recognized and appreciated. To enter into an ensemble without due deference causes dissonance, and this results in a feeling of shame: one is detested for interfering with something that was otherwise going well (*shan* 善). In listening to the tune before joining in, Confucius illustrates once again that deference to form preserves uniqueness by creating the conditions under which that uniqueness can find optimal expression and appreciation.

Confucius is an avid lover and devoted student of music.[13] Ensemble music represents the power to harmonize difference without a loss of uniqueness: a value that is central to Confucius's overall philosophy. Confucius learns the lessons of music from the Grand Music Master of Lu: "Much can be realized through music if one begins by playing in unison, and then goes on to improvise with purity of tone and distinctness and flow, thereby bringing all to completion (*cheng* 成)" (3.23). The culmination (*cheng* 成) that comes with an achieved harmony (*he* 和) carries with it an aesthetic intensity that foregrounds the uniqueness of its parts. Before the background of harmony, uniqueness finds its proper amplification. If the uniqueness disappears into the background, the result is a zeroing of intensity. This would result in a numbing sameness (*tong* 同) to which Confucius is steadfastly opposed: "Exemplary persons seek harmony (*he* 和) not sameness (*tong* 同); petty persons do the opposite" (13.23). Despite his adherence to form, Confucius cares most that the forms he advocates not overwhelm the expression of what is most unique about the person. The richness of human experience must not be allowed to reduce to a bland and insipid sameness.

To summarize: in encouraging deference to form, Confucius intends to secure the means by which the uniqueness that makes life interesting and significant is expressed. Also, in doing so, he intends to expose the duplicity of the counterfeit and frustrate the starched and punctilious formalism of the pedant. In adhering to form, Confucius is less the stern traditionalist and more the forward-thinking aesthete who understands that continuity and harmony are prerequisites for novel significance. Confucius maintains that if one cultivates one's person by arousing sensibilities through the songs, becoming established through ritual, and consummating oneself through music, one maintains uniqueness without frivolity and achieves distinction without arrogance.[14]

Mencius expresses appreciation for Confucius's own uniqueness in words that underscore the aesthetic harmony implied in the project of forming one's person along those lines: "In Confucius, we have a concert of great achievement (*dacheng* 大成). Such an achievement commences with large bells and concludes with jade tubes. The cultivation of coherence (*li* 理) begins with the large bells, and the jade tubes bring that coherence to a close."[15] Confucius surely hoped that his son would achieve such consummate distinction of character in his lifetime; hence, he admonished Boyu to master the tradition in the interest of his own uniqueness. While there is indeed a "profoundly conservative" side to Confucius, it is important to recognize that there is a profoundly progressive side to his teaching as well. Confucius in many ways prioritizes uniqueness over form. This is a crucial part of his overall philosophy, and its inclusion results in a much fuller and more favorable picture.

Notes

1. *Analects* 7.1, 7.20, 7.5, and 3.14.

2. Edward Slingerland, *Confucius: Analects* (Indianapolis, IN: Hackett Publishing Company, 2003), 87.

3. *Analects* 7.18, 17.18, 7.27, 15.11, and 10.8.

4. Ames and Rosemont stress the performative function of the term *zhi* 知. See Roger T. Ames and Henry Rosemont, Jr., *The Analects of Confucius* (New York: Ballantine Publishing Group, 1998), 55.

5. David Schaberg, "Song in the Historical Imagination in Early China," *Harvard Journal of Asiatic Studies* 59, no. 2 (1999): 339.

6. Ibid., 308.

7. Cf. ibid., 337.

8. Slingerland, *Confucius: Analects*, 173.

9. I borrow this example from James's *Pragmatism*, where it is used in another context and stated differently. See his lecture "Some Metaphysical Problems Pragmatically Considered" in William James, *Pragmatism* (Indianapolis, IN: Hackett Publishing Company, 1981), 52–53.

10. James Legge, *The Chinese Classics*, 5 vols. (Hong Kong: University of Hong Kong Press, 1994), vol. 1, 414. Translation is my own.

11. Legge, *Chinese Classics*, vol. 5, 684. Translation is my own.

12. The program was launched in 1993 and soon became a hit in Japan. It has also become popular internationally. At the time of writing, the program is still produced by FujiTV and distributed internationally via the Food Network. There is an American version as well, entitled *Iron Chef America*.

13. *Analects* 3.25 and 7.14.

14. *Analects* 8.8 and 13.26.

15. *Mencius* 5B: 1. Translation is my own.

Three Corners for One: Tradition and Creativity in the *Analects*

5

Sor-hoon Tan

> *If on showing students one corner they do not come back to me with the other three, I will not repeat myself.*
>
> —*Analects 7.8*

Is Confucius merely a more demanding teacher than others in asking for three corners after supplying only one, rather than asking for one corner after supplying three? This passage is more thought provoking than that. The "one corner" given cannot possibly determine the other three without specifying the size of the square: there are infinite sets of three corners that could be offered as appropriate responses. There is no one "correct" answer; although some answers are wrong since it must be a square (implied but not actually used in the passage, the square [*fang* 方] has normative connotations of model or direction). This underdetermination of responses in pedagogical situations leaves more room for creativity in Confucianism than has usually been recognized.

Confucianism and Iconoclastic Attacks on Tradition

Confucianism is more often considered hostile to creativity. After all, in the *Analects*, Confucius says of himself: "Following the proper way, I do not forge new paths (*shu er bu zuo* 述而不作)"[1] Wing-tsit Chan renders this passage as "I transmit but do not create." Other translations of *zuo* include "innovate," "invent," "make up something new."[2] The Han dynasty lexicon *Shuowen jiezi* glossed *zuo* as "to arise (*qi* 起)," "to begin (*shi* 始)," "to make (*wei* 為)"; though different in meaning, it resembles "to give birth to (*sheng* 生)."[3] Given that novelty is part of the definition of creativity (for example, "ability to bring something new into being" or "to create is to act in the world, or on the world, in a *new* and significant way"),[4] whereas tradition involves the transmission of something from the past, and therefore old, to the present, tradition and creativity are often opposed in terms of the opposition between old and new.

Confucius is unequivocal about his love for the past. After declaring that he only transmits but does not create, he continues, "with confidence I cherish the ancients" (7.1; see also 7.20). He holds up past personalities or practices as exemplars for the present (3.16; 4.22; 14.40; 15.25) and compares contemporary phenomena unfavorably with those of the past (14.24; 17.16). Confucius claims that, for a state to be viable, it should "introduce the calendar of the Xia dynasty, ride on the large yet plain carriage of Yin, wear the ceremonial cap of Zhou" (15.11). Of these three early dynasties, Confucius is particularly fond of the Zhou. Many understand his admission that he "follows Zhou" (3.14) as a desire to restore the clan-based social organization and government of the early Zhou dynasty by reviving the ritual practices which were supposedly instituted by the Duke of Zhou.[5] Such interpretations paint Confucius as a traditionalist intent on preserving the past, rendering Confucianism incompatible with progress, modernity, and modernization.

The traditionalist view of Confucius's teachings is reinforced by the attack on tradition during the May Fourth movement in early twentieth-century China. Confucianism was blamed for the stagnation of Chinese society and "Down with the Confucian shop" was a favorite slogan of May Fourth intellectuals in their quest for science and democracy.[6] Chen Duxiu's December 1916 article, "The Way of Confucius and Modern Life," which appeared in *The New Youth*, rejected the way of Confucius as incompatible with modern life: "The ethics [Confucius] promoted is the ethics of a feudal age. . . . The objectives, ethics, social norms, mode of living, and political institutions did not go beyond the privilege and prestige of a few rulers and aristocrats and had nothing to do with the happiness of the great masses."[7] This is certainly undemocratic in not even achieving government for the people, let alone government by the people. More significantly, Chen singled out "Confucian teachings of filial piety and obedience to the point of the son not deviating from the father's way even three years after his death and the woman obeying not only her father and husband but also her son" for making impossible the democratic participation and individual independence that define modern life.[8]

The perceived contradiction between tradition and modernity often includes a contradiction between tradition and creativity, as the importance of creativity in Western thinking is often linked to the processes of modernity, especially the exaltation of freedom accompanying the rise of individualism. Daniel Miller argues that the continuous and rapid change under modernity demands creativity in humanity, who must now "forge for itself the criteria by which it will live."[9] The legacy of May Fourth anti-Confucianism is still evident in contemporary attitudes toward the effect of Confucianism on creativity. A recent *International Herald Tribune* special report on China grapples with the widespread perception that the country lacks the capacity for academic originality, and excels only at imitation rather than innovation. In the article, China's Confucian heritage, especially Confucianism's emphasis on hierarchy and deference to elders, heads the list of factors responsible for the country's relative lack of creativity.[10]

Similarly, a Singaporean writer explains that Asians are less creative because their societies differ from "the liberal individualistic societies of the West," as a result of their outmoded Confucian ways of bringing up children.

> In the Confucian societies of the East, *filial piety* is of paramount importance. . . . The cultural emphasis on filial piety means that children from a traditional Asian family are raised in terms of whether their conduct meets some external moral criteria. . . . Dependence of the child on the parents is encouraged, and breaking the will of the child, so as to obtain complete obedience, is considered desirable. There is less interest in encouraging the child's expression of opinion, autonomy and independence."[11]

Ng's aim in his book is to promote creativity in Asian society by learning from the West; he emphasizes that neither Asian nor Western societies are homogeneous entities, and that perhaps some Western scholars will write a book about what Western societies could learn from Asian societies to complement his. Still, the view of Confucian filial piety in Ng's book, though not an uncommon one in East Asian societies, ignores the complexity of the tradition and the actual teachings found in the texts. More in-depth studies of filial piety and other aspects of the Confucian heritage hopefully will counter such oversimplification.[12]

Benjamin Schwartz criticizes the simplistic opposition of tradition and modernity for its misplaced concreteness. Such dualism treats tradition "as a kind of static setting whose features can be described in terms of a few well-chosen propositions," failing to recognize that it is "a short-hand way of referring to vast inchoate and by no means internally integrated areas of human experience."[13] Few of those who attacked or defended tradition during the May Fourth period offered in-depth comprehensive analysis of the Chinese tradition; perhaps they did not have an adequate language for doing so.[14] Most May Fourth attacks on tradition were influenced by the static conception of tradition opposed to modernity that was prevalent in the work of many nineteenth-century Western thinkers. However, in the second half of the twentieth century, scholars have questioned the assumption that "modern societies, being oriented to change, were anti-traditional or nontraditional, while traditional societies, by definition were necessarily opposed to change."[15] The works of Edward Shils and others argue that tradition is not simply an obstacle to change but an essential framework to creativity.[16]

A rehabilitation of tradition has also occurred in philosophy. Hans-Georg Gadamer rejects the Enlightenment's prejudice against tradition and argues that rather than always subjecting us to blind prejudices and limiting our freedom, tradition as "the commonality of fundamental and enabling prejudices" is neither irrational nor always unfree. "The fact is that in tradition there is always an element of freedom and of history itself. Even the most genuine and pure tradition does not persist because of the inertia of what once existed. It needs to be reaffirmed, embraced, cultivated."[17] From a different philosophical perspective and for different purposes, Alasdair MacIntyre emphasizes the importance of tradition in making sense of morality. Objecting to ideological use of the concept by conservative political theorists following Edmund Burke, who contrasts tradition with reason and the stability of tradition with conflict, MacIntyre argues that "all reasoning takes place within the context of some traditional mode of thought, transcending through criticism and invention the limitations of what had hitherto been reasoned in that tradition. . . . Moreover when a tradition is in good order it is always partially constituted by an argument about the goods the pursuit of which gives to that tradition its particular point and purpose."[18]

The Meaning of *Chuan Tong* (Tradition) in Confucianism

It is against the background of these inspiring philosophical, historical, and sociological studies of tradition that I propose to examine the relationship between tradition and creativity in the *Analects*. A more nuanced understanding of tradition and its continued importance is not limited to Western scholarship. Chinese scholars who have reflected critically on whether and how Chinese tradition could transform itself to meet new challenges of the twentieth century also have offered conceptions of tradition as creative and liberating. Xu Fuguan defines *chuantong* (a neologism for "tradition" adopted from Japanese) as "the way of life and ideas of a group or a people passed from generation to generation. . . . there is orderly continuity in time . . . there is unity in space."[19] Xu distinguishes between low-order tradition and high-order tradition. The former includes all customs and habits of the people; it is concrete and passive, lacking the capacity for self-criticism and self-transformation. High-order tradition is the intellectual and spiritual crystallization of low-order tradition; it is the creation of founders of religions, sages, artists, and thinkers. High-order tradition is critical of low-order tradition and reflectively links the past with present and future. It is idealistic and dynamic and constantly evolving. In inheriting the past, it simultaneously transcends the past. This idea of high-order tradition is important in the context of Confucianism; it consists of not whatever has been passed down for many generations but only a very selective part of the past that has been deliberately cultivated, preserved, and transmitted because it is considered valuable.

The characters *chuan* 傳 and *tong* 統 were not found together in either the *Analects* or the *Mencius*. They are associated (but not used as a single term) only in the *Xunzi*. In his criticisms of Zisi and Mencius, Xunzi condemns the "stupid, indecisive, and deluded Ru" of his day who, in receiving and passing on (*chuan* 傳) the teachings of Mencius and Zisi on the *wuxing* 五行,

are fragmentary in following the model of ancient kings and do not know its *tong* ("guiding principles").[20] The most significant use of *tong* in early Chinese thought is probably in the idea of *dayitong* 大一統, the great unification, which refers not only to political unification, but also to a comprehensive definitive moral order uniting all under heaven that came to be understood as the Confucian order. This idea is central to Dong Zhongshu's arguments in favor of the famous policy of "abolishing and dismissing the hundred schools; venerating only the Confucian arts (*bachu baijia duzun rushu* 罷黜百家獨尊儒術)" in the Han dynasty that sets Confucianism on the course of cultural and political hegemony. To Dong, the Confucian way represents the constant defining order of the cosmos ("the constant warp of heaven-earth," *tiandi zhi changjing* 天地之常經) and the fitting connection of past and present (*gujin zhi tongyi* 古今之通誼).[21] We also find the idea of moral-political order in Mencius's view that the empire could be "settled through unity" and Xunzi's assertion that "The world does not have two ways, and the sage is not of two minds."[22] It is worth noting that Mencius's point about unity is not about eliminating diversity but to emphasize that those who resort to violence could never achieve such unity. Given Xunzi's syncretism, his "one way" is a unity of diversity.

Implicit in the idea of a unified moral order is a concern with orthodoxy, which became explicit in the concept of *daotong* 道統. Apparently this concept was first used explicitly by Zhu Xi 朱熹.[23] The political reversals of Zhu Xi's school of thought reveal only too well the ideological opportunism behind official interest in orthodoxy. Some scholars considered *daotong* to be the center of Chinese traditionalism.[24] According to Shils, "traditionalism is the self-conscious deliberate affirmation of traditional norms, in full awareness of their traditional nature and alleging that their merit derives from that traditional transmission from a sacred origin."[25] While the ideological and extremist tendencies of traditionalism are always a threat, the debates over orthodoxy more often than not problematize legitimacy within the Confucian tradition, even as it is being used as a means of legitimating. Julia Ching's discussion of *daotong* shows that the determination of the line of transmission was problematic from the start given "the contradiction inherent in a 'lineal' transmission of 'insights' into a dynamic truth."[26] Non-circular criteria are fundamentally lacking for such determination. Dialectical contest among leading Confucians over the transmission is how the tradition advances and renews itself over time, while the use of orthodoxy as a device for legitimating political rule threatens the tradition with stagnation. As Ching observes, "as a doctrine, Confucianism had always been eclectic until officially approved and made thereby to stagnate."[27]

Some consider the idea of orthodoxy already germane in the *Analects*' description of the "succession" from Yao to the House of Zhou (20.1). While linking this succession with priorities that coincide with Confucius's teaching about authoritative conduct (17.6) indicates that Confucius is transmitting the way of the sage kings Yao and Shun, the *Analects* gives us little reason to believe that he is as dogmatic and intolerant toward other teachings as some later Confucians defending orthodoxy.[28] I consider it significant that the character *tong* does not even appear in the *Analects*, especially in conjunction with Confucius's openness in his own transmission of the past. He refuses to insist on certainty and rejects inflexibility (9.4); and discussing the action of those who would rather die in exile than serve a ruler with questionable legitimacy or ethics, Confucius says, "I do not have presuppositions as to what may or may not be done" (18.8).[29]

The most famous *Analects* passage that is usually cited to prove Confucius's traditionalism used *shu* 述 instead of *chuan*: "The Master said, 'Following the proper way (述), I do not forge new paths; with confidence I cherish the ancients—in these respects I am comparable to our venerable Old Peng'" (7.1). The character *chuan* was used in two passages; neither involves Confucius. Zengzi says, "Daily I examine myself on three counts. . . . In what has been passed on (*chuan* 傳) to me, have I failed to carry it into practice?" (1.4). Criticized by a fellow student for teaching his students superficial skills "without roots," Zixia responds, "On the path of the exemplary person (*junzi* 君子), what is passed on first and what must wait until maturity, can be compared to plants which must be nurtured differently according to kind. . . . It is the sage alone who walks this path every step from start to finish" (19.12). What is transmitted is meant to be put to use, and moreover, it is sometimes open to question whether something is really important and *worth* transmitting through learning and teaching.

The implication of transmitting only what is worthy is also implicit in the two appearances of *shu* outside *Analects* 7.1. In 14.43, Confucius scolds Yuan Rang for *zhang er wu shu yan* 長而无述焉—"growing up without having accomplished anything at all to pass on" (Ames and Rosemont) or "to have passed on nothing worthwhile when grown up" (Lau). In 17.19, Confucius expresses a desire to give up speech, prompting this appeal from Zi Gong, "If you do not speak, how will we your followers find the proper way?" (Ames and Rosemont), or "What would there be for us, your disciples, to transmit?" (Lau)—*ze xiaozi he shu yan* 則小子何述焉? The latter passage also indicates that for Confucius's followers, and probably for Confucius himself, transmission is deliberate and understood in terms of an articulated set of teachings.

The *Shuowen jiezi* glosses *shu* 述 as *xun* 循, with the meaning of following the footsteps or a path.[30] In the *Analects*, the character *xun* appears in Yan Hui's description of Confucius as a teacher, "he is good at drawing me forward *a step at a time* (*xun xun ran* 循循然)" (9.11). And again in a description of Confucius's ceremonial behavior as "the lord's envoy," "his steps were short and measured as though *following a line* (*you xun* 有循). Such following of footsteps or path clearly implies deliberate practice with strong ethical-aesthetic overtones; it is not, however, a matter of indiscriminate blind following. The character *shu* 述, with the meaning of following a path, is a homonym and cognate of *shu* 術,

and according to the *Shuowen jiezi*, it sometimes substitutes for *shu* 術 meaning "art(s)" as in the "Confucian arts (*rushu*)" that Dong Zhongshu urged the Han emperor Wu to promote over all other teachings. If such substituting is already common in Confucius's times, it reinforces the deliberate and ethical-aesthetic character of Confucius's idea of the practice of transmission in the *Analects*. And even if this substituting is no earlier than the writing of the Han lexicon, it can still illuminate our interpretation of the *Analects* passages and our understanding of Confucius's practice of transmission.

The Western Tradition of Creativity

One could argue that the deliberateness of transmission and the concern with the worth of what is transmitted render agency and choice significant in the process, even if agency and choice are not key Confucian philosophical concerns. Having to choose what to transmit introduces a certain type of freedom into tradition. This freedom would render tradition compatible with creativity.[31] Freedom is certainly central to the Western tradition of creativity. According to Augustine, "God did not create under the stress of any compulsion."[32] God's act of creation is absolutely free since his "effective" power, "cannot be made but can only make," and he "does not create from material which he himself did not make, nor does he employ any workmen except those of his own creation."[33] It is not coincidental that this tradition of *creatio ex nihilo*, wherein man's soul is created in the image of God, conceives of humanity in terms of autonomous individuality. Mason's study of how creativity became a value in European thought identifies two different views of creativity in Western history. The Judeo-Christian and Neo-Platonic tradition gained dominance and obscured, without being able to totally eliminate, an alternative Promethean tradition.[34] Despite the tension—mainly in terms of the relation of creativity to morality—between these two Western traditions, the importance of autonomy surprisingly is a common feature they share. Autonomy is a key link that facilitates the shift of creativity from the divine or superhuman to the human.

From being a divine prerogative, "creating" was only explicitly applied to man in eighteenth-century Europe.[35] The paradigm of human creativity then was that of the artist as creator who creates something original. The creator was guided not by reason or rules, but by feeling and sentiment and by intuition and imagination in a process that is essentially mysterious. Thus, originality is the property of genius. According to Kant, "genius is the exemplary originality of a subject's natural endowment in the *free* use of his cognitive powers."[36] "If an author owes a product to his genius, he himself does not know how he came by the ideas for it; nor is it in his power [*Gewalt*] to devise such products at his pleasure, or by following a plan, and to communicate [his procedure] to others in precepts that would enable them to bring about like products."

No determinate rule can be given for the original products of genius, which "give the rule to art." The creativity of the genius may be understood in terms of self-justifying autonomy. Products of genius "must be *exemplary*; though they do not themselves arise through imitation, still they must serve others for this, i.e., as a standard or rule by which to judge."[37] Acting creatively is to act wholly autonomously in the sense that the action cannot be judged by any existing criteria, but only by those values the action itself or the original work it produces brings into being.

The autonomy of the genius became opposed to tradition in its requirement of complete independence not only from social constraints, but also from all external frameworks or forces.[38] It would, however, be a mistake to see Kant as being hostile to tradition as one such external framework, even though he contrasts learning that is "nothing but imitation" with genius that is "the opposite of a *spirit of imitation.*" Kant allows that learning could be far superior to genius; furthermore, he emphasizes the need of taste to discipline genius in the production of works of fine art. Though fine art is the product of genius, "there is no fine art that does not have as its essential condition something mechanical, which can be encompassed by rules and complied with, and hence has an element of *academic correctness.*"[39] Kant's aesthetics support Robert Jauss's argument that "the Royal road of aesthetic experience is thus not the alleged aesthetic preference for the new, but the mediation of the new through the old!"[40]

T. S. Eliot's 1917 article "Tradition and the Individual Talent" highlights the interdependence of tradition and creativity. Contrary to our bias in identifying a poet's talent and creativity with that which breaks with tradition and is unique in his work, Eliot suggests, "not only the best, but the most individual parts of his work may be those in which the dead poets, his ancestors, assert their immortality most vigorously."[41] Rather than being purely contradictory, tradition and creativity are interdependent. It is not just a matter of tradition nourishing creativity; creativity also transforms tradition in the process, so that "the past should be altered by the present as much as the present is directed by the past."[42] Interdependence between creativity and tradition means that one "lives in what is not merely the present, but the present moment of the past," and is "conscious, not of what is dead, but of what is already living."[43]

Paul Kristeller also argues that the excellence of works of art and of other human endeavors is usually not due to creativity alone but to a combination of originality and tradition. Advocates of creativity who claim that the pursuit of novelty requires us to free ourselves and others from tradition usually set up the latter as a straw man. They often misconceive tradition as completely stable or rigid and never admitting change; such tradition, Kristeller maintains, is humanly impossible and has never existed. They also misrepresent the process of artistic creation, for example, by ignoring the need for artists to be trained in those skills and techniques that can be taught and that are pertinent to their craft, to be exposed to the rules that have been considered by their predecessors to be useful without being obliged to follow them blindly and uncritically, and to learn to appreciate some of the masterpieces of the recent and distant past from which they may derive a standard of artistic quality without trying to imitate details that no longer fit their time or their own characters. Originality may be necessary for artistic excellence, but it is not sufficient.[44]

Kristeller mentions Alfred North Whitehead's use of the term "creativity" in *Religion in the Making* (1927) and *Process and Reality* (1929) and conjectures that "given the great influence of this last work, . . . he either coined the term or at least gave it wide currency."[45] For Whitehead, the concept of creativity is not confined to aesthetics, but central to his process philosophy, which takes creative becoming rather than mere being as the most inclusive mode of reality.[46] Whitehead's influence is evident in George Allan's meditation on the authority of tradition, which also brings out the interdependence of creativity and tradition. The search for "enduring importances of the past," for an understanding of tradition, is about:

> the creation of an environment favoring extraordinary kinds of creative accomplishment. . . . Whenever I do anything important, anything truly valuable, I stand on the shoulders of giants who agree to hold me aloft only if I will do their bidding. The distinctive way by which I carry out that bidding, my misinterpretation of their command, gives novelty and refreshment to the world. But in the absence of these blackmailing giants, my novelty although unbounded will inevitably be unrefreshingly trivial.[47]

The Creativity of Confucian *Chuantong* (Tradition)

Given the recognition of the interdependence of tradition and creativity in Western thought, I am not positing a simple contrast between the Confucian and the Western tradition when I argue that tradition as understood in the context of the *Analects* has a creative dimension. However, the freedom we find in the *Analects* is not Kantian autonomy associated with the individualism of Western modernity. Instead of a necessary presupposition that makes experience possible, freedom in the Confucian context *emerges* in experience—freedom is the product of self-cultivation. The path to Confucius's freedom of "giving his heart-mind free rein without overstepping the boundaries" begins with learning and spans four and a half decades (2.4).[48] Rather than "initiating new paths while still not understanding them (*bu zhi er zuo* 不知而作)," he advocates "learning much, selecting out of it what works well, and then following it" (7.28). By Western standards of heroic creation, contrasted with mere "making," one would have to agree with Michael Puett that although Confucius allows that sages do *zuo*, such an act is not one of creation.[49] But this understanding of creativity is unnecessarily limited. Instead of *creatio ex nihilo* as a limiting concept, the creativity we find in the *Analects* is *creatio in situ*.[50] The creativity of Confucius's way is the creativity of understanding as interpretation. It is also the creativity of pragmatic intelligence using past experiences to meet new experiences and shape a better future.[51]

Chad Hansen notes, "Confucius' apparent innovation was to transform the focus of his *Ru* group from pure ritual mastery to include the study of texts."[52] Confucius is one of the masters around whom a scholarly tradition (or "school") developed during the Warring States period. According to Mark Lewis, such scholarly traditions were a new form of social organization distinct from and often opposed to the state; they generated authority through the activities of writing and transmission of texts. In the *Mencius* and the *Xunzi*, *chuan* 傳 is sometimes used to introduce quotes that were supposedly from some unidentified old texts (Knoblock translates this term as "the tradition").[53] Though important, texts do not confine Confucius's teaching or practice. In *Analects* 3.9, Confucius claims that he is able to speak on Xia and Yin rituals, presumably with edifying results, despite inadequate textual evidence in the descendent states of those dynasties. Although he is confident that had textual evidence been available, they would support his views, the important thing is, he is prepared to advocate those views without textual support.[54]

In the *Analects* (9.15), Confucius mentions revising the *Book of Music*, and putting the "Songs of the Kingdom" and the "Ceremonial hymns" in order after returning to Lu from Wey. One possible reason Confucius considers himself only a transmitter is that he does not write any "original" works; his literary labors are confined to editing, revising, and "putting in order" texts handed down from the past.[55] However, even as a transmitter, Confucius clearly does more than imitate the past; editing, revising, and putting in order involve interpretation and critical selection, both of which are informed by consideration of pragmatic efficacy rooted in actual experience. The combination of interpretation, reflective selection, and pragmatic efficacy introduces into the Confucian tradition from the very beginning a creative space that is necessary for its continued flourishing.

Confucius often urges his students to study the *Songs* (*Shi* 詩), which forms part of the *Ru*'s textual tradition.[56] "For close at hand it allowed one to serve one's father, and away at court it enabled one to serve one's lord" (17.9). During the Spring and Autumn period, songs from the Zhou dynasty served as a form of refined speech employed primarily in diplomatic missions in the practice of "presenting songs (*fu shi* 賦詩)."[57] In this respect, the emphasis in studying the *Songs* is not the preservation of something old per se but rather its practical use in current and often novel situations. "The Master said, 'if people can recite all of the three hundred *Songs* and yet when given official responsibility, fail to perform effectively, or when sent to distant quarters, are unable to act on their own initiative, then even though they have mastered so many of them, what good are they to them?'" (13.5). Effective use of the songs would be creative in that it would be an exercise of intelligence in Dewey's sense, using the past to shape the future by reconstituting a present unique situation. Among other things, citing known verses claims kinship of spirit in the assumption that the listener would recognize quotations and understand their import. Communication works by locating speaker and listener within a common tradition. Quoting from the transmitted songs illuminates a particular situation and transforms the speakers' and listeners' views of the possibilities. Successful presentation of the *Songs* requires appreciating both differences and similarities of past and present, and bringing them into dynamic tension to create new possibilities.

The *Zuo Zhuan* describes the practice of "presenting *songs*" as fundamentally a matter of "breaking apart the stanza to extract the meaning (*duan zhang qu yi* 斷章取義)"—the meaning imparted to a quoted stanza in the scene of presentation is often different from its presumptive "original" meaning. Hans-Georg Gadamer's philosophical hermeneutics is useful to allay worries about "distorting" the meaning of tradition and bring out the importance of creativity in such practice. Gadamer argues that the meaning of a text is not fixed by the intention of the author, nor by the understanding of some ideal contemporary reader. "Every age has to understand a transmitted text in its own way, for the text belongs to the whole tradition whose content interests the age and in which it seeks to understand itself. . . . Not just occasionally, but always, the meaning of the text goes beyond its author."[58] To understand at all, we always understand *differently*, and if there had been an "original" meaning, it would have no special priority or significance in the process.

Furthermore, Gadamer rejects the distinction between understanding, interpretation, and application salient in the early tradition of hermeneutics. Not only is understanding always interpretation, but also "understanding always involves something like applying the text to be understood to the interpreter's present situation." As a result, the text "must be understood at every moment, in every concrete situation, in a new and different way. Understanding here is always application."[59] Such application is not merely reproductive, but always productive. Understanding as application will be successful only if one avoids over-hastily assimilating the past to our present expectation of meaning or purposes by acquiring "the right horizon of inquiry for the questions evoked by the encounter with tradition."[60]

Richard Rorty's challenge to the distinction between interpretation and use adds a further insight to this perspective with an alternative distinction that highlights the difference between methodical and inspired readings of texts: "This is between knowing what you want to get out of a person or thing or text in advance and hoping that the person or thing or text will help you want something different—that he or she or it will help you change your purposes, and thus to change your life."[61] In using the *Songs* in a practice such as *fu shi*, one is participating in what Gadamer calls an "event of tradition," "an event of continual reawakening and reappropriating," wherein one's horizon of the present is continually being formed as it fuses with one's projected historical horizon. "What occurs in human being through the event of tradition is a continual reacquisition."[62] Success of application brings about a self-understanding that renews tradition by creating a present and future. And because hermeneutics is not merely about the studying and interpreting of texts, but aims for an integration of understanding, interpreting, and applying into a process wherein both texts and self interact as subjects in the fullness of experience, this self-understanding is at the same time a self-realization.

To Confucius, the *Songs* gives us a language. "If you do not study the *Songs*, you will be at a loss as to what to say" (16.13). Effective use of this language can create something new. Instead of merely repeating words invented by others, we respond to possible thoughts and expressions already formulated by others in a common language in such ways that at times expand the horizon of what is sayable and thinkable. Contrary to Lewis, the *Analects* passages showing use of the *Songs* does go beyond *proclaiming* their usefulness.[63] While clearly employing the *Songs* as a source of authority, they also bring out the creativity in the process of transmission. Among Confucius's students, Zi Xia is particularly gifted in the study of the *Songs*. In *Analects* 3.8, following Confucius's rather mundane answer to his question regarding the meaning of a song, Zi Xia asks a further question about rituals. Zi Xia's question expands the horizon of understanding by linking two subjects that at first glance are unconnected. The beauty of a lady described in the song becomes a metaphor for ritual. Confucius praises Zi Xia for having stimulated (*qi* 起) his thoughts.[64] As noted before, the *Shuowen jiezi* glossed "creating" (*zuo* 作) primarily in terms of "arising" (*qi* 起) (see note 3). D. C. Lau translates *qi* as having "thrown light on the text"—creativity is necessary to understanding. New thoughts and understandings have arisen, that is, have been created, in the exchange that enhances understanding.

What Confucius wants from his students is not passive acceptance and regurgitation of the transmitted songs. Understanding begins with the questioning of tradition that simultaneously applies it to the present. In the *Analects*, consequently, learning as transmission of tradition is not simply rote learning. Confucius is concerned when students do not question him, and once thought that his favorite student Yan Hui was stupid because the latter seldom asked questions. He changes his mind only after observing how Yan Hui's speech and action outside his presence "illustrate perfectly" what he has been saying (2.9). Perfect illustration, *fa* 發, is not mechanically doing what the teacher says, but involves developing or expanding the meaning of what is taught. Such creative learning is also illustrated by another discussion of the *Songs* between Confucius and Zi Gong, which ends with the master saying: "Zi Gong, it is only with the likes of you then that I can discuss the *Songs*! On the basis of what has been said, you know what is yet to come" (1.15).

In the same spirit, Confucius requires that his students return with three corners after supplying them with one (7.8). Yan Hui is praised for exceeding even the master himself because "learning one thing, he will know ten" (5.9). In such exemplary learning, the fusion of historical horizon with the horizon of the present "opens up" the future, which I offer as a hermeneutic explication of the Chinese idiom *ji wang kai lai* 繼往開來. The extension of the learner's horizon through the productive tension between past and present is central to Confucius's idea of teaching and learning: "Reviewing the old as a means of realizing the new, such a person can be considered a teacher" (2.11). Clearly Confucius's "transmission" is not simply imposing the past on the present that resists change completely. Rather, his transmission is a dynamic process of meeting new challenges with resources accumulated in the past, which become revitalized and renewed in being made useful and relevant to the present.

The nature of the *Analects* further expands the creative space within the textual tradition. As Lewis points out, though Confucius is a historical figure, the master in the texts is always to some degree an "invention." In the *Analects*, we come to know Confucius through his followers' descriptions and discussions. The text is a social creation that has passed through numerous hands and reproduced within itself the disagreements among Confucius's followers and their different interpretations of the master's words and deeds. There is evidence of factional splits in the *Analects*.[65] Hansen argues that the *Analects* is a dialogue containing various tensions, because "disciples were quoting Confucius to support their contrasting, partisan interpretations of what Confucianism holds."[66] Such tensions are creative. It is because the disputes are not and cannot be settled once and for all that the tradition is dynamic and open-ended.

According to Lewis, Confucius's own worry over the inadequacy of language also adds to the dynamic and open-ended character of what became the Confucian tradition. His insistence on giving only one corner and expecting students to return with the other three implicitly recognizes that the more the master speaks, the less the students will think. The master's reticence is built into the structure of the *Analects* and, together with his expectation that students should be desperate to understand, it "established a ground where creative work could be carried out in the guise of following authority." Lewis also observes, "the entire structure of the *Lunyu* problematizes language, since it is devoted to presenting and explaining 'what the master said.' This is an issue because the sayings are not transparent; they do not explain their own meanings."[67] Before one could transmit what Confucius teaches, one must understand, that is, interpret and apply his teachings.

The "creative work carried out in the guise of following authority" is not limited to Confucius's students who compiled the *Analects*; the same hermeneutical dynamics and possibilities apply to those who study and teach the *Analects* in different ages. The ancient text, like the rest of the Confucian tradition, can be preserved only through ever-newer realizations. Ancient texts such as the *Analects* continue to be worthy of transmission because it is possible, in every concrete situation of encountering Confucius in the *Analects*, to understand his teachings in new and different ways, that is, in acts of interpretation-application that make the teachings our own. Such encounters contribute to our self-realization, which is in itself a form of creativity, through an understanding that extends our horizons of past and future, thereby making the present more meaningful and significant.

Notes

1. *Analects* 7.8. Subsequent citations will give book and chapter numbers in parentheses in the main text. Unless otherwise indicated, translations are from Roger T. Ames and Henry Rosemont, Jr., eds., *The Analects of Confucius: A Philosophical Translation* (New York: Ballantine Books, 1998).

2. Wing-Tsit Chan, *A Source Book in Chinese Philosophy* (Princeton: Princeton University Press, 1963), 31; D. C. Lau, trans., *Confucius: the Analects.* (Middlesex: Penguin, 1979); Simon Leys, trans., *The Analects of Confucius* (New York: Norton & Co., 1997); Arthur Waley, trans., *Confucius: the Analects* (Ware, Hertfordshire: Wordsworth, 1996).

3. Xu Shen, *Shuowen jiezi zhu* 說文解字注 (Shanghai: Guji chubanshe, 1981), 374a.

4. This definition of creativity is from John Hope Mason, *The Value of Creativity: The Origins and Emergence of a Modern Belief* (Aldershot: Ashgate, 2003), 7. It has the advantage of recognizing that an action as much as an artifact can manifest creativity. On the various definitions of creativity since it became a popular research area, see Calvin W. Taylor, "Various Approaches to and Definitions of Creativity," in *The Nature of Creativity*, ed. Robert J. Sternberg, 99–124 (New York: Cambridge University Press, 1988). For a definition of creativity that contrasts with rather than requires innovation, see Jon Elster, "Fullness and Parsimony: Notes on Creativity in the Arts," in *Explanation and Value in the Arts*, ed. Salim Kemal and Ivan Gaskell, 146–72 (Cambridge: Cambridge University Press, 1993).

5. Li Zehou 李澤后, *Zhongguo gudai sixiang shi* 中國古代思想史 [History of ancient Chinese thought] (Taipei: Sanmin shuju, 1996), 7. A. C. Graham, *Chuang-tzu: The Inner Chapters* (London: Unwin, 1986), 4. In his *Disputers of the Tao* (La Salle: Open Court, 1989, 12–13), Graham still describes Confucius's thinking as a "conservative reaction" to the breakdown of the world order decreed by heaven in ancient China, though he noted that Confucius was selective and critical in his attempt to rebuild the past. Contrary to traditionalist interpretations, Mark Lewis analyzes passages from the *Analects* wherein "the Three Dynasties appear not as demonstrations of political impermanence, nor as exemplary models, but rather as proofs of the constant adaptation of rites, and as resources to be drawn on." Mark Edward Lewis, *Writing and Authority in*

Early China (Albany: State University of New York Press, 1999), 109. For other arguments that Confucius is progressive rather than conservative or traditionalist, see Herlee Creel, *Confucius: the Man and the Myth* (New York: John Day, 1949), 143–44; Herbert Fingarette, *Confucius: The Secular as Sacred* (New York: Harper & Row, 1972), 57–70; Julia Ching, *Mysticism and Kingship in China* (New York: Cambridge University Press, 1997), 69–74.

6. For the genesis of this slogan, see Hu Shih's preface to Wu Yu, *Wu Yu wenlu* 吳虞文錄 [Collected essays] (Shanghai: Oriental Press, 1922), 7. Leaders of the May Fourth movement recognized that this slogan, "Down with the Confucian Shop," while serving an important purpose in their political struggles, is less than fair to Confucius and Mencius. Yu Ying-shih, "The Idea of Democracy and the Twilight of the Elite Culture in Modern China," in *Justice and Democracy*, ed. Ronald Bontekoe and Maria Stepaniants, 199–215, 204 (Honolulu: University of Hawai'i Press, 1997).

7. Chen Duxiu 陳獨秀, "Kongzi zhi dao yu xiandai shenghuo" 孔子之道與現代生活 [The Way of Confucius and modern life], *Xin qingnian* 新青年 [The new youth] 2, no. 4 (1916): 3–5. Translated and compiled in William Theodore de Bary, Wing-tsit Chan, and Chester Tan, *Sources of Chinese Tradition* (New York: Columbia University Press, 1960), 2:153–56.

8. For Confucius's explication of filial piety as "not changing the father's ways" see *Analects* 1.11 and 4.20. See also similar point by *Zengzi* in *Analects* 19.18. The *Analects* does not mention the doctrine of women's "three obediences" (*sancong* 三從), which is found in the *Book of Rites*; this became an important part of Confucian teachings from the Han dynasty onwards. D. C. Lau and F. C. Chen, eds., *A Concordance to the Li Ji* (Hong Kong: Commercial Press, 1992), 11.25/72/12. For discussions of the extent to which Confucianism is sexist, see Chenyang Li, *The Sage and the Second Sex* (Chicago: Open Court, 2000); Karyn Lai, "Feminism and Chinese Philosophy," special issue of *Journal of Chinese Philosophy* 27, no. 2 (2000): 155–200, 215–40; Sor-hoon Tan, "Filial Daughters-in-law: Questioning Confucian Filiality," in *Filial Piety in Chinese Thought and History*, ed. Alan K. L. Chan and Sor-hoon Tan, 226–40 (London: Routledge, 2004).

9. Daniel Miller, *Modernity: An Ethnographic Approach* (Oxford: Berg, 1994), 62; Robert Paul Weiner, *Creativity and Beyond* (Albany: State University of New York Press, 2000), chap. 7; Mason, *Value of Creativity*, 5–6.

10. Ted Plafker, "China Seeks Way to Nurture Creativity," *International Herald Tribune*, special report on International Education, 21 October 2003, 20. It is not the foreign journalist but a Chinese academic from Qing Hua University, one of the top universities in the country, who blamed the lack of creativity on China's Confucian legacy. Many educated Chinese probably share this view.

11. Ng Aik Kwang, *Why Asians Are Less Creative* (Singapore: Prentice-Hall, 2001), 29.

12. One such recent study is Chan and Tan, *Filial Piety in Chinese Thought and History*.

13. Benjamin I. Schwartz, "The Limits of 'Tradition Versus Modernity' as Categories of Explanation: the Case of the Chinese Intellectuals," *Daedalus* 101 (1972): 71–72.

14. For an account arguing this, see Jiang Yuanlun 蔣原倫, *Chuantong de jiexian* 傳統的界限 [The boundaries of tradition] (Beijing: Beijing Teachers University Press,1998), 108–12.

15. S. N. Eisenstadt, "Intellectuals and Tradition," *Daedalus* 101 (1972): 3. On the prevalence of this conception of tradition in the nineteenth-century founders of sociology such as Durkheim, Weber, Marx, de Tocqueville, and others, and the continued confrontation of modern and traditional in sociological and historical analyses for the first half of the twentieth century, see Eisenstadt, "Intellectuals and Tradition," 1–19.

16. Edward Shils, "Tradition and Liberty: Antinomy and Interdependence," *Ethics* 68 (1958): 153–65; Edward Shils, *Tradition* (Chicago: University of Chicago Press, 1981).

17. Hans-Georg Gadamer, *Truth and Method* (London: Crossroads Publishing, 1989), 281. (Revised edition of 1975 translation, German text published in 1960.)

18. Alasdair MacIntyre, *After Virtue*, 2nd ed. (London: Duckworth, 1985), 221–22.

19. Xu Fuguan 徐复觀, "Lun chuantong" 論傳統 [On tradition], in *Xu Fuguan ji* 徐复觀集 [Collected writings], ed. Huang Kejian and Lin Shaomin (Beijing: Qunyan chubanshe, 1993), 619. Originally published in *Dong feng* 東風 [East wind], 1962.

20. John Knoblock, trans., *Xunzi* (Stanford: Stanford University Press, 1988), 1:224. Knoblock, following Arthur Waley's interpretation, actually reads this paragraph to mean that the "stupid, indecisive, and deluded" Ru "offend against Zisi and Mencius" rather than "this was the crime of Zisi and Mencius," mentioned as an alternative in his notes (n.51, 303). Given that book 6 is "Contra Twelve Philosophers," it seems more likely that Zisi and Mencius are also being blamed for the problem.

21. Ban Gu, *Han shu* 漢書 [History of the Han] (Beijing: Zhonghua shuju, 1997), *juan* 56, "Dong Zhongshu zhuan" 董仲舒傳 [Biography of Dong Zhongshu], 2523.

22. *Mencius* 1A6, in D.C. Lau (trans.), *Mencius* (London: Penguin, 1970), 53. Knoblock, *Xunzi*, 3:100.

23. For discussions of the idea of *daotong*, see Wing-tsit Chan, "Zhuzi daotong guan zhi zhexue *xing*" 朱子道統觀之哲學性 [The philosophical nature of Zhu's view of *daotong*], in *Dongxi wenhua* 東西文化 [Eastern and Western cultures] 15 (1968): 25–32; Julia Ching, "Truth and Ideology: the Confucian Way (Tao) and its Transmission (Tao-T'ung)," *Journal of History of Ideas* 35, no. 3 (1974): 371–88.

24. Wei Zhengtong 韋政通, *Zhongguo wenhuan gailun* 中國文化概論 [An outline of Chinese culture] (Taipei: National Central Library Press, 1994), 39.

25. Shils, "Tradition and Liberty," 160.

26. Ching, "Truth and Ideology," 379.

27. Ibid., 387.

28. "Tracing" the idea to the *Analects* may not extend its history. E. Bruce Brooks and A. Taeko Brooks attribute books 17 to 20 of the *Analects* to Zi Shen 子慎 (c. 293–237 BCE), the sixth and last head of the Kong school in the pre-Qin period. They date book 20 to around 249 BCE, which roughly makes it contemporaneous with the

Xunzi. Brooks and Brooks, *The Original Analects* (New York: Columbia University Press, 1998), 195.

29. Wei Zhengtong acknowledges that there is generally greater appreciation of change before the Han dynasty (*Outline of Chinese Culture*).

30. *Shuowen jiezi zhu*, 70a. The character *xun* 循 is in turn glossed as *xing* 行, to walk (76a).

31. Shils goes so far as to claim that innovation is the inevitable result of any system of liberty. "Tradition and Liberty," 156.

32. St. Augustine, *The City of God*, trans. Henry Bettenson (Middlesex: Penguin, 1984), book 11, chap. 24, 457. See also Milton C. Nahm, "The Theological Background of the Theory of the Artist as Creator," *Journal of History of Ideas* 8 (1947): 363–72.

33. Augustine, *City of God*, book 12, chap. 27, 505–6. Augustine also argues that "If they admit that the world was made by an omnipotent God they must admit that he made what he has made out of nothing." John Burleigh, trans., *Augustine: Earlier Writings*, Library of Christian Classics, vol. 6 (London: SCM Press, 1953), 354.

34. Mason, *Value of Creativity*, chap. 2.

35. The term "creativity" has a more recent history. See note 45.

36. Emphasis in original. Immanuel Kant, *Kant's gesammelte Schriften* [1793], *Akademie* edition (Berlin: Königlich Preußische Akademie der Wissenschaften (1908–13), 5:307–8; translated in Werner S. Pluhar, *Critique of Judgment* (Indianapolis: Hackett Publishing, 1987), 186.

37. Kant, *Critique of Judgment*, 307–8 (Pluhar, 174–75).

38. Mason, *Value of Creativity*, chap. 6.

39. Kant, *Critique of Judgment*, 310 (Pluhar, 178); see also 307–8 (Pluhar, 176–77) and 319–20 (Pluhar, 188–89).

40. Han Robert Jauss, "Tradition, Innovation and Aesthetic Experience," *Journal of Aesthetics and Art Criticism* 46 (1988): 375.

41. T. S. Eliot, *Selected Essays 1917–1932* (London: Faber & Faber, 1932), 14.

42. Ibid., 15.

43. Ibid., 22.

44. Paul O. Kristeller, "Creativity and Tradition," *Journal of the History of Ideas* 44: (1983): 105–113.

45. Kristeller, "Creativity and Tradition," 105. According to Kristeller, the word "creativity" became part of the accepted English vocabulary only between 1934 and 1961. This conjecture is contradicted by Weiner who claims that the term was invented in 1875. Weiner, *Creativity and Beyond*, 89.

46. A sense of creative being and a concern with creativity is also evident in the philosophy of American pragmatists C. S. Peirce, William James, and John Dewey. Charles Hartshorne goes so far as to argue that "creativity itself as a philosophical category of cosmic significance" is a major theme in the American philosophical tradition. Charles Hartshorne, *Creativity in American Philosophy* (Albany: State University of New York Press, 1984), xii.

47. George Allan, *The Importances of the Past: A Meditation on the Authority of Tradition* (Albany: State University of New York Press, 1986), 223–34. Whitehead has also been a favorite with comparative philosophers who have recently discussed creativity in the Confucian context. John Berthrong, *Concerning Creativity: A Comparison of Chu Hsi, Whitehead, and Neville* (Albany: State University of New York Press, 1998); David Hall and Roger Ames, *Focusing the Familiar: a Translation and Philosophical Interpretation of the* Zhongyong (Honolulu: University of Hawai'i Press, 2001), 13–15, 30–35.

48. For a detailed discussion of the "authoritative freedom" one could attribute to Confucius, see Sor-hoon Tan, *Confucian Democracy: A Deweyan Reconstruction* (Albany: State University of New York Press, 2004), chap. 5.

49. Michael Puett, *The Ambivalence of Creation: Debates Concerning Innovation and Artifice in Early China* (Stanford: Stanford University Press, 2001), 40–51. According to Puett, there is a notion of heroic creation in the use of *zuo* in texts and inscriptions in the Bronze Age. Puett discusses the creation of culture, relationship between culture and nature in debates about the nature of innovation and artifice as well as narratives concerning the initial emergence of the state, from the Warring States period to the early Han dynasty. For the purpose of this article (though probably of no consequence to his own), it is unfortunate that he takes for granted that creativity means innovation in a heroic act contrasted with mere making, and ignores some important nuances of the history of the concept in Western thought as well as the possibility of expanding our understanding of creativity.

50. The contrast between Confucian creativity as co-creativity or *creatio in situ* and a Western conception based on *creatio ex nihilo* is discussed in Hall and Ames, *Focusing the Familiar*; Roger Ames, "Making this Life Significant," in *Metaphilosophy and Chinese Thought: Interpreting David Hall*, ed. Ewing Chinn and Henry Rosemont, Jr. (New York: Global Scholarly Publications, 2005), 59–78.

51. For more on this pragmatic conception of intelligence, see John Dewey, *Reconstruction in Philosophy* (1920), in *John Dewey: The Middle Works*, ed. Jo Ann Boydston (Carbondale: Southern Illinois University Press, 1982), 12:134.

52. Chad Hansen, *A Daoist Theory of Chinese Thought* (Oxford: Oxford University Press, 1992), 58.

53. On the generation of authority in texts and the relation of the scholarly traditions with the states, see chapter 2 in Lewis, *Writing and Authority*. Lewis also notes an increase in quotations from titled texts in both the *Mencius* and the *Xunzi*, compared with the *Analects*, which indicates the increasing importance of textual authority (105–7).

54. Tradition for Confucius is of course not confined to texts; it could include anything in the past that, according to Alan Chan, "serves as the unifying ground of Confucius' ethico-spiritual vision." "Philosophical Hermeneutics and the *Analects*: The Paradigm of Tradition," *Philosophy East and West* 34 (1984): 430. Using a Gadamerian framework wherein tradition forms the ultimate horizons of our being and understanding, Chan elucidates the notion of tradition in the *Analects* in a way that avoids the extremes of a static traditionalism and an equally one-sided antitraditionalism. Another fruitful comparison of Confucianism with hermeneutics on tradition is A. T. Nuyen,

"Filial Piety as Respect for Tradition," in Chan and Tan, *Filial Piety in Chinese Thought and History*, 203–24.

55. Though *zuo* was not used explicitly to refer to authorship in the *Analects*, the *Mencius* uses it in that sense when referring to the *Spring and Autumn Annals* (*Mencius* 3B9, 4B21). This meaning was included in the *Shuowen jiezi*'s gloss on the character (374a), citing an example from the *Shi jing*. In modern mandarin, authors are *zuojia* 作家.

56. The canonical *Shi jing* is a collection of songs preserved from the Zhou period and perhaps supplemented by later imitations.

57. Yang Bojun, *Chunqiu zuo zhuan zhu* 春秋左傳注 [Zuo's commentaries to the Spring and Autumn Annals with annotations], 襄公 (Duke Xiang) 28th year (Beijing: Zhonghua shuju, 1981), 1145–46. For an extended discussion of the use of verse in the *Zuo zhuan*, see Lewis, *Writing and Authority*, 156–58. Lewis compares the oral use of verse in *fu shi* practice depicted in the *Zuo zhuan* with the Ru tradition's written presentation of verse as a form of testimony to one's character, which became part of the Ru educational program (148).

58. Gadamer, *Truth and Method*, 296.

59. Ibid., 308, 309.

60. Ibid., 302.

61. Richard Rorty, *Philosophy and Social Hope* (Middlesex: Penguin Books, 1999), 145.

62. Hans-Georg Gadamer, "The Verse and the Whole," in *Hans-Georg Gadamer on Education, Poetry, and History: Applied Hermeneutics*, ed. Dieter Misgeld and Graeme Nicholson, trans. Lawrence Schmidt and Monica Reuss, 88 (Albany: State University of New York Press, 1978). Gadamer talks about the need of European civilization to learn to "live in poetry" to find self-fulfillment. Living in poetry involves "rediscovery of what *memoria* is able to grant to human life. *Memoria* is preserving [*Bewahren*]—not external orders or institutions, but all of what we are. Preserving is not an unquestioning clinging to what is. . . . we must continually renew what we hold to be true" (91).

63. Lewis, *Writing and Authority*, 164.

64. See *Mao shi* 57, translated in James Legge, *The Chinese Classics* (Hong Kong: Hong Kong University Press, 1960), 4:95. The third line quoted does not appear in the extant *Songs*.

65. Lewis, *Writing and Authority*, 58.

66. Hansen, *Daoist Theory*, 60.

67. Lewis, *Writing and Authority*, 84.

PART 3

Self-Cultivation
in Confucius

The "Golden Rule" in the *Analects*

6

Philip J. Ivanhoe

The idea that one's own desires give one at least some sense of what other people might want must be true. Part of our concept of what it is to be a person includes certain assumptions about a range of important needs and desires that all human beings share. If we encounter people who do not eat when hungry, do not rest when weary, do not protect and care for their own children, or willingly sacrifice their own lives, we feel there *must* be special reasons for such behavior. This search for an explanation is founded on our shared conviction that such actions are inconsistent with the needs and desires we expect all human beings to have. If we ever meet people who exhibit such behavior but offer no explanation and find our search for explanation curious and strange, we would be inclined to think they are not really human at all.

Human beings must have common basic needs and desires in order to recognize each other and to organize themselves into larger groups and societies. If we combine these facts about human nature with some level of sympathetic concern for others, we have a promising basis for a certain conception of ethical life. According to such a conception, a good life is one in which a person on the one hand works to satisfy her own needs and desires and on the other constrains her search for satisfaction when it actively harms or inhibits the ability of others to live well, and makes at least some effort to help others attain what they desire. An initial conception of one's own good can lead one to an appreciation of the good of others, and back to an expanded and enhanced sense of what constitutes one's own good.

Such a view of the ethical life entails the idea that one's treatment of others should at least to some degree be governed by the principle of *reversibility*. Stated as a constraint, I should never treat others in ways that I would not want to be treated. Stated as a recommendation, I should work to treat others in the ways that I would like to be treated. These intertwined ideas are the heart of the so-called Golden Rule—the notion that one's own desires can serve, by analogy, as a guide for how one should treat others. It is found in various forms throughout the world's cultures.[1] One of its oldest statements is found in the *Analects* of Kongzi ("Confucius").

Kongzi's version of the Golden Rule has been studied by a number of prominent scholars and continues to draw the attention of contemporary philosophers who work on classical Chinese thought. Several years ago, I offered my own attempt to interpret and explain Kongzi's Golden Rule.[2] I began with a review of some of the most influential analyses available and sought to show their various strengths and weaknesses. In light of this discussion, I then offered my own interpretation. In the years since my original essay was published, a number of scholars have offered important criticisms of my earlier view and alternative interpretations of their own. In light of their insights and suggestions and as a result of my own ongoing attempts to understand early Confucian thought, my interpretation of Kongzi's Golden Rule has changed.

In the present essay, I revisit my earlier review of some of the most influential analyses of the Golden Rule. I have thoroughly revised my discussion in order to bring out more clearly some of my reservations about these alternative interpretations. I also have organized my discussion around three primary questions that I believe all accounts of Kongzi's Golden Rule must answer. First, why does Kongzi employ two different terms, *zhong* and *shu*, to describe the "one thread" of his Way? Second, does a given interpretation explain the apparent order and relative degree of difficulty that Kongzi seems to attribute to *zhong* and *shu*? Third, what role does the interpretation of the Golden Rule play in a larger account of Kongzi's ethical philosophy? After reexamining earlier, influential interpretations of the Golden Rule in light of these questions, I present a new interpretation of the "one thread" that many have thought runs throughout Kongzi's Way. In the course of my discussion, I incorporate and respond to several more recent scholars who have written on this perennially fascinating topic.[3]

Earlier Interpretations

Kongzi's version of the Golden Rule most often is described as consisting of two notions, 忠 *zhong* and 恕 *shu*. In *Analects* 4.15, Kongzi claims these as the "one thread" running through his Way.[4]

> The Master said, "Shen! My Way has one thread running through it"
> Zengzi replied, "Yes!"
> After the Master had left, the other disciples asked, "What did he mean?"
> Zengzi replied, "Our Master's Way is *zhong* and *shu*, nothing more."

Recently, some scholars have questioned whether this particular passage really reflects Kongzi's teachings or even if it forms a part of any consistent point of view in the *Analects*. Others have argued that perhaps *shu* alone represents Kongzi's version of the Golden Rule.[5] I will comment on these and other claims in the course of my discussion. But I would like to begin by considering the earlier interpretations of four eminent and influential scholars who sought to explain what *zhong* and *shu* mean and how they can be understood as the two strands of Kongzi's "one thread."

As is so often the case when it comes to the modern philosophical study of Chinese thought, our story begins with the work of Feng Youlan. He presents a succinct and elegant interpretation of Kongzi's version of the Golden Rule in his book *A Short History of Chinese Philosophy*.[6] Feng understands *zhong* and *shu* as representing "positive" and "negative" aspects of the notion of reversibility. That is to say, *zhong* concerns those things that I should do to others, because I would like to have them done to me, while *shu* describes those things I should not do to others, because I would not like to have them done to me. They are two aspects of a single principle and together form the one thread of Kongzi's Way. As Feng describes his own view:

> In the *Analects* we find the passage: "When Zhonggong asked the meaning of *ren*, the master said: '. . . Do not do to others what you do not wish yourself. . . .'"(12.2) Again, Kongzi is reported in the *Analects* as saying "The man of *ren* is one who, desiring to sustain himself, sustains others, and desiring to develop himself, develops others. To be able from one's own self to draw a parallel for the treatment of others; that may be called the way to practice *ren*." (6.28)
>
> Thus the practice of *ren* consists in consideration for others, "desiring to sustain oneself, one sustains others; desiring to develop oneself, one develops others." In other words: "Do to others what you wish yourself." This is the positive aspect of the practice, which was called by Kongzi *zhong* or "conscientiousness to others." And the negative aspect, which was called by Kongzi *shu* or "altruism," is: "Do not do to others what you do not wish yourself." The practice as a whole is called the principle of *zhong* and *shu*, which is "the way to practice *ren*."[7]

Feng's interpretation offers a systematic account of a variety of passages connected to the problem of the Golden Rule and explains both *zhong* and *shu* in terms of the single notion of reversibility. There is strength in the comprehensiveness of his explanation and elegance in its symmetry. But Feng's interpretation faces some difficulties in answering the three questions I have described above.

Recall that the first question is why would Kongzi have used two terms to describe his "one thread"? Feng's answer is that there are "positive" and "negative" expressions of reversibility: *zhong* concerns "conscientiousness to others" while *shu* describes "altruism." But there is no logical difference between the "positive" and "negative" versions that Feng describes. Any action that I can describe as a "positive" recommendation, I can just as easily describe as a "negative" prohibition. For example, "Always tell the truth" can be expressed as "Never lie." If *zhong* and *shu* both express the principle of reversibility, we should expect some more substantial reason for distinguishing between the "positive" and "negative" forms.

The second question that any interpretation must answer concerns the apparent relative order and degree of difficulty between mastering *zhong* and *shu*. Feng treats *zhong* and *shu* as equal expressions of the principle of reversibility. Nevertheless, on several occasions Kongzi describes people who are *zhong* but who have not yet achieved the state of being *shu*. And he never describes anyone as being *shu* who is not *zhong*. It is reasonable then to understand him as holding that being *shu* tends to follow and is more difficult to achieve than *zhong*. Feng's interpretation does not account for these aspects of *zhong* and *shu*.

The third question concerns the role that the interpretation of *zhong* and *shu* play in an overall account of Kongzi's philosophy. In the case of Feng's explanation, it is not clear how the principle of reversibility can be reconciled with Kongzi's pervasive and consistent emphasis on the importance of classical study and the practice of 禮 *li* "rituals" or "rites"—aspects of Kongzi's philosophy that Feng himself recognizes are critically important. If one can really determine how one ought to treat others by consulting the standard of one's own heart and mind, Kongzi's advocacy of classical study and ritual practice seems largely superfluous. Why would one need to study, practice, and reflect upon the Golden Age of the Zhou if one has within one's own heart and mind the Golden Rule of reversibility?

I would now like to turn to the interpretation provided by D. C. Lau in the introduction to his translation of the *Analects*.[8] Lau understands *zhong* and *shu* to be related in a different way. According to Lau, *shu* is a method of drawing an analogy between oneself and others that identifies which actions pass the ethical criterion of reversibility. *Shu* purportedly tells us *both* what we should do and what we should not do to others. *Zhong* does not directly involve the notion of putting oneself in another's place. Rather, it is a standing imperative to "do one's best" at implementing the course of action revealed through *shu*. As Lau tells us, "*Zhong* is the doing of one's best and it is through *zhong* that one puts into effect what one had found out by the method of *shu*."[9]

Lau's interpretation provides a clear response to our first question. The two terms represent distinct concepts that serve very different functions in Kongzi's ethical philosophy. According to Lau, *shu* plays a purely epistemological role. It involves a process of drawing an analogy between oneself and others that purportedly reveals how one should treat them. Only *shu* expresses the principle of reversibility. *Zhong* does not involve drawing an analogy between oneself and others. It is an imperative to implement *to the best of one's abilities* what is revealed through the exercise of *shu*. Lau seems to be following a certain reading of Zhu Xi's (1130–1200) gloss on *shu* and *zhong*. Zhu explains *shu* as 如 心 *ru xin* "as one feels in one's heart" and *zhong* as 盡己 *jin ji* "fully exerting oneself."[10]

Lau's interpretation expresses an order and perhaps implies a relative degree of difficulty between *shu* and *zhong*. There is clearly an order to *shu* and *zhong*, for one first must know what one should do and then exert oneself to implement this knowledge. It is not clear whether it is easier to know or to act properly though Lau seems to imply that knowledge comes more naturally than action. These aspects of Lau's interpretation imply a connection to a venerable debate among Chinese thinkers concerning whether it is easier to *know* what is right or to *act* properly.[11] But this aspect of Lau's interpretation is not well substantiated by the textual evidence we find in the *Analects*. In fact, his account contradicts important passages concerning *zhong* and *shu* that describe *zhong* as a preliminary stage of ethical development, prior to the higher state of *shu*. For example, as we shall see, Kongzi clearly regards his disciple Zigong as *zhong*. But he also insists that Zigong is incapable of *shu*. In other passages we find Kongzi judging people to be *zhong* but arguing that this alone is not sufficient evidence to proclaim that they are 仁 *ren* "fully good." There are also passages in which Kongzi describes *ren* in terms of fulfilling the twin principles of *zhong* and *shu*. All of this points to the view that I will argue for below. *Zhong* is a necessary and preliminary stage of ethical development that must be refined and guided by *shu* and only those who follow both strands of Kongzi's one thread achieve the goal of being *ren*.

Lau's interpretation gives priority to *shu* and this reverses the proper order between *zhong* and *shu*. It also presents problems for our third and final question. According to Lau, *shu* opens up large parts of the ethical landscape by revealing how we should treat others. We come to understand how we *ought* to treat others by appreciating what we ourselves want. But, as many philosophers have pointed out, this can lead to some rather unhappy consequences. For if one happens to desire bad things for oneself, this conception of the Golden Rule provides a warrant for inflicting one's faults upon others. Such a rule would encourage a drug addict to provide drugs to others, for this is surely what *he* wants. A good Confucian would do more than frown upon such behavior. In order to avoid such problems one might insist on the qualification that when drawing an analogy between oneself and others, one must always be acting as an ideal moral agent. But, taken in this direction, the Golden Rule loses much of its luster. For it renders the imaginative act of analogy pointless. One should simply act as an ideal moral agent.

Another way to avoid the unhappy consequences of appealing to unsavory desires is to argue that our "real" or "authentic" nature is good. If we were good by nature, then we could discover the proper way to treat others by consulting our true nature and following its guidance. Later Confucians such as Zhu Xi advocated different variations of this kind of view and Mengzi (c. 391–308 BCE) held a distinct but related early version of the theory that human nature is good and provides us with ethical guidance. But there is no clear evidence that Kongzi held any such view.[12] Kongzi's only recorded statement on human nature is found in *Analects* 17.2, "By nature human beings are close to one another but through practice they grow far apart." This *could* be read as endorsing a Mengzian-style view but it is more easily interpreted as supporting something closer to Xunzi's (c. 310–218) competing theory that human nature tends to be bad. Kongzi's statement clearly gives pride of place to *practice* over *reflection*. It seems to endorse what T. C. Kline calls an "outside-in" program of moral cultivation.[13] The goal of self-cultivation is to take on a good second nature through a protracted course of study, practice, and reflection rather than to develop and express any innate inclination to follow and enjoy moral action.

We find additional evidence that Kongzi held something closer to Xunzi's view of moral self-cultivation throughout the *Analects*. Kongzi placed great emphasis on classical study and ritual practice. These are indispensable to his program of learning. He also emphasized the role teachers play in guiding their young charges toward the moral life. We do not find him advocating the idea that human beings start out in life with any tendency or taste for morality, nor do we find him urging his students to begin their course of learning by looking within their own hearts and minds. Quite to the contrary, in *Analects* 2.15, he warns us, "To study without reflecting is a waste; to reflect without study is perilous." Xunzi (but not Mengzi) paraphrases this passage in his "Encouraging Learning" chapter. As was the case with Feng Youlan, Lau's interpretation seems to make Kongzi's overwhelming emphasis on the classics and ritual study secondary if not altogether superfluous. According to Lau, our primary guide to the moral way is found within our own hearts and minds. If *shu* can provide one with such extensive moral knowledge, then it is not clear why one needs the classics, the rites, and the sages. This is precisely what exasperated Xunzi about Mengzi's teachings and why Xunzi criticized him for betraying Kongzi's original message.

Herbert Fingarette presents his interpretation of Kongzi's Golden Rule in his article "Following the 'one thread' of the *Analects*."[14] He believes that a revealing parallel exists between Kongzi's Golden Rule and the Biblical version found, among other places, in Matthew 22:35–40, where Jesus is asked, "'What is the greatest commandment of the law?' Jesus replied, 'Love thy Lord your God with all your soul and with all your mind. That is the greatest commandment. It comes first. The second is like it: Love your neighbor as yourself. Everything in the law and prophets hangs on these two commandments.'"[15] The *greatest commandment*, "Love thy Lord your God with all your soul and with all your mind" corresponds to *zhong* and the *second commandment*, "Love your neighbor as yourself" corresponds to *shu*. According to Fingarette, *zhong* does not involve drawing any kind of analogy between oneself and others. It is a kind of "interpersonal good faith and loyalty" mediated by the *li* "rites." *Zhong* is one's personal loyalty to — one's love of — the *dao* or Way and corresponds to the Christian's loyalty to — love of — God. *Shu* involves the "direct analogizing of self with other" and is supposed to condition or govern the interpersonal good faith and loyalty of *zhong*.

Like earlier philosophers who have discussed the Golden Rule, Fingarette worries that the "direct analogizing of the self with other" can lead to wholly inappropriate or paternalistic treatment of others. We can project our worst desires onto others or impose our own tastes upon them and exacerbate such wrongdoing by portraying our action as *good* for those who must suffer such treatment. Fingarette tries to avoid the problem of taking one's own bad desires as the standard for one's treatment of others by first requiring us to exhibit interpersonal good faith in and loyalty to the *dao*. We must establish ourselves as dedicated followers of the rites in order to follow the one thread of Kongzi's Way. He attempts to avoid the problem of paternalism by arguing that when I draw an analogy between myself and others, "I must not imagine *myself* being in your situation; I must imagine *being you*."[16] In other words, I must try to imagine what someone with your needs, desires, and personal history would want. At the same time I don't just try to *become* you, I subject what I come to understand through this imaginative act to my own critical judgment. This kind of dual vision—imaginatively entering into the heart and mind of another while maintaining my own ethical sensibilities—enables me to appreciate your particular needs and desires while maintaining my own critical perspective.[17]

Fingarette's interpretation is original, creative, and philosophically interesting. But there are problems with at least one of its details. Fingarette claims that *zhong* represents a "hybrid notion, *zhongxin*," which means something like "interpersonal good faith and loyalty." But within the *Analects*, *zhong* always means something more like "to be conscientious" in fulfilling one's role-specific duties as described by the *li* "rites." The root sense of the word 信 *xin* is something like "being true to one's word" and by extension often means "to be trustworthy" or "to have trust in." It is an important moral concept that also involves holding oneself to a moral standard, specifically, keeping one's word. But *xin* is not part of Kongzi's "one thread" and the word does not occur in passages that concern the Golden Rule.[18]

Turning now to the first of our three questions, we find that Fingarette can explain why there are two terms rather than just one. According to him, *zhong* is very different from *shu*. It does not involve the idea of drawing an analogy between oneself and others or the idea that one's treatment of others should be governed by the standard of reversibility. *Zhong* is "a kind of interpersonal loyalty and good faith" that exists between those committed to the Way. But this loyalty and good faith must be governed by a critical sensitivity to each individual's particular needs and desires through the exercise of *shu*. Since *zhong* and *shu* play distinct yet interdependent roles in identifying and guiding one along the moral way, it makes good sense that Kongzi would describe them with different terms.

It is less clear how Fingarette would respond to our second question. His interpretation seems to imply that *zhong* is prior to *shu* and perhaps more difficult as well. If *zhong* describes a Confucian's love of and loyalty to the *dao* and is parallel to a Christian's love of and loyalty to God, then *zhong* would seem to be both prior and more difficult. On such a reading the function of *shu* is primarily as a guard against an overzealous and insensitive application of one's love and loyalty to the good. But Fingarette might argue that one cannot truly love and be loyal to the *dao* if one does not focus upon and develop sensitivity to the particular situations of others. If this is how we understand him, then *zhong* and *shu* require one another, are to be practiced simultaneously, and may be equally difficult to achieve. Either reading would seem to have some problems accounting for the order and relative difficulty we find described in several passages in the *Analects*.

Fingarette's interpretation of *zhong* and *shu* is amenable to providing a persuasive response to our third question, for it incorporates and points toward a more comprehensive account of Kongzi's ethical philosophy. For example, according to Fingarette, *zhong* relies on the mediation of *li* "rituals," which most scholars agree are a central and critical feature of Kongzi's ethical philosophy. But if I have understood Fingarette's account of Kongzi's version of the Golden Rule properly, it strikes me as in serious tension with his well-known views about the role of "ritual" in Confucian learning. In his stimulating and influential book *Confucius: The Secular as Sacred*, Fingarette argues that Kongzi's philosophy does not rely upon appeals to moral psychology or the cultivation of interior mental states.[19] Throughout this work he conceives of being disposed to behave in accordance with ritual as Gilbert Ryle described qualities like brittleness—not as an inner state but simply in terms of certain characteristic behavior under certain conditions.[20] Nevertheless, Fingarette's account of the Golden Rule relies on a rich, and in many ways compelling, account of moral psychology and the cultivation of interior mental states. It points toward a more comprehensive account of Kongzi's ethics, but not the one that Fingarette defends in his most well known work.

The fourth and final interpretation I would like to discuss is by David S. Nivison. In "Golden Rule Arguments in Chinese Moral Philosophy," Nivison traces the notion of the Golden Rule throughout the course of Chinese history.[21] Nivison's work is the most historically minded and comprehensive essay on the subject available. But given the purposes of this study I will focus exclusively on his account of Kongzi's notion of the Golden Rule.

Nivison's interpretation is built around an intriguing claim concerning the hierarchical structure of *zhong* and *shu*. According to Nivison, *zhong* governs conduct toward one's peers and social superiors. It involves the act of imaginatively putting yourself in the position of one's equal or superior and, in light of the *li* "rites," seeing how one would want to be treated. *Zhong* brings into focus my role-specific duty toward them. I am then to exert myself to fulfill that duty as best I can. This aspect of Nivison's account gains support from the fact that one of the common meanings of *zhong* is "loyalty"—not in the sense of blind obedience but as a critical and morally informed commitment to serve others. Kongzi is explicit on this last point in *Analects* 14.7, "Can one be *zhong* to others without instructing them?"[22]

Shu supplies the other half of Kongzi's Golden Rule and is directed toward one's peers and subordinates. It is the feeling of care and concern that one should adopt when in a position of authority. The *li* "rites" prescribe what is proper but the practice of *shu* ensures that in exercising the prerogatives of our position, we temper our application of the rules. We should be kind and considerate in what we demand from others. Nivison sums up his interpretation in the following way.

> *Zhong* then is the quality of reliably following one's duties towards superiors of equals. *Shu* on the other hand is a quasi-supererogatory virtue—that is, it had to do with things that are not strictly required of one; it will mean that in dealing with equals or inferiors as our respective roles may require, I will be polite and considerate. The distinction is implicit again in a familiar early text, *Analects* 3.19, not usually brought into this discussion: "A ruler employs subordinates according to the rites; subordinates serve their ruler with *zhong*."[23]

Nivison's claim concerning the hierarchical nature of both *zhong* and *shu* has not persuaded many contemporary scholars.[24] Heiner Roetz flatly claims that Nivison is wrong and offers what he considers to be a clear counterexample to the claim that *zhong* is always directed toward social peers or superiors.[25] Roetz does not prove quite what he claims to prove. He is right, though, to question this aspect of Nivison's analysis, which I also endorsed in my earlier account of Kongzi's Golden Rule.

Roetz rejects Nivison's claim regarding the hierarchical nature of *zhong* and *shu* on the basis of a passage from the *Zuozhuan*, which he offers as a counter-example to the claim that *zhong* means to be loyal and is always directed toward one's peers or superiors.[26] The critical lines are: 所謂道，忠於民而信於神也。上思利民，忠也。祝史正辭，信也. Roetz seems to interpret the first line as saying, "What I mean by the *dao* is to be *loyal to* the people and *faithful to* the spirits." This of course would be a counterexample to Nivison's claim that *zhong* means loyalty and is always directed toward social peers or superiors. But I don't believe the line should be read as Roetz seems to suggest.

The first thing that should strike one about Roetz's reading is that it is anachronistic. The notion of a ruler being *loyal to* his people makes good sense in a democracy but it is hard to understand what this might mean in the context of pre-Qin China.[27] In fact *zhong* is not best understood as "loyalty" in this passage. Rather here, as in many passages in early Chinese texts, *zhong* means something like "conscientiousness." This is how Feng Youlan translated the term and he was correct to do so. D. C. Lau's translation, "doing one's best," which follows the gloss of Zhu Xi, is close to this meaning as well. But we must add an important proviso to both of these earlier interpretations. In these contexts, "to be conscientious" means to carry out one's role-specific duties to the best of one's abilities. I am a conscientious minister when I carry out my duties to my superiors. As Nivison pointed out, *Analects* 3.19 tells us that, ". . . a minister serves his lord with *zhong* 'conscientiousness.'" In such contexts, the word does connote something like an ethically charged sense of "loyalty." But it is better understood as describing how the minister carries out *his duties* and not how he relates to *his lord*. This sense of *zhong* was understood clearly by traditional commentators who often gloss *zhong* with the word 誠 *cheng* "integrity." This is the first definition of *zhong* in Morohashi's *Dai Kanwa jiten* and he offers this very passage from the *Zuozhuan* as an example of this sense.[28]

The real problem with Nivison's claim lies with seeing too tight a fit between *zhong* and "loyalty"—even if we take "loyalty" in the morally charged sense. He is right to insist that a superior cannot be "loyal" to an inferior. But a superior can be *zhong* in regard to the duties that he owes to social inferiors. This is the sense of *zhong* in the passage that Roetz cites. The passage does not show that a ruler can be "loyal" to his people; it shows why we should understand and translate *zhong* as "conscientiousness."[29]

If I am a good father, I am conscientious *in regard to* my children. In such contexts it would be very odd to say that I am "loyal" to my children. We might be loyal to certain children's interests if say we are their guardians. But in both ancient and modern China such fidelity tends to be expressed in terms of integrity and conscientiousness, that is, how well I perform my role-specific duties in regard to others. This idea is captured in another well-known passage, *Analects* 12.11, "Let rulers be rulers, let ministers be ministers, let fathers be fathers, let sons be sons. . . ." The passage Roetz cites from the *Zuozhuan* should be translated something like:

> What I mean by the *dao* is to be conscientious in regard to the people and faithful in regard to the spirits. When superiors concentrate on benefiting the people, this is to be conscientious. When officials in charge of sacrifice address [the spirits] in the correct manner, this is to be faithful.

As is the case in this passage, *zhong* almost always concerns doing what one is supposed to do. That is, it is primarily concerned with proper action and behavior. As noted in our earlier discussion of Fingarette's interpretation, *xin* concerns being true, faithful, or in general correct, in regard to what one says.[30] In regard to the spirits, someone is *xin* if they address the spirits in the proper way, that is, if they give a *faithful* reading of the ceremony, and prove true to what they say. Such a worshipper is both proper and reliable. In general such a person is "trustworthy," which is a primary sense of *xin*. This division of labor, if you will, between *zhong* and *xin* helps to explain why the two terms sometimes occur together, as in the *Zuozhuan* passage. Someone who is reliable in both word and deed is good to find. Nevertheless, as noted earlier, these are distinct virtues.

Nivison's claim regarding the strict and symmetrical hierarchy of the concepts *zhong* and *shu* is difficult to defend. While as a matter of practice, it may well be true that one encounters more opportunities to exercise *zhong* while looking up to superiors or across to equals and that one has more occasions to express *shu* toward peers or subordinates, there is nothing inherent to these notions that restricts them from being applied as guides to one's conduct in general. Let us now see how Nivison's interpretation fares in providing answers to our three questions.

Like Feng Youlan, Nivison offers an elegant and symmetrical account of *zhong* and *shu*. *Zhong* purportedly has more to do with a certain conception of "loyalty" while *shu* is a "quasi-supererogatory virtue" associated more with benevolence. *Zhong* functions to keep me attentive and actively concerned with my duties to peers and superiors, while *shu* encourages me to show compassion, flexibility, and understanding to peers and subordinates. Given the nature of Nivison's understanding of *zhong* and *shu* it makes good sense that there are two distinct terms, for they describe substantially different concepts with distinctive functions in guiding us toward a moral life.

Nivison does not directly address the issue of the apparent order and difficulty of *zhong* and *shu*. But his interpretation does seem to imply that, at least as a practical matter, *zhong* is prior to *shu* and *shu* is more difficult and elusive than *zhong*. In terms of pedagogy, Kongzi seems to have emphasized *zhong* as in some way primary and foundational. We have to learn our role-specific duties and develop effective ways to fulfill them. *Shu* seems to come later and is needed in order to refine and humanize our performance of duty. At least this seems to be what Nivison's account implies concerning the questions of order and difficulty.

Since Nivison's account of *zhong* and *shu* relates both to the practice of *li* "ritual," and in particular to the role-specific duties that the *li* describe, it is easy to see how his interpretation is connected to a more comprehensive interpretation of Kongzi's ethical philosophy. While Nivison has not offered an overall account of Kongzi's ethical views, what he has said about Kongzi and other early Confucian thinkers presents them as virtue ethicists. Nivison has written illuminating and influential essays on the nature and cultivation of virtue and the rich resources of moral psychology to be found among early Confucians. His account of *zhong* and *shu* fits in neatly with this cluster of philosophical concerns.

A New Proposal regarding *Zhong* and *Shu*

Bryan W. Van Norden has presented some good reasons for doubting the authenticity of some of the passages that have been used to support earlier interpretations of Kongzi's Golden Rule.[31] Since I rely on some of these passages in arguing for my own theory, it is appropriate to offer some comments about the concerns he has raised. First, as Van Norden himself points out, even if we doubt the authenticity of certain passages, they might still accurately represent Kongzi's views. A passage need not *come from* Kongzi in order to accurately *represent* his thought. Second, anyone offering an interpretation of the *Analects* should admit that it is impossible to be wholly confident about what the authentic views of Kongzi are and should be clear about the hermeneutical standard they are employing for deciding this issue.

Of course, some passages in the *Analects* must be discarded or at least given much less weight on the basis of historical or philological reasons or because they clash dramatically with the bulk of the material in the text. But even after eliminating passages that are clearly suspect, all we can do with the remaining material is to work to identify themes, ideas, and arguments that hang together in consistent, revealing, and interesting ways. If there are such themes, ideas, and arguments and we have no clear and decisive historical or philological reasons for rejecting the passages that support them, we can attribute these themes, ideas, and arguments to "Kongzi." I believe that the passages concerning *zhong* and *shu* constitute such a group and that the only proof one can offer concerning whether it is reasonable to attribute these themes, ideas, and arguments to Kongzi is to *make the case*. The one thing of which we can be certain is that almost every thinker within the Confucian tradition has believed that *zhong* and *shu* somehow constitute the "one thread" of Kongzi's teaching. My effort is an attempt to contribute to this ongoing conversation with the text.

Analects 4.15 is the only passage in the text that explicitly mentions *zhong* and *shu* together. There is a great deal of traditional and modern commentary on this passage and particularly on two apparent "problems" with it. The first purported problem is that the claim that *zhong* and *shu* are the "one thread" of Kongzi's Way is not made by Kongzi but by one of his disciples. The second is that the "one thread" seems to have two strands (not one).

The arguments for rejecting the passage because it is attributed to Zengzi all rest on speculative stories about competition and intrigue among the disciples after the death of the Master.[32] According to such accounts, passages were added to the core of the *Analects* in order to bolster or challenge the relative status of disciples. The problem with such explanations is that there is no way either to confirm or refute their claims. Moreover, even if such passages came to be in the *Analects* for such "political" reasons, this alone does not mean that they do not accurately reflect the views of Kongzi. Regardless of the truth of claims about the purported provenance of certain passages, the most sensible way we have to assess the worth of a given passage is to consider whether what it says hangs together with other claims. In other words, one is driven back to considering whether or not it is consistent with other themes, ideas, and arguments that we take as representing the central teachings of Kongzi.[33]

The second concern has been used on one hand to establish particular readings of this passage as well as the rest of the *Analects* and on the other to cast suspicion on the passage itself as a reliable guide to Kongzi's philosophy.[34] Although we do not have time to explore the diverse and complex arguments that whirl around this issue, it will help to comment on the question that has generated most of the commentary, why the "one thread" is expressed in terms of the two notions *zhong* and *shu*? This would be at least initially perplexing if the "one thread" were some single substance or guiding principle for then we would have to show how *zhong* and *shu* could somehow be reduced to a single substance or guiding principle. But, if we could do *that*, then we would have to explain why Kongzi felt a need to use two terms to refer to this single substance or guiding principle. Many traditional commentaries are primarily attempts to resolve this apparent tension, and one can easily hear the echoes of this debate in some of the modern interpretations I have discussed above. But all such explanations are working much too hard. As we shall see, Kongzi regularly links *zhong* and *shu* to a single ideal which *every* commentator recognizes is in fact the overall goal of Kongzi's ethical teachings, namely, *ren* "perfect goodness."[35] Once we see that *zhong* and *shu* are distinct yet interrelated ethical dispositions, each of which is necessary but neither of which is sufficient for *ren*, then the apparent paradox of "how can one be two?" dissolves. As it dissolves we see how these two notions are related not only to each other, but also to Kongzi's overall philosophy. Seen in this light, *Analects* 4.15 is not a *problem*, but rather a key to Kongzi's ethical teachings. This of course is just what Zengzi claims it is and how it has been regarded throughout the traditional commentarial tradition.[36]

We now must turn to the question of what *zhong* and *shu* mean and how together they offer sufficient criteria for *ren* "perfect goodness." I will argue that both *zhong* and *shu* involve the imaginative act of putting oneself in the place of others and being guided by the principle of reciprocity to see how one should treat them. *Zhong* differs from *shu* in being focused on moral self-discipline. It keeps us focused on our general role-specific duties, as defined by the *li* "rites" and other norms of Confucian life, and helps us to understand what we must do to fulfill them in the particular cases of actual life. *Zhong* is something we must practice before *shu*; practically speaking, it is prior to *shu* in the process of self-cultivation. This is because *zhong* plays a critical role in developing the sensibilities needed to exercise *shu*.

Shu is concerned with moral discretion. It keeps us focused on the needs, desires, and feelings of those directly affected by the actions we perform in the course of our role-specific duties. *Shu* helps us to appreciate the impact our actions have upon others and how the performance of our duty is perceived by those affected. Specifically, *shu* shows us the way to adjust the performance of our duties in order to avoid inflicting unnecessary suffering or offense upon others. *Shu* refines and enhances the practice of *zhong*. Practically speaking, it is something that comes into play after one has begun to master the rites and norms of Confucian life. We need to understand what it is to perform our duties to others before we come to appreciate how to fulfill our obligations in a caring and sensitive manner. Since one must already be *zhong* in order to be *shu* there is a clear sense in which the latter is a more difficult and advanced state to achieve.

Ritual practice and the general study of culture are central features of Kongzi's ethical philosophy.[37] For example, there is *Analects* 6.25, "The gentleman studies culture extensively and restrains himself with the rites. In this way he makes no transgressions."

In *Analects* 12.1, Kongzi describes the critical task of restraining oneself and submitting to the rites by saying,

> Do not look at anything that is not in accord with ritual.
> Do not listen to anything that is not in accord with ritual.
> Do not speak if it is not in accord with ritual.
> Do not act if it is not in accord with ritual. . . .

As important as 學 *xue* "learning" is for Kongzi, it would be a terribly insensitive caricature of his philosophy to describe his ideal in terms of programming people to behave according to some set of fixed prescriptions. For Kongzi, the study of culture and the practice of ritual are valuable as a critical means for cultivating a range of sensibilities and sense of style for humane living and as the medium through which to express one's humane character.[38] The aim was to cultivate and exercise a certain kind of character, broadly construed. In order to achieve this end one needed to grasp not only the letter of the lessons one studied but their sense or spirit as well. Kongzi regularly complained about the hollow performance of ritual. For example, consider *Analects* 17.9, "They talk about ritual! They talk about ritual! Is ritual nothing but gems and silks?"[39] Some of his harshest criticisms were directed at pretenders to the Way, "the honest men of the village" which he called "the thieves of virtue."[40]

While Kongzi's goal is to cultivate character, the early stages of learning are guided by lessons, practices, and ideals located outside the self.[41] In the opening stages of moral cultivation one's greatest need is to pay attention to performing one's role-specific duty to the very best of one's ability. This not only preserves one from acting contrary to the Way, it offers one regular opportunities to develop an understanding of and get a feel for what moral life is all about.[42] Consider the contemporary example of teaching a child to greet others. While parents can sound rather mechanical in their insistence on proper greeting rituals, they never intend simply to program their children to mechanically greet others. They encourage their children to understand and appreciate that when we greet others we are recognizing their importance and expressing our concern for them.

What I am suggesting is that *zhong* is the call to conscientiously follow such ritual prescriptions and that this regularly entails the imaginative act of putting oneself in the other person's place. We teach our children greeting rituals by encouraging them to do precisely this. On the one hand we often simply instruct them in how to behave, but as part of our instruction we urge them to imagine how the other person feels about the greeting they are receiving. Particularly when children fail to greet someone properly, we ask them to put themselves in that person's place in order to teach them what is wrong and how to correct it. In complex situations we all must engage in such imaginative exercises in order to adjust and refine our performance of ritual. *Zhong* is the call to adhere to and practice ritual by keeping in mind how one would like to be treated. We can understand how to serve others, by asking ourselves how we would like to be served. As *Analects* 6.28 tells us: "Wanting to take one's stand [at court], one helps others to take their stand; wanting to advance [one's career], one helps others to advance. To be able to make the analogy from one's own case can be called the method of *ren* 'perfect goodness.'" In the case of *zhong*, one's imaginative act is focused through an understanding of one's role-specific duties defined by the *li* "rites" and the general norms and expectations of Confucian life. Even someone who knows in the abstract what she ought to do may not be paying enough attention to her duty at a particular moment and may not be clear about how this abstract knowledge should be applied in the case at hand. *Zhong* draws my attention to the practical application of moral knowledge and makes me aware of what I need to do in order to fulfill my role-specific obligations. For example, I know that as a parent I should attend to, support, and encourage my children. But, on a given occasion, I may be tempted to ignore or perform this duty in a perfunctory manner. I also may be uncertain about how to implement this general knowledge effectively without putting myself in the place of my children and seeing how to achieve these broadly defined goals.

Zhong helps me to perform the duties that I know are mine. While in many contexts it is not wholly inappropriate to translate it as "loyalty" such a translation risks promoting misconception. First, as we saw in our earlier discussion of the passage from the *Zuozhuan*, *zhong* can refer to the proper attitude one should have in service to social subordinates. Second, even when the interaction is with someone who is my peer or superior, *zhong* aims at focusing my role-specific duty through a distinctively moral lens. It describes the proper disposition one should have toward one's duties, not the proper relationship one should have toward others. We see this in regard to friendship in *Analects* 12.23,

> Zigong asked about friendship.
> The Master said, "Conscientiously advise them and skillfully lead them [to do what is proper]. If they do wrong, do not join them in it. Do not disgrace yourself."

None of the passages concerning *zhong* explicitly describe it in terms of putting oneself in another's place. But they firmly establish that *zhong* involves paying attention to and conscientiously seeking to fulfill one's role-specific duties as defined by the *li* and other norms of Confucian culture. For the reasons I have outlined above, it makes good sense to think that this regularly requires imaginative analogizing between self and other. And so philosophical charity plays a substantial role in my claim regarding this aspect of the concept of *zhong*. Such an understanding of *zhong* also is supported by passages in which we see a notion precisely like the conception of *zhong* that I have argued for paired with the concept of *shu*. I will return to this additional evidence below, after presenting my interpretation of *shu*.

The notion of *shu* is explicitly defined in *Analects* 15.23, "Do not do to others, what you do not want done to yourself." Many scholars have pointed out that this golden rule is cast "negatively," in terms of a prohibition, rather than "positively," as a recommendation. Earlier I noted that either prohibition or recommendation can be translated into its opposite. But, since Kongzi consistently expresses *shu* as a kind of prohibition or warning, we should prefer interpretations that can offer a convincing reason for this feature of his teaching. Following several other scholars who have made similar arguments, I believe that this aspect of *shu* reflects the fact that it is concerned with becoming sensitive to cases in which it is appropriate to modify and soften the application of rituals or norms. *Zhong* concerns moral self-discipline, it keeps me conscientious regarding my duty and helps me to understand how to carry out my duty. *Shu* concerns moral discretion, it helps me to be sensitive to the lives of those who are directly affected by my actions.

Shu involves an important type of moral judgment; it prevents me from imposing morality upon others in ways that are neither ethically desirable nor pedagogically effective.[43] Kongzi's overall goal is *ren* "perfect goodness" and a defining feature of such a life is the sensitive and humane treatment of others. This idea is clear throughout early Confucian writings and is made explicit in *Analects* 12.22, where Kongzi characterizes *ren* as "caring for others." *Shu* leads me to see when it is appropriate to amend, bend, or even suspend the performance of duty in order to fulfill the greater imperative to care for others and treat them humanely.

At times, insisting on the strict letter of the law can severely undermine interpersonal trust and care. In the course of our moral lives, we regularly encounter opportunities where we can make exceptions, relax requirements, or make extra efforts to help others in order to ensure that they know *we care* about them. Without an active concern of this kind, we run the risk of becoming faceless enforcers of a moral code rather than fellow human beings. *Shu* or "sympathetic concern" is designed to keep us aware that on many occasions, it is perfectly permissible and highly desirable to demand less of others.

I have claimed that in terms of practice *zhong* is prior to *shu* and *shu* is more difficult to master, and that these features of Kongzi's "one thread" have not been fully appreciated or adequately explained by earlier scholars. We see strong textual evidence for these claims about *zhong* and *shu* in a cluster of passages concerning the disciple Zigong as well as elsewhere in the *Analects*. Traditional and modern commentators agree that Zigong represents a specific and important persona in the *Analects*. He is a devoted and energetic disciple who is committed to making progress along the Way. He is a moral "eager beaver," a paragon of *zhong* "conscientious" behavior.[44] At the same time, Kongzi regularly criticizes him for being too stiff and mechanical in his pursuit of the good. For example, he is famously chided for being of limited "capacity" in *Analects* 5.4.

> Zigong asked, "What to you think of me?"
> Kongzi replied, "You are a vessel."
> Zigong inquired, "What kind of vessel?"
> Kongzi replied, "A jade sacrificial vessel!"[45]

In *Analects* 14.29, Kongzi criticizes Zigong for being *too critical and demanding* of others.

> Zigong often criticized others.
> The Master said, "What a worthy man Zigong must be! As for me, I have no time for that sort of thing."

From these passages, we can gain a good sense of the respects in which Zigong falls short of ideal *ren* behavior. Our picture of Zigong's character is made vivid and clear in *Analects* 5.12. In this passage Zigong declares that he has mastered the practice of *shu* but Kongzi explicitly rejects his claim.

> Zigong said, "I do not do to others, what I do not want done to myself."
> The Master said, "Oh Si [Zigong]! That is something you have yet to achieve!"[46]

Taken together, this set of passages reveals a great deal not only about Zigong, but also about *zhong* and *shu*. Specifically, they show that in terms of practice *zhong* is prior to *shu*, that *shu* is more difficult to master, and that together they constitute the ideal of *ren*. This feature of the relationship between *zhong*, *shu*, and *ren* is also seen in *Analects* 5.19.

> Zizhang asked, "Ziwen was appointed as Prime Minister three times and showed no sign of joy. He was dismissed from office three times and showed no sign of resentment. Each time [he was dismissed] he informed the incoming Prime Minister about the business of his office. What would you say of him?" The Master said, "He was *zhong*." Zizhang asked, "Was he *ren*?" Kongzi replied, "I don't yet see how one could judge him to be *ren*."

Ziwen had mastered *zhong*; he held himself to his role-specific duties even when many would have been tempted to slack off and malinger. He treated the incoming Prime Minister as he would like to be treated. Such behavior is a necessary part of *ren* "perfect goodness," but it is not sufficient. Kongzi hesitates to declare that Ziwen is *ren* because he has not been given any evidence that Ziwen also embodies *shu* "sympathetic concern" for others. This makes perfect sense if, as we have argued earlier, *zhong* is a form of moral self-discipline, a kind of strictness in regard to our role-specific duties while *shu* concerns moral discretion and encourages the flexible and humane application of moral norms.

These last points concerning *zhong* and *shu* also make sense if, as has been argued, the cultivation of *shu* requires a prior appreciation of *zhong*. It seems quite sensible to insist that one cannot begin to learn how to amend, bend, or suspend the demands of role-specific duties until one thoroughly grasps not only what these duties are, but how they work when applied to actual situations. Such an interpretation avoids notorious and well-known problems concerning how one is to regulate the application of *shu*. For *shu* does not come into play until one has already developed a strong and sophisticated commitment to and understanding of the rites and norms of Confucian life. In a similar way, in appropriate situations we expect judges to exercise something like the humane discretion of *shu* when they pass judgment. But we feel that such discretion cannot exist in someone who is not committed to and has not mastered the intricacies of the law.

In addition to *Analects* 4.15, which explicitly mentions both *zhong* and *shu* and claims them as Kongzi's "one thread," there are passages in the text that appear to describe both ideals as parallel to and complementing one another. For example, in *Analects* 12.2, Kongzi is asked what constitutes *ren* "perfect goodness" and replies that it requires one both to fulfill one's role-specific duties (*zhong*) and to exercise sympathetic concern (*shu*) toward others.

> Zhong Gong asked about *ren* "perfect goodness." The Master said, "When in public, act as if you were the official host for an important state guest. When managing the affairs of the common people, behave as if you were in charge of performing a great sacrifice. What you do not want for yourself, do not impose upon others. . . ."

Serving as the official host for an important state guest and officiating at the performance of a great sacrifice are both examples of following the *li*. In this case two examples of ritual action are used to describe one's role-specific duties toward both superiors (one's ruler) and inferiors (the people). The idea is that one must be "conscientious" in regard to all of one's role-specific duties. The final line in the citation above quotes the description of *shu* seen in *Analects* 15.23.

We find additional evidence for the proposed interpretation in other texts as well. For example, in the *Zhongyong*, we find the following:

> *Zhong* and *shu* are not far from the Way. . . . What you do not want for yourself, do not do to others. . . . What you would like to receive from your son, use in serving your father . . . what you would like to receive from your subordinate, use in serving your superior . . . what you would like to receive from your younger brother, use in serving your elder brother . . . what you would like to receive from your friend, use in serving your friend.[47]

One of the virtues of the interpretation offered here is that it enables us to appreciate that Kongzi's one thread is woven into the background of other passages in the *Analects*. We can see that even short and enigmatic passages are rich and revealing expressions of a systematic and developed philosophical view. An example is *Analects* 15.15: "The Master said, "Demand much of yourself, but ask less of others, and you will keep resentment at a distance." Here we are told that the way to "keep resentment at a distance" (which is something that only those who are *ren* are able to do) is to "demand much of yourself" (that is, be *zhong*) and "ask less of others" (that is, be *shu*).

The present interpretation can provide direct and clear responses to all three of our earlier questions. Recall that the first question is why Kongzi employs two terms, *zhong* and *shu*, to describe the "one thread" of his Way. The answer is that these terms describe related but distinct ideals, which serve different functions within Kongzi's ethical philosophy. *Zhong* "conscientiousness" is an ethical disposition concerned with self-discipline. It keeps us focused on performing our role-specific duties and helps us to develop an overall sense of the Way. *Shu* "sympathetic concern" is an ethical disposition concerned with moral discretion. It reminds us that the performance of duty is aimed at producing a more caring and humane society.[48]

The second question concerned the apparent order and relative degree of difficulty that Kongzi seems to attribute to *zhong* and *shu*. One of the distinctive features of the interpretation offered here is that it recognizes and incorporates this important aspect of *zhong* and *shu*. In terms of practice, *zhong* is prior to *shu*. Only through the conscientious practice of the rites and norms of Confucian society can one possibly develop an understanding of the values that such a life affords. As one masters and comes to appreciate the goods internal to such a life, one then must work to pay greater and greater attention to the impact one's actions have upon others. This is where *shu* becomes critical. *Shu* helps us to tune our performance of the rites and season our fidelity to the Way so that we can realize the humane ideal defined by *ren*.

The reading offered here is not only more true to the text, it helps us to avoid a notorious philosophical problem. Anyone who gives *shu* pride of place in an interpretation of Kongzi's Golden Rule must explain how from birth human beings could possibly have a clear and reliable sense of what is right and wrong.[49] Such interpretations are surprisingly common. But, as I argued earlier, they read back into Kongzi's philosophy ideas that originate with his later follower Mengzi and find full expression more than one thousand years after Kongzi's death in the movement known as Neo-Confucianism. They are made plausible only by ignoring Kongzi's extensive, explicit, and distinctive advocacy of culture and learning.

The third and final question concerned the role that one's interpretation of the Golden Rule plays in a larger account of Kongzi's ethical philosophy. The present interpretation takes the practice of the rites and other norms of Confucian society as central to the concept of *zhong*. It is through the conscientious practice of the rites and norms, informed by drawing analogies between oneself and others, that one comes to understand and appreciate the purpose and practice of the Confucian Way. *Shu* works to ensure that one's practice of the Way is humane and caring. It serves to guide and soften the practice of *zhong* in order to realize the greater goal of *ren*. In these respects, my interpretation of Kongzi's Golden Rule is systematically embedded within a comprehensive account of his ethical philosophy, one that I have sought to describe and defend in several other works.[50]

Conclusion

I have reviewed and criticized certain aspects of four impressive modern explanations of *zhong* and *shu* in light of three primary questions that any interpretation should answer. First, why does Kongzi employ two terms, *zhong* and *shu*, to describe the "one thread" of his Way? Second, does a given interpretation explain the apparent order and relative degree of difficulty that Kongzi seems to attribute to *zhong* and *shu*? Third, what role does the interpretation of the Golden Rule play in a larger account of Kongzi's ethical philosophy? I also have discussed these four interpretations in light of certain perennial problems associated with all versions of the Golden Rule. Most important among these is the question of how one's own desires can possibly serve as a reliable guide to how one should treat others.

In the final sections of my essay I offered a new interpretation of *zhong* and *shu*. I suggested that *zhong* is a disposition concerned with moral self-discipline and aimed at keeping one attentive to the performance of one's role-specific duties. Those who are *zhong* are "conscientious" about their obligations and seek to understand and fulfill them by imagining how they would like to be served by others. In terms of practice, *zhong* is prior to *shu*, for one must first steep oneself in the Way in order to understand and appreciate the goods internal to this distinctive form of life.

Shu complements the practice of *zhong*. It is a disposition concerned with moral discretion, designed to keep one sensitive to how the practice of one's role-specific duties are affecting those around one. By imagining how one would like to be treated if one were in the other's place, we can be led to see when it is appropriate to amend, bend, or even suspend the practice of the rites and norms of the Way. *Shu* can lead us to make exceptions or soften the requirements we place on others or lead us to see that we need to do more in order to ensure that our fellow human beings feel our concern for them. Together *zhong* and *shu* enable us to discern and make progress along the Way and toward the harmonious and humane ideal of *ren* "perfect goodness."

Zhong is the attitude a beginning student should bring to any discipline of study. If one is learning to play the piano, one does not start out improvising; one begins by conscientiously practicing one's scales, eventually seeking to master a canon of works and emulate the skill of accomplished musicians. But once our student has mastered her instrument she might want to play as part of an ensemble. If she takes this step, she will come to see that the success of the group will require her to be sensitive to the contributions of the other members. She will learn to adjust her performance in order to complement the play of the other musicians. She will have to modify and soften her own performance in order to augment and enhance the collective result. At this point, something like *shu* will become indispensable for her and the others in her group. For only if she and they train themselves to become *zhong* and *shu*, will they play both conscientiously and with sympathetic concern for one another and thereby realize the musical expression of perfect goodness.

Notes

In quoting the work of other scholars, I have converted the romanization they used to *Pinyin* in order to make comparison easier for those who may not be familiar with the multiple ways in which scholars of the Chinese language represent Chinese words in English.

Unless explicitly noted, all translations are my own. I do this in order to bring out the particular ideas that I see as central to understanding the relevant texts. At several points in the course of my presentation and in the notes below I refer to Edward Slingerland's translation of the *Analects*, *Confucius: Analects* (Indianapolis: Hackett, 2003), which is, in my opinion, the most scholarly and insightful work on this topic available in English.

Thanks to Erin M. Cline and Justin Tiwald for helpful criticisms and suggestions on an earlier draft of this essay.

1. In addition to the studies that focus specifically on the Confucian Golden Rule that I mention below, I recommend Jeffrey Wattles's *The Golden Rule* (New York: Oxford University Press, 1996) and the discussion in R. M. Hare, *Freedom and Reason* (Oxford: Clarendon Press, 1963) as general studies of the history and philosophical aspects of the Golden Rule.

2. See my "Reweaving the 'One Thread' of the *Analects*," *Philosophy East and West* 40, no. 1 (January 1990): 17–33.

3. Given the limitations of the present essay, I am not able to offer a full response to all of the careful and insightful criticisms of my earlier attempt. I will make reference to specific authors and criticisms along the way, which should make evident how much I have learned from these colleagues.

4. In *Analects* 15.3 Kongzi tells his disciple Zigong that his Way is not just an aggregate of disjointed pieces of knowledge but it bound together by a single thread.

5. Building on the work of E. Bruce Brooks and A. Taeko Brooks, Bryan Van Norden raises both textual and philosophical challenges of the first sort in his essay, "Unweaving the 'One Thread' of *Analects* 4:15" in *Confucius and the Analects: New Essays*, ed. Bryan W. Van Norden (New York: Oxford University Press, 2002), 216–36. See also E. Bruce Brooks and A. Taeko Brooks, *The Original Analects: Sayings of Confucius and his Successors* (New York: Columbia University Press, 1998). In her essay on Kongzi's version of the Golden Rule, Sin Yee Chan offers a qualified defense of the claim that *shu* alone serves as Kongzi's guiding moral principle. See "Can *shu* be the One Word that Serves as the Guiding Principle of Caring Actions?" *Philosophy East and West* 50, no. 4 (October 2000): 507–24.

6. Feng Youlan, *A Short History of Chinese Philosophy*, trans. Derk Bodde (New York: Macmillan Co., 1953), 43–44.

7. Feng, *Short History*, 43–44.

8. D. C. Lau, trans., *The Analects* (New York: Dorset Press, 1979).

9. Lau, *Analects*, 16.

10. See the commentary on *Analects* 4.15 in *Sishu jizhu* 四書集注.

11. For a revealing study of this problem, see David S. Nivison, "The Problem of 'Knowledge' and 'Action' in Chinese Thought Since Wang Yang-ming," in *Studies in Chinese Thought*, ed. Arthur F. Wright (Chicago: University of Chicago Press, 1953), 112–45.

12. I have argued that later neo-Confucians hold dramatically different metaphysical beliefs about the character of human nature than we find in the *Analects*. This is a theme in two of my works: *Confucian Moral Self Cultivation*, rev. 2nd ed. (Indianapolis: Hackett, 2000) and *Ethics in the Confucian Tradition: The Thought of Mengzi and Wang Yangming*, rev. 2nd ed. (Indianapolis: Hackett, 2002). I also believe that Mengzi's theory that human nature is good is a distinctive development if not a departure from Kongzi's earlier teachings.

13. For this distinction, see Kline's essay "Moral Agency and Motivation in the *Xunzi*," in *Virtue, Nature and Agency in the Xunzi*, ed. T. C. Kline III and Philip J. Ivanhoe (Indianapolis: Hackett, 2000), 157. For Xunzi's theory of human nature, see my "Human Nature and Moral Understanding in Xunzi," in the same volume, 237–49.

14. Herbert Fingarette, "Following the 'One Thread' of the *Analects*," *Journal of the American Academy of Religion: Thematic Issue*, 47.3s (Sept. 1979): 373–405.

15. Fingarette, "Following the 'One Thread,'" 374.

16. Fingarette, "Following the 'One Thread,'" 384.

17. Nel Noddings has done some of the best work describing why caring must involve an active and attentive consideration of the needs of the "cared for" on the part of the "one caring." I have learned a great deal from her insightful and sensitive treatment of this important aspect of our ethical lives. At the same time, I believe that her analysis suffers from too great an emphasis on the perspective of the "cared for." While we must work to understand and remain attentive to and concerned about the needs and desires of others, in some cases these considerations are either impossible to know or in conflict with genuine caring. I can care for someone who is comatose even though I cannot consult her concerning what she might need or desire. I can care for small children or fellow humans in the grip of addiction or some other psychological disorder without needing to heed their advice about what they need and desire. I must always be aiming at what is genuinely *in their interests* and often they are the best source for finding out what this is. It makes sense to insist that I must do my best to consult with and understand their point of view. But, while an important source of information, the opinion of the "cared for" is not always necessary or definitive. For Noddings's view see her seminal *Caring: A Feminine Approach to Ethics and Moral Education* (Berkeley: University of California Press, 1984). In her essay, "Can *shu* be the One Word that Serves as the Guiding Principle of Caring Actions?" Sin Yee Chan defends a version of Fingarette's claim regarding the nature of *shu* in the *Analects*. See below for my reservations about such a reading. Chan also criticizes aspects of Noddings's account but for different reasons than I provide above. See "Can *shu* be the One Word," 518.

18. Van Norden raises similar criticisms of this aspect of Fingarette's analysis. See his "Unweaving the 'One Thread,'" 227. See also my comments below on the passage that Roetz cites from the *Zuozhuan*. One of the reasons *xin* is not part of Kongzi's conception of the Golden Rule is that there is no robust role for analogizing between oneself and others guided by the notion of reversibility. *Xin* reminds me to be true to my word and worthy of trust, but I do not need to put myself in other people's places in order to see how to carry this out.

19. Herbert Fingarette, *Confucius: The Secular as Sacred* (New York: Harper and Row, 1972). In his commentary on Fingarette's essay, Herrlee G. Creel also notes that the position Fingarette advocates concerning the Golden Rule seems to differ from what he presents in *Confucius: The Secular as Sacred*. But Creel does not specify exactly what differences he has in mind. See "Discussion of Professor Fingarette on Confucius," in *Journal of the American Academy of Religion: Thematic Issue* 47.3s (Sept. 1979): 408–15.

20. Benjamin Schwartz offers a thorough criticism of this aspect of Fingarette's view

in *The World of Thought in Ancient China* (Cambridge, MA: Harvard University Press, 1985), 56–134. I too have offered criticisms of this aspect of Fingarette's analysis and explicitly defend the view that Kongzi is a kind of virtue ethicist. Such an understanding of Kongzi's ethical theory seems more in line with Fingarette's analysis of *zhong* and *shu*. See chapter 1 of my *Ethics in the Confucian Tradition* and "The Shade of Confucius: Social Roles, Ethical Theory, and the Self," in *Polishing the Chinese Mirror: Essays in Honor of Henry Rosemont, Jr.*, ed. Ronnie L. Littlejohn and Marthe Chandler (ACPA Series on Chinese and Comparative Philosophy, forthcoming).

21. "Golden Rule Arguments in Chinese Moral Philosophy" in David S. Nivison, *The Ways of Confucianism: Investigations in Chinese Philosophy*, ed. Bryan W. Van Norden (Chicago: Open Court, 1996), 59–76.

22. Compare *Mengzi* 3A4.

23. Nivison, "Golden Rule Arguments," 66.

24. It is though surprising how few actually argue against his claim and how many mis-describe it. For example, Sin Yee Chan claims that, ". . . Nivison and Ivanhoe believe that *shu* is the prerogative of social superiors in dealing with their subordinates, a view with which I disagree." First, neither Nivison nor I in my earlier work ever endorsed the view that *shu* only concerns superiors and subordinates. Second, Chan does not tell us why she disagrees with this view. Third, she *must* have meant to say that she objects to the view that it *only* concerns the relationship between superiors and their (peers and) subordinates. Since she thinks *shu* applies to all interpersonal interactions, she must believe it governs these as well. As should be clear, I no longer advocate this aspect of Nivison's view.

25. See Heiner Roetz, *Confucian Ethics of the Axial Age: A Reconstruction under the Aspect of the Breakthrough toward Postconventional Thinking* (Albany: State University of New York Press, 1993). On p. 312, n. 159, Roetz claims that the passage he cites shows that it is wrong to claim, as I did in my earlier work, that "A person can never be *zhong* to a subordinate." As I will argue, I don't think that the passage shows that this claim is wrong. But, on p. 142, he is right to disagree with the related claim that ". . . *zhong* exclusively refers to relationships with equals or superiors."

26. *Zuozhuan*, Duke Huan, Year Six. For a different yet complete translation, see James Legge, trans., *The Chinese Classics*, vol. 5, *The Tso Chuen*, repr. (Hong Kong: Hong Kong University Press, 1970), 48.

27. I don't believe that the early Chinese had a conception of *faith in* the spirits either. This idea is post-Buddhist and is first seen in texts like the *Awakening of Faith in Mahayana*. It does become important for certain neo-Confucians, among them Wang Yangming. But it is wrong to read such notions back into pre-Qin thought. See my entry "*xin* (trustworthiness)" in the *Routledge Encyclopedia of Philosophy*, ed. Edward Craig (London: Routledge, 1998), 9:816–17.

28. Morohashi, Tetsuji, *Dai Kan-Wa jiten* (Tokyo: Taishukan shoten, 1965).

29. On p. 142, Roetz says, "I do not see any reason not to interpret *zhong* in its ordinary meaning 'loyalty' or 'benevolence.'" He claims that a passage from the *Xinshu* supports the translation "benevolence." This is not a widely accepted understanding of

the word. I know of no other scholar who defends such a reading. More puzzling is how "benevolence" and "loyalty" can be understood as interchangeable concepts.

30. Even the form of the character suggests this idea, though of course that alone proves little.

31. See Van Norden, "Unweaving the 'One Thread,'" 222–23.

32. This kind of argument is characteristic of the work of Brooks and Brooks in *The Original Analects*. See also Van Norden, "Unweaving the 'One Thread,'" ibid.

33. Edward Slingerland has made similar points in his excellent review of *The Original Analects*. See "Why Philosophy is not 'Extra' in Understanding the *Analects*," *Philosophy East and West* 50, no. 1 (January 2000): 137–41. Brooks and Brooks respond and Slingerland adds a rejoinder on pages 141–47.

34. See Van Norden, "Unweaving the 'One Thread,'" 222. For a good sense of the range of diversity to be found among traditional scholars on this topic, see Slingerland's comments on *Analects* 4.15, etc.

35. In his comment to *Analects* 4.15, Edward Slingerland makes a similar point though through a different route. He argues that Kongzi's "one thread" is more a matter of "consistency in action" rather than some unified theoretical principle. If we interpret him as saying that the "one thread" points toward a form of life then our points are very close. Slingerland does not specifically identify the goal as *ren* but he does recognize that *ren* describes Kongzi's overall ethical goal. See *Confucius Analects*, 34.

36. Van Norden suggests that modern scholars may be particularly fascinated with the concepts of *zhong* and *shu* because of their particular fascination or perhaps obsession with finding formal systems of thought. See "Unweaving the 'One Thread,'" 230–31. This may be true. But it is worth noting that traditional Confucian thinkers have shown an enduring interest in explaining these same concepts. Given the diversity of their opinions on the matter, modern scholars are simply joining their Confucian forebears in a common quest for Kongzi's holy grail. Nivison's essay, discussed above, offers a good introduction to some of the most influential and interesting attempts by traditional Chinese Confucians to understand the concepts of *zhong* and *shu*.

37. On this issue, see my *Confucian Moral Self Cultivation* or chapter 1 of *Ethics in the Confucian Tradition*.

38. Joel Kupperman has written insightfully on the importance of style in ethics in general and in the thought of Kongzi in particular. See his *Character* (New York: Oxford University Press, 1991) and "Confucius and the Problem of Naturalness" in *Learning from Asian Philosophy* (Oxford: Oxford University Press, 1999), 26–35.

39. See also *Analects* 2.7, 3.3, etc.

40. *Analects* 17.11. Compare *Mengzi* 7B37.

41. The issue of how norms and ideals that are outside the self can come to be internalized and incorporated into an individual's own motivational structures is lucidly explored and explained by Richard Wollheim. See for example, "Experiential Memory, Introjection, and the Inner World" and "From Voices to Values: The Growth of the Moral Sense" both in *The Thread of Life* (New Haven: Yale University Press, 1984).

42. Though he did not explicitly discuss the need for analogizing between self and

other, Aristotle advocated something like this idea as well. He thought one needed to be well acquainted with proper practices in order to appreciate what many of the goods of the good life were like and that our common human nature would lead to considerable consensus about the constituents of the good life. For a revealing discussion of this aspect of Aristotle's thought, see M. F. Burnyeat, "Aristotle on Learning to Be Good," in *Essays on Aristotle's Ethics*, ed. Amélie Oksenberg Rorty (Berkeley: University of California Press, 1980), 69–92.

43. As a form of moral self-discipline, *zhong* helps me to understand and carry out the letter of the rites. In contrast, *shu* requires me to make judgments about how to follow the spirit of the rites. (Thanks to Justin Tiwald for helpful comments on how to bring out this difference between *zhong* and *shu*.) We get some sense of what *shu* means from the use of the word 施 *shi* "to hand down to" which is part of the definition of *shu* in *Analects* 12.2 and 15.24. While I do not believe that this implies that our actions are always directed at peers or subordinates, it does convey the sense of "imposing" one's actions upon others. See Nivison's discussion, "Golden Rule Arguments," 65.

44. As Slingerland points out in his very helpful note to *Analects* 5.4, Zigong was successful in both politics and business. He was also known as an excellent speaker. Nevertheless, he comes in for considerable criticism by the master on a number of occasions. For a thorough and revealing discussion of this issue, see Slingerland, *Confucius Analects*, 40.

45. *Analects* 2.12 informs us that a gentleman is not a vessel. That is to say, he is not to serve a limited "capacity" (the pun is intended). A gentleman is not just technically competent; he has the character, judgment, and sensitivity to realize the Way in a variety of novel or difficult circumstances. In terms of the interpretation I advocate, a gentleman is not just *zhong*; he must be both *zhong* and *shu* in order to realize *ren*.

46. This passage should be read alongside *Analects* 15.24, "Zigong asked, 'Is there one teaching that can serve as a guide throughout life?' The Master said, 'Is it not *shu*? Do not impose upon others what you do not want for yourself.'" In this passage, Kongzi is offering Zigong advice that is directed specifically at his particular weakness. Zigong might even be understood as seeking not a general maxim that *all* people should follow but a single teaching that *he* should follow.

47. *Zhongyong*, chapter 13. For a different but complete translation, see James Legge, trans., *Confucian Analects, The Great Learning, The Doctrine of the Mean, The Chinese Classics*, vol. 1, repr. (Hong Kong: Hong Kong University Press, 1970), 394. The *Zhongyong* of course was composed several hundred years after Kongzi's death.

48. Kongzi's paradigm for society is a warm, well ordered, and harmonious family. As is true of such families, interpersonal relationships within his ideal society are to be regulated as much by love as a sense of justice. As I understand him, Kongzi combines a call to role-specific duties, which of course involves a sense of what people are owed and can claim, with an overarching ideal of care. Compare the view described by Avishai Margalit in his *The Decent Society* (Cambridge, MA: Harvard University Press, 1996).

49. In a recent essay on Kongzi's Golden Rule, Professor Bo Mou has raised some objections to my earlier interpretation. While my new account avoids some of these

criticisms, for example, the criticism concerning the hierarchical nature of *zhong*, some of his criticisms would apply to my new interpretation as well. The most important criticism concerns my claim that one's moral sense emerges through the practice of ritual and engagement with the norms and ideals of Confucian society. He seems to think that there is some special problem with how this could happen. But, unless one appeals to something like Mengzi's notion of moral sprouts or Neo-Confucian beliefs about innate moral minds, the mystery is how one could possibly possess anything like a reliable moral sense from birth. Philosophers such as Wollheim have presented philosophically powerful accounts of how the "outside-in" process might work (see above, note 41). In my view such an interpretation of Kongzi's views are both more historically accurate and in many ways more philosophically compelling. Professor Mou further objects that my view cannot explain how *shu* could serve as the governor of *zhong* "at the very beginning" of the self-cultivation. My answer is that my view has always been and remains that *shu* does not serve this role until *after* one has developed a reliable moral sense. See Bo Mou, "A Reexamination of the Structure and Content of Confucius' Version of the Golden Rule," *Philosophy East and West* 54, no. 2 (April 2004): 218–48, especially p. 232.

50. For examples, see *Confucian Moral Self Cultivation* and *Ethics in the Confucian Tradition*.

Crafts and Virtues: The Paradox of *Wu-wei* in the *Analects*

7

Edward Slingerland

The spiritual ideal of *wu-wei*, or "effortless action," is portrayed in the *Analects*[1] as a kind of unselfconscious, effortless mastery of ritual and other Confucian practices attained through a lifetime of rigorous training in traditional cultural forms. One who has in this manner mastered the Confucian Way comes to love it for its own sake and takes a kind of spontaneous joy in its practice. What I have elsewhere called the "paradox of *wu-wei*"[2] appears in the *Analects* as the problem of how one can be trained to spontaneously, unselfconsciously love the Way if one does not love it already. If one is born already loving the Way (as is apparently the case with the disciple Yan Hui or the sage-king Shun), it would seem that the Confucian soteriological project is unnecessary. If such a feeling needs to be instilled through training, however, we have the problem of how one can try not to try: how one can force oneself to love something one does not already love.

Because *wu-wei* is a term that has traditionally been associated more with Daoism than Confucianism, I will first spend some time arguing for the importance of *wu-wei* as a spiritual ideal in the *Analects*, the end-goal of a long process of self-cultivation. I will then suggest that the conceptual paradox contained within this ideal is concretely manifested in terms of a tension between two incommensurable conceptual metaphors[3] for self-cultivation that one finds in the text, the more internalist SELF-CULTIVATION AS ADORNMENT and the more externalist SELF-CULTIVATION AS CRAFT REFORMATION. The two metaphors for self-cultivation seem to serve important functions in compensating for the shortcomings of the other, but they do not themselves seem to be compatible. This tension in the *Analects* will be related to the problem of virtue as identified by Aristotle in the *Nicomachean Ethics*—that, in order to perform a truly "just" action, one must already be just—and the introduction of the adornment metaphors into the *Analects* will be presented as at least partially a response to the important disanalogy between virtues and craft production identified by Aristotle. The broader role of *wu-wei* in East Asian religious traditions and the so-called virtue ethics tradition in the West will also be briefly explored in the conclusion.

Wu-wei as Conceptual Metaphor

Before discussing *wu-wei* in the *Analects*, it is necessary to say a little about the concept itself, which will involve discussing the schemas commonly used to conceptualize the self. Perhaps one of most common abstractions we need to conceptualize and deal with in everyday decision-making is ourselves (our "selves"). Lakoff and Johnson have mapped out some of the basic schemas we employ in English to conceptualize and reason about the self, and almost all of these schemas are found as well in Warring States classical Chinese. With regard to conceptions of the self in modern American English, Lakoff and Johnson note that there is no single monolithic way that speakers of English invoke in order to conceptualize inner life. We rely upon a variety of metaphoric conceptions to understand ourselves. These various metaphors do, however, draw upon a fairly small number of source domains such as space, object possession, exertion of physical force, and social relationships.[4] Although these various schemas are at times literally contradictory, they are generally not incompatible—that is, they serve to supplement one another and thereby fit together to form a coherent conception of self. In elucidating the structure of the *wu-wei* metaphor, we will have reason to discuss several of these schemas.

To begin with, it is necessary to examine the most general metaphoric structure for conceptualizing the self, first identified by Andrew Lakoff and Miles Becker and elaborated by Lakoff and Johnson: the SUBJECT-SELF schema.[5] After examining a wide variety of metaphors for the self in modern American English, Lakoff and Becker concluded that English speakers fundamentally experience themselves in terms of a metaphoric split between a Subject and one or more Selves. In this SUBJECT-SELF schema, the Subject is always conceived of as personlike and with an existence independent from the Self or Selves; it is the locus of consciousness, subjective experience, and our "essence"—everything that makes us who we are. The Self encompasses everything else about the individual, and can be represented by a person, object, location, faculty, physical organ, body, emotion, social role, personal history, and so forth. Consider, for example, the expression, "I had to force myself to do it." What Lakoff and Becker are arguing is that this phrase is based upon a conceptual split between a metaphoric Subject ("I")—the ever-present locus of consciousness—and a separate Self ("myself") that has to be "forced" to do what the Subject wants it to do. This is the Subject-Self split at its most basic. In an expression such as, "My fear overwhelmed me," the Self is an emotion ("my fear"), distinct from the Subject ("me") and conceptualized as a physical force not under the Subject's control, whereas in the phrase "I was able to step outside of myself," the Self is conceptualized as a metaphoric location (a kind of container) where the Subject normally resides, but which the Subject can leave when it needs to "observe itself." What makes all of these expressions metaphoric is the fact that (1) they are not literally true (e.g., there is no "me" that is literally separate from an "I" that can be physically "forced" to do something); and (2) that (as we will explain shortly) they draw upon concrete source domains—object relations, physical forces, physical locations, or containers—in order to describe and reason about the abstract realm of "the self."

Many of the metaphors for self we will describe below are merely special cases of this single general metaphor system.[6] Phenomenologically, this is very significant; as Lakoff and Johnson note, "this schema reveals not only something deep about our conceptual systems but also something deep about our inner experience, mainly that we experience ourselves as a split."[7] The precise manner in which this split is conceptualized then depends upon the concrete source domain that is invoked. Some of the more common source domains— and the more specified versions of the Subject-Self metaphor that go along with them—will be described below as we relate the generic SUBJECT-SELF schema to the metaphor of *wu-wei*.

*   *   *   *   *

Manipulating physical objects is one of the first things we learn how to do and is also something we continue to do frequently throughout our lives. We should thus not be surprised that object manipulation serves as the source domain for many of the SUBJECT-SELF metaphors, including that of *wu-wei* itself. The basic schema is SELF-CONTROL IS OBJECT CONTROL, and since the most common way to control an object is to exert force upon it, this schema is often formulated as SELF-CONTROL IS THE FORCED MOVEMENT OF AN OBJECT, which can be mapped as follows:

SELF-CONTROL IS THE FORCED MOVEMENT OF AN OBJECT

A Person	→	The Subject
A Physical Object	→	The Self
Forced Movement	→	Control of Self by Subject
Lack of Forced Movement	→	Noncontrol of Self by Subject

Examples from English given by Lakoff and Johnson include: "I *lifted* my arm. The yogi *bent* his body into a pretzel. I *dragged* myself out of bed. I *held* myself *back* from hitting him."[8] This schema of self-control and object movement informs the most basic metaphorical conception of *wu-wei*, that of "effortlessness."

Primary Wu-wei *Metaphor: Effortlessness*

Generally, control of the object Self by the Subject is desirable, but even in English we sometimes speak of noncontrol of the Self in a positive sense, as when a person who—perhaps after much effort and no progress in learning how to dance—at last succeeds and explains, "I was finally able to *let* myself *go*." This is the sense in which we are to understand the metaphor conveyed by the phrase "*wu-wei*" itself: literally meaning "no doing/effort/exertion," it refers metaphorically to a state in which action is occurring even though the Subject is not exerting force. "*Wu-wei*" thus serves as the most general metaphoric expression of the concept of effortlessness or lack of exertion. Sharing its conceptual schema structure are two main "families" of metaphoric expressions, both of which fall under this rubric of "effortlessness" but differ from each other slightly in conceptual structure.

The first of these is the "following" family, whereby the Subject surrenders control and physical impetus to the Self. The most common of these are:

following (*cong* 從)

following/adapting to (*yin* 因)

leaning on (*yi* 依)

flowing along with (*shun* 順)

In these metaphoric expressions, the Subject is able to be free of exertion because the Self is allowed to do all of the work. An alternate family of metaphors, the "at ease" family, expresses the same concept of effortlessness, but in a slightly different form. Here the focus is solely upon a unitary Subject, who is portrayed as simply resting or not exerting force, with no mention of the Self. Metaphors in this family include:

at ease/at rest (*an* 安)

relaxed (*jian* 簡; *shu* 舒)

still (*jing* 靜)

at rest (*xi* 息; *she* 舍; *xiu* 休)

wandering/rambling (*xiaoyao* 逍遙, *fanghuang* 彷徨)

playing/wandering (*you* 遊)

Here there is no explicit inclusion of the Self as an agent of action, although of course it would be a logical entailment—based upon our knowledge of physical objects and movement—that the Subject is able to "rest" only because someone or something else has taken over. Conceptually, then, the difference in structure between the "following" and "at ease" families is slight and, as a result, the two types of metaphors are often used together and in a more or less interchangeable fashion.

Secondary Wu-wei *Metaphor: Unselfconsciousness*

These two families of metaphors, both having to do with lack of exertion or effortlessness, form the core of the *wu-wei* constellation and determine its basic conceptual structure. In turn, though, the entailments of this basic structure motivate other sets of conceptually related metaphors, the most prominent example being the "losing/forgetting" family.

This set of metaphors is based upon an alternate conception of self-control, that of object possession, found in English[9] as well as classical Chinese. This schema can be mapped as follows:

SELF-CONTROL IS OBJECT POSSESSION

A Person	→	The Subject
A Physical Object	→	The Self
Possession	→	Control of Self
Loss of Possession	→	Loss of Control of Self

Examples from English include "losing yourself" or "getting carried away," and this is generally understood in a negative sense. Nonetheless, this phenomenon is not always given a negative valuation, for "losing oneself" in the enjoyment of a book or work of art, for instance, is a desirable and pleasurable experience. In cases such as this, the ordinary state of metaphorically "possessing" the self is conceived of as a restriction or burden, and the elimination of possession understood as a kind of release. Although the literal structure of the OBJECT LOSS schema can be distinguished from the "effortless" metaphors described above, the two schemas are closely linked conceptually as a result of our experience of the world. That is, since physical effort requires concentration and focus, an entailment of effortlessness—one that follows quite naturally for anyone familiar with the domain of physical exertion—is an accompanying state of unselfconsciousness. It is thus not surprising that the two schemas are often associated with one another in English. We see this phenomenon, for example, in the conceptual equivalence of the concepts of "letting yourself go [in enjoying an activity]" and "losing/forgetting yourself [in an activity]." Here, the Subject ceasing to exert force on the Self ("letting yourself go") is conceptually equivalent to the Subject "losing" or "forgetting" (that is, losing from consciousness) the Self.

A basic entailment of "forgetting" is that, once you have forgotten something, you no longer know it. This entailment allows us to bring the common literal expression of unselfconsciousness, *buzhi* 不知 ("unaware"), into the losing/forgetting family. Another association is provided by the fact that the experience of strong emotions often induces a kind of unselfconsciousness, as the Subject is overwhelmed by the Self (in the form of an emotion). We thus find strong emotion being linked to the losing/forgetting family throughout Warring States texts. To jump ahead to *Analects* 7.19, for instance, we see the conceptual link between joy, forgetting, and literal unselfconsciousness very elegantly illustrated in a single line where Confucius describes himself as, "He is the type of person who is so passionate that he forgets (*wang*) to eat, whose joy (*le*) renders him free of worries, and who grows old without noticing (*bu-zhi*) the passage of the years."[10] We can thus classify all of these metaphors or literal expressions as being members of what we will call the "losing/forgetting" family:

forgetting (*wang* 忘)

losing (*shi* 失; *yi* 遺; *sang* 喪)

not knowing/unaware (*buzhi* 不知)

joy (*le* 樂) or other overpowering emotion.

Understood metaphorically in terms of the Object Loss schema, unselfconsciousness is thus closely linked to effortlessness schemas as one of its entailments. Together, effortlessness and unselfconsciousness represent the two conceptual, metaphorical hallmarks of what we will be calling *wu-wei* activity.

The Ideal of *Wu-wei* in the *Analects*

With this preliminary groundwork on the metaphorical structure of the *wu-wei* concept in place, we are now in a position to understand its pervasive role in the *Analects*. Although the term *wu-wei* itself only appears once in the *Analects* (in a relatively late passage, 15.5), we find instances of the *wu-wei* families of metaphors throughout the text. Perhaps most well known is the account of Confucius at age seventy in 2.4, where he is said to be able to "follow [his] heart's desires without overstepping the bounds of propriety." Here we have a classic example of the first hallmark of *wu-wei*, lack of exertion by the Subject (Confucius), who surrenders control and follows (*cong* 從) the promptings of the Self (the desires of his heart). Most commonly, however, the *Analects* expresses the idea of lack of exertion through the "at ease" (*an* 安) family of metaphors, often in combination with metaphors for the second hallmark of *wu-wei*, unselfconsciousness. While the text at times employs the more common metaphors for "loss of self"—"forgetting" (*wang* 忘) and "not knowing" (*buzhi* 不知)—its favorite metaphorical expression of this aspect of *wu-wei* is spontaneous "joy" (*le* 樂): a state of completely unselfconscious enjoyment of one's activities. The graphic pun between "joy" (樂 AC: **lak*) and "music" (樂 AC: **ngåk*) also sets up a quite elegant link between joy/unselfconsciousness and musical performance and dance, a metaphor for *wu-wei* that makes its debut in the *Analects* but becomes a favorite among later Confucians.

For a concise summary of the Confucian soteriological path, we can do no better than to turn to Confucius's spiritual autobiography, as recorded in *Analects* 2.4:

> The Master said, "At fifteen I set my mind upon learning; at thirty I took my place in society; at forty I became free of doubts; at fifty I understood Heaven's Mandate; at sixty my ear was attuned (*ershun* 耳順); and at seventy I could follow my heart's desire without overstepping the bounds of propriety (*ju* 矩; lit. carpenter's square)."

We can see this spiritual evolution as encompassing three pairs of stages. In the first pair (stages one and two), the aspiring gentleman commits himself to the Confucian Way, submitting to the rigors of study and ritual practice until these traditional forms have been internalized to the point that he is able to "take his stand" among others. In the second pair, the practitioner begins to feel truly at ease with this new manner of being, and is able to understand how the Confucian Way fits into the order of things and complies with the will of Heaven. The clarity and sense of ease this brings with it leads to the final two stages, where one's dispositions have been so thoroughly harmonized with the dictates of normative culture that one accords with them spontaneously. As Zhu Xi glosses the description of Confucius at age seventy, "Being able to follow one's heart's desires without transgressing exemplary standards means that one acts with ease (*an* 安), hitting the mean without forcing it (*bumian er zhong* 不勉而中)."[11]

Effortlessness

We see in this commentary the first of the two main hallmarks of *wu-wei*, effortlessness, being conceptualized in terms of both the "following" (*cong* 從) and (in Zhu Xi's commentary) the "ease" (安) families of metaphors. In 2.4, the Subject (Confucius) is able to relinquish control and simply "follow" the Self (his heart's desires) without being led outside of the bounded space of morality, and one aspect of the Self (the ear) is described as merely "going along with the flow" (*shun* 順). There has been some commentarial controversy concerning what it means for one's ear to be able to "flow along," but most interpretations take it to mean that Confucius at this point immediately apprehends the teachings he hears and/or that there is no conflict between his dispositions and the teachings of the sages—thereby more clearly linking it with the stage that follows. The Jin Dynasty commentator Li Chong combines both explanations:

What it means for Confucius to say that his "ear flowed along" is that upon hearing teachings concerning the models of the former kings, he immediately comprehended their Virtuous manners. He could follow (*cong*) the models handed down by the Lord without any aspect of them going against (*ni* 逆) his heart. His heart and ear were perfectly in sync (*xiangcong* 相從; lit. followed one another), and this is why he says that his "ear flowed along."[12]

At this stage, one takes joy in the teachings of the ancients, and so accords with them in a state of effortless release. This joy and sense of ease in turn serves to further strengthen the feeling of certainty derived from understanding the Mandate of Heaven, which in turn fosters resoluteness and further liberates one from both doubts and external distractions.

Metaphors from the "following" and "ease" families abound in the text. In 7.6 the Master describes the ideal way of being in the world as follows: "Set your heart upon the Way, rely upon (*ju* 據) Virtue, lean upon (*yi* 依) Goodness, and explore at ease (*you* 游; lit. 'wander in') in your cultivation of the arts." Similarly, the "complete" person—one who genuinely possesses the virtue of Goodness—feels "at home/at ease in Goodness" (*anren* 安仁), unselfconsciously embodying it in his every action. Yan Hui was apparently very close to this stage, and in any case far ahead of his fellow students. As Confucius says of him in 6.7, "Ah, Yan Hui! For three months at a time his heart did not stray from Goodness. The rest could only sporadically maintain such a state." That the Master himself transcended even this state is discernable not only from 2.4, but is also suggested in passages such as 5.26:

> Yan Hui and Zilu were in attendance. The Master said to them, "Why do you not each speak to me of your aspirations?"
>
> Zilu answered, "I would like to be able to share my carts and horses, clothing and fur with my fellow students and friends, without feeling regret."
>
> Yan Hui answered, "I would like to avoid being boastful about my own abilities or exaggerating my accomplishments."
>
> Zilu then said, "I would like to hear of the Master's aspirations."
>
> The Master said, "To bring comfort (*an* 安) to the aged, to inspire trust in my friends, and be cherished by the youth."

What we have here is clearly a progression in nobleness of aspiration or intention. Zilu is overly focused on externalities and what might be called the outer branches (*mo* 末) of the tree of virtue (rather than the roots). Yan Hui is clearly a cut above this: he shows a settled aversion to actions that would violate Goodness, and so has internalized this virtue to a certain extent. Confucius, however, reveals his superiority to even Yan Hui by casting his commitment in positive terms: to bring peace, to trust, and to cherish. I think that Zhu Xi—who explicitly links this passage to 6.7—is correct in summing up the differences between the three answers in this way: "The Master felt at ease in Goodness, Yan Hui did not violate Goodness, and Zigong actively pursued (*qiu* 求) Goodness."

The implication is, of course, that if one has to actively pursue it, one does not truly get it—the genuinely cultivated person does not *have* to try. The Confucian Way should effortlessly permeate every aspect of one's life. This is why even in moments of leisure Confucius appears "composed (*shenshen* 申申) and yet fully at ease (*yaoyao* 夭夭)" (7.4), and why he only begins to worry about himself when the Way of the Zhou no longer penetrates even into his dream-life: "How seriously I have declined! It has been so long since I have dreamt of meeting the Duke of Zhou" (7.5).

Unselfconsciousness

In 6.11, Confucius praises his favorite student, Yan Hui, because his dire economic situation does not detract from his joy (*le* 樂) in the Way, and in 7.16, the Master rhapsodizes upon his own freedom from luxuries or external comforts: "Eating plain food and drinking water, having only your bent arm as a pillow—certainly there is joy to be found in this! Wealth and eminence attained improperly concern me no more than the floating clouds." This sort of joy arises spontaneously once the dispositions have been harmonized with the demands of practice, and allows the experience of a genuine sense of satisfaction in one's activity. We see such joy manifested when the Master hears the music of the great sage-king Shun and is so enraptured that for three months he "did not even notice (*buzhi* 不知; lit. did not know) the taste of meat" (7.14). We see here an association between music, joy, and forgetfulness that is also echoed by the graphic pun between the words for "joy" and "music" in ancient Chinese, which are both represented by the character 樂. The joyous rapture inspired by sublimely beautiful music—involving as it does a kind of unselfconscious ease and a loss of a sense of self—thus serves as a powerful metaphor for *wu-wei* perfection.

We see a similar association of joy and forgetfulness in 7.19, cited above, where a local ruler asks the disciple Zilu about Confucius. Confucius advises him: "Why did you not just say: 'He is the type of person who is so passionate that he forgets (*wang* 忘) to eat, whose joy renders him free of worries, and who grows old without noticing (*buzhi* 不知) the passage of the years.'" Here we see all three of the main metaphors for Confucian unselfconsciousness nicely combined in one passage: forgetting, joy, and "not knowing" or "not being conscious of." It is precisely this joyful unselfconsciousness that distinguishes a true practitioner from one who has not yet seen the Way. In 6.20 Confucius describes the progression of affective states that a Confucian practitioner must experience: "One who knows it [that is, the Confucian Way] is not the equal of one who loves it, and one who loves it is not the equal of one who takes joy in it." That is, it is not enough to have a merely intellectual or practical understanding of the meanings of the rites and the contents of the canon (the Way), and even loving (*hao* 好) the Way involves too much conscious focus upon the object. The goal is to become so immersed in the practice that all distinction between self and object is forgotten.

This emphasis on spontaneity and joy is the reason that Confucius is reluctant to pronounce others Good only upon accounts of their exploits. Virtuous deeds can be faked, but true virtue is a stable disposition that endures over time and shines forth in the subtlest details of one's everyday life. The virtue of the truly accomplished Confucian sage—subtle in its detail, and flowing forth as it does so effortlessly—is a mysterious thing that is sometimes invisible to the common person. The Confucian sage is thus at times in the *Analects* described in terms that, in their apparently paradoxical juxtaposition of opposites, call to mind the ideal of the Daoist sage: "Master Zeng said, 'Able, and yet asking questions about abilities that one does not possess; using what one has much of in order to ask about what one lacks; having, yet seeming to lack; full, yet seeming empty; offended against, and yet feeling no need to retaliate. I once had a friend who was like this'" (8.5). Although this paradoxical character of the Confucian sage will be echoed in texts such as the *Laozi* and *Zhuangzi*, the metaphorical valuations are quite different, with the Daoists trying to genuinely *empty* the CONTAINER SELF rather than fill it. Nevertheless, we cannot help but see an affinity between the perfected Confucian and Daoist sages, sharing as they do this sort of unconscious ease and accordance with others. Consider, for example, 14.13, where a certain Gongshu Wenzi is rumored to have never spoken, laughed, or taken anything. His disciple explains that this is not literally the case, but that the rumor has arisen because of the utter genuineness and spontaneity of his master's actions: "My master only spoke when the time was right (*shiran* 時然), and so people never grew impatient listening to him. He only laughed when he was genuinely full of joy, and so people never tired of hearing him laugh. He only took what was rightfully his, and so people never resented his taking of things." We see here a new term: *shi* 時 or *shiran* 時然 ("timely"). The metaphor concerns the Subject's relationship to the world, portraying the Subject's actions as "fitting" circumstances. We will conclude our discussion of Confucian *wu-wei* with an examination of this metaphor.

Timeliness and Flexibility

We have seen that the "completed" Confucian gentleman is portrayed as having struck a balance or achieved a kind of harmony between his natural dispositions (his "native stuff") and external cultural forms ("adornment"). This balance allows him to follow his spontaneous impulses while still remaining within the bounds of morality. Because the moral action of the gentleman arises effortlessly out of the Self, the Subject is able to display a level of autonomy and flexibility impossible for one who is merely "going by the book." Indeed, one cannot be said to be perfected or completed until one knows how to apply traditional forms skillfully and in a context-sensitive manner. As Confucius notes in 13.5: "Imagine a person who can recite the several hundred odes by heart but, when delegated a governmental task, is unable to carry it out, or when sent abroad as an envoy, is unable to engage in repartee. No matter how many odes he might have memorized, what good are they to him?" The goal is to develop a *sense* for traditional culture, and not to focus too exclusively on its formal qualities.

Similarly, clinging too rigidly to codes of moral conduct will cause one to lose sight of morality itself; it is better to hold fast to a developed sense for what is right (*yi* 義) and respond with flexibility to the situations that present themselves. "With regard to the world, the gentleman has no predispositions for or against anything," Confucius explains in 4.10, "He merely seeks to be on the side of the right." Having over the course of a long process of self-cultivation internalized the rules and conventions that define such practices as the rites, a gentleman such as Confucius is able to display a degree of autonomy in applying—or even potentially evaluating, criticizing, or altering—them. Hence we have the famous passage, *Analects* 9.3, where Confucius accedes to a modification in the rites:

> The Master said, "A ceremonial cap made of linen is prescribed by the rites, but these days people use silk. This is frugal, and I follow the majority. To bow before ascending the stairs is what is prescribed by the rites, but these days people bow after ascending. This is arrogant, and—though it goes against the majority—I continue to bow before ascending."

It is certainly possible to exaggerate the iconoclastic character of this passage: the ritual modification involved is rather minor, and Confucius is not himself proposing it, but simply going along with a popular practice, perhaps with a hint of reluctance. Nevertheless, we can appreciate the sense of it without ignoring Confucius's profound conservatism: rites are expressive of a certain sense or feeling, and thus an alteration in the actual rite is permissible if it will not—in the opinion of one who has fully mastered ritual and thus internalized it—alter its essential meaning.

*   *   *   *   *

In addition to *yi*, a discussion of flexibility and autonomy in Confucian practice must also encompass the virtue of *shu* 恕, which seems to serve an analogous counterbalancing function in the *Analects*. The importance of *shu* in Confucius's thought is quite clear. In 4.14, coupled with *zhong* 忠 (role specific duty) it is described by a disciple as the "single thread" tying together all that Confucius taught. In 15.24, it is described as the "one word that can serve as a guide for one's entire life" and is defined by Confucius as "Do not impose on others what you yourself do not desire." The similar idea of being able to take what is near at hand (that is, oneself and what one does and does not desire) as an analogy is described in 6.30 as the "method of Goodness," and in 5.12 Zigong explains that he aspires to what is no doubt a paraphrase of *shu*: "What I do not wish others to do unto me, I also wish not to do unto others." Understanding what is entailed in *shu* is therefore quite clearly essential if one is to comprehend Confucius's soteriological vision, and 4.14 makes it apparent that any understanding of *shu* will involve explicating its relationship to *zhong*.

The definition of these two concepts has been a source of a great deal of controversy among modern scholars, but the definitive position seems to me to be that of David Nivison, as modified by P. J. Ivanhoe.[13] In this interpretation, *zhong* is understood as the virtue of properly fulfilling one's ritually dictated duties in service to others, whereas *shu* is seen as the complementary virtue that "humanizes" *zhong*. *Shu* involves the ability to amend or suspend the dictates of *zhong*—or to apply them flexibly—when holding to them rigidly would involve "imposing on others what you yourself do not desire." Understood in this manner, it might be rendered as something like "sympathetic understanding." This interpretation is supported by 12.2, where (as Ivanhoe has suggested in chapter 6 of this volume) we can see another implicit pairing of *zhong* and *shu* by Confucius in response to a question about Goodness:

> Zhonggong asked about Goodness.
>
> The Master said, "When in public, comport yourself as if you were receiving an important guest, and in your management of the common people, behave as if you were overseeing a great sacrifice. Do not impose upon others what you yourself do not desire. In this way, you will encounter no resentment in your public or private life."

The first two injunctions refer to fulfilling role-specific duties, and are apparently to be supplemented by the injunction that serves as the definition of *shu* in 15.24. The "sympathetic understanding" of *shu* thus seems to be an indispensable complement to role-specific dutifulness, as well as an essential aspect of the overall virtue of Goodness.

Representing as it does a type of situation-specific disposition rather than a maxim or rule, *shu* cannot be characterized formally, but must rather be illustrated by means of role models or exemplars from the past. This is part of Confucius's function in the *Analects*, for he serves throughout the text as an exemplar of this sort of context-sensitivity. Indeed, the entirety of book 10—an extended account of Confucius's ritual behavior—can be seen as a model of how the true sage flexibly adapts the principles of ritual to concrete situations. While this chapter is often skipped over in embarrassment by Western scholars sympathetic to Confucianism but nonetheless appalled by the seemingly pointless detail and apparent rigidity of behavior ("The gentleman did not use reddish-black or maroon for the trim of his garment, nor did he use red or purple for his informal dress. . . . With a black upper garment he would wear a lambskin robe; with a white upper garment he would wear a fawnskin robe; and with a yellow upper garment he would wear a fox-fur robe"—10.6), this discomfort is based upon a fundamental misunderstanding. While the scope and detail of Confucian ritual certainly (and quite rightly) seems alien to a modern Westerner, it is important to understand that what is being emphasized in this chapter is the ease and grace with which the Master embodies the spirit of the rites in every aspect of his life—no matter how trivial—and accords with this spirit in adapting the rites to new and necessarily unforeseeable circumstances.

That Confucius's flexibility in applying the rite is the theme of book 10 is made clear in the last passage, 10.27: "Startled by their arrival, the bird arose and circled several times before alighting upon a branch. [The Master] said, 'This pheasant upon the mountain bridge—how timely (*shi*) it is! How timely it is!' Zilu saluted the bird, and it cried out three times before flying away." This poetic, somewhat cryptic passage seems like a non sequitur at the end of a chapter devoted to short, prosaic descriptions of ritual behavior—unless, that is, it is seen as a thematic summary of the chapter as a whole. "Timeliness" (*shi* 時) is Confucius's particular forte, and indeed he is known to posterity (through the efforts of Mencius) as the "timely sage"—the one whose ritual responses were always appropriate to circumstances. As Mencius explains in 5B.1:

> When Confucius decided to leave Qi, he emptied the rice from the pot before it was even done and set out immediately. When he decided to leave Lu he said, "I will take my time, for this is the way to leave the state of one's parents." Moving quickly when it was appropriate to hurry, moving slowly when it was appropriate to linger, remaining in a state or taking office when the situation allowed—this is how Confucius was. . . . Confucius was the sage whose actions were timely.

The Paradox of *Wu-wei:*
Adornment versus Craft Reformation

As we can see from this discussion of Confucian *wu-wei*, Confucius places a great deal of emphasis upon the importance of "naturalness" in the moral life. One who has to force morally acceptable behavior is not, in the Confucian view, a truly moral person: a truly moral person dwells in morality as comfortably as in his own home, and the genuinely Good person can thus follow the spontaneous promptings of the heart/mind (*xin*) without overstepping the bounds. The fact that there is something of a paradox involved in this vision—submitting to a lifetime of ritual training in order to reach a state where one can finally act "naturally"—has not escaped the notice of scholars of Chinese thought. Joel Kupperman, for instance, asks of Confucius's program of self-cultivation: "How can highly ritualized behavior, which requires much training, practice and self-control, be said to involve 'naturalness'?"[14] He approaches the problem by noting that "naturalness" or "natural" can have more than one sense, and exploits this ambiguity in proposing a solution to the paradox of *wu-wei* as he sees it in the *Analects*. "Naturalness" for Confucius, he argues, is not to be understood as following the "nature" one is born with; rather, the sort of "naturalness" advocated by Confucius is an *artificial* naturalness produced by a complete transformation of our original emotions, dispositions, and sensitivities:

> It may seem paradoxical to speak of naturalness in a sense in which "nature is art." The paradox disappears, however, once we stop thinking of education as merely placing a *veneer* over our original "nature." Once we realize that education can *transform* what a person is, we realize that it can in a sense transform people's natures. What comes naturally is very much a product of training and habit.[15]

I would argue that what Kupperman is sensing here in this contrast between two models of education is the tension between two sets of metaphors for self-cultivation that we find in the *Analects*.

Despite Kupperman's dismissal of the first model of education ("placing a veneer over our original nature"), Confucius *does* at times portray cultural refinement as a sort of decoration laid on top of a well-shaped substrate. This is the SELF-CULTIVATION AS ADORNMENT schema, which informs the metaphor pair of "native stuff" (*zhi* 質) and "cultural refinement" (*wen* 文; lit. lines, strokes), as well as the most common term for self-cultivation itself, *xiu* 修—literally, decorating or adorning a surface.[16] This metaphor exists side-by-side with a second metaphor, SELF-CULTIVATION AS CRAFT REFORMATION, where the process of education is understood as an actual transformation of the "stuff" of the Self rather than the adornment of a surface. The two metaphors are not entirely compatible. One of the entailments of the SELF-CULTIVATION AS CRAFT REFORMATION metaphor is that, in order for the raw material to be fashioned into something beautiful or properly formed, it will be necessary for external force to be applied, and this application of force will result in a sometimes violent reshaping of the original material. A fair amount of energy and exertion will also be required to perform such a difficult task. The SELF-CULTIVATION AS ADORNMENT schema possesses some of these entailments—the need for time, for instance, and the external application of effort—but also possesses its own unique and somewhat contradictory entailment. Since painting or adorning do not—like craft reformation (carving, bending)—actually alter the "stuff" upon which they are applied, it is a prerequisite of these processes that a suitable surface or substrate be present. Unlike the craft metaphor, then, the adornment metaphor involves a substrate material that is not a shapeless mass to be cut or trimmed, but that instead helps to determine the final shape of the "product."

The tension between these two metaphorical models forms the basis of our discussion of paradox of *wu-wei* as it appears in the *Analects*. Below we will see the appeal of each model—that is, what sort of conceptual work it does for the author(s) of the *Analects*—and also explore in more detail their points of incompatibility.

The Adornment and "Root" Metaphors

Part of the appeal of the adornment model of self-cultivation can be explained by a tension in early Confucian thought identified by David Nivison and referred to by him as the "paradox of Virtue."[17] In pre-Confucian times, the suasive power of charismatic Virtue (*de* 德) was something given by Heaven as a reward to a sagely ruler—that is, one who displayed perfect, *wu-wei* ritual behavior, which in turn required infusing ritual practice with genuine generosity, self-restraint, self-sacrifice, and humility. At the same time, the attractive power conferred by Virtue was perceived as something necessary for the ruler to have if he is to function effectively as a ruler. The paradox here, as Nivison sees it, is that Virtue is something that cannot be strategically *sought* after by an aspiring ruler, since if he is performing "good" acts merely with an eye toward obtaining Virtue, these acts are then not really good. Truly virtuous acts must be done for their own sake, not with an eye toward strategic gain. This means that true Virtue can only be embodied in a completely unselfconscious manner, which engenders a paradox: it seems that one must already be virtuous in order to acquire Virtue.

This paradox of Virtue is inherited by Confucius, in the sense that the virtue of Goodness, as well as the Virtue that comes with it, can only be realized by one who truly *loves* the Way for its own sake. If, however, one already truly *does* love virtue or the Way, then one already has them. As Confucius declares in 7.30, "Is Goodness really so far away? If I simply desire Goodness, I will find that it is already here." Nivison likens this tension to the paradox of learning discussed in the *Meno*:

> *Wanting* to be moral—being disposed or being sufficiently disposed to perform the role that you and everyone else knows you should perform—is the essential part of *being* moral. But if the teacher is to teach this disposition, to impart it, the student must already be disposed to accept the instruction, and so, apparently, must already have it. The problem is structured like Socrates's paradox of learning in the *Meno* (to be taught, one must recognize the thing taught as something to be learned, and this requires that in some sense one already knows it); but in the Chinese moral education form it is far more convincingly and distressingly real.[18]

We might thus expect to find in the *Analects* something structurally similar to the Platonic idea of "recollection," and indeed we find throughout the text suggestions that self-cultivation involves merely the beautification of tendencies already present within the self.

The most common general term for self-cultivation is a metaphor referring to the adornment of a surface, *xiu* 修, and self-cultivation is also often conceptualized in terms of some cultural "adornment" (*wen* 文) being applied to preexisting "native stuff" (*zhi* 質). This entailment is clearly expressed in an exchange between Zixia and Confucius in 3.8:

> Zixia asked, "[An ode says,]
>> 'Her artful smile, with its alluring dimples,
>> Her beautiful eyes, so clear,
>> The unadorned upon which to paint.'
> What does this mean?"
>> The Master said, "The application of colors comes only after a suitable unadorned background is present."
>> Zixia said, "So it is the rites that come after?"
>> The Master said, "It is you, Zixia, who has awakened me to the meaning of these lines! It is only with someone like you that I can begin to discuss the *Odes*."

Ritual training is here portrayed metaphorically as applying cosmetics to an otherwise unadorned face. Just as all of the cosmetics in the world are of no avail if the basic lines of the face are not pleasing, so is the refinement provided by ritual practice of no help to one lacking in good native substance. It is this entailment that explains both Confucius's concern that cultural adornment be firmly rooted in its native substrate and his preference to err on the side of simplicity:

> Lin Fang asked about the root of ritual.
>> The Master exclaimed, "What a noble question! When it comes to ritual, it is better to be sparse than extravagant. When it comes to mourning, it is better to be excessively sorrowful than fastidious." (3.4)

The "native stuff" of the basic emotions serves as the "root" (*ben* 本) of ritual forms, and it is important that this form never lose touch with its organic origins. This organic metaphor appears also in 1.2, where filiality and respect for one's older brother (*xiaodi* 孝弟) are described as the "roots of Goodness," and where Yuzi notes that "the gentleman applies himself to the roots; once the roots are firmly established (*li* 立), the Way will grow (*sheng* 生)."

Supplementing these "adornment" and "root" metaphors, we can find several passages in the text that suggest the existence of some kind of innate tendency toward the Good. For instance, we read in 16.9 that some are "born knowing it," and although Confucius does not count himself among them (7.20), it is apparent that Yan Hui, at least, has some sort of intuitive grasp of the Way. In 2.9, Confucius describes how Yan Hui listens somewhat passively all day to his teachings in a manner that suggests he is somewhat stupid. When Confucius then secretly observes Yan Hui's private behavior, though, he finds that it manifests perfectly the Confucian Way. "That Yan Hui is not stupid at all," Confucius concludes. The implication is that Yan Hui did not ask questions because he already had some grasp—at least at an intuitive level—of what was being taught to him. This interpretation is strengthened by 5.9:

> The Master said to Zigong, "Who is better, you or Yan Hui?"
>
> Zigong answered, "How dare I even think of comparing myself with Hui? Hui learns one thing and thereby understands ten. I learn one thing and thereby understand two."
>
> The Master said, "No, you are not as good as Hui. Neither of us is as good as Hui."

Although in these passages Yan Hui is portrayed as requiring some instruction, he seems to have been something of a moral genius naturally inclined toward the Way. If nothing else, he possessed a kind of passion for learning that apparently cannot be taught, and which is unfortunately rare among Confucius's contemporaries. In 6.3, Confucius is asked by a ruler which of his disciples loves learning, and he replies somewhat wistfully: "There was one named Yan Hui who loved learning. He never misdirected his anger, and never made the same mistake twice. Unfortunately, his allotted life span was short, and he has passed away. Now that he is gone, there are none who really love learning—at least, I have yet to hear of one." That a moral elite among humans possess some sort of natural inclination toward the Way is also suggested in the observation in 17.3 that "the very wise. . . . do not change (*yi* 移; lit. move)," and in 19.22 we even find the suggestion that such innate orientation toward the good is a universal quality: "The Way of Wen and Wu has not yet fallen to the ground, it still exists in people (*zairen* 在人). . . . There is no one who does not have the Way of Wen and Wu in them." Although this late passage may reflect the beginnings of a Mencian-like internalist sect of Confucianism, we can see that it is not without precedents in the earlier strata of the text.

Of course, these internalist-leaning passages raise problems. If all that is necessary to possess Goodness is to love it, then why is Yan Hui, who is clearly even more naturally gifted than Confucius, told by Confucius in 12.1 that Goodness consists of "overcoming/defeating (*ke* 克) the self and returning to the rites," and why does he need to be so strictly warned: "Do not look unless it is in accordance with the rites; do not listen unless it is in accordance with the rites; do not speak unless it is in accordance with the rites; do not move unless it is in accordance with the rites." Let us turn now to the alternate set of metaphors, those of craft reformation and effort, that serve to correct some of the problematic entailments of the adornment-organic metaphors, but that in turn raise problems of their own.

The Craft and Effort Metaphors

The occasional celebrations of innate endowment that we see above are over-shadowed in the *Analects* by passages that stress the difficulty of self-cultivation. There are, for instance, several passages that explicitly deny that virtue is the result of innate ability. For instance, in 3.16 Confucius notes that, as set down in antiquity, "in archery, one does not emphasize piercing the hide of the target, because people's strength differs." That is, the ancients designed the practice of archery to recognize and celebrate acquired skill (proper aim), not some merely inborn quality such as physical strength. The fact that it is effort and perseverance—not inborn talent—that counts in self-cultivation is also indicated in Confucius's comment that he "has never seen a person whose strength was insufficient" (4.6). The problem is merely that people do not *try* hard enough.

Understood in terms of the SELF-CULTIVATION AS CRAFT REFORMATION metaphor, the purpose of ritual training is to restrain or regulate (*jie* 節) the inherent emotional "stuff" of human beings, which would tend toward excess if left to develop on its own: "The Master said, 'If you are respectful but lack ritual you will become exasperating; if you are careful but lack ritual you will become timid; if you are courageous but lack ritual you will become unruly; and if you are upright but lack ritual you will become inflexible'" (8.2). We see the craft metaphor in the characterization of a certain disciple in 5.10 as a piece of "rotten wood" or a "dung wall" that cannot be made into something beautiful, and it appears systematically throughout the text. In 15.10 an aspiring gentle-man's seeking out of virtuous company is compared to a craftsman (*gong* 工) sharpening his tools, and in 19.7 Zixia compares the learning of the gentleman to the work of the "hundred craftsmen" in their shops. We see the reshaping entailment appear in 5.21, where the "wild" youth of Confucius's home state are described as lacking the means by which to "trim" (*cai* 裁) themselves, as well as in 12.22, where something resembling the "press-frame" metaphor that becomes so prominent in the *Xunzi* is invoked: "Raise up the straight and apply them to the crooked, and the crooked will be made straight." The metaphor of "straightness" (*zhi* 直) is a common one, referring sometimes to a specific virtue (often rendered as "uprightness") but also, as in 12.22, to general moral "straightness." Another metaphor that becomes a favorite of Xunzi's is that of carving and polishing jade or bone, which are extremely difficult and time-consuming materials to work. In 1.15, Zilu quotes the lines from Ode 55, "As if cut (*qie* 切), as if polished (*cuo* 磋); as if carved (*zhuo* 琢), as if ground (*mo* 磨)," to describe the perfected person, and is consequently praised by Confucius. In 9.19, self-cultivation is compared to building up a mountain or leveling ground, both grueling tasks that allow no respite (*zhi* 止; lit. stopping), and in 9.17 Confucius praises the indefatigability of the flowing river, which "does not rest day or night."

That a slacking off of effort can be metaphorically conceptualized as "stopping" or "resting" indicates a conceptual link between the craft metaphor and the schema, SELF-CULTIVATION AS LONG JOURNEY. In 8.7, the process of becoming a gentleman possessing the virtue of Goodness is likened by the disciple Master Zeng to a difficult, lifelong journey: "A scholar-official must be strong and resolute, for his burden heavy is and his Way is long. He takes up Goodness as his personal burden—is it not heavy? His way ends only with death—is it not long?" The two schemas are combined in 9.11, where Yan Hui laments the arduousness of the task of self-cultivation: "The more I look up, the higher it seems; the more I delve into it, the harder it becomes. Catching a glimpse of it before me, I then suddenly find it at my back. . . . Though I desire to follow it, there seems to be no way through." The coordination of the craft metaphor with the journey metaphor serves to reinforce and supplement the entailments discussed above. Since the journey is long and difficult, one cannot expect instant results. This is why Confucius criticizes those who want "quick success" (*sucheng* 速成) (14.44), and notes that "those who crave speed will never arrive" (13.17). Like a road, the task of self-cultivation has a definite beginning and a clear end (19.12), and one must forge ahead in a determined manner and avoid distractions or "byways." "Although the byways (*xiaodao* 小道) no doubt have their own interesting sights to see, one who wishes to reach a distant destination fears becoming mired," Zixia notes in 19.4 concluding: "This is why the gentleman avoids the byways." Indeed, as his spiritual autobiography in 2.4 indicates, even Confucius himself apparently did not attain the state of truly loving Goodness—in the sense of being able to fully embody it in a *wu-wei* fashion—until after fifty-five years of intensive self-cultivation. Hence Confucius's description of himself in 7.34: "How could I dare to lay claim to either sageliness or Goodness? What can be said about me is no more than this: I work at it (*weizhi* 為之) without growing tired and encourage others without growing weary."

The response of one of Confucius's disciples, Gong Xihua, to this comment of the Master's indicates, however, one of the internal tensions in the craft-effort model. Commenting on Confucius's tireless devotion to the Way, he notes, "This is precisely what we disciples are unable to learn." This is a very revealing observation. In order to keep oneself moving forward on the "long journey" of self-cultivation it is necessary that one genuinely desire to reach the destination. How, though, does one *teach* such desire to a person who does not already possess it? This is no doubt the source of much of Confucius's frustration with his current age, expressed most succinctly in 15.13: "I should just give up. I have yet to meet a man who loves Virtue as much as female beauty." A similar sense of exasperation shows through in 9.24:

> The Master said, "When a man is rebuked with exemplary words after having made a mistake, he cannot help but agree with them. However, what is important is that he change himself in order to *accord* with them. When a man is praised with words of respect, he cannot help but be pleased with them. However, what is important is that he actually *live up* to them. A person who finds respectful words pleasing but does not live up to them, or agrees with others' reproaches and yet does not change—there is nothing I can do with one such as this."

Nominal assent to the Confucian Way is thus insufficient—if *wu-wei* perfection is to be attained, the student must *love* the Way, not merely understand it. How, though, do you teach someone love? As Confucius remarks somewhat impatiently in 15.16, "I have never been able to do anything for a person who is not himself constantly asking, 'What should I do? What should I do?'" The problem, of course, is that it is hard to see how the teacher could instill this sort of passion or love in a student to whom it simply does *not* occur to ask, "What should I do?" In short, if unselfconscious, *wu-wei* perfection is the soteriological goal, the student cannot learn from the teacher unless he or she is passionately committed to learning, and this would seem to entail already possessing a genuine love for the Confucian Way. Here we have Confucius's version of the Meno problem.

It is in response to this problem of motivation that we find the author(s) of the *Analects* falling back upon the adornment-root metaphors. Consider, for instance, *Analects* 5.10, where the disciple Zai Wo is observed by the master sleeping during the daytime. "Rotten wood cannot be carved, and a wall of dung cannot be plastered," the Master remarks disdainfully. "As for Zai Wo, what would be the use of reprimanding him?" Here, someone like Zai Wo, who presumably "gives assent" to the Confucian project but nonetheless lies sleeping in bed all day, is dismissed by Confucius as a piece of "rotten wood" that cannot be "carved." Although the most salient metaphor here is SELF-CULTIVATION AS CRAFT REFORMATION, notice that the emphasis is upon the need for quality "stuff." As I argued above, it is in response to precisely this problem of motivation that the adornment-root metaphors find a place in the text. On the other hand, craft metaphors need also be invoked as a counterbalance to the adornment metaphors, entailing as they do the openness of the Confucian Way to everyone and the need for education, traditional forms, and effort. Therefore, both the adornment and craft metaphors serve crucial functions in compensating for the shortcomings of the other, but the two sets of metaphors are themselves not fully compatible.

The Paradox of *Wu-wei* in a Broader Context

One might try to explain away the incompatibility between the adornment and craft metaphors for self-cultivation by attributing them to different strata of the *Analects*—different wings of the early Confucian school—and there may be some truth to this idea. Mencius and Xunzi, for instance, can be seen as focusing upon one or the other of these primary metaphors for self-cultivation and attempting to consistently elaborate them. As I have argued in *Effortless Action* (2003), however, neither the Mencian nor Xunzian attempt proves ultimately successful, and the tension between incompatible metaphors for self-cultivation that we find in the *Analects* is in fact reproduced in various forms throughout the later Chinese philosophical tradition. It might be helpful to provide a brief sketch of the early Chinese responses to this tension—as well as the sorts of problems these responses encountered—in order to suggest how the ideal of *wu-wei* and its paradox can not only serve as a powerful lens through which to view the development of early Chinese thought, but also give us insight into the more general problem of human moral education.

Mirroring the split between the more internalist adornment metaphors and externalist craft metaphors in the *Analects*, attempted "solutions" to the paradox in the later tradition can be generally be characterized as predominantly internalist or externalist.[19] Each response merely chooses a horn of the dilemma upon which to impale itself. The internalists answer the question of how one can try not to try to be good by gravitating toward the "not trying" horn: at some level, they claim, we already *are* good, and we merely need to allow this virtuous potential to realize itself. Zhuangzi, Laozi, and Mencius fall into this camp. The externalists, exemplified by Xunzi (and arguably by the dominant position in the *Analects* as well), maintain on the contrary that it is essential that we *try* not to try. That is, they claim that we do *not* possess the resources to attain *wu-wei* on our own and that *wu-wei* is a state acquired only after a long and intensive process of training in traditional, external forms. Toward this end they formulate a rigorous training regime designed to gradually lead us from our original state of ignorance to the pinnacle of spiritual perfection. Unfortunately, neither of these responses to the paradox proves entirely satisfactory or even internally consistent, and both are plagued by superficial and structural difficulties.

For instance, the Confucian internalist Mencius is confronted with the superficial problem that, by placing the locus of moral authority within the individual, he has apparently undermined the need for traditional Confucian ritual practices and the classics. These cultural resources are often portrayed as merely helpful aids to moral self-cultivation, dispensable in a pinch and ultimately subordinate to the individual's own inner moral guide—the heart/mind.[20]

This becomes the focus of the Xunzian critique of Mencian thought, but is less of a problem for the Daoist thinkers, who are in any case already doctrinally committed to undermining traditional Confucian institutions.

The deeper, structural problem faced by any internalist—Confucian or Daoist—is the question: if we *are* already fundamentally good, why do we not *act* like it? The fact that we are not, in our current fallen state, actually manifesting our "innate" goodness calls into question the internalist position and makes the externalist solution seem more reasonable. We apparently need to do *something* in order to eventually be able to "not-do." The result is that all early Chinese internalists feel the need to fall back occasionally into an externalist stance, making some kind of reference to the need for effort and even externalist practice regimens. This deeper, structural tension manifests itself in texts such as the *Mencius* in terms of a conflict between metaphor schemas for self-cultivation that possess incommensurable entailments. Mencius relies primarily upon the SELF-CULTIVATION AS AGRICULTURE schema as his dominant model for the process of education, and the entailments of this metaphor support his professed internalist position: without the need for external instructions, seedlings spontaneously tend to grow into full-grown plants at the urging of their innate *telos*, and all that they require to realize this internal *telos* is a supportive, protected environment. Unfortunately, this model does not account for the fact that following our supposed "true" innate promptings (that is, becoming good) is in practice a real struggle for human beings—in other words, the fact that, in order to become moral, we have to try quite hard to be "spontaneous" in the way Mencius desires us to be.

It is in response to this perceived tension that Mencius occasionally supplements his internalist metaphors with externalist schemas that possess entirely different and incompatible entailments: SELF-CULTIVATION AS CRAFT REFORMATION, for instance, where human behavior is portrayed as something that needs to be guided by the standards supplied by external measuring tools (4A.1, 4A.2).[21] Similarly, the authors of the *Laozi* and *Zhuangzi* temper their faith in our spontaneous, natural tendencies— expressed by various effortless or "wild nature" metaphors—with hints of external practices and structured disciplines that are necessary if one is to actually realize *wu-wei*, expressed in terms of "grasping," "cultivation," or other effort-related metaphors. In this respect it is quite revealing that, regardless of whether or not such cryptic phrases as "block the openings and shut the doors" (*Laozi*) or instructions to "fast the mind" (*Zhuangzi*) originally referred to concrete, physical practices, they were certainly understood in this sense by later Daoist practitioners, and were subsequently developed into elaborate externalist systems of yogic, meditative, alchemical, and sexual regimens.

The practical difficulty of self-cultivation might thus make the externalist position seem more attractive. This position, however, is plagued by its own superficial as well as structural problems. Xunzi, for instance, is faced with the more superficial difficulty of trying to explain how, if human beings are completely bereft of innate moral resources, morality gets its start, since as a Confucian he is doctrinally committed to the position that the sage-kings who created the rites and wrote the classics were themselves human beings just like us. That this problem is superficial is indicated by the fact that Christian externalists in the West are able to circumvent it by locating the source of morality in an extrahuman realm.

The deeper problem faced by externalists who are concerned with moral self-cultivation—Confucian as well as Christian—is the question of how the novice is to be *moved* from the precultivated state to the state of moral perfection when genuinely moral action seems to require some sort of preexistent (or at least coexistent) internal disposition. Despite the power of the SELF-CULTIVATION AS CRAFT REFORMATION metaphor, there is an important *disanalogy* between a craft skill and moral virtue, as Aristotle succinctly pointed out:

> What is true of crafts is not true of virtues. For the products of a craft determine by their own character whether they have been produced well; and so it suffices that they are in the right state when they have been produced. But for actions expressing virtue to be done temperately or justly [and hence well] it does not suffice that they are themselves in the right state. Rather, the agent must also be in the right state when he does them.[22]

Genuinely moral action involves not only producing the right external "product" (behavior), but doing so while also possessing the right internal disposition. The problem of moral virtue confronting an externalist, then, is that it seems that the student must in some sense already *be* virtuous—or at least have the beginnings of virtuous inclinations—in order to act in a genuinely virtuous manner. It is precisely this difficulty that any externalist teacher of virtue must try to circumvent, the mystery being how the student is to make the transition from merely acting out morality to actually *becoming* a moral person. The common danger is that this transition will not be made and that the training regimen will thus produce nothing more than a moral hypocrite who merely goes through the motions of morality. It is this potential danger—one felt by the Confucians no less than the Daoists—that explains the perennial appeal of the internalist position.

That this was a subject of concern for both the compilers of the *Analects* and Xunzi is evidenced by the *Analects'* concern about the so-called village worthy—the "thief of virtue," or counterfeit of the true Confucian gentleman, who observes perfectly all of the external forms of virtue but is completely lacking in the proper internal dispositions—and by Xunzi's recognition that truly moral action must be accompanied by "sincerity" (*cheng* 誠) and a genuine love for the Way. In both the *Analects* and the *Xunzi* this concern for proper moral dispositions results in a degree of metaphoric incommensurability, with both thinkers being motivated to supplement their dominant externalist metaphors for self-cultivation with occasional internalist ones. As we have seen above, this metaphoric tension is more pronounced in the *Analects*, and this is perhaps less surprising considering the mixed provenance of the text. Most likely cobbled together over time by different—and perhaps even rival—groups of disciples, the mixing of externalist and internalist metaphors in the *Analects* could perhaps be attributed to doctrinal conflicts within the early Confucian school. What is more revealing and significant is the appearance in the *Xunzi*—for the most part representing the writings of a single, careful thinker quite consciously and explicitly opposed to internalism—of such internalist metaphors as "natural" response or moral "taste."

It seems that the early Chinese tradition was never able to formulate a fully consistent or entirely satisfying solution (whether internalist or externalist) to the tensions created by one of its central spiritual ideals. Historically, the tensions inherent in the early Chinese spiritual ideal of *wu-wei* were subsequently transmitted to later East Asian schools of thought that inherited *wu-wei* as an ideal. They resurface in Chan Buddhism in the form of the sudden-gradual controversy, in Japanese Zen Buddhism in the form of the debate between the Rinzai and Soto schools, and in East Asian neo-Confucianism in the form of the conflict between the Cheng-Zhu and Lu-Wang factions. The tenaciousness of this tension is illustrated by its resistance to being resolved by doctrinal fiat. The victory of the Southern (sudden) school of Chan Buddhism, for instance, was designed to settle the problem in an internalist/subitist fashion: all human beings originally possess pure, undefiled Buddha-nature, which means that practice and other external aids to enlightenment (scripture, etc.) are essentially superfluous. Yet the problem refuses to be so easily conjured away and simply reemerges both in Buddhism and neo-Confucianism (which also adopts the Buddhist "solution" of an originally pure nature) in the subsequent splits between the more internalist, "sudden-sudden" Rinzai and Lu-Wang schools and the more externalist, "gradual sudden" Soto and Cheng-Zhu schools. The continued, stubborn reemergence of this split—ultimately related to a failure to produce an entirely consistent or satisfying internalist or externalist position— suggests that the paradox of *wu-wei* is a *genuine* paradox and that any "solution" to the problem it presents will therefore necessarily be plagued by the sort of superficial and structural difficulties described above.

Indeed, the implications of the *wu-wei* problematic extend beyond its contribution to our understanding of Chinese or East Asian thought, because the tensions produced by the paradox of *wu-wei* are to be found not only in Aristotle's claim that "to become just we must first do just actions" but also in Plato's belief that to be taught one must recognize the thing taught as something to be learned—the so called "Meno problem." It seems that something resembling the paradox of *wu-wei* will plague the thought of any thinker who can be characterized as a virtue ethicist—that is, anyone who sees ethical life in terms of the perfection of normative dispositions. In this respect it is revealing that the significance of Aristotle's paradox and Plato's Meno problem have been "rediscovered" by Alasdair MacIntyre in the course of his retrieval of our own lost virtue ethical tradition. Consider, for instance, his discussion of a deep tension to be found in the Augustinian educational system:

> In medieval Augustinian culture the relationship between the key texts of that culture and their reader was twofold. The reader was assigned the task of interpreting the text, but also had to discover, in and through his or her reading of those texts, that they in turn interpret the reader. What the reader, as thus interpreted by the texts, has to learn about him or herself is that it is only the self as transformed through and by the reading of the texts which will be capable of reading the texts aright. So the reader, *like any learner within a craft-tradition*, encounters apparent paradox at the outset, a Christian version of the paradox of Plato's *Meno*: it seems that only by learning what the texts have to teach can he or she come to read those texts aright, but also that only by reading them aright can he or she learn what the texts have to teach.[23]

We might thus be justified in seeing the tensions circling about the paradox of *wu-wei* as having significance not only for early Chinese thinkers, but also for any thinker concerned with the problem of self-cultivation—that is, with the problem of not merely winning from the individual rational assent to a system of principles but actually *transforming* them into a new type of person. Seen in this way, this discussion of a tension between metaphors for self-cultivation in the *Analects* takes on a significance that goes beyond the merely sinological, for it can serve as a window through which we can gain new insight into the ideals and problematiques of our own early tradition.

Notes

1. As the reader is no doubt aware, there is a consensus among contemporary scholars that the *Analects* is a somewhat heterogeneous collection of material from different time periods, although scholars differ in their identification of the different strata, as well as in the significance they attribute to these differences. It is my own opinion that, although representing different time periods and somewhat different concerns, the various strata of the *Analects* display enough consistency in terminological use, conceptual repertoire, and general religious viewpoint to allow us to treat the text as a whole as presenting a unified vision—a representation of the state of the "School of Confucius" before the innovations of Mencius and Xunzi. The reader is referred to Edward Slingerland, "Why Philosophy Is Not 'Extra' in Understanding the *Analects*, a

review of Brooks and Brooks, *The Original Analects*," *Philosophy East and West* 50, no. 1 (January 2000): 137–41, 146–47, for more on this issue, framed as a response to the more radical views of the text put forth by Brooks and Brooks, *The Original Analects* (New York: Columbia University Press, 1998).

2. This chapter is a modified excerpt from chapter 2 of Edward Slingerland, *Effortless Action: Wu-wei as Conceptual Metaphor and Spiritual Ideal in Early China* (New York: Oxford University Press, 2003), and the reader is referred to that work for more on the argument that a network of *wu-wei* metaphors having to do with effortlessness and unselfconsciousness pervade "mainstream" Warring States Chinese texts, and that the "paradox of *wu-wei*"—most simply, the problem of how one might try not to try—serves as a main motivating force in pre-Qin secondary theory formation.

3. The term "conceptual metaphor" refers to cross-domain cognitive projections, whereby part of the structure of a more concrete or clearly organized domain (the *source* domain) is used to understand and talk about another, usually more abstract or less clearly structured, domain (the *target* domain). For instance, when talking and reasoning about our lives, we commonly draw upon a projection whereby the features of physical journeys are mapped onto our lives: we can *make progress* in our work, feel that we are *falling behind*, or *come to a crossroads* in our careers. This is known as the LIFE AS JOURNEY metaphor, and it is this sort of projective mapping that is meant by the term "conceptual metaphor," which—understood in this way—encompasses simile and analogy as well as metaphor in the more traditional sense. George Lakoff and Mark Johnson are the most prominent advocates of the view that conceptual metaphor plays a central role in human cognition, and serves one of our primary tools for reasoning about ourselves and the world—especially about relatively abstract or unstructured domains. For introductions to conceptual metaphor theory, see George Lakoff, "The Contemporary Theory of Metaphor," in *Metaphor and Thought*, 2nd ed., ed. Andrew Ortony, 202–51 (Cambridge: Cambridge University Press. 1993); George Lakoff and Mark Johnson, *Metaphors We Live By* (Chicago: University of Chicago Press, 1980); and George Lakoff and Mark Johnson, *Philosophy in the Flesh: The Embodied Mind and its Challenge to Western Though* (New York: Basic Books, 1999). For more on applications of metaphor theory to the study of Chinese thought and comparative religion in general, see Slingerland, *Effortless Action*; Edward Slingerland, "Conceptual Metaphor Theory as Methodology for Comparative Religion," *Journal of the American Academy of Religion* 71, no. 1 (March 2004): 1–31; and Edward Slingerland, "Conceptions of the Self in the *Zhuangzi*: Conceptual Metaphor Analysis and Comparative Thought," *Philosophy East and West* 54, no. 3 (July 2004): 322–42. After Lakoff and Johnson, I will designate conceptual metaphors with small capital letters.

4. Lakoff and Johnson, *Metaphors*, 267.

5. Andrew Lakoff and Miles Becker, *Me, Myself, and I* (manuscript, University of California, Berkeley, 1992); Lakoff and Johnson, *Philosophy in the Flesh*, 268–270.

6. Lakoff and Johnson claim that *all* metaphors for the self are based upon this schema, but this is overstated; in both Warring States Chinese and modern English we

often find a unitary subject interacting metaphorically with an external entity, such as the world. Consider, for example, the comment, "I simply went along with the flow."

7. Lakoff and Johnson, *Philosophy in the Flesh*, 269.

8. Lakoff and Johnson, *Philosophy in the Flesh*, 271.

9. Lakoff and Johnson, *Philosophy in the Flesh*, 272–73.

10. All translations from the *Analects* are my own, taken from *Confucius: Analects* (New York: Hackett, 2003) (translation with running traditional commentary, glossary, and extensive introduction).

11. Cheng Shude 程樹德, *Lunyi Jishi* 論語集釋 (Beijing: Zhonghua Shuju,1996), 78.

12. Cheng Shude, *Lunyi Jishi*, 75.

13. See David Nivison, "Golden Rule Arguments in Chinese Moral Philosophy," in *The Ways of Confucianism*, by David Nivison, ed. Bryan Van Norden (Chicago: Open Court. 1996), 59–76; and Philip J. Ivanhoe, "Reweaving the 'One Thread' of the *Analects*," *Philosophy East and West* 40, no. 1 (1990): 17–33; and Ivanhoe's update of his position in his contribution to this volume.

14. Joel Kupperman, "Confucius and the Problem of Naturalness," *Philosophy East and West* 18 (1968): 177. Scott Cook makes a similar point when he notes that, with regard to musical perfection in the Confucian scheme, there is a "fundamental paradox between the hardship and incessant discipline of constrained practice leading up to it and the spontaneous freedom of performance or the perfected embodiment of artistry marked by its complete attainment." *Unity and Diversity in the Musical Thought of Warring States China* (PhD dissertation, University of Michigan, 1995), 131.

15. Kupperman, "Confucius," 180; emphasis added.

16. The radical for *xiu* is *shan* 彡, which the *Shuowen* defines as "to draw or write with a hair-brush." Another meaning of *xiu* is "to sweep" (i.e., with a broom), and the *Shuowen* defines *xiu* itself as *shi* 飾, "to adorn," "to brush or sweep," or "to clean" (the radical of *shi* is *jin* 巾, meaning "canvas," "napkin," "cloth"). While it is always possible to read too much meaning into a character's radical, the basic meaning of *xiu* can be said to be adorning or painting a surface with a brush or burnishing or cleaning a surface with a cloth.

17. Nivison, *Ways of Confucianism*, 31–43.

18. Nivison, *Ways of Confucianism*, 80.

19. When we pick up the debate in the early Chan tradition, we find that self-cultivation internalism has become the unquestioned orthodoxy, and the tension is therefore formulated in terms of a "sudden-gradual" split. It is interesting to note, though, that although internalism becomes a theological commitment, we can still see the paradox as creating an internalist-externalist split with regard to soteriological strategies. That is to say, the gradualist school of Chan Buddhism also endorses what look like more externalist soteriological techniques, and the Cheng-Zhu versus Lu-Wang debate can arguably also be characterized along self-cultivationist externalist internalist lines, even though both schools were theologically committed to internalism.

20. Consider the discretion displayed by the Mencian gentleman in adapting or even violating the dictates of the rites if they fail to accord with what is "right" for the situation (3B.10, 4A.17, 4A.26, 5A.2) or following his intuition in reinterpreting or even rejecting portions of the classics (5A.4, 7B.3).

21. See also 3A.4 and 6A.20.

22. *Nicomachean Ethics* 1105a27–31; Terence Irwin, trans., Aristotle's *Nicomachean Ethics* (Indianapolis: Hackett, 1985), 39–40.

23. Alasdair MacIntyre, *Three Rival Versions of Moral Inquiry* (Notre Dame: University of Notre Dame Press, 1990), 82; emphasis added.

Slowing Death Down: Mourning in the *Analects*

8

Amy Olberding

Contemporary American funerary practices, with their elaborate material provisions for burial and their curious display of the embalmed body, mark the United States as a society that struggles to articulate a meaningful program for honoring the dead and managing bereavement. Given a culture that seems committed to avoiding reminders of death, what Jessica Mitford deems the "full-fledged burlesque" of the American funeral is a particularly peculiar phenomenon.[1] We are a society that appears unable to reconcile conflicting urges. We wish not to confront death directly, yet we can neither easily nor completely abandon our dead without ceremony. In consequence, our practices often neglect sustained reflection on the significance of loss and seek instead to answer pain with the all too familiar material extravagance that marks much of American culture. We may often find ourselves uneasy with the economics of the contemporary funeral industry and, in particular, the way in which the material provisions of funerary ritual are uncoupled from a coherent program for incorporating mourning into a robust ethos of human flourishing. For this, Confucius offers a resource.

While Confucius addresses mourning throughout the *Analects*, in what follows I focus on what might best be considered a failure of mourning, the arrangements made for the funeral and burial of Confucius's beloved student Yan Hui.[2] The passages concerning Yan Hui's death and burial are particularly useful for they afford the opportunity to examine Confucius's claims about the efficacy and meaning of mourning *in situ*, in a circumstance in which Confucius himself painfully struggles to apply his own strategies for handling grief. Moreover, insofar as the rituals surrounding Yan Hui's death can be counted a failure, the ways in which they fail are instructive for inhabitants of a culture where the expressions of grief most ready to hand are those of ostentatious display. Confucius's protests at the material extravagance of Yan Hui's funeral suggest a broader critique of ostentation in funerary practices and point the way toward a model of more robust mourning.

It is instructive, from the outset, to distinguish mourning from grief.[3] In its most rudimentary form, mourning is an activity, or body of activities, that is designed to commemorate loss and is, in some measure, culturally sanctioned as an appropriate expression of bereavement. Grief, in contrast, is a response to loss that is striking in its immediacy. Genuine grief comes unbidden, and while it is informed by antecedent belief, it is not something that, at the moment of loss, we summon into existence. We are, rather, "stricken" by grief. It is a feeling or complex of feelings, and its attendant behaviors are largely unpremeditated: we weep, we wail, we speak in unaccustomed ways or mutely suffer. Mourning, in contrast, lacks this immediacy and is not feeling but affect. It consists in a body of practices such as funerary ritual or the adoption of specific clothing and adornments that are socially symbolic. Unlike grief, which may be wholly private, mourning is culturally constructed and has its home in the public space where the meanings of its various signs and ritualized behaviors reside. It is, in this sense, wholly artifice, and its activities are constructions that formalize and regulate the expression of sorrow.

In distinguishing grief and mourning thus, it is perhaps tempting to see grief as involuntary, as simple reaction, and to see mourning as a reflective, more thoughtful endeavor, as a formulated and premeditated response. In some respects this would be an accurate description of a fundamental difference. Where grief overtakes us and imposes itself upon us, to be in mourning is to assume a particular public posture. However, while this distinction may be, at times, conceptually useful, as a practical matter it is often less clear. While it is true that grief simply comes upon us, this is not to say that it comes from nowhere. Grief has its origins in beliefs about loss and these beliefs, far from coming unbidden, require at least our tacit, if not explicit, assent. To grieve, that is, I must have an antecedent conviction about the value of what is now lost. Although I may abdicate thoughtful consideration and evaluation of these beliefs, they are nonetheless the products of a certain species of consent. Thus, while grief, *when it arrives*, may be characterized as a nonreflective reaction, it is, in this sense, a formulated response. I grieve because I have shaped my life, self-consciously or not, in such a way that it is governed by convictions about value that make grief possible. Confucius's therapy for loss is predicated on the view that there are a variety of "reasons" or antecedent beliefs, not all of equal merit, that may create the conditions for grief. Thus, while it is important to recognize the way in which grief comes unbidden at the moment of loss, its origins in the ways we choose to formulate value must not be neglected.

That mourning may be contrasted with grief on the grounds that the activities of mourning display a level of choice that grief does not may likewise be a misleading or reductionistic characterization. For, as a practical matter, the "decision" to mourn is often reflexive rather than thoughtful. As a socially recognized and encouraged means of commemorating loss, mourning may serve as a simple refuge from the need to self-consciously choose behaviors. Mourning provides a set of norms to which one may acquiesce in the confusion and upheaval of grief. Although to acquiesce in such a fashion is certainly a tacit choice, it is important when using the language of "choice" in this context to be conscious of its limitations as a description of what the bereaved actually do in the midst of grief. Their level of deliberation or reflection may actually be quite minimal. Recognizing the way in which the postures of mourning are often adopted unreflectively in the extremity of grief is of great import for understanding Confucius's counsel for his recommendations regarding mourning hinge on his desire to see mourning entered into in a way that is far more thoughtful than may be the norm. He wishes mourning to be conceived as both permitting and requiring a greater measure of meditative care than a merely acquiescent "choice" can sustain. Thus, while grief and mourning may be distinguished according to the degree of deliberation that each seem to permit, this distinction serves well only when qualified by a recognition of its somewhat ambiguous character in the context of bereavement.

Given that many in his audience likely would already see such activities as the socially expected and thus appropriate response to loss, Confucius's recommendations can appear merely to sanction what is ordinary. Indeed, that these activities are such an ordinary and typical mechanism for managing grief appears to be one of the reasons that Confucius recommends them. Much of Confucius's technique as a philosopher consists in harnessing the prosaic to an enriched understanding. Because of this technique, according to Francois Jullien, "the richness of the Confucian lesson comes from its refusal of original-ity, from its not seeking to make itself conspicuous in its ideas. Its profundity lies in its formulating the obvious."[4] However, while Confucius sanctions the ordinary and transmits tradition, his use of both ordinary and traditional prac-tice serves to imbue them with a reflective philosophical sensibility. For what he encourages is that the activities of daily life and the inherited practices of the community become, in Herbert Fingarette's idiom, an endeavor rooted in a spiritual and aesthetic appreciation of community.[5] This sensibility is evident in Confucius's advocacy of formal mourning. In urging mourning, Confucius urges his audience to a vigorous and enlightened participation in activities that are already well established and familiar to Confucius's contemporaries. What is innovative in Confucius's counsel then is not *what* he advises his audience to do, but what he suggests about *how* they do it. In describing a life articulated through relations with others, Confucius recommends a manner of life that is imperiled by the possibility of loss. While such a peril is, in Confucius's idiom, an ineluctable feature of a flourishing life, this is not to say that there is nothing to be done about it. The capacity to experience intense grief is, in Confucius's view, a laudable trait that stems from our ability to recognize and honor the significance of others in a flourishing life. Yet the very values that grief consum-mates demand that we treat our grief, when it comes, not as a final destination, but as a particularly difficult terrain through which we must pass.

If grief is to function in such a way that it honors the significance of our relations with others, any steps we might take to secure relief must be designed to manage grief while simultaneously preserving its worth as an affirmation of value. Confucius's counsel prosaically acknowledges that loss constitutes an injury, yet the risk that loss poses to our well-being cannot be evaded if we are to live well and richly. For if we take our relations with others to be constitutive elements in an enriched life and character, we sanction for ourselves a life made finely vulnerable to the possibility of loss and we cannot detach our own well-being from that of our companions. Thus any technique that would relieve our pain by repudiating it as unwarranted or sanctioning a retreat from our attachments constitutes a betrayal of that which most stands to secure a flourishing life. In this regard, Confucius's strategy for the management of grief offers a resource for loss. His strategy is a counsel that is helpful both in what it positively offers for the relief of pain and, notably, in what it declines to offer.

Confucius's strategy for the management of grief is less a remedy for pain than a technique for enduring it. Indeed, in its most ambitious formulation, Confucius's strategy may be seen as a technique for *relishing* the pain of bereavement as a significant and forceful manifestation of one's fullest self.[6] Confucius does not deny the severity of the injuries that loss may inflict upon us, but neither does he wholly seek to eradicate pain. Rather, he seeks to root our relief in what is, in some measure, an *appreciation* of pain. To appreciate our pain is to decline any relief that would abnegate its cause and to seek instead the perhaps more arduous task of managing damage while maintaining a life that permits the possibility of further injury. Mourning enables us to exercise a species of control in which these sometimes apparently competing needs can be met. When his beloved student Yan Hui died, Confucius was undone by sorrow. He claimed that his bereavement constituted his destruction (11.9), and appeared to have abandoned his typical self-command (11.10). Given the extremity of Confucius's pain in this circumstance, the manner of mourning that followed the death of Yan Hui is of particular interest. For in his mourning, Confucius's claims about the efficacy and meaning of mourning may be examined *in situ*, in a circumstance in which Confucius himself painfully struggles to apply his own strategies for handling grief.

The formal activities surrounding the death of Yan Hui are described in two passages of the *Analects* that concern the material provisions made for Yan Hui's funeral ceremony and burial. What is initially most striking in these passages is that in both cases we are shown a Confucius who is reluctant to embellish the funeral arrangements made for Yan Hui with any extravagant display. In the first passage, Yan Hui's father has requested that Confucius sell his carriage in order to purchase an outer coffin for Yan Hui's burial (11.9). Confucius declines the request, noting that when his own son died, he had made no such provision—his son was buried in a simple coffin because it would be inappropriate for a man of Confucius's status to have no carriage and be obliged to "travel on foot." Confucius sympathetically intimates that he understands the desire of Yan Hui's father because it is natural for a father to wish the best for a son. However, he declines nonetheless.

A similar sentiment is evident in the second passage concerning Yan Hui's funeral. Here it is Confucius's other students who express the desire to provide

Yan Hui with an extravagant burial. Although Confucius objects, complaining that this would be inappropriate, the students disregard Confucius's wishes, proceed with their plans, and Yan Hui is buried in rich fashion. Confucius's reaction to the ceremony bespeaks a sense of betrayal so intense that it leads him to disown the ritual, protesting, "Hui regarded me as a father, yet I have not been allowed to regard him as a son. This is not on my account, but is the work of these others" (11.11). The ritual procedures attending Yan Hui's death, because they were so extravagant, frustrate Confucius. In particular, they have created an environment in which Confucius is alienated from both Yan Hui and his surviving students. In the context of an elaborate ritual, Confucius cannot be to Yan Hui what he was when Yan Hui still lived. Neither can he find comfort in his remaining students. Far from discovering a refuge in shared pain, Confucius seems wholly without community. His students have become reduced to "these others," that is, to individuals whose actions apparently supplement, rather than salve, Confucius's pain. The example that Confucius here offers appears negative. It is a case in which mourning has apparently failed. Understanding the way in which it constitutes a failure provides a foundation for a description of successful, restorative mourning and offers a model for appropriation in our own strategies for mourning.

What the ceremony provided by Yan Hui's fellow students lacks is not grief, for clearly Yan Hui's father, Confucius, and the students rue his death. What the ceremony lacks is, put simply, Yan Hui. For while the rituals of mourning serve, in a general fashion, to symbolize grief, grief itself is never general. Grief originates, rather, in the specific and idiosyncratic relations that death so abruptly severs. We grieve specific others and, if ritual is to commemorate loss, it must reflect not *that* we have lost, but *what* we have lost. At its most basic level, the loss of Yan Hui is the loss of a man who lived a modest life (11.19), a man who refused to complain when he had but a serving of rice to eat and whose good cheer was unaffected by the meanness of what life materially afforded him (6.3). On these grounds alone, it is evident what Confucius finds so ill fitting in the extravagance of Yan Hui's burial. There is nothing of Yan Hui, or who Yan Hui was to those who loved him, in his burial. It is instead a ceremony marked by what can only be deemed generic and rather ill-conceived symbols of "importance." Rituals marked by material ostentation may thus serve to announce to larger society, in symbols it will readily recognize, that Yan Hui was someone significant. Yet in making the provisions for this social recognition, Confucius's students have rendered Yan Hui unrecognizable to those who most immediately loved and cared for him. Yan Hui has become the generic dead and, because grief is not generic, a ritual designed in such elaborate fashion is condemned to missing its target. It fails both as meaningful ritual and, more specifically, as a remembrance of Yan Hui.

The lack of a ceremony that distinctively acknowledges Yan Hui is problematic because of the way in which it fails to serve the living who, whatever may become of Yan Hui, must struggle to reconcile themselves to his absence and what that absence signifies for their lives. The figurative absence of Yan Hui from the ceremonial observances that mark his death can only accentuate the actual absence of Yan Hui in the lives of those who grieve him. In particular, it serves as a magnification of pain for Confucius who, one might imagine, finds himself not only bereft of his beloved student, but also, in consequence, bereft of the one pupil who would be most likely understand his objections to the ceremony that the other students offered. The ritual emphasizes, in a superfluous and thus cruel fashion, that there is no one who can hear and understand what Confucius endures. That Confucius, who elsewhere displays a remarkable humor and patience with his students' failings,[7] goes so far as to repudiate the ritual indicates how bitterly alienated he is and how little the ritual has achieved in reconciling Confucius to the loss of Yan Hui.

In longing for what he conceives as an appropriate mourning ritual for Yan Hui, Confucius expresses a longing common to any who grieve. The pain of loss demands to be addressed and demands some sort of relief. Yet Confucius understands (and his students fail to understand) that any release from pain cannot be purchased with the coin of practices indifferent to the identity of their participants and the specificity of loss. If ritual is to have efficacy in providing release from pain, it must answer to it. However, while the actual rituals of mourning must be specifically oriented to acknowledge the unique identities of the dead and those who survive them, the function of mourning itself does permit a more general analysis and this provides a necessary foreground for understanding what specificity in ritual can accomplish.

The pain that accompanies loss is, at least in part, attributable to the way in which death so abruptly severs the relation between the living and dead. Whether death comes quickly or results from a prolonged illness, the physical reality of death is such that, whether it is anticipated or not, its effect is immediate and sudden. Breath ceases, animation deserts the body, and what in one instance was living body is, in the next, inert corpse. Physically, death is instantaneous, unambiguous, and final. Yet the physical event is but one element of death. What is empirically evident as a radical physical transformation serves to transform the living in ways that likewise occur in an instant but that defy instantaneous comprehension.

In a recent set of essays on his experience as an undertaker, Thomas Lynch observes the way in which death is, in the lived experience of the bereaved, not a singular event, but divisible. Death is an end but it is not, for the bereaved, over. Lynch distinguishes between two distinct aspects of death: "the death that happens and the death that matters."[8] In Confucius's idiom a similar distinction obtains. When queried about death, Confucius asks his interlocutor, "Since you do not yet understand life, how could you understand death?" (11.12). While Confucius here explicitly insists that understanding life must take priority, his claim likewise indicates a direction for our energies where death intrudes upon us in the form of bereavement. There is that death which is physical and incompletely understood, and about which we may (vainly, Confucius suggests) speculate. The "death that matters," however, is the province of the living. This death is constituted by the forced recognition of the significance and reach of loss. Death here belongs to the bereaved for whom the physical death marks both an end and a terrible new beginning. It constitutes the termination of a world defined by the living presence of the beloved and the inauguration of a new world defined as much by what it lacks as by what it positively offers.

As a salve for the pain of loss, mourning serves as a technique for managing "the death that matters." Recognition of the fact of loss may swiftly follow the death of a beloved. Yet the substance of such an immediate recognition is largely unformed and its content, insofar as it lends itself to any expression, is raw and spare: She is gone. We shall not grow old together. These simple facts, however, provide what is only the onset of understanding, for they fail to capture just how, and how extensively, life has been transformed. The bare fact of loss, like death itself, arrives quickly, but the significance of loss is only revealed over time. The "death that matters" thus does not have the character of an event. It is, rather, a process through which the reality of lived relation is painfully and gradually supplanted in the consciousness of the survivor by a new and unfamiliar reality. This too is evident in Confucius's loss of Yan Hui.

Insofar as a human life can be conceived as a journey across a landscape, there are certain paths that Confucius, upon the death of Yan Hui, can no longer traverse. Yan Hui's death forecloses each of these routes just as decisively as it severs Confucius from Yan Hui himself. However, unlike the spare fact of death, the recognition that these highly particular avenues of possibility have been closed cannot be accomplished in a moment. Confucius's relation to Yan Hui, we may infer, included, as any close relationship must, ways of being in the world, and the way in which these features of relationships operate in our lives rarely rises to the level of conscious awareness. They are the stuff of the idiosyncratic personal history we share with another and of habituated manners of interaction developed organically and gradually. They are just those aspects of a relationship that are most resistant to abstract characterization and thus are the most difficult to shed when loss severs them from us. Indeed, we may not even know what they are until they are no longer available.

These less tractable features of relations are exposed each time I begin to say, "Remember when we . . . ," and realize that I alone am left to remember. They are exposed each time I make a gesture that my companion would have known but that now passes unrecognized. They are exposed each time I frame my experience in terms of how I will recount it to my companion and apprehend that there is no one left to tell. In short, relationships develop their own vocabularies, modes of interaction that are idiosyncratic, private, and formed from a body of shared experiences. Such vocabularies resist easy abandonment. Our relation with another makes them, yet they are also the making of our self-understanding. Loss is renewed and pain returns afresh each time I reflexively appeal to this vocabulary and find that the one who would understand it is gone. At such times, I am forced to acknowledge the absence of my companion and the consequent uncertainty about who I am or can be without her.

Death comes quickly; the task of mourning is to *slow things down*. Appropriate mourning, as a body of both practices and attitudes, serves to prolong and sustain in time what would otherwise pass more swiftly. Formal mourning, by its very nature, extends loss across a broader temporal span and prolongs engagement with loss. Through mourning, death is transformed from a discrete and abrupt event into an enlarged space in which the bereaved may dwell until such time as they are prepared to relinquish the dead. What it means to prolong the experience of sorrow and how it benefits the bereaved must be read at two distinct and separable levels. The first of these levels is constituted by what might be deemed a reparative therapy.

Particular features of mourning function to guard the bereaved as they adjust to the new reality into which death has thrust them. Mourning can assist the bereaved in resolving the dissonance that obtains between who they have been and who they must now become. The deployment of rituals that are embedded in tradition is but one of the ways in which this is accomplished. For participation in traditional practices acknowledges one of the ways in which we are situated in the world, providing an arena in which a much-needed sense of continuity with the past can be achieved. In grief the bereaved suffer the disorientation of one who is suddenly and dramatically lost, unsure of where she stands and where she must go. Traditional ritual operates as an orienting landmark that uniquely represents both the living and the dead. It announces that others have passed this way before, and that we are not wholly alone in our sorrow.

The public nature of mourning likewise serves to aid in the repair of loss. For it ensures that the bereaved do not suffer the sort of isolation that merely reinforces the dislocation of identity that accompanies loss. Because it implicitly acknowledges the significance of what the living endure, mourning extends the reach of death or, rather, acknowledges that it is already extended. Death ceases to be contained in its barest physical manifestations and is instead tacitly reconceptualized as a phenomenon that involves the entire community of the bereaved. That one must, in the public practices of mourning, interact with others in one's grief highlights surviving relationships and encourages the location of a continuity through what is already established, and remains so in spite of loss. Some of this dynamic is curiously on display in Confucius's dissatisfaction with his students over the funeral of Yan Hui. In this model, it becomes clear that there need not be something so simple as succor offered by others. What others may offer, as is the case with Confucius's students, may be as mundane as a reminder of habitual irritations. When Confucius's students plan an elaborate burial for Yan Hui, they are in many ways acting as they often do. They frequently err in their judgments and incompletely understand Confucius's counsel. Thus when Yan Hui dies and Confucius's students act in a somewhat feckless manner, they are acting in a way that is strangely and reassuringly familiar. As irritating as this may immediately be for Confucius, it likewise serves to announce that all is not irrevocably altered. There is a constancy articulated even in human weaknesses and the attempt, in the mutuality of affectionate relations, to struggle with one another regarding those weaknesses.

What most distinguishes mourning as a technique for recovering from the destructive nature of grief is the way in which it sustains an attentive engagement of the living with the dead. Where physical death dictates an instant transformation of relations, mourning broadens the interstice between past and future. In the activities and attitudes of mourning, the bereaved resolutely maintain the dead and the relationship that is lost as the exclusive locus of attention. In so doing, they are able to assert a certain species of control within the upheaval of loss. They are able, through an insistent attention upon what is absent, to simulate a presence of sorts, a way in which the dead may be allowed to linger beyond their lives. Thus within the space of mourning, the dead are *not quite dead*. They persist as an ineluctable part of life as those who survive them act to preserve them through self-consciously adopting behaviors and attitudes that sustain the relation.

In order for mourning to function in this way, it is necessary that certain conditions be met and highlighting these conditions is, in part, Confucius's project. To describe the ways in which mourning may fail is largely to describe ways in which the maintenance of the dead in life can fail. Where the bereaved are ostentatious in their design of mourning, attention to the dead is divided by superfluous material concerns; where ritual is not appropriated to reflect the specific identities of the dead and bereaved, the dead are lost in generic display. To most effectively use mourning to repair the injury of loss, one must insist upon making it an occasion for careful and thoughtful reflection upon the significance and identity of the dead. Ritual and the material provisions it entails should, when properly used, be mechanisms for achieving this heightened attention. Thus when Confucius objects that his students' actions have prevented him from acting as a father to Yan Hui, he indicates that the material provisions they have made create an environment in which Yan Hui's presence cannot be simulated. Yan Hui is one who has no place in ostentation. The vocabulary in which Confucius and Yan Hui dwelled, a vocabulary of simplicity and what Jullien terms the "barest indications,"[9] cannot be maintained in a ceremony that lacks all subtlety and is more akin to a shout than the pregnant silences that marked the living relation. In this painfully alienating circumstance, mourning has not slowed death down, but instead accelerated its effect. Yan Hui is abruptly and bluntly gone. His friends act as they could not were he still present and even Confucius's formidable attention cannot overcome the absence.

What all of these aspects of mourning do to alleviate the pain of loss rests in the assertion of a gradualism that supplants the suddenness of death. Where physical death operates like a swift vanishing, the beloved abruptly just gone, in mourning the dead do not simply vanish. Rather, they recede from life just as someone walking away from us recedes from view. The bereaved are thus afforded the power to relinquish what has been, rather than having it stripped from them. Mourning allows the living to maintain, for a longer duration than the blunt facts themselves permit, the living roles by which the richness of life has been defined.

When Confucius expresses his frustration at the failure of mourning for Yan Hui, it is in terms that highlight this dimension of mourning. "I was prevented from being a father to him," Confucius complains. While Yan Hui's death robs Confucius of the capacity to act as such in life, restorative mourning would have allowed him to be as a father in death. When this possibility is denied, the abrupt pain and upheaval of loss is unassuaged and unanswered. In such circumstances, the peril is something of a paradox. The living are left without the means to sacralize and relinquish what death has taken. Yet while they cannot elevate, through human activity, the loss of the beloved, neither can they make it ordinary. For while mourning invests death with human meaning and value, it simultaneously serves to make loss ordinary. Even as we maintain the dead in awareness and explore the significance of what is lost, we tacitly adjust ourselves to their absence by subtly transforming death's significance in the consciousness of the bereaved. That is, while mourning serves to preserve the dead in awareness, it likewise prepares the living to accept the dead *as dead*, as presences that only the memory of the living can summon. In keeping the dead as a locus of attention, we cannot but keep their absence—that which generates the need for this heightened attention—in mind as well. The bereaved thus become less liable to suffer revisitations of pain, for the source of pain is always before them. That life and flourishing relations include suffering loses the power of a sudden revelation visited upon the bereaved each time they are reminded of loss. For in mourning, nothing stands to remind them painfully of what they do not, through their attention to loss, *already know*.

To speak of mourning thus—as a means to preserve not only the dead, but also, in some sense, the *pain* of loss—is to enter into a somewhat more ambitious program for mourning. The restorative function of mourning is most concerned with the way that the provisions of mourning enable the living to answer the pain of loss, and this is what I would wish to describe as the more modest program that Confucius offers. His is a technique that stands to benefit even those who may not fully appreciate the way in which its various procedures and techniques stand to help and where the origins and nature of that relief are only dimly understood.[10] There is, however, a second, more ambitious level of mourning that Confucius appears to describe and, unlike restorative mourning, it requires a rare species of understanding for its fulfillment.

It is with the more ambitious program of mourning implied in Confucius's counsel that a strategy not for the alleviation, but for the appreciation, of pain clearly emerges. In this more ambitious program, the general function of mourning is much the same. It still serves to slow down that which comes upon us quickly. The practices associated with mourning still serve to simulate a species of presence of the dead in the lives of their survivors. However, where restorative therapy primarily is engineered to alleviate immediate suffering, the aim of this more formidable version of mourning is to discover in the pain of loss a richly aesthetic vision of life. To make clear the nature of this vision, it is necessary to return briefly to the phenomenon of death and the way in which it is recognized by the living.

The moment in which the living realize the death of a beloved other is, in both Confucius's counsel and behavior, a moment necessarily infused with a certain horror. For many, this experience is short-lived and quickly replaced by a benumbed sorrow. The immediate experience of loss devastates but the engulfing shock must soon pass, for to retreat from this experience is an almost instinctual necessity. One withdraws from it as one would withdraw one's hand from a flame. The shock is simply too much to be endured as a raw sensation of pain. In its most ambitious formulation, Confucius's counsel suggests that *this too* be prolonged; that this moment be brought into the crosshairs of thought and feeling; that we not withdraw from this feeling but studiously target it with the entirety of our energies and attention.

Confucius describes Yan Hui's death as his "destruction." It is a moment not when death has gone wild, but when *life* is revealed to be wild. Confucius often likens human life to the traversing of a path, yet here is where the path abruptly terminates, leaving the traveler suddenly and unwittingly losing all footing to be plunged over the side of a cliff. Existence at the moment of realizing the death of the other becomes a frantic clawing at a spur of rock, the rock of a hoped-for self, an achieved self. Yet death denies this achievement. To slow down and prolong this experience is to forego retreat, to spurn any saving numbness, and to remain, suspended in a place where nothing can block a lonely thought. One's beloved companions, one's projects, and the very contours of one's life are here revealed as wholly fragile. To linger in the pain of this recognition is to see the vista opened by death. To linger here is to understand that all one is and loves, that the human condition itself, is not just now but has always been finely vulnerable. To linger in this recognition is to realize that there can be no protection against death's transformative power and that to live is to have no purchase.

The appreciation of pain becomes possible as the horror of what I now endure enables to me to realize that the moment of my loss is also that instance in which I am most exquisitely human. For in loss, any complacency I may have about what life may afford is unseated. My bold resolutions and faithful affections read as pledges against contingency. Whatever I may achieve and whatever I may become, my limit resides outside myself and is entrusted to an uncertain future and companions whose well-being I desire profoundly but cannot vouchsafe. To sustain loss in this fashion is to experience my humanity as a sublime condition. In prolonged attention to loss, I may divine the means by which my pain is valorized. There is a boundary that I may reach but not surpass. I know who I was and who I cannot continue to be. I know the limitations of my self, and the tenuousness of any control I may achieve. In the very transience of life resides the value of pleasures made richer for their end, moments made dense with meaning because they shall pass, and affections made finer because they abide in spite of all that is temporary. When loss is prolonged, I may achieve the liminal awareness that in my humanity I hand myself over to a world in which a vital instability makes possible more meaningful commitments. For in having pledged myself and who I can be to another, I have resolved to tread a path while discerning that a firm step is impossible. To prolong the experience of loss is not to flinch from the full import of human mortality, both the limit that it sets and the value it bestows. To draw out grief through mourning is to sustain the recognition that, as Confucius explains in recalling Yan Hui, "there are, to be sure, young plants that bear no flowers and flowers that bear no fruit" (9.22).

Notes

1. Jessica Mitford, *The American Way of Death Revisited* (New York: Vintage Books, 1998), 149.

2. All references to the *Analects* (*Lunyu*) give chapter and passage number as they appear in *A Concordance to the* Analects (Harvard-Yenching Institute Sinological Index Series, no. 16). The translations throughout are mine. Hereafter citations are given in the text and designated by book and passage.

3. See, for example, *Analects* 3.26 and 19.4 in which Confucius takes care to distinguish grief and mourning, and demarcates the conditions under which the emotive features of grief may be properly wedded to the affective demeanors of mourning.

4. Francois Jullien, *Detour and Access*, trans. Sophie Hawkes (New York: Zone Books, 2000), 197.

5. See Fingarette, Herbert, *Confucius: The Secular as Sacred* (New York: Harper & Row, 1972), esp. chap. 1.

6. See *Analects* 19.17, in which Zengzi recounts Confucius's claim that mourning one's parents may function to draw out one's best self.

7. *Analects* 9.12 offers a particularly apt example. Here Zilu has directed some of

Confucius's students to pose as retainers while Confucius is ill, presumably to impress upon any visitors their master's importance. When Confucius begins to recover, he affectionately criticizes Zilu for this and notes that while he lacks real retainers, so long as he is among friends, he shall not be dying bereft "by the side of the road."

8. Thomas Lynch, *The Undertaking: Life Studies from the Dismal Trade* (New York: Vintage Books, 1997), 21.

9. Jullien, *Detour and Access*, 202.

10. While Confucius is arguing for a more thoughtful manner of conducting the rituals of mourning, it likewise seems that achieving this as a broader social goal is something that can occur even where individual mourners do not appreciate the richer subtleties of Confucius's counsel. That those in a position to serve as role models act more thoughtfully would likely serve as an elevating influence for the larger society, regardless of varying levels of understanding exhibited by its individual members.

PART 4

SPIRITUAL CULTIVATION IN CONFUCIUS

An Unintegrated Life
Is Not Worth Living

9

Henry Rosemont, Jr.

The Analects of Confucius is a singular text in a number of ways, not the least of which is that it provides instructions for how to teach it to others. Clearly the book, like any other book over two millennia old, is of great antiquarian interest, but by no means should it be seen solely as the property of (Sinological) antiquarians; as Confucius himself said: "Reviewing the old as a means of realizing the new—such a person can be considered a teacher" (2.11).[1] For myself, a signal criterion for measuring our understanding of the text is an increasing desire to follow the Master's pedagogic practices and share the text with others whom we believe also share our basic concerns about how best to lead our all-too-human lives.

That is to say, while the *Analects* has a great deal of intrinsic historical value, it also speaks clearly about the problems of the present to those who listen carefully, a present which is becoming, in my view, ever more fragmented aesthetically, morally, and politically, and barren spiritually—with violence more the rule than the exception today.

Far too many human beings are visiting unspeakable horrors on other human beings in far too many parts of this fragile planet at present, and while the root cause of much of the violence is economic in nature, nevertheless efforts to develop moral and political visions to which all peoples might subscribe is necessary if a more peaceful and just world is to be realized. If, however, new (or very old) moral and political visions are to make claims of worldwide applicability, as they should, they must become increasingly multicultural in both scope and content. While it is not impossible that the members of any one culture have either discovered or created the (or a) value system to which all decent people everywhere could give allegiance, it is certainly not very probable, and consequently political visions and ethical theories developed in comparative cross-cultural perspective should be strong candidates for serious international consideration.

In addition to ethical and political concerns, there is, at a deeper level, much in the *Analects* of religious significance, another area in which examining the old can aid us in realizing the new. All religions provide guidelines for leading lives that are not only morally and politically but also spiritually meaningful (and aesthetically satisfying). There is much in the sacred texts of each religion that can speak to everyone. But the more distant from our own specific faith, the more difficult it is to profit from the spiritual instructions offered by other religious traditions, because they are so often intertwined with ontological, cosmological, and theological beliefs that are remote from our own, and incompatible with a number of pronouncements of modern science. (Of course, the adherents of these other religious traditions face the same problems in attempting to understand the spiritual instructions in *our* texts.)

In other work I have argued that the differing ontological, cosmological, and theological claims associated with the world's religions obscure the fact that the spiritual instructions for disciplines of self-cultivation are very similar in all of them.[2] I will not belabor that point herein, except to underscore my insistence on the importance of the *Analects* cross-culturally: *none* of the lessons the Master can teach us require acceptance of any beliefs incompatible with the ontological, cosmological, or theological beliefs of any other religion, or scientistic atheists for that matter; learning from the *Analects* does not require acceptance of any beliefs that fly in the face of physics or biology.

This fact by itself makes Confucius unique as a religious thinker, but we must go further: for the Master, our moral and political lives are not and cannot be distinct from our spiritual development, but rather are essential to it. Alone among the world's religions, classical Confucianism has no monks, nuns, anchorites, or hermits in the tradition. *Only* by doing what is appropriate in your manifold relational roles as child, parent, neighbor, sibling, friend, student, spouse, and others, can you develop spiritually, as Confucius points out the path ("human way," 人道 *ren dao*) in the *Analects*.

And just as we cannot appreciate fully the spiritual guidance Confucius offers apart from his ethical and political concerns, so, too, must we weigh his ethical and political views against the ultimately spiritual nature of the "Human Way." But before weighing the ethical and political (and aesthetic) in the context of the spiritual, let me rehearse the latter path briefly.[3] Confucius speaks approvingly of several categories of persons in the *Analects*, three of which, I have argued, should be seen as linked, even though they are not explicitly so linked in the text itself: the *shi*, "scholar-apprentice," *junzi*, "exemplary person," and *sheng*, *sheng ren* (聖), "sage" or "sage persons."

Twelve passages make reference to the *shi*. One of these (18.11) merely says that during the early Zhou period, four pairs of twins were *shi*. (They were all distinguished men.) In two other passages, the disciples Zigong and Zilu respectively ask about the qualities of the *shi*. To the first, Confucius answers: "Those who conduct themselves with a sense of shame and who, when sent to distant quarters, do not disgrace the commission of their lord, deserve to be called *shi*" (13.20). And he tells Zilu that "persons who are critical and demanding yet amicable can be called *shi*. They need to be critical and demanding with their friends, and amicable with their brothers" (13.28). In another passage, Zizhang asks how scholar-apprentices (*shi*) become prominent, and Confucius tells him: "Those who are prominent are true in their basic disposition, and seek after what is most appropriate. They examine what is said, are keen observers of demeanor, and are thoughtful in deferring to others" (12.20).

These remarks suggest that the *shi* are indeed apprentices of some kind. They are to be formal, precise, polite, deferential. They have already extended their ways of relating to others beyond the family, for in no passage of the *Analects* is *xiao*—family reverence[4]—linked to the *shi*.

This interpretation of the *shi* is reinforced by Zizhang's description of them in the opening chapter of book 19:

> Those *shi* are quite acceptable who on seeing danger are ready to put their lives on the line, who on seeing an opportunity for gain concern themselves with what is appropriate, who in performing sacrifices concern themselves with proper respect, and who in participating in a funeral concern themselves with grief.

Moreover, while the syntax of these passages, when rendered into English declarative statements, suggest that the *shi* are being described, I believe the sentences should be read rather as imperatives, as instructions for what the *shi* should do to become true *shi*. They have set out on a path (*dao*), but they still have a long way to go, and there is much yet to be done. As the senior disciple Zengzi says, "the *shi* cannot but be strong and resolved, for they bear a heavy charge and their way (道 *dao*) is long. Where they take authoritative conduct (仁 *ren*) as their charge, is it not a heavy one? And where their way ends only in death is it not indeed long?" (8.7).

By describing the *shi* as those who have assumed the burden of authoritative conduct, or authoritativeness, we get a hint that it is not only a moral and political apprenticeship the *shi* are serving, but a spiritual one as well, for the *ren* of Confucius is the highest and most encompassing of excellences, not radically different from the Socratic good.[5] In another passage we see that the *shi* are placed in conjunction with authoritative persons: "The Master said, 'For the resolute scholar-apprentice (*shi*) and the authoritative person (仁人 *ren ren*), while they would not compromise their authoritative conduct to save their lives, they might well give up their lives in order to achieve it'" (15.9).

Further evidence that it is a spiritual as well as moral and political path the *shi* are following is found in two additional passages in which negative instructions are given, the thrust of which is to not take material well-being as a major goal. First, "The Master said, 'The *shi* who cherishes material comforts is not worthy of the name'" (14.2). And: "The Master said, 'The *shi* who, having set their purposes on walking the way (*dao*) are ashamed of rude clothing and coarse food, are not worth engaging in discussion'" (4.9).

There are, of course, numerous other positive instructions the Master proffers not only for the *shi*, but also for others: become steeped in poetry and in history; study and practice rituals; listen to, play, become absorbed in good music; perform public service when it is appropriate to do so; above all—by engaging in all of these efforts—extend one's human sympathies beyond one's family, clan, and village and learn to become benefactor and beneficiary[6] within ever-enlarging circles. Again, the *shi* are never instructed in the proper behavior and demeanor due their parents; they have already learned that filial piety is not confined to parental or to merely material needs:

> Zixia asked about filial conduct. The Master replied, "It all lies in showing the proper countenance. As for the young contributing their energies when there is work to be done, and deferring to elders when there is wine and food to be had—how can merely doing this be considered being filial?" (2.8)

If this reading of these passages has merit, it follows that the major goal toward which the *shi* are striving is to reach a higher stage in life. And that stage must be to become a *junzi*, the paradigmatic human exemplar for Confucius who is mentioned sixty-eight times in the *Analects*. A few examples:

> The Master said, "Exemplary persons (*junzi*) cherish their excellence; petty persons cherish their land. Exemplary persons cherish fairness; petty persons cherish the thought of gain." (4.11)

> The Master said, "In the niceties of culture I am perhaps like other people. But as far as personally succeeding in living the life of the exemplary person, I have accomplished little." (7.33)

> The Master said, "The path (*dao*) of the *junzi* has three conditions that I am unable to find in myself: The authoritative (*ren*) are not anxious; the wise (*zhi*) are not in a quandary; the courageous are not timid."
> Zigong replied, "This is the path that you yourself walk, sir." (14.28)

If the *shi* does, the *junzi* more nearly *is*. In the text, *junzi* are almost always described, not instructed. They have traveled a goodly distance along the way, and live a multiplicity of roles (5.16). Benefactors to many, they are still beneficiaries of others like themselves (7.31). While still capable of anger in the presence of evildoing, they are in their person tranquil (12.4). They know many rituals and much music, and perform all of their functions not only with skill, but also with grace, dignity, and beauty, and they take delight in the performances (12.8). Still filial toward parents and elders, they now work on behalf of others (12.16), especially the needy (6.4). Always proper in the conduct of their roles, that conduct is not forced, but rather effortless, spontaneous, creative (8.4, 11.26). There are, in sum, very strong aesthetic, ethical, and political dimensions to the life of a *junzi*, and a sense of the religious as well. They are indeed exemplars:

Confucius said, "Exemplary persons always keep nine things in mind: in looking they think about clarity, in hearing they think about acuity, in countenance they think about cordiality, in hearing and attitude they think about deference, in speaking they think about doing their utmost (忠 *zhong*), in conducting affairs they think about due respect, in entertaining doubts they think about the proper questions to ask, in anger they think about regret, in sight of gain they think about what is appropriate conduct (義 *yi*). (16.10)

For most of us, the goal of *junzi* is the highest to which we can aspire. In an important sense, however, it is a "goal" that is unachieveable: Human perfectability is what the texts exalt, but the authors know well there are no perfect human beings, and there never will be. Hence it is better to think of exemplary persons in terms of the attitudes, perspectives, emotions and creativity with which they enact their roles; not so much a goal of life as a way of *living* our lives—in *this* world, not another.

There is, however, an even loftier human "goal," to become a *sheng*; but in the *Analects* it is a distant goal indeed. There are eight references to *sheng* or *sheng ren* in the text. In one passage Confucius dared not rank himself a *sheng* (7.33), in another he lamented that he never had, and probably never would, see one (7.25), and in still another he gently chastises Zigong when the latter likens him to a *sheng* (9.6). And later, even though Mencius allows that the man in the street can become a Yao or Shun (Sage kings of high antiquity), he, too suggests strongly that this goal is beyond the reach of most mortals (6B.2).

Yet the goal is there, and it is attainable. There are *sheng*. They have risen beyond the level of *junzi*, because 16.8 describes the *junzi* as those who stand in awe of the words of the *sheng*. From 6.30 we learn that those who confer benefits on and assist everyone are *sheng*. Clearly such persons have extended their human feelings and thoughts to embrace the entire human race. *Junzi* may be said to take the stance described above with respect not only to those they know personally, but all others in the human community as well. But even more, the *sheng* can take this stance with all those who have come before us, and all those who will follow: in 19.12, Zixia says that not even the *junzi*, but the *sheng ren* alone, are capable of uniting, in themselves, with that which comes first and that which comes last:

Ziyou said, "The disciples and young friends of Zixia are quite all right when it comes to housekeeping, taking care of guests, and standing in attendance, but these are just the tips of the branches. What do you do about the fact that they have no roots?"

Zixia heard about this, and responded, "Ah! Ziyou is mistaken! On the path (*dao*) of the *junzi*, what is passed on first and what must wait until maturity, can be compared to plants which must be nurtured differently according to kind. How can he so misrepresent the path of the *junzi*? And it is the *sheng ren* alone who walks this path every step from start to finish."

To summarize this brief reading of the qualities of, and relations between, the *shi*, *junzi*, and *sheng*: all *sheng* are *junzi*, and all *junzi* were formerly *shi*, but the converse does not hold. These are, in other words, ranked types of persons, and the ranking is based on a progression from scholarly apprenticeship to sagehood: *shi* are, relatively speaking, fairly numerous; *junzi* are scarcer, and *sheng* are very few and very far between, owing to "the heaviness of the burden, and the distance of the journey" (8.7). The *shi* have willed (知 / 智 *zhi*) to follow the *dao* as it is embodied in the *li*—customs, rituals, traditions—that govern the interpersonal relations definitive of the *shi*'s several roles. The *shi* know some of the *li*, and are engaged in the ongoing activity of learning and practicing more, concomitant with the interactions appropriate to their new and continuing stations. Much farther along this learning and doing continuum we have the *junzi*, who know the *li* thoroughly enough to follow the spirit of the *li* even in the absence of precedent. They have integrated their roles masterfully, deriving a deep satisfaction from the grace, dignity, effortlessness, and creativity with which they have come to conduct themselves with others, acquaintances and strangers no less than kin and neighbors.

And at the upper end of this continuum are the *sheng*. In addition to possessing all of the qualities of the *junzi*, the *sheng* appear to see and feel customs, rituals, and tradition—the *li*—holistically, as defining and integrating the whole of human society, and as defining and integrating as well the human societies of the past, and of the future. This seeing and feeling can be described in our terms (not Confucius's) as transcendent understanding,[7] the capacity to go beyond the particular time and place in which we live, coming to a union not only with our contemporaries, but again, with all those who have preceded us, and all those who will follow; a union, in other words of self and all others, at-one-ment.

If this interpretation can be sustained, and is at all faithful to the tests, it must follow that the charge of narrow particularism against early Confucianism is woefully misplaced. Even the novice *shi*, while remaining rooted in specific duties, must nevertheless begin their trek along the (Human) Way by broadening their social horizons, and interactions with others, and in doing so are cultivating the aesthetic, moral, political, and spiritual dimensions of their lives. To repeat an earlier point: a unique feature of the classical Confucian persuasion is that spiritual self-cultivation *requires* others; it is overwhelmingly not a solitary exercise, as it is outlined in the classical texts. Herbert Fingarette has stated the matter cogently: "For Confucius, unless there are at least two human beings, there are no human beings."[8]

Much more, of course, needs to be said about all of these matters, but if the "homoversal"[9] vision inherent in the tradition is brought to the fore, much more *can* be said about them. Unless everything I have said up to this point is mistaken, it is altogether wrong-headed to suggest that Confucius did not have a strong sense of, empathy with, and concept of humanity writ large.

All of the specific human relations of which we are a part, interacting with the dead as well as the living, will be mediated by the *li*—the courtesy, customs, manners, and traditions as well as more formal rituals—that we come to share as our inextricably linked histories unfold. By fulfilling the obligations defined by these relationships we are, for early Confucians, following the *ren dao*, the human way. In his "Essay on Rituals" Xunzi makes clear the role of the *li* in our treading of the spiritual path: "only the *sheng* fully comprehend the *li*. The *junzi* are at ease in their performance, and the *shi* are careful to maintain them."[10] Thus rituals—and customs, manners, traditions—are an essential element of a comprehensive human way. By the manner in which we interact with others our lives will clearly have a moral dimension infusing *all*, not just some, of our conduct. By the ways in which this ethical interpersonal conduct is effected, with reciprocity, and governed by civility, respect, affection, custom, ritual, and tradition, our lives will also have an aesthetic dimension for ourselves and for others. And politically, by specifically meeting our defining traditional obligations to our elders and ancestors on the one hand, and to our contemporaries and descendants on the other, the *Analects* aids us spiritually in developing our human capacity to go beyond the specific spatiotemporal circumstances in which we exist, giving our personhood the sense of humanity shared in common, and again, thereby a sense of strong continuity with what has gone before and what will come later. There being no question for Confucius of the meaning *of* life, we may nevertheless see that his view of what it is to be a human being provided for everyone to find meaning *in* life. The burden is indeed heavy, the Way indeed long (8.7); but the prize is great. If we are truly social beings, and if this is the only life we have to live, then it seems clear that the text can have much to say today as we continue the search for answers to the question of how we should live out these, our all-too-human lives, and why.[11]

There are several major obstacles to appreciating fully the contemporary aesthetic, ethical, political, and spiritual relevance of the *Analects*. First, for most of the past two thousand years Chinese society has been seen as more or less a Confucian society, and that society was rigidly hierarchical, paradigmatically sexist, and almost unrelievedly homophobic. Moreover, Chinese history reveals an ample measure of authoritarian rulers, self-serving officials, exploitative parents, dull pedants, and more.

But a defense of the Confucian vision is no more a justification or apology for the sorrier dimensions of Chinese history than a defense of the moral and spiritual vision of Christianity entails a justification or apology for the Crusades, Inquisition, Thirty Years War, and other sorry episodes in Western history. Clearly the moral and spiritual ideals of Confucianism were seldom realized, even approximately, in imperial China any more than Christian ideals have been much realized in Western history.

Moreover, without in any way minimizing the facts of female oppression in imperial China, we can note that the sexist dimensions of early Confucianism *as a belief system* has been exaggerated. Michael Nylan, who has studied this issue at some length, has this to say:

> If the extant historical [Han Dynasty] records, which Sinologists so rarely mistrust, have any accuracy at all, then Han elite women tended to be strong-willed, well educated, and physically courageous. More importantly, they were specifically lauded for these qualities by the official histories composed by elite men. . . . This is not to deny that there were contemporary debates over the "proper place" of women in elite society, as the Han sources can attest; it is rather to suggest that in such debates the elites—including many committed Confucians—confirmed the value of women.[12]

Whatever the final verdict on what the early Confucian thinkers believed women's roles should be, clearly any and all efforts at re-appropriating and re-authorizing the Confucian persuasion in the light of our contemporary moral, political, and spiritual concerns must excise any elements of the commentarial tradition that assign women inferior roles. This excision—or perhaps in some cases exorcism—must in the first instance be evidenced throughout society, because good reasons can no longer be given for restricting the liberty to develop one's own capacities to the fullest on the basis of biologically or otherwise constructed sex differences.

The task of modifying the Confucian persuasion to accord with contemporary moral sensibilities may not, however, be an altogether Herculean effort conceptually. Admitting the downplaying of the abilities and accomplishments of women in classical Confucianism, I nevertheless hold that the thrust of that tradition was not competitive individualism—associated in the West with the masculine—but rather other-directed nurturing, associated throughout Western history with the feminine.[13] And when we come to appreciate that the modern Western tradition only negatively celebrates qualities and attributes associated with the feminine, we might cautiously opine that the demand for gender equality could well be brought into Confucianism without doing violence to its basic insights and precepts.[14]

We might go even further in this regard, revising but keeping the central role of the family that dominates the tradition. We can certainly have not only the concept of the family alongside the concept of sexual equality; we can also expand yet still keep the concept of the family by allowing for two and perhaps more parents or nurturers of the same sex. Homophobia was, and still is, as characteristic of Chinese history as sexism was, but gays and lesbians, too, are the sum of the roles they live within and outside of the family, and the conceptual framework of Confucianism would surely be as impoverished by their exclusion as it would be enriched by their inclusion. Intergenerational interactions are crucial to the Confucian tradition; the gender and sexual preferences of the interactors much less so.

To see these points in another way, consider a related criticism against Confucianism, that it is hierarchical and, consequently, elitist. I believe the charge is misplaced, for two reasons. First, although elitism does directly entail a hierarchy, the converse does not hold, and hence the two concepts are not logically equivalent. Consider, for example, a happy, nurturing family, a well-run and productive classroom, a scientist supervising the research of her graduate students, or a family doctor working with the patients he has come to know well. All of these and other social situations are in a sense clearly hierarchical, but to label them "elitist" guarantees that we will not understand them. I did not think of myself as having power over my daughters when I was teaching them to read, nor do I think my doctor is "lording it over me" when he tells me to reduce my intake of red meat.

Second, the charge against the hierarchical ordering of Confucianism is usually couched in terms of human relationships based on roles that are described as holding between "superiors" and "inferiors," or between "superordinates" and "subordinates." But when we look closely at the Confucian texts for guidance in how to properly fulfill our roles as parents and children, teachers and students, as friends, siblings, neighbors, and so on, and when we keep in mind the central role of *reciprocity* (恕 *shu*) in early Confucianism, we might want to change the descriptive terms of the relationships as holding not between "superiors" and "inferiors" (the usual rendering of *shang* 上 and *xia* 下 respectively), but as relating with others as *benefactors* and *beneficiaries*, as noted briefly earlier. And if we keep equally in mind that all of us are some of the time benefactors and some of the time beneficiaries in our relations, then much of the sting of the accusation of hierarchy or elitism goes away. I would maintain that this account is a fairly realistic one: what I am and do depends significantly on whom I am interacting with, and when: I was largely a beneficiary of my parents when young, then their benefactor when they aged, and the converse holds with my children. Indeed, I would argue that upon close inspection, virtually *all* human interrelationships can be cogently analyzed in this way, as between benefactors and beneficiaries. And is there not a deep satisfaction that comes from having the opportunity to be a benefactor to one who has been a benefactor to you?

Except for committed cynics and thoroughgoing historicists, I believe these obstacles to appreciating the Human Way mapped out in the *Analects* can and will be overcome. Another problem, already hinted at, will be much more difficult, because it fundamentally involves our deepest Western conception of ourselves, which we tend to regard as a given, accepting it as an inheritance from the Enlightenment and the development of capitalism. The spiritual path Confucius sketches in the *Analects* is, as we have seen, linked closely to the ethical and political instruction he also gives us. But there is a catch: his instructions are given to students who see themselves fundamentally in relation to others, as role-bearers in community first and foremost. Hence his signposts of the integrated path will be hard to discern for those who define themselves and others most fundamentally as rationally choosing, free, autonomous, self-interested individuals—the Enlightenment vision gone awry.

Everyone in the West with eyes to see is aware of the manifold problems attendant on an altogether individualistic orientation, but I do not believe we take those problems seriously enough at the conceptual or experiential level. First-generation human rights, for example, grounded in the concept of freely choosing autonomous individuals, may indeed offer protection from the whims of despotic governments, but they also now serve to maintain a gross and growing maldistribution of the world's wealth by providing legal justification for transnational corporations to do pretty much as they wish. The result is an increasing loss of community, especially in the developed capitalist nations. Relatedly, as autonomous individuals, it is extremely difficult for us to contemplate seriously that there may be a higher good independent of our conception of it, and we will continue to insist, in the public sphere at least, that justice continue to be defined procedurally rather than distributively. Worse, as autonomous individuals, "they"—the Other—all too easily become radically other, and even "we"—those very similar to us—become Other in a global society wherein competition is the norm in a series of zero-sum games; if you get the golden ring, I do not.[15]

Classical Confucian spirituality, on the other hand, leads us to see ourselves not as autonomous individuals, but as co-members of several communities, who, through sustained effort, are increasingly integrated into an ever-larger community, something larger than ourselves, which, for want of a better term I would call the human project. We must come to see ourselves as fundamentally, not accidentally, intergenerationally bound to our ancestors, contemporaries, and descendants. It is not that we are to become selfless, that is, altruistic, for this would imply a pure, isolated, or isolatable self to be surrendered, the existence of which any Confucian would find impossible to take seriously. Rather we must come to see and feel our personhood as dependent on others for its uniqueness and well-being, just as others must depend on us for their uniqueness and well-being. In order to *be* a friend, or a lover, I must *have* a friend or a lover; and "freedom" must be seen not as a state of being, but as an ongoing achievement for each of us.[16] So long as I feel I *must* meet my defining obligations I am obviously not free. Only when I come to *want* to meet them, enjoy doing so, and come to feel at one with my fellows past, present, and future, can I have a true sense of freedom, and make spiritual progress.

A final difficulty in appreciating the Confucian vision fully is linked closely to these others. It is virtually a commonplace that the *Analects* advocates an ethical particularism based on kinship, which perhaps can teach us a thing or two about how to deal with family members and neighbors. But not being universal in describing what we ought to do, Confucius seemingly cannot give us firm guidelines or even precepts for dealing with strangers, and consequently cannot contribute to developing a comprehensive ethical or moral theory, and consequently in turn must be rejected as possibly applicable to the contemporary world of six-billion-plus human beings.

There is an important element of logical and philosophical significance in this last criticism. If we accept the concept of the fundamentally relational self presupposed by Confucius, and accept as well the importance of the particularity of the specific other(s) with whom we interact, then it does seem to be very difficult to insist on *ethical grounds alone* that we can have significant moral obligations to the grandparents of strangers no less than to our own. It is for this reason that I can only interpret the *ren dao*, the Human Way of Confucius, as a *religious* path, and that its ethical dimensions, important as they are, have to be construed in the end as spiritual requirements for treading that path fully. For him, my self-cultivation *requires* that I expand my appreciation of, and feelings for, my grandmothers to yours, and thence, ever more expansively, to all other grandparents (friends, children, neighbors, and others).

I submit that this vision or sense is, in all of its moral, political, and religious multidimensionality, one of the most important lessons we may learn from close and careful readings of the *Analects*. The proponents of "holy" or "just" war [*sic* twice] always put forward abstract, moral, political, and/or religious principles to justify our killing the enemy, but know well those abstract principles seldom suffice for morale to be maintained; in modern warfare most clearly, the enemy must be dehumanized as well. But with the help of Confucius, we can come to recognize that every one of the purported "enemy" is someone's son or daughter, grandson or granddaughter; many of them will also themselves be parents, grandparents, teachers and students, lovers, friends, and more. And when we recognize the "enemy" in this way, killing them becomes much harder to do, no matter how many moral, political, or religious abstract principles are invoked by the propagandists and other warmongers to justify our doing so. If we engage in dialogue with our loved ones when disputes arise rather than slaughter them, perhaps we can learn to do the same with strangers.

In this way the Confucian persuasion, if it became more widespread, could surely make a significant contribution toward making the twenty-first century a less murderous one than the twentieth, and an equal contribution toward the development of moral and political theories and policies with greater cross-cultural applicability, helping to generate a rank ordering of human values and rights to which all people of good will might give their allegiance, no matter what differing religious and cultural traditions they inherited and cherished. And we should have some optimism that Confucianism really can make this contribution, because in the end, the "role ethics" vision contained in the canonical texts is *not* a theory—moral or otherwise—and hence is not, when understood correctly, in competition with other theories. It is simply an integrated life being advocated for all.

I personally believe the overwhelming majority of the peoples of all traditions, if asked what they thought they ought to do, and found deep satisfaction in doing, would say something like the following: "I would like to bring peace and contentment to the aged, to share relationships of trust and confidence with my friends, and to love and protect the young"—an intergenerationally integrated life aesthetically, morally, politically, and spiritually, lived actively in the world of human experience. The words are from Confucius (5.26), but I believe most everyone would say pretty much the same thing, making his vision no less important now than when it was first put forth over two millennia ago in a land no longer as distant from us as it once was.

Notes

I am deeply indebted to David Jones for inviting me to participate in this volume, for having the patience of Job as I missed promised deadlines, and for his clear editorial eye, which has done much to improve my text, as has the equally careful eye of Cindy Pineo, my editor at Open Court. My life partner in attempting to tread the Human Way described in these pages, JoAnn Rosemont, has once again turned my increasingly illegible scrawls into a polished and more coherent manuscript.

1. All translations from the *Lunyu* are from *The Analects of Confucius: A Philosophical Translation* (New York: Ballantine, 1998), by Roger Ames and myself.

2. Henry Rosemont, Jr., *Rationality and Religious Experience* (Chicago: Open Court, 2001).

3. The next several pages are taken, with changes, from my "Is there a Universal Path of Spiritual Progress in the Texts of Early Confucianism?" in *Confucian Spirituality*, ed. Tu Weiming and M. E. Tucker, vol. 1 (New York: Herder and Herder/Crossroad Publishing Company, 2003). See also Ames and Rosemont, "Introduction to the *Analects*," *Analects of Confucius*, 62–63.

4. For a detailed analysis of the role *xiao* plays in the articulation of the early Confucian vision, and its significance in self-cultivation, see the forthcoming *Chinese Classic of Family Reverence*, translated by Henry Rosemont, Jr., and Roger T. Ames (Honolulu: University of Hawai'i Press, 2008).

5. Whence my title. It is that section of the *Apology* in which Socrates insists on the necessity of seeking the good that he says, "An unexamined life is not worth living." Both the similarities and the differences between the progenitors of the two traditions are stark.

6. For the significance of these terms, see below, p. 161.

7. It is only in this nonmetaphysical sense that I speak of "transcendence." The *locus classicus* for cogent arguments denying the existence of a transcendental realm in early Chinese thought is *Thinking Through Confucius* by David Hall and Roger Ames (Albany: SUNY Press, 1987).

8. Herbert Fingarette, "The Music of Humanity in the Conversations of Confucius," *Journal of Chinese Philosophy* 10 (1983): 217. Equally required reading is his *Confucius: The Secular as Sacred* (New York: Harper and Row, 1972).

9. As opposed to "universal," which means "throughout the universe." My somewhat more modest neologism has been inspired by my studies of generative grammar with Noam Chomsky, and I intend the term to mean "for all human beings, mentally and physically constituted as they are." See my "Against Relativism" in *Interpreting Across Boundaries*, ed. Gerald Larson and Eliot Deutsch. (Princeton, NJ: Princeton University Press, 1987).

10. Translation modified from Burton Watson's *Hsun Tzu: Basic Writings* (New York: Columbia University Press, 1963), 110.

11. For details, see Rosemont, *Rationality and Religious Experience*.

12. In her splendid essay "Golden Spindles and Axes: Elite Women in the Achaemenid and Han Empires," in *The Sage and the Second Sex*, ed. Chenyang Li (Chicago: Open Court, 2001), 204. See also Michael Nylan, "A Problematic Model: The Han 'Orthodox Synthesis' Then and Now," in *Imagining Boundaries: Confucian Doctrines, Texts, and Hermeneutics*, ed. Kai-wing Chow, On-cho Ng, and John B. Henderson (Albany: SUNY Press, 1999). For an overview of Western scholarship specifically on women in China, see Jinhua Emma Teng, "The Construction of the 'Traditional Chinese Woman' in the Western Academy: A Critical Review," *Signs* 22, no. 1 (1996).

13. I have taken up these feminist issues in "Classical Confucian and Contemporary Feminist Perspectives on the Self: Some Parallels and their Implications" in *Culture and Self*, ed. Douglas Allen (Boulder, CO: Westview Press, 1997). The following two pages are largely taken from that paper, which includes additional references.

14. While long aware of the evolutionary nature of the commentarial tradition in the history of Confucianism, I did not appreciate fully its philosophical significance until reading Phillip J. Ivanhoe's incisive review of Kwong-loi Shun's work on the *Mencius* in the *Journal of Asian Studies* 57, no. 3 (1998).

15. To be skeptical of the moral basis for grounding human rights only in first-generation rights—as the U.S. Government and legal system tend to do—is not in any way to defend some kind of "Asian authoritarianism," as I have argued on several occasions. See, for example, "Which Rights? Whose Democracy? A Confucian Critique of the Western Liberal Tradition" in *Philosophy and the Public Realm*, ed. Douglas W. Shrader, Oneonta Philosophy Series (Binghamton, NY: Global Academic Publishing, 2001), which contains other references.

16. In claiming that "freedom" is more an achievement than a stative term I am following the several keen insights of Eliot Deutsch on this concept. One example: "[F]reedom is an achievement that is always embodied as a quality of an action." *Creative Being: The Crafting of Person and World* (Honolulu: University of Hawaii Press, 1992), 171. See also the succinct account of freedom in an early Confucian context in Peimin Ni, *On Confucius* (Belmont, CA: Wadsworth, 2002), 70–76.

Gongfu—A Vital Dimension of Confucian Teaching

10

Peimin Ni

For a long time in Western universities, Confucianism was taught either in East Asian studies departments, in world religions courses, or in most schools, not at all. The last century, especially the last decade or so, has witnessed great efforts to justify a place for Confucianism in philosophy curricula and in academic philosophy scholarship. These efforts have won for Confucianism a visible presence in many philosophy conferences, publications, and curricula. However, many have contributed to this effort by pushing Confucianism in the direction of mainstream Western philosophy—interpreting it using familiar Western philosophical terminology, picking out concepts that can be fit into the familiar frameworks of philosophical issues, and articulating them in a familiar discourse style featuring clear definitions, logical argumentative structures, and intellectual consistency. Even those who insist on differences between mainstream Western philosophy and Confucianism tend to interpret the latter in intellectualistic ways. The consequence, in many cases, is that the more Confucianism is accepted by mainstream Western philosophy, the less it is itself. Ironically, those who pushed Confucianism in this direction thought, either consciously or subconsciously, that they were doing it a favor. By carefully filtering Confucius's sayings, leaving out anything that appeared to be mystical or otherwise "irrelevant" to philosophy, by placing the selected sayings in the context of Western philosophical debates and by creating a logical order for them, many scholars thought that they were rescuing Confucian philosophical wisdom from obscurity.[1]

One vital dimension of Confucianism is a casualty of this general trend. The *gongfu* dimension has been sympathetically neglected, even though no one seems to deny that it is quite obviously present in Confucianism. In this essay, I would like to call attention to the *gongfu* dimension, and will use mainly the *Analects* to illustrate that we can draw rich layers of significance and enhance our appreciation of Confucian teachings by taking up the *gongfu* perspective. I believe that the *gongfu* perspective will simultaneously correct the overintellectualizing of Confucianism and expand our notion of philosophical practice. By doing this, I do not mean to reject the value of reading Confucianism from other viewpoints, but rather to point out that our understanding will be severely inadequate if we neglect this important dimension.

Gongfu Approach
versus Philosophical Approach

Song 宋 and Ming 明 Confucian scholars frequently used the word *gongfu* (工夫 or 功夫, formerly known as *kungfu*) in their articulation and discussion of Confucianism. Most people nowadays (whether in the West or in the East) understand the word narrowly to mean martial arts,[2] but traditionally the word *gongfu* has at least six different yet interrelated senses. The most common meaning of the term, which is still popular in ordinary Chinese today, is the time spent on something, as in the expressions such as "the *gongfu* of a cup of tea" or "the *gongfu* of a meal." A natural extension of the meaning is the effort spent on something, as in expressions like "the *gongfu* [effort] of learning 為學工夫" and "the *gongfu* of rectifying the heart-mind and cultivating the person 正心修身工夫." A third meaning is the proper and effective way of making an effort or spending time, or particular instructions on how to make such an effort. Some examples of this way of using the term are "the *gongfu* [way] of *The Great Learning*《大學》工夫" and "the *gongfu* of the *Zhongyong*《中庸》工夫." The word can also mean the ability to make efforts in a proper way, as in the case of "*gongfu* [embodiment of abilities] and original formation [or body] are one and the same 本體工夫合一."[3] This way of using the word is close to how the word is understood widely today, but with an extension that goes far beyond the martial arts. *Gongfu* is also used to describe the level of the abilities. The last meaning associated with the word *gongfu* is the function, effect, or manifestation of the abilities. For example, Wang Yangming was asked, "I recently found myself having less inappropriate ideas, . . . is this *gongfu* [effect or manifestation of abilities]? 近來妄念也覺少 . . . 不知此是工夫否?"[4]

These different meanings of *gongfu* are mutually connected, and the connection justifies the ambiguous use of the word in different contexts. When one spends time or effort on something, there has to be a way in which the time or the effort is spent. No one can make an effort without specific content. So for instance, when someone wants to spend *gongfu* (time or effort) on learning, the person may appeal to the instructions of the *Great Learning* or of the *Zhongyong*. These specific ways give the *gongfu* (time or effort) a specific content, so the ways can be called the *gongfu* of the *Great Learning* or the *gongfu* of the *Zhongyong*. This naturally leads to the extension of the word *gongfu* to mean special embodied abilities. As a way of making effort, *gongfu* is not something merely employed or applied, like a tool being used for a certain purpose. A tool does not necessarily require the user to have skills (today we see many sophisticated tools designed specifically to reduce the requirement of having skills to use them). *Gongfu* requires a special talent or ability on the part of the agent. In other words, not all the ways of doing things can be called *gongfu*. Only the ways for handling things that are difficult to accomplish and require special embodied abilities of the agent can be called *gongfu*. Since abilities can admit degrees, so also people talk about levels of *gongfu*. Special abilities are displayed or manifested in their functions and results, and thus the functions and results are nothing but the presence of *gongfu*, the abilities. The execution of the ability is the same process in which the functions of the practice are shown. Sometimes people use different words to specify the last four of the six inter-related meanings. They use *gongfu* 功法 to mean methods or ways of making an effort, *gongneng* 功能 or *gongli* 功力 to mean embodied abilities (*gongneng* is for kinds of abilities, and *gongli* is for strength of the given abilities), and *gongxiao* 功效 for the outcome or manifestation of the abilities. However, the general term for all the five is still *gongfu*.

Reading Confucianism as a *gongfu* system means to take Confucian teachings as instructions or prescriptions about how to conduct one's life, rather than as descriptions of facts or as ethical rules of conduct. It means to take Confucianism as a system of knowledge about "how," rather than a system of knowledge about "what." The actual matter is certainly more complicated, and can hardly be as simple as an "either/or" proposition, but outlining a fundamental difference between the two is helpful before investigating their connections.

The matter of claiming Confucianism as a *gongfu* system can be taken in two ways, one from a theoretical approach and the other from a practical approach. A theoretical approach to a *gongfu* system entails the recognition that the system is instructional rather than descriptive, and it involves philosophical study of the *gongfu* system to reveal the unique messages that the system conveys and the philosophical implications of these messages. For instance, we do not say an instruction is true or false; instead, we say it is good or not good, effective or ineffective, with regard to the objectives that it sets out to achieve and the means it uses for achieving those objectives. Obviously, if Confucianism is a *gongfu* system, then treating it as a descriptive theory about what the world is, what a person is, and what our moral duties are would be a gross misreading of it, and comments and criticisms based on the misreading will be simply irrelevant to what the texts are about. For many statements in the classic texts that are obviously instructional, such misreading is less likely, though their importance may escape our attention. For many other statements that are less clearly instructional, failure to grasp their instructional meaning will cause us to miss the message and lead the scholarship in an entirely wrong direction.

This approach is still theoretical in the sense of engaging in critical examination of hidden basic assumptions, implications, and structures of a system—in this case, a *gongfu* system. It does require us to stretch the conventional Western notion of philosophy beyond the search for objective validity. It suggests that besides the three major areas of philosophy, namely, metaphysics, epistemology, and ethics, we should add a fourth one: praxiology—an area of philosophical study of praxis.[5] But this approach remains interpretive. To take a *gongfu* system with a theoretical approach is still different from taking it with a practical approach, though the latter itself can be an object of philosophical reflection. Even the saying "Confucianism is a *gongfu* system" is itself not a *gongfu* reading in the full sense, for one still looks only at *what* the text is rather than *how* to conduct oneself with one's reading of the text. In a short article about how to read the *Analects* and *Mencius*, Zhu Xi 朱熹 says:

> In reading the *Analects* and *Mencius* one should not aim at merely understanding the theory and the meanings of the texts. One should make careful reflection and put the teachings into practice. . . . If one were to aim simply at having the books read, one or two days would be quite enough. However, if one wants to use them in one's own practical life, making careful reflections about how they will work in practice, then one day would only be enough for reading a few or even just one or two passages. Reading the *Analects* and *Mencius* must be related to one's own life. Take the saying "repeatedly apply what you have learned" for example. How do we relate this to our own practical life? You should ask yourself this question with regard to every saying [in the *Analects* and *Mencius*], and then you will be benefited. . . . Mr. Fu of Qingyuan says, if a person who reads the books can relate the sages' sayings to his own person and examine them through his own embodied practice, his time (*gongfu*) will surely not be spent in vain. Every day will bring you the result (*gong* 功) of the day. If one only takes the books as collections of sayings, that would be merely the learning of the mouth and the ears.[6]

朱子曰，論孟不可只道理會，文義得了便了。須子細玩味，以身體之。…二書若便恁地讀過，只一兩日可了。若要將來做切己事，玩味體察，一日多看得數　或一兩　爾。讀論孟須是切己。且如學而時習之，切己看時，曾時習與否，句句如此求之，則有益矣。…慶源輔氏曰，讀書者能將聖人言語切己體察，則定無枉費工夫。一日當有一日之功。若欲只做一話説，則是口耳之學耳。

Cheng Yi 程頤 illustrates the same point in another way: "Nowadays people no longer know how to read. When they read the *Analects*, for instance, they are the same kind of people before they read the book and after they read the book. This is no different from not having read the book 今人不會讀書，如讀論語，未讀時是此等人，讀了後又只是此等人，便是不曾讀."[7] When asked about how to read the *Analects*, Zhu Xi says, "You should neither be in a hurry nor slow. The reason I say you should not be in a hurry is that the result (*gongxiao* 功效) cannot be obtained in a hurry. The reason I say that you should not be slow is that your effort (*gongfu*) cannot be spared 這也使急不得，也不可慢，所謂急不得者，功效不可急。所謂不可慢者，工夫不可慢."[8] These instructions are all about reading the books as practical *gongfu* guidance, not simply as objects of theoretical research. The former requires one to make self-reflection and to apply the teachings in practice, while the latter only requires one to realize intellectually what the books say and mean. The former leads to self-transformation, while the latter, in its worst, only lets the reader "hear the words with the ears and talk about the words with the mouth."

For the convenience of discussion, in the following discussion I shall use "*gongfu* perspective" to mean the perspective with a philosophical awareness of the *gongfu*, and "*gongfu* approach" to mean the approach of taking a text practically as *gongfu* instructions.

Metaphysics as *Gongfu*

Instructions about how to conduct one's life necessarily entail a certain understanding of what the world, self, and life are, and our understanding of the world, self, and life inevitably shape our praxis. Understanding and conduct cannot be totally separated. In the introduction to their philosophical translation of the *Analects*, Roger Ames and Henry Rosemont stress the importance of reading the *Analects* from the perspective of a "nonsubstantialist" and "relational" metaphysics. Their interpretation helps readers avoid reading into the *Analects* metaphysical assumptions that are foreign to its authors. The preoccupation of seeking the essence of things in Western philosophy, based on the separation of reality and appearance, of one thing from another, and of the knower and the known, is put in contrast in the Chinese tradition of seeing things relationally and in the process of change. Hence, this explains why in the West philosophers are chiefly concerned with describing the "things" in the world and why in traditional China the main concern is always on the "events" and on the guiding discourse (*dao* 道) for achieving harmony (*he* 和). This also helps to "explain why Chinese philosophers in general, and Confucius in particular, were teachers in a very different way than their peers steeped in the Greek and Abrahamic traditions. For Chinese teachers do not seem to have been so much concerned with describing and thereby conveying knowledge about the world as they were to have their students learn *how to get on* in the world, which is clearly reflected in the written texts."[9] This *how to get on* is what the *gongfu* method is about—of course not in the sense of getting a career and making a living, but in the sense of how to conduct one's life. Ames and Rosemont are quite insightful in tracing the different orientations to their metaphysical roots.[10] Since an event/relational metaphysics is embodied in the *Analects* but not discussed or articulated in it, Ames and Rosemont's introduction serves the important function of preparing readers for a proper reading of the *Analects*. However, some may assume that metaphysics is concerned only with knowledge about the world rather than with how to get on in the world, and that the purpose of the introduction of a book is to summarize the most important messages of the work. The long discussion about the contrast between thing/essence metaphysics and event/relation metaphysics may leave these readers with the mistaken impression that the central philosophical significance of the *Analects* is its embodied metaphysics rather than the instructions about how to get on.[11]

To illustrate that the metaphysical dimension in Confucianism is always subordinated to the *gongfu* dimension, let us take a closer look at a puzzling passage in the *Analects*.

> Zigong said, "We can learn from the Master's cultural refinements, but do not hear his discourse on subjects such as our 'natural disposition (xing 性)' and 'the way of *tian (tiandao* 天道).'"[12]

This passage is puzzling for a couple of reasons. One is about the reason why people did not get to hear the Master's discourse on these subjects. P. J. Ivanhoe makes a survey of major commentaries of the *Analects* that contain a number of different explanations: some believed that the Master did not talk about these topics because they are by nature transcendental and ineffable, and should therefore be understood "silently" or intuitively; some believed that these things require a high level of intelligence to understand and so would not be taught by the Master to the general assembly of his students; and some felt that abstract metaphysical ideas tend to mislead people and cause them to turn away from the actual phenomenal world in their search for the Way.[13] These observations have considerable plausibility, but they seem inadequate to explain another puzzle related to the passage: why did Mencius and the *Zhongyong*, contrary to Confucius, talk extensively on these subjects? With no intent to offer a full account of the existing interpretations of the passage myself, since it is beyond this essay's scope, I would simply point out how one interpretation seems to have escaped Ivanhoe's careful attention. There is one remark by Cheng Yi 程頤, "性與天道非自得之則不知,"[14] which is rendered by Ivanhoe as "If one does not 'attain a personal understanding of them [natural disposition and the way of *tian*]' then one does not understand."[15] The word *de* 得 in the sentence is translated as an attainment of an understanding of what the Way of *tian* and human nature are. But the original Chinese sentence does not have a word "understanding" between "attain (*de* 得)" and "them (*zhi* 之)." The sentence simply states, "if one does not attain them in person, then one does not understand." Clearly, it makes more sense to take the word *de* 得 to mean direct embodiment of the Way of *tian* and the natural dispositions. In the same article where Zhu Xi quotes the above remark, Zhu offers another quote from Cheng Yi: "Only because Zigong was able to reach the principle (*li* 理) in person, could he then make such admiring remarks, saying that the others could not hear it 唯子貢親達是理，故能為此歎美之辭，言眾人不得聞."[16] The word "reach" (*da* 達), again not followed by "understanding," suggests an attainment of the natural disposition and the way of *tian* directly, not an intellectual understanding about them. Reading the statements in this way, natural disposition 性 and the Way of *tian* 天道 are both no longer objects of intellectual knowledge (knowledge of "what" is there), but *gongfu* (way of life) to be attained and fully embodied, which is a prior condition for understanding them. Even the understanding one obtains from embodying *gongfu* is more likely an understanding of the effects, *gongxiao* 功效, than an intellectual (metaphysical) understanding of what they are.

This interpretation also can explain why the *Mencius* and the *Zhongyong* are able to talk extensively about both natural dispositions and the Way of *tian* without being considered as contradicting Confucius. The difference would simply be a matter of different methods (*gongfu*) for reaching the same goal. Song dynasty commentator Zheng Ruxie 鄭汝諧 says:

> Natural disposition and the Way of *tian* are extremely difficult to talk about. Confucius entailed them in his cultural refinements, and only Zigong was able to hear them. When it came to Mencius, he earnestly talked about the goodness of human nature and about the Way of *tian*. Confucius showed people the beginning, and wanted to let the followers attain the rest by themselves. Mencius articulated the secret for everybody, so that all under heaven can get to know it. Confucius's way of teaching is to provide the primordial energy so that when nurtured with rain and dew everything will grow by itself. Mencius's way of teaching is to nurture all things. He not only plants them but also waters them. The aims of Confucius and Mencius are one and the same, but what makes them sages is different.[17]

性與天道，至難言也。夫子寓之於文章之中，惟子貢能聞之。至孟子則諄諄然言性善，言天道。夫子示人以其端，欲學者至於自得。孟子闡其祕以示人.欲天下皆可知。夫子之設教元氣也，雨露所滋，萬物自遂。孟子之設教生物也，既栽培之，又灌溉之。孔孟之心則一，所以為聖賢者固有分量也。

Were Confucianism primarily a theory about the Way of *tian* and human nature and only secondarily applied theory to practice, the difference between Mencius and Confucius would be much more troubling. The fact that the difference did not even lead to much discussion in the classical commentaries is itself an indication of how the matter was taken.

Equally if not more revealing is the fact that both Mencius and Xunzi were accepted as Confucians even though they had opposing views about human nature. It shows that Confucianism may accept both as different *gongfu*—different ways for achieving the same goal. The *gongfu* orientation has no intrinsic admonition against metaphysical speculation, and it can accept different interpretations of the world, measured by their constructiveness to and effectiveness for the given objectives. In this regard, I believe Confucianism is far more "pragmatic" than the contemporary pragmatic Richard Rorty. Rorty makes great contributions by disabusing people of intellectualist preoccupations and guiding them toward the practical usefulness of life. However, he is still trapped in the framework of epistemology that he himself is famous for calling to an end in his landmark work *Philosophy and the Mirror of Nature*.[18] To him, a statement either can be empirically confirmed or cannot be confirmed;[19] there is either a tribunal to make a verdict of whether the given statement is true or false or there is none, and if the latter, then it is simply contingent. But the Confucian *gongfu* approach displays a third option: a metaphysical statement or concept can serve the function of being the goal of *gongfu*, as in the case of the unity between heaven and human (*tianren heyi* 天人合一) or a *gongfu* method, as in the case of the concept of sincerity (*cheng* 誠), or both. In serving these functions, statements that contain metaphysical concepts would be neither subject to empirical confirmation or disconfirmation (as true or false), nor simply contingently created. Such statements can be acts of recognition or recommendation, rather than acts of cognition or arbitrary creation. Here I am using the word "recognition" differently from the way Rorty uses it.[20] He uses the term as recognition of a fact, while I use it in the sense of recognition of a status. The latter is a performative act; it can be an act of both cognizing a certain fact, and an act through which a status of the fact is established (e.g., an umpire's announcement). The recognition can be a recommendation of an objective or a method of achieving a goal. In this sense it is also different from a contingent creation. A recommendation needs to have a rational basis of being effective.

Moralistic View
versus *Gongfu* Objective

The main objective of Confucian learning is clearly not to reveal some ultimate metaphysical truth about matters of fact. It is less clear, however, whether the main objective is to set up moral values or to reach a state of existence that, though undoubtedly having a lot to do with morality, can nevertheless not be summarized in moralistic terms. Let us take the often-quoted passage that tells us where Confucius himself reached at the final stage of his life as a reference point to look into this issue since it can be taken as an indication of the objective of Confucian learning. The Master says, "At seventy I could give my heart-mind free rein without overstepping the boundaries" (2.4). This is a state of freedom different from the so-called freedom of indifference. Freedom of indifference is practically impossible, since no one can be entirely free from any dispositions; it is also undesirable even if one could be in a state of absolute indifference, since if so there would be nothing that can help the agent to make a nonarbitrary choice. Freedom of indifference cannot be considered a *gongfu* in any sense of the term outlined above. On the other hand, the Confucian freedom indicated in the passage is also different from the Kantian absolute spontaneity in which pure reason governs our heart and its desires and aversions. In Kantian absolute spontaneity, pure reason is not in harmony with inclinations, and is therefore constantly under the threat of being overridden by the natural forces of the heart. Actually it appears as if one can be free in the Kantian sense only when pure reason is separated from and stands in opposition to one's heart. The Confucian sense of freedom is a cultivated spontaneity, a state of freedom when one's heart (natural desires and aversions) is attuned and moral reasoning "materialized" through embodiment. Unlike Kantian spontaneity that still has moral activities partially against the agent herself (her natural inclinations), Confucian freedom allows the activities to fully arise from the agent herself and yet stay within moral boundaries.[21] In this regard, we can say that Confucian *gongfu* sets its sights higher than Kantian *gongfu* does, that is, if such a thing can be said at all.[22] The Confucian aim demands more cultivation of the person than does the Kantian version. Not only does it require one to "overcome the self" (which the Kantian *gongfu* also requires) and "to return to the observance of rites" (12.1), but also it aims at a consummation of the self. At its perfection, one should be completely at one with oneself and let one's heart-and-mind take free rein without overstepping the proper boundaries. This is a state where one will have no more need to make choices since one will naturally be doing the right kind of things.

From the *gongfu* perspective, the "right kind of things" is different from a normal understanding of ethics, because here "right" does not mean that one has a moral obligation to do the right kind of things, though it does not exclude one's moral obligation to do so. If one wants to use Kantian terminology here, one might say that they are hypothetical imperatives that are in accord with one's moral duty, and at its ideal state they are fully embodied as one's cultivated inclinations, so one does not even feel like following any imperatives at all. The objective of the "right kind of things" is, from the *gongfu* point of view, not for the sake of moral duty, but rather for the consummation of oneself (為己之學). As Tu Wei-ming says:

> If we prefer to use the word "good" to designate a quality that can be distinguished from other desirable qualities such as wise and creative, we may have to redefine the primary Confucian concern in more neutral terms such as "learning to become more authentically or more fully human." . . . To learn to become an authentic person in the Confucian sense is certainly to be honest with oneself and loyal to others, but it also entails a ceaseless process through which humanity in its all-embracing fullness is concretely realized.[23]

This view is much closer to the Aristotelian notion of morality as the formation of good habits—"good" in the sense of being conducive to achieving the *telos* of a human being. To live a life fully as a human sounds very much like Aristotle's aim of *eudaimonia*. But this "authenticity" is not merely an expanded moralistic notion of what is to be fully human. Or to put it in another way, Confucius is not merely trying to tell us that there is a *telos* that we are morally obligated to honor. This authenticity entails what a human being is able to achieve. As another articulation of the highest objective of the Confucian learning says, a well-cultivated person should be able to "wander in the arts 游於藝" (7.6), though this saying by no means entails a moral requirement that everyone is obligated to follow.

Unlike common conceptions of art that associate artworks with studios and galleries, the Confucian conception of art is the artistic way of life itself. This means to take everyday activity as artistic creativity, as recreational wandering, and to be cocreators of the universe along with Heaven and Earth. Confucius was known as "a person who keeps trying although he knows that it is in vain" (14.38). He kept trying in the face of constant defeat because the Master had found the meaning or the worth of life right from within, from the effort itself, which was at the same time a source of aesthetic enjoyment. For example, "The Duke of She asked Zilu about Confucius, but Zilu did not reply. The Master said, 'Why didn't you just say to him: As a person, Confucius is driven by such eagerness to teach and learn that he forgets to eat, he enjoys himself so much that he forgets to worry, and does not even realize that old age is on its way'" (7.19). This enjoyment makes moral responsibility almost irrelevant—having a good life is not conceived as fulfilling a list of joyless moral obligations. When the person enters an aesthetic realm, life itself becomes artistic creation. The Master says, "I find inspiration from intoning the songs; I learn where to stand from observing ritual propriety; and I find complete fulfillment in art and enjoyment (*yue* 樂)" (8.8). This shows that artistic enjoyment in creativity is the highest aim of Confucian learning!

The shift from a moralistic view to a *gongfu* perspective means that we can take all moral teachings of Confucius as statements of a *gongfu* objective, that is, instructions to help the person consummate the self. The shift may generate very different observations. Let us take a look at one example here. "Zengzi says, 'Daily I examine my person on three counts. In my understanding on behalf of other people, have I failed to do my utmost (*zhong* 忠)? In my interactions with colleagues and friends, have I failed to make good on my word (*xin* 信)? In what has been passed on to me, have I failed to carry it to practice?'" (*Analects* 1.4). From the *gongfu* perspective, all three counts are specific *gongfu*; they are methods of making efforts to become a *junzi* and not perform merely out of moral obligations. Nothing seems particularly controversial here. But when we associate this passage with 4.15 of the *Analects*, and look at the two from a *gongfu* point of view, a striking conclusion emerges: Confucius sees the deficiency of Zengzi's method! He told Zengzi, "My way (*dao* 道) is bound together with one continuous strand." In other words, the Master's way, when taken separately as Zengzi does on three counts, becomes disintegrated. Wang Yangming remarks that it is like a tree and its leaves. One is the root of the tree, and the "continuous strand" is the connection of the leaves. One is the body or formation, and the continuous strand its function. Zengzi places his *gongfu* (effort) in three separate counts (*gongfu*). That is equivalent to trying to capture the individual leaves (functions) without grasping the root (the Way) that keeps all the leaves alive. Zengzi does not know that these functions all came from one origin; therefore his way is not good enough.[24]

This reading may strike many as unusual since normally both passages 1.4 and 4.15 are read positively as statements of Confucian principles. Passage 4.15 is even read as a favorable depiction of Zengzi's privileged status. The passage says that when Confucius left the room, another disciple asked, "What was [the Master] referring to [by saying that my way is bound together with one continuous stand]?" Zengzi said, "The way of the Master is doing one's utmost (*zhong* 忠) and putting oneself in the other's place (*shu* 恕), nothing more" (*Analects* 4.15). This seems to imply that Zengzi knows what the Master meant. Bryan Van Norden, seeing that "there is never, for example, a passage [in the *Analects*] in which Zengzi is commended by Confucius for his insight, in the manner that Confucius commended Zixia (3.8) or Zigong (1.15)," suspected that 4.15 is an interpolation by the followers of Zengzi to boost his image.[25] But the *gongfu* reading suggests that Zengzi is not even presented in the passage favorably. His explanation of the Master's saying seems to indicate that he still did not get what the one strand is, since his answer still entailed two *gongfu* methods: *zhong* and *shu*.[26]

Of course this "one strand" does not mean that Confucius taught only one single *gongfu*. It refers to the strand that links all his *gongfu* together. It is possible that the Master did not say what the one strand is because the inter-connectedness of all the *gongfu* is not itself a separate *gongfu*. If this were the case, it would be mistaken to take one of them as central, and denounce others.[27] Take the notion of filial piety (*xiao* 孝) as an example. In passage 1.2 Youzi says, "Exemplary persons (*junzi* 君子) concentrate their efforts on the root, for the root having taken hold, the way (*dao* 道) will grow therefrom. As for filial and fraternal responsibility, it is, I suspect, the root of human-hearted conduct (*ren* 仁)." Here filial piety is not presented merely as a moral virtue that one has an obligation to have, or as a rule of conduct that one has to obey. Neither is Youzi saying that it is the most important virtue, and the rest can be logically inferred from it. Filial piety is presented as a *gongfu* for becoming a *ren* person—a basic method that will causally lead to others. This does not exclude the possibility that other methods can have the same function. If the various *gongfu* are interconnected, one can cut in from any of the key *gongfu* and the others will naturally follow. In the *Analects* we see a number of key *gongfu* such as ritual propriety (*li* 禮, 12.1), what is appropriate (*yi* 義, 4.10, 4.16), putting oneself in the other's place (*shu* 恕, 15.24), centering the commonality (*zhongyong* 中庸, 6.29), and to "let no thought deviate toward the inappropriate" (*si wu xie* 思無邪, 2.2).[28] ("Letting no thought deviate" is the forerunner of the key *gongfu* in the *Zhongyong*, sincerity [*cheng* 誠]). With the *gongfu* perspective, we shall be able to see more clearly how each of these important terms in the *Analects* can be viewed as *gongfu*, and how they are connected with others in a way different from how parts of a descriptive theory are connected.

Social and Political Philosophy as *Gongfu*

To further illustrate the significance of the *gongfu* perspective, in this section, I will take a few passages from the *Analects*, all related to social and political philosophy that are difficult for contemporary Confucian scholars to defend to show how the *gongfu* perspective can shed new lights on them.

From the very beginning, Confucius's teaching of filial piety has been criticized for advocating partiality to one's own family and lacking universality. Typically, defenders of Confucian love-with-gradation argue that it is more natural for a person to love one's own inner circle than to love outsiders. Modern feminism and pragmatism also argue from the same point that our love of one of "us" over others is a basic fact of human life, and thus a morality based on the acceptance of this fact is natural.[29] However, what if filial piety is in conflict with social justice? Modern Confucian scholars are often silent on passage 13.18,[30] because it appears bluntly consanguineous:

> The Governor of She in conversation with Confucius said, "In our village there is someone called 'True Person.' When his father took a sheep on the sly, he reported him to the authorities." Confucius replied, "Those who are true in my village conduct themselves differently. A father covers for his son, and a son covers for his father. And being true lies in this."

Looking from the *gongfu* perspective, however, this passage can be viewed more than as a simple adherence to what is "natural" (which is not necessarily moral) or a moral obligation toward one's own family circle. When asked about why the Moist "love without discrimination" is not taken as human-heartedness (*ren* 仁), Wang Yangming responds:

> *Ren* is the principle of productivity (*sheng* 生). Though it permeates everywhere, its dissemination is gradual, . . . and therefore has a beginning. Only because it has a beginning, can it develop; only because it can develop, can it never be exhausted. Take an example of a tree. It begins with a sprout. This is where the tree starts to develop. Once it has a sprout, it begins to develop a stem, and then branches and leaves, one after another. If there were no sprout, how could it have stem, branches, and leaves? Having a sprout means that there is a root underneath. With the root, the tree can live, without it, the tree dies. . . . The love between father and son and between brothers is the place where the productivity of the human heart begins, just like the tree's having a sprout. From there the love of humanity and the care for everything develops, just as the tree's having branches and leaves. The Moist love without discrimination treats one's own parents and brothers just like a stranger, and therefore loses the starting point. Since it does not have a sprout, we know that it does not have a root, and hence will not be generative.[31]

While whether a *gongfu* reading resolves the possible conflict between filial piety and social justice is certainly still questionable, such a reading sheds light on the issue, for it reveals that for the Confucians, filial piety is the very root of social justice. Filial piety and social justice are linked rather than simply opposed to one another as conflicting universal principles. Just as something that nourishes a person in general can also harm one's health, when looking from a *gongfu* perspective, the possible conflict between filial piety and social justice are practical difficulties in achieving ideal results without compromising some objectives. It is a matter of exercising practical wisdom and keeping the "root" of humanity at the cost of some "branches." The logic of "either/or" is not appropriate here, because according to the Confucians, they are not upholding one and abandoning the other. Sacrificing some immediate objectives for securing the same objectives in the long run is very different from simply choosing one over the other.

Another passage difficult for modern Confucian scholars to defend is 17.3, where the Master instructs, "Only the most wise (*zhi* 知) and the most stupid do not move." This is widely taken as a discriminative statement because the words rendered "most wise" and "most stupid" are "*shang zhi* 上智" and "*xia yu* 下愚*." "*Shang* 上*"* means superior, upper, above, and "*xia* 下*"* means inferior, lower, and below. Critics therefore read this passage as, "Those of the upper class are wise and those of the lower class are stupid. That never changes." From the *gongfu* point of view, however, *shang* and *xia* mean superior and inferior rather than upper and lower social classes. The proper reading of 17.3 should be, "Only the most wise and the most stupid do not want to move." As Wang Yangming comments, "Not that they cannot move. It is rather that they do not want to."[32] The wisest don't want to move because they have found the way and do not want to deviate from its correct path; the stupidest do not see the need to improve, and so they don't want to move either. This is a warning not to be the most stupid, not a description of fact, and has nothing to do with discrimination against any social class. Cheng Yi says, in interpreting this passage,

> The so-called 'most stupid' are of two kinds: The self-abusers 自暴 and the self-deniers 自棄. With willingness to cultivate oneself with goodness, no one is impossible to move. Even the most stupid and confused can gradually strive to be better. But the self-abusers refuse to believe [that they can improve], and the self-deniers refuse to act [on the belief that they can improve].[33]

Still another passage that many modern Confucians are reluctant to mention is 8.9: "the common people can be made to follow a path, but not to know." Critics of Confucianism often cite this passage as evidence that Confucianism is authoritarian, elitist, and opposed to human freedom and democracy. But again this is in part because the saying is taken descriptively rather than instructively. It is taken to be saying that, timelessly and universally, the common people are low in social status and they are incapable of knowing what is good for them. But when considered as a *gongfu* instruction, it becomes entirely different. The following is a *gongfu* interpretation from Dai Xi 戴溪 of the Song Dynasty:

> The saying that "the common people can be made to follow a path" does not mean to be afraid of the common people's being smart and therefore want to keep them dumb. Neither does it mean that the common people are so stupid that they cannot be made to know. This passage is about the sage's way of transforming people—it can make the common people follow, just like having an invisible spiritual force that excites and motivates people. This is like when the common people plow the land to get their food, dig their well to get their water, they don't know what the power of their Emperor has anything to do with them. If there were something for the common people to know, it means that my way is still visible and not very effective in transforming the people. The way of the sage kings is transparent and broad; that is what "follow" means. The way of tyrants is to make people nervous; that is what "know" means. It is better for the fish to live in rivers and lakes and be able to forget about each other than for them to be in a dry pond and have to moisten each other with their spit.[34]

> 民可使由之，不是恐民之智，將以愚之，亦不是匹夫匹婦之愚，不可與知。此一段自是論聖人動化之道，可使民由之。所謂鼓舞震盪，忽焉若神，耕食鑿飲，不知帝力於我何有之類是也。若使民知之，則是在我未免有形迹，而道化之在民者，亦淺矣。王者皥皥，所謂由也。霸者譁虞，所謂知也。水涸，魚相煦以濕，相濡以沫，不如相忘於江湖。

In other words, this is the Confucian method of *wuwei* 無為. The most effective parental guidance takes place when the children do not even know that they are disciplined. The most well-governed society is one in which common people do not even feel the need to know the laws.[35]

No passage in the *Analects* embarrasses contemporary Confucians more than 17.25. Confucius says, "It is only women and petty persons who are difficult to provide for. Drawing them close, they are immodest, and keeping them at a distance, they complain." Modern advocates of Confucianism, like their opponents, take the saying to be descriptive, and hastily denounce the saying completely as sexist. The common strategy to get around it is to argue that even though this saying is sexist, the salient spirit of Confucianism is the nurturing care that is associated in the West with the feminine.[36] However, there is an instructive message underneath the passage. Qing dynasty Wang Xuan 汪烜 says in his *Sishu Quanyi* 《四書詮義》 with regard to this passage, "This is saying that in cultivation of the person and regulating the family, nothing can be taken lightly or taken for granted. Do not think that servants and concubines are low in social status and therefore can be used in anyway I like, without caring about how to treat them 此言修身齊家者不可有一事之可輕，一物之可慢，毋謂僕妾微賤，可以惟我所使，而忽以處之也."[37] What this means from the *gongfu* perspective is that the passage is not describing how women and people in low social status are difficult to provide for, but rather that one ideally should be able to make even those who are most difficult to provide for pleased, if they are close, and attracted, if they are at a distance (近者說, 遠者來, 13.16). As Song dynasty scholar Lü Zuqian 呂祖謙 comments on this passage:

> When thinking about how to deal with this kind of people [those who are difficult to provide for], the most difficult thing is to be firm on discipline yet not to appear harsh. Ordinary people cannot be firm on discipline if they do not appear harsh. In order to be firm on discipline, they have to make special deliberate efforts. This is just like being "respectful and yet at ease." Ordinary people usually have to be ill at ease when they want to appear respectful. If they behave without constraint they will not be respectful. Only with deep cultivation of one's nature and disposition can a person be naturally both firm on discipline and respectful. If what is inside of the person is not sufficient, the person will have no way but to appeal to artificial efforts. Those who are ferocious but not commanding also belong to this kind.[38]

> 要當思其所以處之之道，夫不惡而嚴，最人之所難。　常人不惡則不嚴。苟欲其嚴，必作意而爲之。亦如恭而安，尋常人恭敬者多拘束才安，肆則不恭矣。惟性情涵養，則自然嚴恭。苟內不足，則必待造作。威而不猛亦其類也。

Here "respectful and yet at ease 恭而安" is from 7.38 of the *Analects*: "The Master was always gracious yet serious, commanding yet not severe, respectful yet at ease." This "at ease" says even more than "giving the heart-mind free rein without overstepping the boundaries." For not to overstep the boundaries is still about how the cultivation affects a person, that is, how it enables one not to overstep the boundaries. Yet passages 17.25, 7.38, and 13.16 require one to be naturally both firm on discipline and attractive to those who are most difficult to provide for, even in most tedious daily personal life. In these passages, we see three distinctive features of Confucianism that Kupperman finds particularly valuable: that Confucianism provides a scope of ethics broad enough to cover all or almost all of life, rather than merely "big movements"; that Confucianism extends beyond choice-making to character formation; and that it provides sliding scales of moral requirements that stretch to higher aims than ordinary morality.[39] I would just emphasize that these features are not part of a Confucian plot to inculcate people so that a high degree of morality can be implemented in society without any trace of force. Instead, Confucianism is a way of cultivating and consummating the self.

Concluding Remarks

In light of the above explanation and discussion, we may see more clearly why Confucius presented his teachings as he did—he never gave systematic lectures to articulate his views. Most of his teachings took the form of short and direct instructions. Sometimes they were given using the Master's own way of living as an example, showing that the *Analects* has no intention of constructing a theory, but focuses instead on giving guidance. The *Analects* shows that when asked about *ren* by the disciples, Confucius never tried to describe *ren* per se. He talked about what a *ren* person would be like, how he would act, and he gave instructions according to each disciple's particular condition, letting him know how he should start or continue his practice. The teaching method is indeed more typical of *gongfu* masters than of philosophy teachers. If he were to describe and articulate *ren* verbally, it would be like, as the Chinese saying goes, "trying to scratch the feet through boots"—not to the right point. He would be misleading the disciples by a mere intellectual understanding, where the real spirit of *ren* cannot be found.

Teaching Confucian learning through a *gongfu* system implies learning Confucian values, not merely as options to choose from, but as ideals to pursue. The aim of the Confucian learning is, using Kupperman's words, to narrow down their real options or "closing off of possibilities, in that certain things (such as brutal or unjust actions) become unthinkable."[40] Since the aim of *gongfu* is to know "how," to embody abilities and achieve transformation of the person rather than to gain intellectual understanding of "what," understanding Confucianism as a *gongfu* system does not require elaborate verbal articulation of the system. Indeed, it may even be better that little verbal instruction is given because the knowledge about "how" must be acquired through practice and by direct experience. Sometimes Confucius's disciples are even discouraged to ask why, because without trying to experience what is to be understood, a verbal answer could easily mislead the student to think he has already understood the answer from only words.

> The Master said, "I think I will leave off speaking."
>
> "If you do not speak," Zigong replied, "how will we your followers find the proper way?"
>
> The master responded, "Does *tian* 天 speak? And yet the four seasons turn and the myriad things are born and grow within it. Does *tian* speak?" (17.19)

Passages 4.24 and 13.27 of the *Analects* even take slowness of speech (*na* 訥) as an indication of being close to *ren*. Yet the common assumption in the West nowadays is that true knowledge is always describable and capable of being communicated by language. The primary function of a teacher is to present (or represent) facts with words or symbols, to persuade students by appealing to their reason through verbal clarification and argumentation. Students are encouraged to ask "why" as they constantly seek the reason for everything they learn, unless it is seen by reason as self-evident.

Today, the difficulties for understanding Confucianism as a *gongfu* system involve dealing with a complex of mental habits (intellectualist way of thinking, metaphysical outlook of taking things as discrete entities, and so forth), social values (individual freedom of choice, no discrimination on the basis of personal beliefs, and so forth), functions of language (descriptive role versus guiding role), and even social institutions (laws and regulations).

As I demonstrate in this essay, it is possible to take a *gongfu* perspective to look at Confucianism. This perspective is to look at Confucianism praxiologically (or "philosophically," in the sense of including praxiology, in addition to the conventional areas of metaphysics, epistemology, and ethics, as an important part of philosophy) with an awareness of its *gongfu* orientation. Such an orientation can help us gain more insights into Confucian teachings and correct the overly intellectualistic and moralistic reading of Confucian texts. However, the *gongfu* perspective is not a "*gongfu* approach," that is, not yet taking the text as instructions for one's own transformation. It is important to understand that without the latter, the *gongfu* perspective itself can still easily become merely the "learning of the mouth and the ears."

But what can we do?

The Master says, "In expressing oneself, it is simply a matter of getting the point across" (15.41). The point to be gotten across allows us to take each group and each person, including ourselves, as far as we can go. It is essential to Confucian *gongfu* that other teachers will appear for each of us, and we must not let the opportunities for learning from them (learning their *gongfu*) go unnoticed and unappreciated. As Confucius says, "In strolling in the company of just two other persons, I am bound to find a teacher" (7.22)—a teacher who can teach us not only how to live an examined life (like Socrates), but also a cultivated one (like Confucious).[41]

Notes

1. A similar problem exists in teaching other Eastern philosophies as well. Such a problem made Eliot Deutsch hesitant to accept the invitation from Blackwell to edit a volume on *A Companion to World Philosophies*. Can Chinese, Indian, and Islamic traditional thoughts, which are so different from the Western philosophical tradition, be brought under the single category called "philosophy"? Finally the editor at Blackwell convinced him by saying that his way of thinking "was all very fine for those philosophers and students who were already knowledgeable about other traditions, but the actual state of affairs in the field as a whole was still such that the vast majority of philosophers

and students, although now very interested in cross-cultural encounters, knew very little about traditions other than their own." Eliot Deutsch, ed., *A Companion to World Philosophies* (Malden, MA: Blackwell, 1997), xii.

2. In a popular dictionary that most American college students use, the word is defined narrowly as "any of various Chinese arts of self-defense like karate" (*Merriam Webster's Collegiate Dictionary*). This is not merely in the West. A quick search of the Chinese word 功夫 on the internet will show that clearly this is also the way that most people in China understand the word.

3. Wang Yangming,《王陽明全集》[Collected works of Wang Yangming] (Beijing: Hongqi Press 北京紅旗出版社, 1996), vol. 1, 129.

4. Wang Yangming,《王陽明全集》[Collected works], vol. 1, 128.

5. As this is not the place to identify and chart the issues of praxiology, I will merely give a couple of examples. Praxiology studies, for instance, the connection between our model of praxis and our notion of cause (a notion of linear efficient cause, for example, is associated with dominative and manipulative behavior) and our notion of freedom (Sartre's notion of freedom, for example, entails anguish, forlornness, and despair).

6. Zhu Xi, "讀論語孟子法" [On methods of reading the *Analects* and *Mencius*], in《四庫全書》文淵閣本, 經部・四書類・四書大全・論語集註大全 [*Siku Quanshu*, Wenyuange copy, Classics part, Four Books section, Grand collection of the Four Books—Grand collection of commentaries of the *Analects*], 3.

7. Zhu Xi,《四書章句集注》[Collected commentaries of the chapters and sentences of the Four Books] (Shandong: Qilu Shushe 齊魯書社, 1992), "論語集注" [Collected commentaries of the *Analects*], 4.

8. Zhu Xi,《朱子語類》[Collected sayings of Master Zhu], in《四庫全書》文淵閣本, 子部・儒家類 [*Siku Quanshu*, Wenyuange copy, Masters part, Confucianism section], vol. 19, 9.

9. Roger T. Ames and Henry Rosemont, Jr., *The Analects of Confucius: A Philosophical Translation* (New York: Ballantine. 1998), 33.

10. One example of the relevance of metaphysics is the conception of self. Martha Nussbaum, for instance, insists that "separateness of individuals is a basic fact of human life" in her defense of liberal individualism in response to feminist challenges, and in doing this, she takes Buddhist and Confucian notions of the self as targets of her criticism, presumably because feminism is relatively new and has yet to develop its own metaphysics. See Martha Nussbaum, "The Feminist Critique of Liberalism," in *Sex and Social Justice* (New York: Oxford University Press, 1999), 10, 62.

11. I had the similar worry with Roger Ames and David Hall's new translation of the *Zhongyong* also, as the *gongfu* dimension of the book is eclipsed by their emphasis on metaphysics. See Peimin Ni, "Reading *Zhong Yong* as *Gongfu* Instruction: Comments on Ames and Hall's *Focusing the Familiar*," *Dao: A Journal of Comparative Philosophy* 3, no. 2 (2004):189–203.

12. Ames and Rosemont, *Analects*, 5.13. Quotes from the *Analects* will be mainly from the Ames and Rosemont translation, often with slight modifications. Hereafter, they will be cited in the text with chapter and section number. All other translations are mine.

13. P. J. Ivanhoe, "Whose Confucius? Which *Analects*?" In *Confucius and the Analects: New Essays*, ed. Bryan Van Norden (New York: Oxford University Press, 2002), 119–33.

14. Zhu Xi,《論語精義》[Subtle meanings of the *Analects*], vol. 3, part 1, in《四庫全書》文淵閣本, 經部 · 四書類 · 論孟精義 [*Siku Quanshu*, Wenyuange copy, Classics part, Four Books section, Subtle meanings of the *Analects* and *Mencius*], 20.

15. Ivanhoe, "Whose Confucius?" 122.

16. Zhu,《論語精義》[Subtle meanings], vol.3, part 1, 21.

17. Zheng Ruxie 鄭汝諧,《論語意原》[Original meanings of the *Analects*], vol. 1, in《四庫全書》文淵閣本, 經部, 四書類 [*Siku Quanshu*, Wenyuange copy, Classics part, Four Books section], 31.

18. Richard Rorty, *Philosophy and the Mirror of Nature* (Princeton: Princeton University Press, 1979).

19. Rorty made a subtle yet important correction of my interpretation of him, though the correction does not affect the validity of my argument. He wrote, "I agree with Ni that my 'sweeping rejection of theories of human nature' is 'partly the result of a simplistic dichotomy created by epistemology.' Simplistic though it may be, I think it is very useful. The dichotomy I prefer to wield, however, is not (as Ni puts it) between a claim that has a truth value and one that is simply created. It is a dichotomy between claims that can be empirically confirmed and those that cannot." (See *Morality, Human Nature, and Metaphysics: Rorty Responds to Confucian Critics*, edited by Yong Huang. Forthcoming, SUNY Press). I made a correction in my statement here accordingly. My point is that, though useful, the dichotomy limits our vision of the *gongfu* dimension.

20. Richard Rorty, *Contingency, Irony, and Solidarity* (Cambridge: Cambridge University Press, 1989), 196.

21. See my article "The Confucian Account of Freedom," in *The Examined Life: Chinese Perspectives; Essays on Chinese Ethical Traditions*, ed. Xinyan Jiang, 119–40 (Binghamton, NY: Global Publications, 2002) for a more detailed discussion on this topic.

22. I can envision that a Kantian may argue that one also needs *gongfu* to reach the Kantian state of absolute spontaneity, for it requires one to detach from one's own natural inclinations.

23. Tu Wei-ming, *Confucian Thought: Selfhood as Creative Transformation* (Albany: SUNY Press, 1985), 52.

24. Wang Yangming,《王陽明全集》[Collected works], vol. 1, 34.

25. Bryan Van Norden, ed., *Confucius and the Analects: New Essays* (New York: Oxford University Press, 2002), 222.

26. Zhu Xi 朱熹's way of handling this passage is quite interesting. He agrees that even though Zengzi was working hard on the functions (*yong* 用) of Confucian *gongfu*, he did not understand the oneness of the formation (*ti* 體). But Zhu Xi thinks that after Confucius pointed this out to Zengzi, Zengzi did get the message, and was able to articulate it. Zhu Xi's way of helping Zengzi to make *zhong* and *shu* into one strand is by using the concept of sincerity (*cheng* 誠). Doing one's best is *zhong*, just as heaven

and earth are sincere, and the manifestation of this sincerity is *shu*, just as everything else gets its proper place in heaven and earth. Since the way of heaven and earth is silent, Zengzi uses its manifestation to make it easier to understand. However, Zhu Xi says that actually beside sincerity, there is no other method, and therefore no need to have another method for manifestation(see Zhu Xi,《四書章句集注》[Collected commentaries],"論語集注" [Collected commentaries of the *Analects*] 34–35.

27. Fingarette, for instance, mistakenly moved toward the direction of contrasting ritual propriety (*li* 禮), something that he sees correctly as having a "magical power," against an equally Confucian *gongfu* of cultivating the person internally. Consequently a vital dimension of Confucian learning, the dimension of personal transformation through cultivation, is omitted or overshadowed by his emphasis on *li*. Herbert Fingarette, *Confucius: The Secular as Sacred* (New York: Harper & Row, 1972).

28. Wang Yangming says, "Not only the 300 poems, but also all the six classics can be summarized in this one short sentence. . . . This is the *gongfu* of one shot to kill all the birds at once."《王陽明全集》[Collected works], vol. 1, 107.

29. Nel Noddings, *Caring: A Feminine Approach to Ethics and Moral Education* (Berkeley and Los Angeles: University of California Press, 1984), 16, and Rorty, *Contingency*, 191.

30. For instance, the passage is mentioned neither in Hall and Ames's *Thinking Through Confucius* (SUNY Press, 1987), nor in Van Norden's *Confucius and the Analects*. The passage and the whole issue related to the apparent conflict between filial love and justice were brought to a heated debate recently, initiated by Liu Qingping of Beijing Normal University. See *Debates on Confucian Ethics: The Mutual Concealment among Family Members*, ed. Guo Qiyong (Wuhan: Hubei Jiaoyu Chubanshe, 2004).

31. Wang Yangming,《王陽明全集》[Collected works], vol. 1, 27. Of course Wang is far from being alone in taking the issue in this way. The analogy of the root of a tree is already in the *Analects*, where it is stated that, with regard to the relation between filial piety and human-heartedness, "Exemplary persons concentrate their efforts on the root, for the root having taken hold, the way (*dao*) will grow therefrom" (1.2). Cheng Yi and Zhu Xi also elaborated the point (See Zhu Xi,《四書章句集注》[Collected commentaries] "論語集注" [Collected commentaries of the *Analects*], 2).

32. Wang Yangming,《王陽明全集》[Collected works], vol. 1, 33.

33. Cheng Yi 程頤,《伊川易傳》*Yichuan Yichuan*, vol. 4, in《四庫全書》文淵閣本, 經部·易類 [*Siku Quanshu*, Wenyuange copy, Classics part, Yi section], 24.

34. Dai Xi 戴溪,《石鼓論語答問》[Shigu questions and answers of the *Analects*,], vol. 2, in《四庫全書》文淵閣本, 經部·四書類 [*Siku Quanshu*, Wenyuange copy, Classics part, Four Books section], 9.

35. The same interpretation is also made in a number of other commentaries. He Yan 何晏, for instance, quotes Zhang Ping 張憑: "Things will all follow their nature if political affairs are conducted with virtue, and everything under the heaven can be left alone for their everyday use. If political affairs are conducted with penal law, then measures will be taken to prevent common people from doing evil. Knowing that measures are taken, the common people will do evil more covertly. This is why [the Master] says

that they cannot be made to know. It is saying that political affairs should be conducted with virtue and simply let the common people to follow, not with penal laws and let them know the measures 為政以德則各得其性，天下日用而可使由之。若為政以刑，則防民之為奸，民知有防，而為奸彌巧。故曰不可使知之，言為政當以德，民由之而已。不可用刑，民知其術也." He Yan 何晏，《論語集解義疏》[Analysis of the collected commentaries of the *Analects*], vol. 4, in《四庫全書》文淵閣本，經部‧四書類 [*Siku Quanshu*, Wenyuange copy, Classics part, Four Books section], 31. See also the interpretation by Song dynasty Chen Xiangdao 陳祥道 in Chen Xiangdao 陳祥道，《論語全解》[Comprehensive explanation of the *Analects*], vol. 4, in《四庫全書》文淵閣本，經部‧四書類 [*Siku Quanshu*, Wenyuange copy, Classics part, Four Books section], 28. Here I am not claiming that there are no other plausible readings of this passage.

36. See Henry Rosemont, Jr., *A Chinese Mirror: Moral Reflections on Political Economy and Society* (La Salle, IL: Open Court, 1991), 75, and Chenyang Li 李晨陽, ed., *The Sage and the Second Sex: Confucianism, Ethics, and Gender* (Chicago: Open Court, 2000), 35.

37. See Cheng Shude 程樹德，《論語集釋》[Collected commentaries on the *Analects*] (Beijing: 中華書局 Zhonghua Shuju, 1990), 1244.

38. Lü Zuqian 呂祖謙，《麗澤論説》[Discourses of Lize,], vol. 2, in《四庫全書》文淵閣本，子部 [*Siku Quanshu*, Wenyuange copy, Masters part], 14–15.

39. Joel Kupperman, *Learning from Asian Philosophy* (New York: Oxford University Press, 1999), v, v, vi.

40. Kupperman, *Learning*, 136.

41. I want to acknowledge my indebtedness to my colleague Stephen Rowe for the concluding point of this paper, and for his numerous other helpful comments on an earlier draft. His book *Living Philosophy* (St. Paul, MN: Paragon House, 2002) is very much of the same orientation as this paper. My gratitude also extends to Professor David Fielding for his insightful comments and suggestions.

The *Ren Dao* of Confucius: A Spiritual Account of Humanity

11

Mary I. Bockover

Confucius is commonly known as a teacher of morality who would therefore belong to the philosophical province of ethics. By extension he is thought of as a "humanist" who speaks to the heart of the human condition and how we may properly respond to it. This is a correct view of Confucius. However, a common misconception taken to follow is that Confucianism is an exclusively humanistic and secular philosophy. The *Analects* is most centrally a moral teaching, but it is wrong to think of it as *only* a moral teaching. I will argue that the spiritual dimension of Confucian principles must be fully acknowledged for the ethics to be understood. Confucian ethics is simultaneously a religion that evokes a deep respect for spirits and spiritual agency, as well as recognition that the human way (*ren dao*) is essentially entailed by, and coextensive with, the way of heaven (*tian dao*). This essay aims to bring out just this connection.

Li 禮

One of the most important principles that Confucius gives us in the *Analects* is *li*, which is translated as ritual, rite, ceremony, propriety, good conduct, and the like. *Li* literally is the "ritual vessel" through which human excellence is realized. *Li* can be lofty and grand, as in the case of an elaborate religious or political ceremony, or *li* can be down to earth, as in the case of a handshake, a bow, or even a smile. But in any case, *li* is learned convention, acts of civility that not only communicate our humanity to others, but that allow humanity to flourish as well. This is the beauty of Confucian ethics: moral conduct, such as *li*, is relational in aiming to elicit an appropriate response that is as twofold in nature as the act (of *li*) that gives rise to it; and when fully accounted for, this twofold "nature" allows us to see the religious dimension of Confucian ethics. First, *li* is learned human convention that serves the central social purpose of allowing us to recognize and respond to each other in a meaningful and civilized way. As such, *li* is the "vessel" for cultivating human relations. But second, *li* is sacred in linking us with the greater way of heaven itself—indeed, in being the very vehicle for its expression. Thus, beyond its social function of cultivating the (five basic) human relations, *li* is also the way that humanity develops through the ages, not the least of which includes rituals for properly revering ancestors in *tian*. This is part of the spiritual function of *li* that is often overlooked in discussions on Confucian philosophy. Confucius represents the magical effect of ritual in ordering things in the following exchange: "Someone asked the Master for an explanation of the *di* imperial ancestral sacrifice, and he replied: 'I don't have one. Anyone who did know how to explain it could rule the empire as easily as having it here.' And he pointed to the palm of his hand."[1]

Both ethical and spiritual dimensions of Confucianism rest on the fact that *li* is rooted in the distinctively human ability to stand simultaneously in relation to the past, the present, and the future. *Li* is more than a vehicle for personal communion; it is the means by which humanity is guided ideally toward the unknown future by virtue of the wisdom of the past. Through *li*, humanity can fine-tune its relation with the natural harmony and grace of the way of being itself (*dao*), but this is a temporal process that depends on our ability to discern from the past what is needed to move efficaciously into the future. Confucian ethics is not just a secular ethic, for *li* is the secular expression of the sacred;[2] *li* is the human way to be aligned with the greater way of heaven and thus to cultivate excellence that continuously and essentially reaches for a higher ideal—even for divine perfection.[3] A critical part of this process is taking what the history of our descendents shows us to be culture at its best into the future by instituting it in the present. This is why Confucius was so concerned with learning "the rites" and "the songs," for the distilled wisdom and beauty of his culture was needed to foster self-improvement. But the fostering of this self-improvement also provides the cultural refinement needed to nurture and sustain future generations.

Another part of the spiritual function of *li* that has often been overlooked concerns the *ren*[4] that *li* necessarily expresses. The human way, or *ren dao*, is a way of *li*—of benevolent conduct ritualized into a particular normative form. The human way is a way of goodness and decency (*ren*) communicated through a more particular normative convention (*li*). Through *li* and the goodness that it transmits, personal authority and power (*de*) are established and then reciprocally expressed through roles that are relevant to one's culture—again through *li*. Its most perfect expression is thought to have issued from divine sages, descendents of heaven like Yao and Shun, who were among the greatest of ancient Chinese emperors. Their greatness culminated in an extraordinary ability to realize the "mandate of heaven," serving humanity with excellence, much like a benevolent father would attend to his family. Therefore we can see the human way (*ren dao*) and the way of heaven (*tian dao*) are linked by the same normative thread that runs from basic human goodness to divine perfection. Through the power and agency of such goodness (*de* is the power of *ren*) the world is transformed into a better place. The sublime, harmonious, balanced, efficacious, and spiritually wholesome relations that we develop, and the wisdom of the ages that we realize in the present, are the means by which *we* can make the way great. In so doing, the human way is an expression of the great way of *tian*: "The Master said: 'Governing with excellence (*de*) can be compared to being the North Star: the North Star dwells in its place, and the multitude of stars pay it tribute'" (2.1).

Ren 仁 and *Ren Dao* 仁道

Ren is the awesome quality of *li* that dignifies human life. The religious character of the *Analects* is captured in seeing humanity as embedded in, and guided by, spiritual forces that issue from the greatest of realities that the ancient Chinese referred to in general terms as *dao*. *Dao* is "the way" of proper relation for all contexts; *dao* orders the hierarchy of relations for heaven, humanity, and earth. Most importantly, the way of humanity is a microcosm of the way of heaven, much as family is a microcosm of humanity.

I have already established that the *ren dao* (or human way) is a way of *li* (ritual) and *ren* (benevolence). But more needs to be said about the religious character of *ren*. First, *ren* is more mysterious than *li*, in being the rarefied, indeed sacred human spirit that *li* must express. *Ren*'s lack of specificity, therefore, should not obscure its importance. A critical and paradoxical point is that despite *ren*'s ephemeral nature, it never stands alone (as purely ephemeral). Indeed, *li* and *ren* can be separated only for the purpose of conceptual analysis, for *ren* is what *li* necessarily expresses. In actuality then, *ren* is an aspect of *li* and *li* is an aspect of *ren*.[5] They are necessarily interrelated aspects of the same larger reality that is irreducible in practice: that of harmonious human activity that, at bottom, is an act of communion.[6]

To understand how *li* and *ren* together make up harmonious, authoritative, even "holy" human activity, we need to remind ourselves what concerned Confucius so much in the *Analects*; what was it that disturbed him so deeply?[7] His world was not following the *ren dao*, but instead was in a state of vast disintegration. It was the time of the warring states, and the question that comes to the fore is how can harmony—the kind of glorious harmony that reigned during China's "golden age"—be restored to the human community in his time. Confucius offered a solution through the concepts of *li* and *ren*; social and spiritual wellbeing were needed to heal the wounds of his day. Western ethics may see these categories (of social and spiritual) as separate, and treat them in turn as separate disciplines altogether, but for Confucius *li* is the social manifestation of *ren*, and *ren* is the spirit of *li*. *Ren* and *li* are unified in practice to make up a way of human flourishing consistent with and descendent from the way of heaven. *Ren* is the integrity, grace, natural order, and beauty of the human spirit—as it derives from its ultimate primal source—that *li* expresses through some normative form or other. *Li* is that form, the socially determined convention that therefore underdetermines the great spirit of humanity, the *ren* that it expresses. It is vital to understand that this is the case even though *li* (to be *li*) must be a true expression of *ren*. Our moral challenge is to learn the *li* so well that these social actions become "actionless," or genuine and fluid expressions of *ren*. *Li* still underdetermines *ren* even in this case because *ren* is a "universal"[8] manifestation of the human spirit that, paradoxically, requires a "particular" (culturally specific) custom, or context, to exist. To the contrary, if *li* does not express *ren* properly, then according to Confucius, it is not really *li*, or not really a *ren* action at all:

> The Master said, High office filled with men of narrow views, ritual preformed without reverence, the forms of mourning observed without grief—these are things I cannot bear to see![9]

> The Master said, "In referring time and again to observing ritual propriety (*li*), how could I just be talking about gifts of jade and silk? And in referring time and again to making music (*yue*), how could I just be talking about bells and drums?" (17.11)

To explain further, *li* and *ren* are not just aspects of a larger reality that I call harmonious human activity; they are aspects of each other as well. One of the most unique qualities of Confucian ethics is that it conceives of moral conduct in a very different way than is traditionally (that is, dualistically) done in the West. *Ren* must be tangibly expressed if it is to exist at all, and so requires a culturally established convention for this purpose. Otherwise people would not be able to understand and respond to each other in a meaningful, cooperative manner. But it is not just that *ren* needs a vehicle for its expression; the expression *is ren* (in some form or another). It is not the case that there is a distinct spirit of communion (*ren*) that finds a tangible ritualized form (*li*), with the two necessarily (inter)depending on one another while still maintaining their practical distinctiveness.[10] To make this point, consider the example of a handshake: a particular normative convention expressing a more universal human greeting. When our attention is drawn to the convention—to what culturally distinguishes us—we speak of *li*. However, when our attention is drawn to the more universal human spirit that the action conveys—the greeting that is a part of all human cultures—we speak of *ren*. In reality, we cannot take the greeting out of the handshake any more than we can communicate a greeting without some culturally relative form. Whether it is a handshake, a bow, a smile, or some other socially prescribed convention, the human spirit it embodies is a cross-cultural or even universal human reality that issues from particular persons, at particular places and times.[11] The practical fact of the matter is that the larger reality in every case requires a distinct and definitive form to be realized. Put another way, in practice *li* and *ren* constitute a *union*, and refer to one dignified action with various features. Consider the simple analogy of a ball that is red, bouncy, round, and so forth; these are all various features of the *same* ball. Similarly, *li* and *ren* can be distinguished for conceptual purposes, but for practical purposes they are really just different aspects of the *ren dao* that is one ultimately unified path of beneficent, human, being.

To restate, *li* and *ren* refer to the same type of action, but are conceptually distinguished in order to bring out different aspects of that action. *Li* is the normative form of moral conduct shaped by culture, and *ren* is the human goodness expressed by that form and simultaneously underdetermined by it. At this point, there are several points that deserve special attention. In his *Confucius: The Secular as Sacred,* Herbert Fingarette addresses one of these points. *Ren* is not an intrapersonal state; it is not an intention or purpose or anything of the subjective kind. *Ren* is an objective part of the action itself in being its conscious aim. I wish to spell this out in a more detailed fashion by the following analysis. As Confucius himself noted, a basic aspect of human activity that distinguishes it from the instinctive actions of "beasts" is that it has objective direction.[12] The intrinsic dignity and superior worth of persons over nonhuman animals derives from just this quality.[13] This superior quality of *ren*, and of human nature more generally, can now be explained in the language of theory that Confucius admittedly did not have at hand, and in terms of this distinction. *Ren* is *intensional* in being the conscious aim that gives a genuinely humane action its objective direction—that makes it a superior human action instead of one lacking the proper spirit. For example, one offers up her hand to have another grasp it and shake, with the conscious aim of *greeting* that person. It need *not* be *intentional* in the sense of having to be deliberated upon, then self-consciously and purposefully chosen, however. To the contrary, the act can be quite spontaneous and unreflective and still be a genuine greeting.[14]

So, *ren* is the spirit of harmonious human activity that should not be confused with any psychological state such as an intention. Consider the difference between intending to, or having the purpose of, committing to another person for life, and actually going through with the actions of getting married, and of maintaining a lifestyle faithful to that commitment. Marriage is an objective, social reality to be distinguished from the intention that psychologically motivates it. We have seen another example so central in the *Analects*—the obligation of performing the ancestral sacrifices, acts that obviously had both profound social and spiritual significance: "The expression 'sacrifice as though present' is taken to mean 'sacrifice to the spirits as though the spirits are present.' But the Master said: 'If I myself do not participate in the sacrifice, it is as though I have not sacrificed at all'" (3.12). Ancestral sacrifice is an act of reverence and a socially prescribed norm, but never just an intention. Even when planned and therefore deliberate, as a social activity, ancestral sacrifice is still an action with a first-order[15] normative aim that has to be realized for the sacrifice to have occurred (as seen in the passage above). Westerners have a hard time grasping this point because their consciousness has been so thoroughly, if not exclusively, internalized by a more dualistic metaphysic.[16] But this viewpoint may well not do justice to the nature of human activity—Confucius offers us a new and different way of thinking about ethics, in any case, by having us think of consciousness as an objective social and spiritual fact (even if this spiritual aspect eludes conclusive identification).[17]

Fingarette's insight included the further point that the "locus of the personal" is a vector between subjects, not inside of them. Henry Rosemont, Jr., has expanded on this point in a variety of places by showing that what it means to be a "person" is also a social reality.[18] We establish ourselves as persons through the meaningful relations we cultivate, for example, a father is a father precisely because he is responsible for children, a teacher is a teacher precisely because he has the responsibility of teaching students, and so forth. *Ren* (like the *li* that communicates it) is established between, not just within, different subjects, making personal development a function of social development. If this is added to my earlier point that *ren* and *li* are different qualities of the same action, what follows is a total elimination of individualistic, self-defining boundaries. Just as a "ball," or a "ritual vessel," is socially constructed or defined according to its function in the community, so is a "person," a "family," a "neighborhood," a "nation." These constructions all are established in accordance with their role in the "larger scheme of things." Consider the following excerpt for the *Great Learning (Da-Xue)* translated by Lydia Gerber:

> Once things are investigated, knowledge will be completed.
> Once knowledge is complete, opinions will be verified.
> Once opinions are verified, minds will be rectified.
> Once minds are rectified, persons will be cultivated.
> Once persons are cultivated, families will be harmonized.
> Once families are harmonized, states will be put in order.
> Once states are in order, there will be peace all under heaven.
> From the emperor to the common people, all must see the cultivation of their own person as the root of all else.
> If roots are in disarray, there will never be healthy branches.[19]

Ren is the unique human quality of harmonizing with, and becoming a necessary part of, greater realities. A family becomes unified when all of its members stand in strong, healthy relation to one another. The person is related to, and to that extent defined by, the family, just as the family is to the larger community.[20] By following the *ren dao* the human community becomes unified, and stands in strong, healthy relation to *tian* and the ancestors who fill it. And to our ancestors we must pay homage in order to maintain our good standing with them and to remain connected to our cultural past. All of these ways of being are essentially co-related, from the nearest relation of parent to child, to the more distant relations of person to ancestor and person to heaven.

Ren dao is embedded in a larger metaphysic that is alluded to in the *Analects*, though it is expressed more fully elsewhere in the ancient Chinese philosophical tradition. In the *Yi Jing*, for example, the general usage of *dao* refers to a way of change (particular to heaven, to earth, and to the humanity that links them). In the *Dao De Jing* of Laozi, we also see that *dao* is the most rarified source and sustainer of all that exists; "It was from the Nameless [*dao*] that Heaven and Earth sprang."[21] For the ancient Chinese, "heaven" or *tian* was conceived as being filled with phenomena that are real and existing: our ancestors who have passed into a more rarified form of being and who are therefore not dead to us. And clearly, we are still obligated to maintain our relations with them if we want things in the human community to be well.[22]

Thus, *dao* can refer to a form of being so rarefied that it escapes ordinary perception and understanding, or to less rarified and more tangible changes that occur in the natural world (i.e., on Earth). *Tian dao* is also a more rarified way than *ren dao*, filled with river ghosts and valley spirits spoken of by the ancients. Heavenly phenomena also seem to have more *de*, or power, so whatever qualities they possessed in this life as human beings, are made more potent by *tian dao*. Much of this is extrapolation when applied to Confucius. What we see in the *Analects* is an utter devotion to ancestors, and a clear sense that ancestral sacrifice is most important because it allows us to maintain our relations with those who have passed before us and still exist in more rarified form. If we fail in our duties to our ancestors, they have great power to create imbalance in our lives. But if we genuinely fulfill our obligations to them with rituals that are proper and reverent, harmony between heaven and earth (cosmic harmony) will be maintained.[23]

> The Master said, "The use of a hemp cap is prescribed in the observance of ritual propriety (*li*) [at the ancestral sacrifice]. Nowadays, that a silk cap is used instead is a matter of frugality. I would follow accepted practice on this. A subject kowtowing on entering the hall is prescribed in the observance of ritual propriety (*li*). Nowadays that one kowtows only after ascending the hall is a matter of hubris. Although it goes contrary to accepted practice, I still kowtow on entering the hall. (9.3)

So to summarize, the spiritual account of Confucianism always sees humanity in relation to the larger scheme of things. Indeed, the world becomes a better place when *ren dao* expresses the harmony and order of *tian dao*, making moral agency and spiritual power inseparable. The "self" or "person" is also established relationally—in connection with family, friends, colleagues, community, nation, and with heaven. *Ren dao* extends from the great harmony or way of heaven to earth insofar as we are noble in spirit (*ren*) and action (*li*). *Ren*, the spirit of harmonious blending, is the greatness that *li* expresses and that makes human life sacred. However, heaven, humanity, and earth all issue from an even "greater" way, one that provides the normative core to all of being, and that at bottom harmonizes, integrates, and sustains it.[24] The distinction between the "secular" and the "sacred" is a false dichotomy for Confucius exactly because the "secular" conventions of ritual express the "sacred" human spirit. This is the way that humanity blends with and becomes an extension of the way of heaven. Spirit and form are inseparable aspects of *dao* on all levels really, as life is inseparable from the roots and branches that carry it to the leaves of a tree.[25]

Another false distinction that can be found in light of this discussion is between the "universal" and the "particular." In a Confucian context, the "universal" spirit of humanity is always expressed in some particular form or another. In fact, I have argued that a Confucian account of "moral" conduct just draws our attention to what in practice is an inseparable union between spirit and form, that is, a larger reality of harmonious human activity that has social and spiritual aspects. On a metaphysical level, with the extension of *dao* through heaven, humanity, and earth, we must see ourselves as being part of a universe that *is* diverse by its very nature. It is all one "way of the world" that has more or less rarified ways of being.[26] All things have a principle or "way" that is different from others only in degree, making the universe co-extensive, mutually defining, and mutually enriching. This is why we can make the way great. As we have seen it conceived from a Confucian standpoint, humanity can enhance (or inhibit) "cosmic" unity and well-being overall. Our power to change things for the better (or worse) creates heavenly phenomena that have even greater power to produce good (or bad) effects for humanity in turn. Moreover, and dangerous as this may be, the emperor was thought to descend from *tian*, to be a divine "prince" or "son" of heaven who sees the all-pervasive unity or wholeness of being, while all of lesser beings see only the differences. He was thought of as being closer to and in more refined alignment with the great way itself, the natural order and harmony pervading the cosmos. Thus, it was thought that he could more effectively bring that order and harmony to the human community through his governance. Through the *li* appropriate to a sage king, the emperor was thought to establish this heavenly mandate on earth without force: "The Master said, 'If anyone could be said to have effected proper order while remaining nonassertive,[27] surely it was Shun. What did he do? He simply assumed an air of deference and faced due south'"[28] (15.5).

Rulers could also lose the "mandate of heaven" by performing poorly or not living up to their natural endowment as descendent of the divine order.[29] Confucius took this quite seriously. His philosophy stressed the importance of moral character because this is how the goodness that extends from *tian* is put into practice on earth. This moral and spiritual uprightness is to be the measure of a person, in this case, a ruler. Many use the same measure today. However, we must be cautious, because, if we take Confucianism seriously, we must not falsely equate good social consequences (at least in terms of how they appear to us) with *ren* action.[30] From a social standpoint, the consequences of a truly *ren* person's actions may be grave, and one may lose fortune, reputation, or even one's life to live up to the name of being *ren*. Confucian philosophy is relevant today because it speaks to the way the world works. We cannot identify or translate the spirit of an action into the cultural convention used to express it (*li*) or the empirical consequences that flow from it, and we cannot determine whether those in positions of authority are *ren* by observing their social and political choices.

The Noble Ruler and War and Peace in the Twenty-first Century

Ren is the real, objective, but nonetheless mysterious quality of moral and spiritual integrity that eludes identification. As discussed above, what makes this Confucian concept of moral integrity unique is that it is not defined by one's intention; *ren* does not require a willful and deliberate aim, but still has conscious direction.[31] Again, *ren* is intensional in having an objective and conscious aim, but this aim is not second-order—it does not need to be reflected upon and then self-consciously chosen. In fact, the Confucian sage is so savvy that such deliberation may mark a lack of moral development, or a lack of connection with the larger, harmonious way of things.

Also, for Confucius all things are folded into the greater divine order and stand in relation to it hierarchically. From the top down, the great way orders all things, and the divine sage, although superior in metaphysical status to those who occupy lesser roles, is still subordinate to *tian dao* in his position as governor (that is, he can lose the mandate of heaven). If this position is well occupied, that is, by a person who is truly *ren* in having taken this all-pervasive "burden"[32] upon himself as his principle and central goal of life, then it will be as if he is "plugged" into the great way and so naturally and spontaneously will see, even foresee, what he needs to do in times of trial and tribulation. This is a first-order conscious activity of directly discerning and then appropriately responding to states of affairs as they come and go. Moreover, in having this rarified ability to discern the nature of things, the Confucian sage cannot be mistaken in his governance and still be considered *ren*. He is always *ren*, never "parting from the way of goodness" (Waley 4.5).

The paradox here is that the divine ruler truly deserves the name, even when social events do not seem to bear this out, and even though *ren* is not based on having good intentions. Divine actions are actually divine, even when their outcomes seem bad to us.[33] The divine ruler's moral integrity establishes the balance needed to bring about a better world by providing the ground for cultural and spiritual development in the human community. Our problem is that we have limited vision, and consequently cannot tell how good a leader is, or was, especially in the short run. We are left trying to look with the hindsight of history to access the greatness of a leader.[34] Time will tell what can be told if we learn the history, but it will still not be enough to determine conclusively that a person is truly *ren*. Even the leaders to whom Confucius refers in the

Analects, such as the great emperors Yao and Shun, were in no small measure the characters of legend and myth. It may also be the case that the farther back in history one goes, the easier it is to overlook the flaws that would lead us to question a leader's integrity.

I would like to offer a contemporary analysis that shows why we can never definitively say that someone is *ren*. A person's overall goodness, which her character possesses and which she offers to the world, remains enough of a mystery to prevent us (humans who are limited in vision) from definitively linking social outcomes that we think have flowed from her actions with her actual integrity. I am using "integrity" in the Confucian sense: *ren* is not an inner psychological state, for a "person" is a *social* or *relational* being who has a more or less rarified moral and spiritual status. *Ren* is that moral-spiritual dimension of our being that connects us with others and the world around us.[35] Paradoxically, there is a connection between historical fact and *ren*, but this connection cannot be fully established for two reasons.

First, all or most historians lack the clarity of the Confucian sage. The degree to which one believes it possible to have perfect clarity into the nature of things will depend on a deeper belief about the perfectibility of human nature itself, which is a different topic and very difficult one. Suffice it to say for now that most people have limited insight into the true nature of things, including into whether another is *ren* or not. This fallibility has led to the cultic deification of some charismatic figures, based on the false view that they are truly great (truly *ren*, divinely inspired, morally and politically upright, etc.)—a human tendency witnessed worldwide. Not surprisingly, these historical figures tend to become the characters of legend and myth. At worse moments in history, some have even persuaded and then exploited others to follow their fraudulent and destructive path. Please understand that my argument is not that being *ren* is impossible. In fact, I think that *ren* actions are quite common, even if *ren* persons are rare. Rather, my argument is that conclusively identifying a *ren* action or a *ren* person as a social or historical fact is impossible. The belief in *ren* is more like an article of "faith"—a testimony to one's belief in the goodness of the human spirit (or human nature).

This leads to the second reason that *ren* cannot be definitively identified, and back to my earlier point that *ren* is underdetermined by its very nature. *Ren* is a mysterious, moral-spiritual quality expressed by some social convention or another.[36] The benevolent activity of *li* has a spirit, or conscious direction, so refined that it has the power to effect extraordinary change in the world. *Ren* is that noble consciousness, but again, it must be communicated by some cultural form (of *li*) or other, but cannot be reduced to, nor identified with, that form which is more particular in nature. Thus, it should come as no surprise that it is much easier to distinguish actions by looking at their more particular empirical aspects than the spiritual agency they have to bring goodness to the world. It should also be clear why Confucius thought of *ren* persons as being so rare, and that most of us cannot live up to the name because we are not able to measure up to the ideal of *ren*. No wonder it is so difficult to speak about *ren*, especially if trying to cite it in practice.[37]

More concretely, a governor with little contest during his time to govern may seem very exemplary, because his society is flourishing. Can we look back in history and say he was truly a man of *ren*? What if this same ruler had been challenged during his charge in a more serious way with events that had more profound social consequences? His moral uprightness and ability to govern may falter, and so he would not be *ren*.[38] Similarly, history may come to embrace a more favorable view of a leader, after the passage of time allows greater hindsight about him and the world in which he lived. In this kind of case, perhaps even long after the fact, we may come to say that his political choices were right after all, or that he was actually a person of great integrity even though seemingly weak or misguided at the time of his governance.

In conclusion, we can much more easily find that a person is not *ren* when we have clear and reasonable evidence that she lacks moral fortitude.[39] Consider some of the examples found in the *Analects* that are not uncommon now, in a more global arena: rulers who are fraudulent, fickle (following what is popular instead of what is in the best interest of state and citizenry), careless, selfish, boastful, egotistical, unintelligent, undisciplined, driven by sexual desire at the expense of what is good for the state or country, or more concerned with personal gain or reputation than with the welfare of people. For Confucius, moral fortitude is inseparable from spiritual fortitude, such that the greatness of a noble ruler affects the world down through the ages, even if we are not able to definitively identify it. What is the measure for such greatness? History can tell only part of the story when it comes to accounting for the human spirit; the rest of the story remains a mystery.

With this said, we can look at the current state of affairs in the world in this early part of the twenty-first century and say we have a mess on our hands.[40] The atrocities perpetuated by human beings upon other human beings in the twentieth century also call into question how much the human race has advanced morally and spiritually through the ages.[41] One guiding principle from the *Analects* is that a great ruler's way is to rule, not to slay. When Confucius was asked, "Suppose I were to slay those who have not the Way in order to help those who have the Way, what do you think of it?" he responded, "You are there to rule, not to slay. If you desire what is good, the people will at once be good" (Waley, 12.19). Presumably, a good ruler would first be a good diplomat, looking for nonviolent ways to resolve even deep conflicts. Today, as globalization continues, I take this state of affairs to require reasonable cooperation with other nations, and with the institutions created to facilitate such cooperation so that largely unilateral and ultimately divisive decisions are not made in error. Of course, human life is not so simple, and it too would be consistent with Confucian principles for a ruler to defend his people against "barbarians," that is, against others who are less enlightened, civilized, or culturally advanced, especially if they pose a direct threat to the security and interests of state and citizenry, or (I think it can be argued) to human interests more generally. In light of this in the year 2007, how might we judge the US invasion and occupation of Iraq by Confucian principles? How might our leadership at this time be judged? This is where the debate begins. As usual, though, history will provide an account of the political choices that we have made, or at least the opportunities that we have had to exert influence on a global level. As subjects of the Great *Dao*, however, this will be only part of the story.

Notes

I would like to heartily thank Henry Rosemont, Jr.—my friend, mentor, former teacher, and present colleague—for his insightful reading and comments on this essay. I would also like to thank David Jones, editor of this volume, for his suggestions and support.

1. Roger T. Ames and Henry Rosemont, Jr., trans., *The Analects of Confucius: A Philosophical Translation* (New York: Ballantine, 1998), 3.11. Hereafter cited in the text. Unless stated otherwise, all quotes from the *Analects* come from this translation.

2. See Herbert Fingarette's *Confucius: The Secular as Sacred* (New York: Harper-Collins, 1972; Prospect Heights, IL: Waveland Press, 1998).

3. The ancients thought that the divine sage descended from heaven (e.g., as in the *Shu Jing*), while Confucius was revolutionary in seeing sagehood as a function of character development.

4. As I have noted elsewhere, the character for *ren* or "benevolence," also translated as "Goodness" by Waley and "authoritative conduct" by Ames and Rosemont, consists of the character for person (*ren*) plus the character for two, signifying *persons* standing in dignified or "sacred" relation. This ability to stand in such sacred relation is what distinguishes persons from "beasts." *Ren* or the (benevolent) spirit of *li* is a conscious (but not self-conscious) act that is good, noble, authoritative, and humane. And it is what makes us distinctively human and uniquely connected to the greater way of heaven itself. See my "The Internet in China: A Confucian Critique," *Religion East and West* 2 (Spring 2002).

5. I have discussed this in various places; see "Internet in China."

6. The word "harmonious" does not quite capture in its fullness the kind of activity *li* and *ren* comprise. The activity is dignified even if markedly simple and spontaneous, noble in its authenticity, wholesome in its connecting people into a larger union of communication, cooperation, or communion. The lofty language should not obscure that this can happen in the most basic of human contexts, for example, parent to child, or friend to friend.

7. See Fingarette's *Confucius*. The *ren* person has developed this noble quality and gains moral authority and power thereby. See Ames and Rosemont, *Analects of Confucius*, for the rendering of *ren* as authoritative conduct.

8. I put this in scare quotes because later I argue that the distinction between the "universal," and the "diverse" or the "particular," is a false dichotomy from the point of view of early Chinese cosmology (or what we in the West would call metaphysics, in assuming a distinction between the physical and the metaphysical). Also, for contemporary purposes and from a cross-cultural perspective we can now make sense of how *ren* can be described as "universal." But Confucius most likely thought of *li* and *ren* as distinctively and even exclusively Chinese, because for the ancients, cross-cultural comparisons were so limited in scope. The tendency would then be not to recognize the *li* of another culture as *li*, or even worse, to see it as "barbarian."

9. *The Analects of Confucius*, trans. Arthur Waley (New York: Macmillan, 1938; repr. Vintage, 1989), 3.26. Hereafter cited in text as Waley.

10. In contrast, Aristotle's distinction between soul and matter in *De Anima* would be such a relation, one that is necessarily interdependent but different in kind. Soul and matter are in no way aspects of one another, while *li* and *ren* are different aspects of the same good action.

11. This universality of *ren* becomes even more relevant to the contemporary world, especially as globalization continues. It is not so clear the Confucius himself thought of *ren* as cross-cultural.

12. The "rectification of names," for instance, rests on the observation that if one does not act like a good person, then one does not deserve to be called by that name. To cite an even more specific application of this same principle, if a man does not act like a father or does not fulfill his basic obligations to his family as is appropriate and "prescribed by *li*," then he is not really a father. The implication has vast importance: a father is a social and not biological reality that has to be realized through proper action. Moreover, the action cannot be accounted for simply in terms of convention, nor is it merely to engage in certain "good" gestures (e.g., see *Analects*, book 2, passages 7 and 8, in both the Waley and the Ames and Rosemont translations). The conscious aim of a father, for instance, is to act responsibly and compassionately. He is to *act* this way, not just intend to do so. But these are things that must be *learned* or culturally transmitted, based on, as well as generating a genuine concern for other people and the world more generally. This is what distinguishes us as human beings.

13. There are many passages in the *Analects* bearing this out (e.g., 18.6 in both Waley, and Ames and Rosemont). Specifically, according to the *Analects*, humans and animals are different in that humans are creatures of culture who can stand in dignified relation to their fellow human beings, while animals are not. We are defined by *ren*, that is, a spirit of beneficence that allows us to care for others and for such noble things as learning for its own sake and the sake of humanity as much or more than we care for ourselves. This is how we are thought to be different from animals driven by the immediate interests of selfish desire only. I try in this essay to theoretically analyze aspects of Confucian philosophy, even though no such analysis appears in the *Analects* itself, to make sense of the kind of reality *ren* is. My view more generally is that Chinese philosophy was pretheoretical during the time of Confucius (circa 500 BCE). Moreover, the distinctions that later philosophy makes never occurred to Confucius and his contemporaries who

genuinely saw, and thought of things more holistically, and therefore, perhaps more realistically in some ways too.

14. In fact, most of our greetings are marked as genuine precisely because they are "actionless" (*wu wei*), or skillful and spontaneous, at the same time without being strained by deliberation or being self-conscious.

15. This is a main theme of this essay: first-order consciousness is simply consciousness directed at, or about, some object or other. Second-order consciousness is one's thinking about one's first-order conscious experience. For example, I can be completely absorbed in a musical performance and enjoying it profusely. This is a first-order experience that involves no awareness that I am having the experience. However, if something makes me self-conscious of the fact that I am listening and enjoying, this is a second-order conscious experience. The same distinction goes for any conscious act. With respect to moral consciousness, if one is *ren*, then one's first-order consciousness is good, moral, or noble. Moreover, benevolent consciousness is directed at the object of moral consideration—the people one wants to help: family, friends, constituents, and so forth. For Confucius and for ancient Chinese philosophers in general, morality was not a second-order business. The West, and some later Chinese philosophy too, turned ethics into a second-order enterprise by applying theoretical principles to objects of moral consideration. Moral consciousness is second-order only when one becomes aware of thinking or feeling morally.

16. This is why I call *ren* the spirit of a good action and not "good will." The concept of "will" naturally leads a typical Westerner to think of an internal psychological state instead of a form of social consciousness.

17. I take this to be the most refreshing aspect of Confucian ethics, and the main thing that makes it a religion or spiritual philosophy: consciousness is not just an internal state but is an objective, external (that is, social and spiritual) reality. *Ren* is more rarified and harder to discern, but its objective direction puts it as much on the outside of a person as on the inside. Consciousness is real, and it is what connects us to everything else (note that this is often a point of mutual fact).

18. For example, see Henry Rosemont's *A Chinese Mirror* (Chicago: Open Court, 1991), especially chap. 3, "Interlude: Modern Western and Ancient Chinese Concepts of the Person."

19. Excerpted from *Reading About the World*, Vol. 1, Harcourt Brace Custom Books, 1999.

20. Critically, a "person" from a Confucian perspective is cultivated by society—family, teachers, friends, neighbors, the rulers who have set the principles to live by, and so forth. (Daoism and Buddhism offer what seems to be a more "individualistic" notion of self-cultivation to China). One is not responsible for independently cultivating oneself in the manner so prevalent in the West, from our philosophies focusing on personal choice and moral individualism to our self-help books in the nonacademic sector. The Confucian person is seen always as a part of a larger whole. The roles we occupy as persons in that larger whole are mutually responsible for creating a genuinely flourishing community.

21. Taken from the first chapter of *The Way and Its Power: Lao Tzu's Tao Te Ching and Its Place in Chinese Thought*, trans. and ed. Arthur Waley (Grove Press, New York, 1958).

22. There are passages in the *Analects* that suggest that Confucius never talked about "prodigies or spirits" (e.g., 7.20 in Waley, or 7.21 in Ames and Rosemont). I take this to be analogous to the passages that say that he never talked about *ren*, which he did many times. I think these passages should be taken to mean that he did not give any specific definition or statement about them that would lead us to think of them as anything less than spiritual and full of power. Clearly, the passages that reference ancestral sacrifice would bear this claim out.

23. This can be as simple as maintaining health and well-being within a family or as complicated as maintaining the well-being of a nation or fostering relations between nations on a global level. Of course, the further implication is that the relation between the past (ancestors), present (humans), and further descendents will be kept in order as well. Heaven and Earth would be in alignment and act in harmonious unison. This is not distinctively Confucian, however. It is very much a part of the belief system that pervades ancient China more generally. Again, see the *Yi Jing* and Laozi's *Dao De Jing*.

24. Laozi expresses this in paradox, as a way so great that it can't be fathomed. He therefore depicts *dao* in terms of "what is not" (heard, seen, and thought), of being "empty," etc.

25. Even on a more mystical reading, such as what can be found in the paradoxical *Dao De Jing*, it is said of *dao* that "latent in it are the forms," "hidden, yet complete," and that "the great form is without shape." Spirit and form still comprise a union, albeit a most rarified one.

26. In fact, *dao* has been translated as One for this reason.

27. As noted by Ames and Rosemont, this is the earliest instance of what is usually taken to be a Daoist idea, "nonassertive action" (*wu wei*). See page 262, note 259.

28. South is the position of the Ruler, and Shun was considered a divine sage.

29. So one is not noble simply be being born into a noble family. His nobility (*ren*) must be actualized. Confucius was revolutionary in stressing the importance of character development over birth line when it came to accounting for *ren* and people with *ren* qualities.

30. Confucius is not just a utilitarian, unless one can include the goodness of the human spirit in the cost benefit analysis. But this is something that cannot be conclusively done and is exactly why we must take the spiritual aspects of Confucian philosophy seriously. For example, see book 4, passages 5 and 6 in both the Waley and the Ames and Rosemont translations.

31. If a person deliberates on an aim, then it has become an explicit object of attention for her, but in the sense that she is aware that she is thinking about matters of great importance, for example, and will be judged by peers in the short run and by history in the long run. In this case, one often becomes more aware of one's *self* in such a position than aware of the substance of the dilemma in question. This is typically not an easy situation to be in since moral dilemmas often offer us no good options, that is, only

ones that are more or less objectionable. The tendency to become concerned about one's self, one's reputation, one's safety, the effect on loved ones, and so forth, cannot help but tempt a person away from doing what morality might require. But a person who is truly *ren* will not waver in her integrity and will aim to benefit those in her charge and not just herself. Moreover, this "benevolent" way of being conscious is *wu wei*, or happens "actionlessly," that is, spontaneously, gracefully, and without being difficult or forced.

32. See *Analects*, in both the Waley and the Ames and Rosemont translation: 4.5; 4.6; 9.10 in Waley and 9.11 in Ames and Rosemont; 15.8 in Waley and 15.9 in Ames and Rosemont.

33. For example, a truly great person may have to lose her life in the pursuit of *ren*. What is more, through her willingness to challenge, and change, the status quo, a troubled period of social instability and unrest may (at least initially) result. Consider the life of Joan of Arc as a possible example.

34. Notice that rather than finding one translation of *ren* that I can consider most apt, I offer various translations that are more or less suitable in bringing out different aspects of this broad concept. I take greatness or even perfection to be degrees of the same principle or concept of *ren*.

35. The moral-spiritual dimension of humanity and its cultural-empirical expressions are linked, but not identifiable. Also, human spirit and culture are linked to produce the overall unity of human evolution that should not be reduced to any single category (such as its scientific aspect).

36. It is appropriate to think of great actions of divine sages as being almost magical for the same reasons. The gesture or ritual (*li*) can bring about even incredible results through spiritual agency (*ren*).

37. See the *Analects*, 14.2 in Waley, and 14.1 in Ames and Rosemont.

38. It is important to say that Confucius sometimes speaks of *ren* as if it were an ideal quality that no one can possess fully, and other times as if all one must do is really *care* about goodness to possess it. I interpret this to mean that morality requires an ideal that a true *ren* person who really cares about goodness will always strive to achieve. It is not as if someone can really believe that he or she has embodied the ideal quality of goodness and be anything less than arrogant. Second, even though *ren* is spoken of as a basic human quality, notice how hard it is really to care about others without cessation. Selfishness or self-interest that takes precedence over what is in the interests of those who stand in relation to us is the rule. *Ren*, or genuine benevolence and concern for others, is the exception to the rule. So being *ren* would be most difficult, even though it is *also* a basic and centrally defining human quality.

39. This counterfactual is meant to support the general view I am here promoting: that spiritual agency is not reducible to empirical, material, or social consequence. Such empirical measures do not adequately capture the spirit of benevolent action, and are typically conceived of as devoid of spiritual or conscious content. My thanks to Richard Schubert for his questions during the June 2004 Society for Asian and Comparative Philosophy that helped me clarify this discussion.

40. As of June of 2004, there were forty-seven wars ongoing according to the United Nations. The UN is one key source that provides information about conflicts going on in the world today. Go to www.un.org for this source.

41. This *is* a question. For example, there have been a numerous discussions, e.g., a 2003 point – counterpoint discussion between Robert Dole and Bill Clinton, that suggest the general state of the world, at least in terms of its political unity, is much better now than it was during the cold war period. The two politicians discussed various issues on the CBS program "60 Minutes" (meeting numerous times between March and May of 2003).

PART 5

MORAL CULTIVATION IN CONFUCIUS

Zhu Xi and the *Lunyu*

12

Kwong-loi Shun

Introduction

Ren (仁) (humaneness, benevolence) is one of the most prominent concepts in the *Lunyu* (*Analects*), and is often used in the text to refer to an all-encompassing ethical ideal. The *Mengzi* (*Mencius*), uses it to refer to one among four ethical attributes *ren*, *yi* (義, righteousness, propriety), *li* (禮, ritual propriety), and *zhi* (智, wisdom). In Han thought, it refers to one among five ethical attributes: *ren*, *yi*, *li*, *zhi*, and *xin* (信, trustworthiness). The neo-Confucian philosopher, Zhu Xi (1130–1200), continues to use *ren* to refer to one among several ethical attributes, along with *yi*, *li*, *zhi*, and sometimes also *xin*. At the same time, he also retains its use to refer to an all-encompassing ethical ideal. How, then, does he reconcile these two ways of using *ren*? Mencius holds the view that *xing* (性, nature) is good, in the sense that human beings share certain ethical predispositions that, when fully developed, lead to the ethical ideal. The idea that *xing* is good is reaffirmed by later Tang thinkers such as Han Yu and Li Ao. Li Ao holds the view that *xing* is perfectly good in its original state, though it can be obscured; the task of self-cultivation is to restore the original state of *xing*. Zhu Xi holds a similar view of *xing*, regarding *ren* as the original state of *xing*. At the same time, he continues to affirm certain observations in the *Lunyu* about the difference between different kinds of people and about how people are close to each other by nature (*xing*). How, then, does he reconcile these ideas with the observations that human beings share an originally good *xing*?

These two questions reflect a task that Zhu Xi often has to confront in developing his own understanding of Confucian thought. He upholds the status of the *Lunyu* as a Confucian canon, and at the same time draws on and synthesizes ideas from later Confucian thinkers and texts. These later ideas, however, often appear at odds with ideas in the *Lunyu*, and he faces the task of having to resolve this apparent conflict. In what follows, I consider how his attempt to resolve the apparent conflict shapes his interpretation of the concept of *ren*, the view of *xing*, and the conception of self-cultivation in the *Lunyu*.

Zhu Xi on *Ren* in the *Lunyu*

To understand Zhu Xi's interpretation of *ren* in the *Lunyu*, let us first consider his own understanding of *ren*. Often, he characterizes *ren* in terms of forming one body (一體, *yi ti*) with all things and in terms of a ceaseless life-giving force (生生, *sheng sheng*).

In early texts, Heaven (天, *tian*), the ideal ruler, and even the ideal person are often described as forming one body with other people and things. The *Liji* (*Book of Rites*) describes the ideal ruler as someone who regards the common people as part of his body,[1] while the *Guanzi* describes him as one who forms one body with the common people.[2] The *Zhuangzi* describes Heaven and Earth (天地, *tian di*) as forming one body, and oneself as being one with the ten thousand things,[3] and similar ideas are found in the *Liezi*.[4] Later Confucian thinkers continue to advocate similar ideas, and characterize *ren* in these terms. Zhang Zai describes the ten thousand things as being one thing and describes *ren* as embodying all affairs just as Heaven embodies all things without omission.[5] The Cheng brothers describe the body of the ten thousand things as my body, and characterize *ren* in terms of forming the same body with all things or regarding the ten thousand things as one body and as part of oneself.[6]

Zhu Xi endorses similar ideas, regarding Heaven and Earth and the ten thousand things as originally forming one body with oneself, and characterizes *ren* in these terms.[7] *Ren*, for him, involves forming one body with all things.[8] Though one may have deviated from this state of existence, the task of self-cultivation is to enlarge one's heart/mind (心, *xin*) until one sees everything as connected to oneself.[9]

Early texts also describe the operation of Heaven (*tian*) in terms of a ceaseless life-giving force. For example, *Xunzi*[10] and *Zhuangzi* (7/1b) refer to Heaven, or to Heaven and Earth (*tian di*), as what gives birth to things. The *Yijing* (*Book of Changes*) highlights the idea of *sheng sheng* (生生), or continuously giving life, and speaks of *sheng* (生, giving life) as the "great virtue" of Heaven and Earth.[11] In later Confucian thought, Zhang Zai describes the *ren* of Heaven and Earth in terms of giving birth to and nourishing the ten thousand things (5/4b), and the Cheng brothers refer to *sheng* (giving life) as the *dao* (道, Way) of Heaven (*Cuiyan* 1/5a). According to the Cheng brothers, the heart/mind of humans should be identical with the heart/mind of Heaven and Earth (*Yishu* 2a/1a), which is to give life to things.[12] This is *ren*, which is compared to the life-giving force of a seed (*Cuiyan* 1/4b, *Yishu* 18/2a). The Cheng brothers even link the idea of ceaselessly giving life to the idea of forming one body with the ten thousand things—in giving life to all things, it is as if all things are part of one's own body (*Yishu* 2a/15b).

Zhu Xi again endorses similar ideas. He describes the heart/mind of Heaven and Earth as one of giving life to things (*Yulei* 4, 1791).[13] This heart/mind of giving life to things is *ren* (*Yulei* 85, 2634),[14] and *ren* is compared to the life-giving force of seeds (*Yulei* 464–5, 2419). And, just like the Cheng brothers, he relates the idea of giving life to all things to the idea of forming one body with Heaven and Earth and with the ten thousand things (*Yulei* 2810).

How, then, does Zhu Xi reconcile the use of *ren* in the *Lunyu* to refer to the ethical ideal in general with its more specific use to refer to one of the four, or five, ethical attributes? Of the five attributes often mentioned together in Han and post-Han thought, *xin* is not highlighted in the *Mengzi*. This absence, according to Zhu Xi, is explained by the fact that *xin* refers to one's truly (實, *shi*) having the other attributes *ren*, *yi*, *li*, and *zhi*, and so is not distinct from these other attributes (*Yulei*, 104, 1296; *Daquan* 74/18b–19b). This is the reason why Mencius speaks of only four sprouts, and does not mention a sprout for *xin* (*Yulei* 255–56).

As for the more specific use of *ren* to refer to one of the four ethical attributes, Zhu Xi reconciles this with the more general use of *ren* by invoking the idea that *ren*, understood in the more general manner, refers to a ceaseless life-giving force. This life-giving force runs through the four more specific attributes in the way that it runs through the life cycle of a plant during the four seasons. It is most conspicuous in the spring when the plant begins to grow, and so the first of the four attributes is also referred to as *ren*. But it also runs though the development of the plant in the summer, autumn, and winter, as the plant flourishes, completes its growth and starts to recede, and then subsides (*Yulei* 109, 112, 2416; *Daquan* 74/18b–19b). Just as Heaven and Earth have this life-giving force as their heart/mind, human beings also have this life-giving force, namely *ren*, as their heart/mind. And just as the life-giving force of Heaven and Earth goes through the four phases described above, *ren* in human beings also manifests itself in the four attributes of *ren*, *yi*, *li*, and *zhi* (*Daquan* 67/20a–21b).

So, while *ren* in the specific sense refers to one of these four attributes, the one that has to do with love (愛, *ai*) and in which this life-giving force is more conspicuous, *ren* in the general sense encompasses all four attributes (*Daquan* 67/13a and see *Yulei* 2634). While Confucius occasionally uses *ren* in the specific sense, as when he associates *ren* with love,[15] he more often uses it in a general sense (*Yulei* 2416). However, according to Zhu Xi, in speaking of *ren* in the general sense, Confucius also is implicitly talking about *ren*, *yi*, *li*, and *zhi*, which it encompasses (*Daquan* 74/18b–19b). Putting this in terms of the distinction between substance (體, *ti*) and function (用, *yong*), *ren* in the general sense refers to the substance of *ren* while *ren*, *yi*, *li*, and *zhi* refer to the different functions or manifestations of this substance. Thus, Zhu Xi reconciles Confucius's and Mencius's different usages of *ren* by observing that Confucius focuses more on substance and Mencius more on function (*Yulei* 115).

Zhu Xi on *Xing* in the *Lunyu*

Zhu Xi expresses his views on *xing* through his conception of the distinction between *li* (理, pattern, principle) and *qi* (氣, material force, vital energies). *Li* (理, pattern, principle) is used verbally in early texts in the sense of "give order to" (*Guanzi* 10/3b).[16] The term is often used in relation to another term *zhi* (治), which means "bring order to" or "be in order" (*Xunzi* 5/7a; *Guanzi* 16/3a;),[17] and is sometimes contrasted with *luan* (亂), or disorder.[18] *Li* (理) pertains to things (*Xunzi* 15/9b; *Huainanzi* 21/3a; *Liji* 11/15a–b; *Zhuangzi* 10/14a), and the ten thousand things differ in *li* (理) (*Hanfeizi* 6/8a–b; *Zhuangzi* 8/30a–b). *Li* (理) is something to be conformed to (*Mozi* 3/3/15–17) or followed (*Guanzi* 13/8b; *Hanfeizi* 20/8a; *Zhuangzi* 10/18a). As such, it is often paired with *dao* (道, Way) (*Hanfeizi* 6/3b; *Zhuangzi* 6/3b, 10/17b) and *yi* (義, propriety) (*Xunzi* 10/8b, 19/3b; *Guanzi* 13/4a; *Mozi* 63/39/33).[19] So, *li* (理) resides in things, is the way things operate, and is also that to which their operation should conform.

This notion of *li* (理) continues to be emphasized by later thinkers. For example, Guo Xiang regards *li* (理) as pertaining to everything, and relates the notion to *fen* (分, proper place), which in turn is related to *xing* in the expression *xing fen* (性分).[20] The difference between these terms is that *li* (理) emphasizes that which resides in a thing and governs its operations, *xing* emphasizes the thing's possession of *li* (理), and *fen* emphasizes the proper place of the thing given its *li* (理). For Guo Xiang, everything has its *xing fen*, and one should follow one's *xing* and live in accordance with one's *fen* (1/1a). By the late Tang and early Song, *xing* has come to be seen by Confucian thinkers as something that is originally good but potentially can be obscured. Li Ao takes this view, regarding *qing* (情, emotions) as that which can potentially obscure *xing* and the task of self-cultivation as one of restoring the original *xing*.[21] Shao Yong emphasizes the idea of responding to things in accordance with their *li* (理), putting this in terms of viewing things with things or with the *li* (理) in things.[22]

Zhu Xi continues to emphasize the notion of *li* (理). *Li* (理) resides in things, and it accounts for the way things are (所以然, *suo yi ran*) (*Yulei* 414)[23] as well as the way things should be (當然, *dang ran*) (*Yulei* 414, 863; *Lunyu Jizhu* 2/11a).[24] Following the Cheng brothers (*Yishu* 22a/11a), he regards *xing* as constituted by *li* (理) (*Yulei* 92–3, 1387, 2427). As *li* resides in human beings and constitutes their *xing*, it takes the form of *ren, yi, li,* and *zhi* (*Yulei* 63–4, 83, 92). Thus, *xing* is identical with *li* (理) and is originally good; that human beings might not be good is due to *qi*.

In early texts, *qi* is viewed as something that fills Heaven and Earth (*Zhuangzi* 3/11a).[25] *Qi* also fills the body of human beings; for example, *qi* grows in a person through the intake of the senses, and the proper balance of *qi* accounts for the proper operation of the senses (*Guoyu* 3/13b). Both Mencius and Xunzi regard properly nourishing *qi* under the guidance of the heart/mind as an important part of self-cultivation (*Mengzi* 2A:2, 6A:8; *Xunzi* 1/8b–9a). By contrast, the *Zhuangzi* advocates emptying the heart/mind so that *qi* in oneself can respond without influence from the heart/mind (*Zhuangzi* 2/7a). Han thinkers such as Dong Zhongshu continue to advocate the proper balance of *qi* in oneself, while Wang Chong speaks of people having different endowments of *qi*.[26] By early Song, Confucian thinkers such as Zhang Zai speak of the purity and impurity of *qi* (2/3b), and refer to *xing* that is constituted by one's endowment of *qi* as material nature (氣質之性, *qi zhi zhi xing*) (2/18b–19a).

Zhu Xi regards things as comprising both *li* (理) and *qi*—*li* (理) does not exist without *qi* and vice versa (*Yulei* 2–3). Thus, though *xing* in a thing is constituted by *li* (理), this *li* (理) must reside in an endowment of *qi* that the thing has (*Yulei* 61, 66). While *xing* in a human being is constituted by *li* (理) and is perfectly good, the endowment of *qi* can be pure or impure (*Yulei* 8, 56, 64–67). This endowment of *qi* accounts for ethical differences between people (*Daquan* 74/20a; *Yulei* 68, 2429). The endowment of *qi* in a person is also part of *xing*, and material nature (氣質之性, *qi zhi zhi xing*) refers to *li* (理) as embedded in *qi* (*Yulei* 67). Accordingly, Zhu Xi endorses the Cheng brothers' distinction between original nature (本然之性, *ben ran zhi xing*) and material nature (*Yulei* 2431); the former is perfectly good while the latter can be not good (*Yulei* 89). This distinction provides the apparatus for resolving the apparent conflict between the Mencian view that *xing* is good and Confucius's observations in the *Lunyu* about different kinds of people and about how people are close to each other by nature (*xing*).

In *Lunyu* 17.2, Confucius observes that people are close to each other by nature (*xing*), though they can come apart through practice. Zhu Xi endorses the Cheng brothers' view that this is an observation about material nature (see Cheng Yi and Cheng Hao *Yishu* 18/19b, 22a/10b–11a). If the passage were about original nature, which is constituted by *li* (理), then people are equally good and it would have been inappropriate to speak of their being close to each other by nature (*Lunyu Jizhu* 9/1b–2a; *Lunyu Huowen* 22/2b–3a; *Yulei* 67–69, 1177–8). While material nature accounts for the ethical differences among people, the differences are not extreme at the start, and it is only through practice that people have come further apart.

There are two passages in the *Lunyu* that describe different kinds of people. In 17.3, Confucius observes that only those of superior intelligence or profound stupidity do not change. And in 16.9, he describes various kinds of people: those who are born knowing, those who know after having learnt, those who learn upon feeling perplexed, and those who do not learn even when perplexed. Again, Zhu Xi takes these passages to describe the difference in the endowment of *qi* among people (*Lunyu Jizhu* 8/12b, 9/2a; *Lunyu Huowen* 21/8a–b). The difference between 17.2 and 17.3 is that 17.2 concerns most people, who are close to each other by nature, while 17.3 describes the extreme cases of those at the highest or lowest end (*Yulei* 1178). Even in the extreme cases, it is not that these people cannot change (*bu ke yi*, 不可移). Those of superior intelligence just follow *li* (理) without effort, and so there is no need to change (*Yulei* 2875). Those of profound stupidity, on the other hand, do not change (不移, *bu yi*) only because they are unwilling to change (不肯移, *bu ken yi*) (*Lunyu Huowen* 22/4a–b; *Yulei* 1178). These are the people described in *Mengzi* 4A:11 as people who do violence to themselves (自暴, *zi bao*) or throw themselves away (自棄, *zi qi*). The former refuse to believe in their ability to change, while the latter refuse to undertake change (*Lunyu Jizhu* 9/2a; cf. Cheng Yi and Cheng Hao *Yishu* 18/17b).

Thus, the distinction between original nature and material nature allows Zhu Xi to explain how people differ despite the fact that they are all fundamentally good. It is the difference in endowment of *qi* that accounts for this difference as described in *Lunyu* 16.9 (*Yulei* 66) and in chapter 20 of *Zhongyong*.[27] According to Zhu Xi, while Confucius is discussing material nature in the passages just considered, he rarely comments on original nature. This accounts for a disciple's observation in passage 5.13 that Confucius rarely discourses on *xing*, which according to Zhu Xi is *xing* as constituted by *li* (理) (*Yulei* 726; *Lunyu Jizhu* 3/5a).

Zhu Xi also uses the distinction between two notions of nature to characterize other views of *xing* found in the history of Chinese thought (*Yulei* 70). According to him, Mencius discusses *xing* as constituted by *li* (理), which is perfectly good.[28] The same is true of the observation in chapter 1 of *Zhongyong* that what is mandated by *tian* is what is meant by *xing* (*Yulei* 67–69; *Zhongyong Huowen* 3/4b–6a). On the other hand, Xunzi's view that *xing* is bad, Yang Xiong's view that *xing* is mixed, and Han Yu's view that there are different grades of *xing*, are all about material nature (*Yulei* 78). This is also true of Gaozi's view that *sheng* (生, life, to give life) is what is meant by *xing*, a view that focuses on what pertains to *qi*, such as consciousness and the operation of the senses (*Yulei* 71, 1375–6, 2425; *Mengzi Jizhu* 6/2a–2b; *Mengzi Huowen* 36/2a). The Cheng brothers comment that to discourse on *xing* without discoursing on *qi* is to lack comprehensiveness, and to do the reverse is to lack understanding. According to Zhu Xi, to talk about original nature without regard to the different endowments of *qi* in which it is embedded is to lose sight of the difference between people and so lacks comprehensiveness. On the other hand, to talk about material nature without regard to the original good nature is to lose sight of the source of goodness, something fundamental to human beings, and so lacks proper understanding (*Yulei* 1387–9, 1493).

Zhu Xi on Self-Cultivation in the *Lunyu*

Zhu Xi's view that human beings are originally good influences his reading of certain important passages in the *Lunyu*. Consider, for example, passage 1.2 in which Youzi observes that being filial to parents and obedient to elders is the basis (本, *ben*) for, depending on interpretation, *ren* or *wei ren* (為仁, practice of *ren*). If human beings are already *ren*, then being filial and obedient cannot be the basis for acquiring *ren*. For this reason, the Cheng brothers think that 1.2 is an observation about the basis for *wei ren*, namely the practice of *ren*, rather than for *ren* (*Waishu* 7/3a; see *Yishu* 11/7a). They take *wei ren* to be about the practice of *ren* (行仁, *xing ren*)—the practice of *ren* starts with being filial to parents and obedient to elders (*Cuiyan* 1/3b; *Yishu* 18/1b). Zhu Xi endorses the Cheng brothers' view (*Lunyu Jizhu* 1/2a; *Lunyu Huowen* 6/10a–b). Not only is being filial toward parents and obedient toward elders not the basis for *ren*, but it is the latter that provides the basis for the former—being filial and obedient is a manifestation of *ren*, which is in one's original nature (*Yulei* 462–3, 471). Because *ren* is first manifested within the family setting in these two qualities, one should start by practicing them so that the manifestation of *ren* will eventually broaden to other areas (*Daquan* 67/12b, 70/20a–20b; *Lunyu Huowen* 6/10a–b).

Thus, Zhu Xi regards 1.2 as about the practice of *ren* rather than about *ren* as such. The same tendency can be seen in the way he interprets many of the passages in the *Lunyu* that apparently are about *ren*—he sees them as primarily about self-cultivation rather than about *ren* itself (*Daquan* 73/46a). And since *ren* is, according to him, used primarily in the *Lunyu* in a general sense that encompasses *ren*, *yi*, *li*, *zhi*, and *xin*, he takes these passages also to be implicitly about these other attributes. For example, 1.2 is also about the basis for the practice of these other attributes. Loving parents (愛親, *ai qin*) is the starting point for the practice of *ren* in the specific sense that focuses on love. Following parents (順親, *shun qin*) and respecting parents (敬親, *jing qin*) are respectively the bases for practicing *yi* and *li* (禮, ritual propriety), while knowing to do these is the basis for practicing *zhi*. One's truly (誠, *cheng*) doing all of the above, on the other hand, is the basis for the practice of *xin* (*Lunyu Huowen* 6/11b).

But if human beings are originally good, why do we need a process that starts with being filial to parents and obedient to elders in the practice of *ren*? According to Zhu Xi, human beings are drawn by external things and can lose what they received from Heaven. As a result, they might no longer be able to practice *ren* without effort, and so have to start with the more intimate relations within the family (*Lunyu Huowen* 6/11a–b). The view that ethical failure is due to the influence of external things can be found in various early texts.

Regarding the heart/mind as the organ that should regulate the senses, the *Mengzi* ascribes ethical failure to the operation of the senses (6A:15). The *Huainanzi* observes how sensory objects can distort the operation of the senses (7/3a) and how it is only under the heart/mind's regulation that the senses attain their proper balance (14/7b). The *Guanzi* observes how external things can distort the operation of the senses (16/3a), which in turn can distort the operation of the heart/mind (13/6a). The "Yueji" chapter of the *Liji* describes how, when human beings come into contact with external things, likes and dislikes arise, and how such likes and dislikes, if not regulated, can do damage to *tian li* (天理) (11/8b–9a). Zhu Xi similarly ascribes ethical failure to distortion that arises when one comes into contact with external things. When the senses come into contact with external things, desires (*yu*, 欲) arise, and desires can become numerous because external things are without limit.[29] When such desires are plenty and unregulated, they become problematic (*Mengzi Jizhu* 7/28a) and one becomes subordinated to external things (*Yulei* 262).

This phenomenon Zhu Xi refers to as *si* (私, private, partial, self-centered), which is contrasted with *gong* (公, public, impartial). *Si*, when used to refer to what has to do with oneself, does not by itself carry any negative connotation. The *Lunyu* speaks of examining Yan Hui's *si* in the sense of examining his "private" life (2.9), and the *Mengzi* talks about attending to one's own (*si*) affairs after having attended to public (*gong*) affairs (3A:3). However, *si* can also be used to describe a focus on oneself that prevents a balanced perspective. For example, *gong yi* (公義), or propriety that is "public" or "objective," is contrasted with resentment that is self-centered (*si*) (*Mozi* 9/8/20), with private (*si*) affairs (*Xunzi* 8/5a) or with selfish (*si*) desires (*Xunzi* 1/13a). Zhu Xi likewise sees *si* as problematic when contrasted with *gong*. *Gong* is compared to being comprehensive, and *si* to forming associations and being swayed by close personal relations (*Lunyu Jizhu* 1/11b; *Yulei* 581). To form one body with the ten thousand things is *gong*, by contrast to *si*, which has to do with focusing on oneself in a way that inappropriately neglects the interest of other people and things (*Yulei* 117; *Daxue Huowen* 1/14a–b). One's being drawn by external things without regulation leads to this inappropriate focus on oneself to the neglect of others.

This understanding of *si* influences Zhu Xi's interpretation of several important passages in the *Lunyu*. In 12.1, in response to a question by Yan Hui about *ren*, Confucius responds that *ren* has to do with overcoming the self and returning to ritual propriety (克己復禮為仁, *ke ji fu li wei ren*). For Zhu Xi, *ke ji* (克己) refers to overcoming or winning over (克, *ke*) the *si* of the self (己, *ji*). *Li* is the embodiment of *tian li* (理), and *fu li* (復禮) refers to one's returning (復, *fu*) to *tian li* (天理) with which one is already endowed and which is embodied in *li* (禮, ritual propriety, rites). *Wei ren* (為仁) refers to the way to practice the *ren* that one has, which involves overcoming one's selfish desires (私欲, *si yu*) thereby returning to *tian li* (天理) (*Lunyu Jizhu* 6/10a; *Yulei* 1045; *Daquan* 67/20a–21b). *Li* (rites) pertains to *li* (pattern, principle), and is contrasted with *ji* (self), which has to do with selfish human desires (*Lunyu Huowen* 17/4a–b); this contrast is the same as that between *gong* (impartial) and *si* (self-centered) (*Lunyu Huowen* 17/2a). While *fu li* (returning to ritual propriety or the rites) follows from *ke ji* (overcoming the self) and is not another process distinct from it (*Yulei* 1060), the two differ in that *ke ji* is a general description of the process while *fu li* emphasizes the details that pertain to daily life (*Yulei* 1046).

In *Lunyu* 12.2, in response to Zhong Gong's query about *ren*, Confucius says: "When traveling behave as if you were receiving an important guest. When employing the services of the common people behave as if you were officiating at an important sacrifice. Do not do to others what you yourself do not desire." Zhu Xi takes the two halves of this remark to be about, respectively, *jing* (敬, reverence, seriousness) and *shu* (恕, reciprocity). *Jing* involves maintaining one's mental focus and attention, while *shu* involves extending oneself to other people and things. By practicing *jing* and *shu*, one eliminates the selfish thoughts (私 意, *si yi*) in oneself—the former prevents selfish thoughts from arising, while the latter prevents them from manifesting themselves in one's interaction with other people and things (*Lunyu Jizhu* 6/11a–b; *Lunyu Huowen* 17/7a). These two aspects of self-cultivation are related—*jing* precedes and is preparation for *shu* (*Yulei* 1071).

The first half of 12.2 describes dealing with others as if receiving an important guest and conducting a sacrifice; the attitude highlighted is directed toward deities and persons, and is often characterized as *jing* in early texts. The *Lunyu*, however, also uses *jing* in relation to affairs (for example, 1.5, 13.19, 15.38, 16.10), and presents it as a way to cultivating oneself (14.42) as well as a quality of the superior person (12.5). Other early texts relate *jing* to *jie* (戒) and to *shen* (慎).[30] Both of these terms have to do with an attitude of being on guard and cautious. So, even in early texts, *jing* has the more general meaning of an attitude of mental focus, caution, and fearfulness. Zhu Xi, following the Cheng brothers (Cheng Yi and Cheng Hao, *Yishu* 15/5a, 15/20a; *Cuiyan* 1/3b), characterizes *jing* as having oneness as master in that the heart/mind is not divided (*Yulei* 2635), so that one is not distracted by other things when focused on one thing (*Yulei* 2464, 2467). *Jing* is an attitude of caution and fearfulness (*Yulei* 2471, 2767) and involves being constantly alert (*Yulei* 494, 2788). This attitude of mental focus prevents selfish thoughts from arising, which Zhu Xi takes to be the point of the first half of the remark from 12.2.

As for the second half, not doing to others what one does not oneself desire is explicitly described as *shu* in 15.24, and *shu* is linked to *zhong* (忠, doing one's best, devotion) in 4.15. Related ideas are also found in 5.12 and 6.30. According to Zhu Xi, *shu* involves extending oneself (推己, *tui ji*) to other things (*Lunyu Jizhu* 8/6a). The extension of oneself to other things flows naturally from the sage without effort, while others in the process of self-cultivation need to exert effort (*Yulei* 672). According to Zhu Xi, the way Zigong describes himself in 5.12 emphasizes the effortlessness of his extending himself to others, and that is the reason why Confucius remarks that what Zigong has described is not yet something Zigong has accomplished. The way it is described in 12.2 and 15.24, on the other hand, uses a term of prohibition *wu* (勿) thereby emphasizing effort (*Lunyu Jizhu* 3/4b–5a; *Yulei* 116, 358; *Lunyu Huowen* 11/30a; see also Cheng Yi and Cheng Hao, *Waishu* 7/3a).[31] Through the exercise of *shu*, one overcomes the *si* (私, self-centeredness) of human desires (*Yulei* 1435–36), and this restores the original state in which one forms one body with all things (*Lunyu Jizhu* 3/18a).

For Zhu Xi, *jing* and *shu* highlighted in 12.2 and *ke ji fu li* (overcoming the self and returning to ritual propriety) referred to in 12.1 mutually support each other (*Yulei* 1072). The former focuses more on positively developing oneself, and the latter on correcting what is problematic (*Yulei* 1073). He compares *jing* (reverence, seriousness) to guarding the doors of one's house and *ke ji* (overcoming the self) to warding off robbers, as well as comparing *jing* to resting to build up strength and *ke ji* to taking medicine to cure one's illness. The former, if successful, preempts the need for the latter; on the other hand, the latter comes into play should the former not do its job (*Yulei* 151). In both cases, the goal is to preempt *si* and to eliminate its presence if it does arise.

On Zhu Xi's interpretation, 12.1 and 12.2 are not directly about *ren*, even though Confucius is responding to queries by disciples about *ren*. He relates *ren* (humanness, benevolence) to *gong* (impartiality), and regards *si* (self-centeredness) as what detracts from *ren* (*Yulei* 2486); the *gong* of *ren* is compared to the way Heaven and Earth nourishes the ten thousand things without discrimination (*Yulei* 2415). However, *ren* is not identical with nor produced by *gong*. Rather, *gong* is identical with the absence of *si* and enables *ren*, which one originally has, to flow and manifest itself (*Yulei* 116–7, 2833–4). Passages 12.1 and 12.2 are not direct characterizations of *ren* but describe the process by which one preempts and eliminate *si*, thereby allowing *ren* to fully manifest itself (*Yulei* 2453). This point he illustrates with the imagery of a mirror. *Ren* is compared to the brightness of the mirror, which is originally there. *Si* is compared to the dust on the mirror, and *gong* to the absence of dust. The absence of dust enables the brightness of the mirror to shine forth, but this brightness is originally there and is not identical with nor produced by the absence of dust (*Yulei* 2454).

This understanding of the contrast between *gong* and *si* in relation to *ren* shapes his interpretation of other passages in the *Lunyu*. Consider as further examples passages 6.3 and 6.7, which comment on Yan Hui; 6.3 describes how Yan Hui does not "transfer his anger." Following the Cheng brothers, Zhu Xi uses the imagery of the mirror to explain this observation. Yan Hui's heart/mind is like a bright mirror. Just as the image in a mirror is a response to things and does not originate from the mirror, Yan Hui's anger is an appropriate response to a situation and does not originate from him. Since his anger is directed only to what appropriately calls for such anger, it would not be transferred inappropriately to other situations (*Lunyu Jizhu* 3/10b; *Yulei* 768, 772). Similarly, he interprets 6.7, which describes how Yan Hui's heart/mind does not deviate from *ren* for three months, in terms of the notion of *si*. Since *ren* already exists, one's heart/mind will deviate from *ren* only as a result of the effect of selfish desires (*si yu*). Just as the absence of dust enables the brightness of the mirror to shine forth, the absence of selfish desires in Yan Hui enables his heart/mind to not deviate from *ren* (*Yulei* 781, 787).

Concluding Remarks

Zhu Xi's interpretation of ideas in the *Lunyu* is shaped by his own version of Confucian thought and by his conception of Confucian orthodoxy as defined by a set of canonical texts. The latter accounts for his explicit attempts to both defend ideas in the *Lunyu* and make these ideas compatible with ideas from other canonical texts such as the *Mengzi*. Our discussion shows how both are at work in his interpretation of ideas in the *Lunyu* related to *ren* (humanness, benevolence), *xing* (nature), and self-cultivation.

In relation to *ren*, he understands *ren* in terms of two related ideas—forming one body with all things, and a ceaseless life-giving force. He also sees the need to reconcile the general use of *ren* in the *Lunyu* with its more specific use to refer to one of several ethical attributes in the *Mengzi* and in later Confucian thought. The view of *ren* as a life-giving force enables him to do this by observing how this life-giving force manifests itself in different ethical attributes, though more visibly in the attribute that focuses on affective concern.

In relation to *xing*, he regards *xing* as constituted by *li* (理) (pattern, principle), while at the same time holding the view that *li* (理) is always embedded in *qi* (material force, vital energies). Thus, there is a distinction between original nature, which refers to *li* (理) as such, and material nature, which refers to *li* (理) as embedded in *qi*. He also sees the need to reconcile Confucius's observations about how people are close to each other by nature and about different kinds of people with the Mencian view that *xing* (nature) is good. He does this by invoking the distinction between original and material nature, claiming that Mencius's view is about original nature while Confucius's view is about material nature.

Zhu Xi's view that the *xing* of human beings is constituted by *li* (理), which is perfectly good, leads him to view ethical failure as a deviation from the original state of human beings. This original state is characterized by *ren*, which involves one's forming one body with all things, and ethical failure is due to one's focusing inappropriately on oneself in a way that separates one from other people and things. This is the phenomenon of *si* (self-centeredness), which is contrasted with *gong* (impartial), a state in which there is no inappropriate focus of this kind. His view that *ren* characterizes the original state of human beings leads him to interpret passages in the *Lunyu* such as 1.2 to be about the practice of *ren* rather than about *ren* itself. And his understanding of *si* also leads him to interpret passages such as 12.1 and 12.2, in which Confucius responds to disciples' queries about *ren*, as observations not about *ren* as such but about the practice of *ren* through the prevention or elimination of *si*. For him, many of the comments on *ren* in the *Lunyu* are not directly about *ren*, but about the practice of *ren*. Even in the case of Yan Hui as depicted in 6.3 and 6.7, he sees these passages as not directly about *ren* in Yan Hui, but about how the absence of *si* enables his *ren* to manifest itself.

Earlier, in discussing Zhu Xi's interpretation of Confucius's and Mencius's different usages of *ren*, we noted that he regards Confucius as focusing more on the substance (*ti*) of *ren* and Mencius more on function (*yong*). Our discussion of Zhu Xi's understanding of self-cultivation in the *Lunyu*, however, also shows that he believes Confucius does not directly talk about the nature of *ren*. That is, while Confucius addresses substance, he focuses on how to enable this substance to manifest itself rather than on the direct characterization of this substance. Zhu Xi's interpretation of passage 5.13 reflects this point by saying that Confucius rarely discusses original nature—Confucius's focus is on material nature, namely *li* (理, pattern, principle) as embedded in the endowment of *qi*. So, Confucius's concern is the practical manifestation of *ren*, and this accounts for his focusing on the practice of *ren* rather than on the nature of *ren* itself when responding to disciples' queries about *ren*. According to Zhu Xi, it is exactly the contribution of the *Mengzi* and the *Zhongyong* that they take the Confucian discourse beyond this practical focus to a more explicit discussion of the fundamental characteristics of the original nature of human beings.

Notes

Materials in this paper are based on research related to a book in progress, *The Development of Confucian-Mencian Thought: Zhu Xi, Wang Yangming and Dai Zhen*, sequel to *Mencius and Early Chinese Thought* (Stanford University Press, 1997).

1. *Liji* (*Sibubeiyao* edition), 17/16a. After first mention, page references to primary sources will be cited in the text.

2. *Guanzi* (*Sibubeiyao* edition), 10/18a.

3. *Zhuangzi* (*Sibubeiyao* edition), 1/18a, 10/21a.

4. *Liezi* (*Sibubeiyao* edition), 8/14b.

5. Zhang Zai, *Zhangzi Quanshu* (*Sibubeiyao* edition), 2/5a, 2/11b.

6. Cheng Yi and Cheng Hao, *Ercheng Cuiyan* (*Cuiyan*), in *Ercheng Quanshu* (*Sibubeiyao* edition), 1/10b–11a; Cheng Yi and Cheng Hao, *Henan Chengshi Yishu* (*Yishu*), in *Ercheng Quanshu* (*Sibubeiyao* edition), 2a/3a–3b; Cheng and Cheng, *Cuiyan* 1/7b.

7. Zhu Xi, *Zhongyong Zhangju* (Sikuquanshu edition), 2b; Zhu Xi, *Lunyu Jizhu* (*Sikuquanshu* edition), 3/18a–b.

8. Zhu Xi, commentary on Zhang Zai's *Ximing* in *Zhangzi Quanshu* (*Sibubeiyao* edition), 1/9b–10a.

9. Zhu Xi, *Zhuzi Yulei* (*Yulei*) (Zhonghua Shuju, 1986), 2518–19.

10. *Xunzi* (*Sibubeiyao* edition), 5/7a, 6/6a, 13/2b.

11. *Yijing*, in *Zhouyi Wang-Han Zhu* (*Sibubeiyao* edition), 7/4a, 8/1b.

12. Cheng Yi and Cheng Hao, *Henan Chengshi Waishu* (*Waishu*), in *Ercheng Quanshu* (*Sibubeiyao* edition), 3/1a.

13. Also Zhu Xi, *Zhouyi Benyi*, 2nd ed. (Tianjinshi Gujishudian, 1988), 142.

14. Also Zhu Xi, *Zhuzi Daquan* (*Daquan*) (*Sibubeiyao* edition), 67/20a–21b.

15. *Lunyu*, following the numbering of passages in Yang Bojun, *Lunyu Yizhu*, 2nd ed. (Zhonghua Shuju, 1980), 12.22.

16. Also *Huainanzi* (*Sibubeiyao* edition), 21/8a.

17. Also *Hanfeizi* (*Sibubeiyao* edition), 6/6b, and *Xiaojing*, in *Xiaojing Zhushu* (*Sibubeiyao* edition), 7/1b.

18. *Mozi*, following the reference system in *A Concordance to Mo Tzu* in the Harvard-Yenching Institute Sinological Index Series, 2nd ed. (1961), 36/25/14.

19. Also *Mengzi*, following the numbering of passages, with book numbers 1A–7B substituted for 1–14, in Yang Bojun, *Mengzi Yizhu*, 2nd ed. (Zhunghua Shuju, 1984), 6A:7; and *Lushichunqiu*, in Xu Weiyu, *Lushichunqiu Jishi*, 4th ed. (Taipei: Shijie Shuju, 1988), 18/19b.

20. Guo Xiang, *Zhuangzi Zhu*, in *Zhuangzi* (*Sibubeiyao* edition), 1/19a, 1/2a, 1/1a, 3/16a.

21. Li Ao, *Liwengong Ji* (*Sikuquanshu* edition), 2/1a–b, 2/3a–3b.

22. Shao Yong, *Huangji Jingshishu* (*Sibubeiyao* edition), 6/26b, 6/26a.

23. Also Zhu Xi, *Mengzi Jizhu* (*Sikuquanshu* edition), 2/6a.

24. Also Zhu Xi, *Lunyu Huowen* (*Sikuquanshu* edition), 9/14b.

25. Also *Guoyu* (*Sibubeiyao* edition), 1/10a.

26. Dong Zhongshu, *Chunqiufanlu* (*Sibubeiyao* edition), 10/3b; Wang Chong, *Lunheng* (*Sibubeiyao* edition), 2/14a–b, 18/4a.

27. Zhu Xi, *Zhongyong Huowen* (*Sikuquanshu* edition), 4/25b–26b.

28. Zhu Xi, *Mengzi Huowen* (*Sikuquanshu* edition), 30/1a.

29. Zhu Xi, *Daxue Huowen* (*Sikuquanshu* edition), 1/5a–b.

30. For example, *Zuozhuan*, in *Chunqiu Zuoshizhuan Dushijijie* (*Sibubeiyao* edition), 16/23a (relating *jing* to *jie*) and 19/23b, citing *Shijing* (relating *jing* to *shen*).

31. Also Cheng Yi and Cheng Hao, *Chengshi Jingshuo* (*Jingshuo*). In *Ercheng Quanshu* (*Sibubeiyao* edition), 6/5a.

Analects 13.3 and the Doctrine of "Correcting Names"

13

Hui-chieh Loy

Although the doctrine of "correcting names" (*zhengming* 正名) mentioned in *Analects* 13.3 is generally considered a cornerstone of classical Confucianism, its precise content continues to elude us.[1] This state of affairs is hardly unique to *zhengming*: almost every significant concept in the *Analects* has been the subject of scholarly dispute, be it *ren* 仁, *yi* 義, or *li* 禮. Unlike these other categories, however, the very phrase *zhengming* appears in exactly only one passage of the *Analects*: 13.3. Though this last fact does not rule out the possibility that something like a notion of *zhengming* can also be found in other parts of the *Analects*, it does imply that any account of the doctrine will depend critically upon the interpretation of a *single* passage in the *Analects*.

For instance, the Master might, as some claim, say inconsistent things with regards to *ren*. But at least one might presume that he is speaking about the same (possibly vague) concept. By collating all that is said concerning *ren* in the *Analects* (taking into account their diverse contexts), it seems possible to reconstruct an overall account of *ren*. It appears also possible to reconstruct, with the same kind of procedures, the interrelations between the various concepts *ren*, *yi*, *li*, and so on. But there will be no simple way to apply the above procedures in the case of *zhengming*, since the phrase does not recur outside 13.3. Consequently, in order to bring together two or more passages in any account of *zhengming*, one will presumably have to first show how each of the cited passages is about *zhengming*. At the very least, one will have to show that these passages are about the same thing as what 13.3 is about. And in order for that to happen, one must first have an interpretation of 13.3.

This essay aims to furnish one necessary component to a reconstruction of the *zhengming* doctrine by an analysis of 13.3. The purpose is to discover what the Master might be driving at in saying that he would first "correct names" should he take up office in the state of Wey 衛, and his reasons for so speaking. To anticipate: it appears that whatever the precise mechanics of the Master's *zhengming* proposal, it is ultimately concerned with people's use of language, quite probably that of the political elite in particular. It seems that there are forms of incorrect naming and speaking that can lead to sociopolitical disorder, such that any attempt to reinstate order in the sociopolitical realm must begin with the imposition of order on the linguistic realm.

Historical Context and Interpretative Pitfalls

Let me begin by quoting 13.3, dividing it into segments following the traditional *zhangju* 章句 organization of the text so as to facilitate later discussions:

[1] 子路曰：「衛君待子而為政，子將奚先？」

[2] 子曰：「必也正名乎！」

[3] 子路曰：「有是哉？子之迂也！奚其正？」

[4] 子曰：「野哉，由也！君子於其所不知，蓋闕如也。」

[5] 「名不正則言不順；言不順則事不成；事不成則禮樂不興；禮樂不興則刑罰不中；刑罰不中則民無所措手足。」

[6] 「故君子名之必可言也，言之必可行也。君子於其言，無所苟而已矣！」

[1] Zilu said, "The prince of Wey is waiting to leave the government of his state to you, what are you going to put first?"

[2] The Master said, "That must be to correct names (*zhengming*)."[2]

[3] Zilu said, "Is that right? Surely you are far [off the mark]. Why consider correcting [names] at all?"

[4] The Master said, "You! How boorish! The gentleman (*junzi*), when faced with something he does not know, is wont to keep his peace.

[5] "When names (*ming*) are not correct (*buzheng*) then speech (*yan*) will not accord (*bushun*); when speech does not accord then affairs will not be effected; when affairs are not effected then the rites and music will not flourish; when the rites and music do not flourish then punishment will not hit the mark; when punishment does not hit the mark then the people will not know where to place hand or foot.

[6] "Hence what the gentleman (*junzi*) names (*ming*) surely can be put into speech (*yan*), what he puts into speech (*yan*) surely can be put into action (*xing*). The gentleman with regard to his speech (*yan*), is careless (*gou*) about nothing."

The conversation between the Master and Zilu appears to be presented as taking place within some *particular*, though not fully specified, context. Throughout the *Analects*, we see the Master speaking to a variety of disciples, political leaders, and princes in a diversity of contexts, each occasion presenting its situational demands upon his pedagogical ability (11.22), patriotic expectations (7.31), and even his humor (17.4). What about 13.3? Two points: first, the Master speaks here to Zilu, a particular character, rather than to some unnamed audience. Second, the disciple's initial question, which sets the theme if not the final direction of the discussion, appears to have very specific points of reference: a particular prince—of Wey—desires your services; what would you, Master, put first if you should take up his offer?[3] The entire conversation is presented as taking place within a fairly specific set of circumstances. That is, some occasion where it makes sense for the disciple to ask such a question.

Unfortunately, the compilers of the *Analects* did not leave us with enough information to further specify this context. That, however, does not rule out the possibility that the passage was composed with some specific context in mind, the details being well known to an earlier audience though obscure to present day scholars. Two questions thus arise: first, whether this lack of direct information can be remedied from sources outside the *Analects*; and second, the extent to which extra-*Analects* information should be allowed to influence the interpretation of 13.3 (and in turn influence any account of *zhengming* in the *Analects*).

With regard to the first question: the majority opinion in traditional scholarship connects 13.3 with the following passage in the *Shiji* 史記 biography of Confucius:[4]

> At that time, the father of the prince Zhe 輒 of Wey was unable to get himself installed [i.e., as the ruler], and thus remained abroad. The feudal princes repeatedly expressed the view that Zhe should yield the throne to his father. Many of Confucius's disciples were serving in Wey and the prince of Wey desired to obtain Confucius for his government. (*SJ* 47/1933–34)

This is immediately followed by an almost verbatim reproduction of *Analects* 13.3,[5] thus suggesting a background to the conversation between the Master and Zilu. By drawing further from the *Shiji* account of the House of Wey (*SJ* 37/1598–99) and the *Zuozhuan* 左傳,[6] roughly the following account can be reconstructed:

> Trouble came to the state of Wey in year 39 of Duke Ling's 衛靈公 reign (496 BCE) when crown prince Kuai Kui 蒯瞶, being at odds with the Duke's principal wife Nanzi 南子, plotted to have her killed.[7] The hired help bungled the attempt and Kuai Kui had to flee his father's anger. He was harbored by the powerful House Zhao 趙 of the state of Jin 晉, and later installed by them in the border city of Qi 戚 (cf. *Zuo*, Ai 2.2). Duke Ling died three years later (493 BCE), and after some confusion over the issue of succession, the people of Wey enthroned Zhe 輒, Kuai Kui's son (Duke Chu 衛出公). The stage was thus set for a showdown between father and son when in the same year, Kuai Kui attempted a comeback with the armed assistance of the Zhao, only to be repulsed. In the following spring, Zhe, with the help of his own great power backer (the state of Qi 齊) laid siege to his father. (cf. *Zuo*, Ai 3.1)[8]

If Sima Qian is right, the Master would have been either in or within the vicinity of Wey during the whole period and thus at least a partial witness to the ensuing family melodrama (cf. *SJ* 47/1933–34). Sometime around the death of Duke Ling he left Wey, returning about 489 BCE when Zhe would have been on the throne for four years. This was the situation indicated in the *Shiji* quotation above, setting the immediate context for the conversation between the Master and Zilu. Perhaps more importantly, the sources also tell us that Zilu was at that time an employee of Zhe and will one day die fighting against Kuai Kui on behalf of his lord (*Zuo*, Ai 15.5; *SJ* 37/1599–1601).[9]

I suppose it makes sense to accept some such account on the authority of Sima Qian (and the veracity of the *Zuozhuan* account) as the assumed background to *Analects* 13.3. Sima Qian may have had access to traditions no longer extant that would justify such a reading. More importantly, as we shall see later, many details of 13.3 do make more sense when seen against these larger events and even the later career of Zilu. It is another question, however, as to what extent this background information should be allowed to influence an interpretation of 13.3.

Given the historical context, it is probable that the Master, in calling for a correcting of *ming*, has "the station or social role" (*mingfen* 名份) of "father" and "son" in mind. He is, after all, talking about the struggle between the father and son: Zhe and Kuai Kui. From here, one might be tempted to make the further inferences that (1) *ming* in 13.3 *signifies* "station or social role" in 13.3; and that (2) "the primary arena for the application of Confucius' doctrine of 'correction of names' was socio-political rank and class differentiation; other names [i.e., that do not refer to station or social roles] were peripheral to this central concern."[10] This, however, will not do.

The first inference requires that we equate the *referent* of a segment of speech—that is, whatever it is in the world that the segment of speech picks out or is about—with its *signification* or *meaning*. This is often not possible. Suppose I speak of an urgent need to change all the furniture in a particular room, and since it so happens that there are only chairs in that room, then it might be said that what I am *referring* to are the chairs when I say "let's change the furniture." But that does not entail that "furniture" and "chairs" are equivalent in meaning, or that what I said is simply equivalent to "let's change the *chairs*." I might, but more evidence is needed—for instance, if the collation of a sufficient sample of my idiolect reveals that the only things I ever refer to by "furniture" are chairs then perhaps a case can be made for construing my use of the word within the more (idiosyncratically) restricted sense.[11]

If the meaning of the *ming* in 13.3 cannot be plausibly restricted to "station or social role," neither can the "primary arena" of any purported doctrine of *zhengming* be restricted to "socio-political rank and class differentiation"— at least not on the basis of 13.3 alone. But even if *ming* means "station or social role" in 13.3, can we infer that the primary concern of the doctrine of *zhengming* is restricted to sociopolitical rank and class differentiation? Two assumptions are needed for such a move: (a) that there exists a certain unified doctrine under the label *zhengming*; and (b) that the discovery of the very signification of the phrase *zhengming* itself unpacks for us the contents of this doctrine.

(a) The first assumption presupposes that the Master uses the phrase *zhengming* in 13.3 either as a technical or quasi-technical term, or a heading under which he groups a specific set of doctrines.[12] But the impression of the passage points in an entirely opposite direction: Zilu asks the Master as to his plans should he take up Zhe's offer, and the Master says that he will first put the names right—whatever that means—and not that he will engage some definite program consistently called by the technical appellation "the correcting of names." This does not mean that the *Analects* does not contain any well-defined teaching about the use of names and speaking in general, on the one hand, and governance and sociopolitical order, on the other. It does mean that any such doctrine need not be somehow referred to by the phrase *zhengming*, and may very well be taught through larger units of discourse, with or without the phrase.

(b) As for the second assumption: suppose there is such as a thing as a *zhengming* doctrine in the *Analects*. Even with this supposition, it is still not obvious that once one knows what the Master *means* when he says "it must be to correct names [in Wey]," much less what he is *referring* to by *ming*, one also possesses an interpretation of "the socio-political import of Confucius' correction of names programme."[13] One will at best have an interpretation of the Master's answer to Zilu. That, surely, will be important—even necessary—in any reconstruction of an *Analects* teaching on *zhengming*; but it is surely not equivalent to an account of the larger teaching.

The above is not meant to imply that the reconstruction of the historical background is completely useless. It is a reminder that interpreting a passage is not the same as recovering its historical background or *Sitz im Leben* ("setting in life"), even if these are necessary for the first. At some point, the mundane task of closely reading 13.3 cannot be avoided.

Reading the Dialogue of *Analects* 13.3

The passage opens with a question from Zilu [1],[14] eliciting an answer from the Master, in fact his *thesis* [2], in turn provoking a *challenge* from the disciple that the thesis be defended [3]. This is followed by a long discourse of the Master [4]–[6].

As already mentioned, Zilu's question has very specific, rather than general, points of reference. The answer it seeks is circumscribed: not politics or governance in general (cf. 15.11), but the particular policy for a particular state in a particular point in time. Some scholars trace Zilu's dissatisfaction with the Master (evidenced in [3]) to the supposed newness of the Master's doctrine, others to the disciple's "lack of sympathy with the Master's philosophical insights."[15] But the disciple is completely in character here. His initial question concerns his acknowledged sphere of expertise—practical politics (cf. 5.8, 6.8, 11.3, 11.24, 13.1, 13.28, 14.22). His forthrightness in criticizing the Master is also attested in other parts of the *Analects* (e.g., 6.26, 17.5, 17.7), most examples of which concern some practical political proposal of the Master. The drift of the criticism here is in keeping with his practical man's distrust of theory (cf. 11.25). Perhaps the Master's reply sounds too impractical to him.[16] Furthermore, by perusing the historical background, we are now aware of Zilu's commitment to the cause of Prince Zhe against Kuai Kui. In this light, Zilu's criticism of the Master becomes readily understood as the indignation of a fervent supporter and employee of Zhe.[17] Perhaps Zilu detects in the Master's initial reply a hint of reproach towards his lord, and by implication towards the disciple as well. It is thus improbable that Zilu replies as he does because the Master is teaching a new doctrine, or because he simply does not understand. In that case the intuitive thing to do is to ask for clarification (cf. 13.1, 14.42). That Zilu should criticize the Master's reply implies that he understands, or thinks he understands enough of what the Master is proposing—enough for him to take offence.[18]

The Master on his part is not slow in rebuking Zilu (cf. 9.12, 11.15, 25). His criticism amounts to the accusation that Zilu does not know what he is talking about, a criticism that, as we will soon see, has much to do with his *zhengming* thesis. His *main argument* justifying the earlier reply to Zilu begins with five interconnected conditional statements [5]. As far as the logical import of the long sentence is concerned, what is said in [5] can be concatenated as "if names are not correct, then the people will not know where to place hand or foot."[19] On one level at least, this abbreviation summarizes more or less the *logical* contribution of the Master's argument.

Where one might expect the conclusion "hence the need to correct names," bringing closure to the dialogue, the Master concludes with [6], which comes in two parts. First, "hence what the gentleman names surely can be put into speech, what he puts into speech surely can be done." This is supposed to follow from segment [5]: "hence" (*gu* 故). This obscure sentence is not left unexplained because the Master restates it immediately, "the gentleman with regard to his speech is careless about nothing (*wu suo gou* 無所苟)."[20] That is, the gentleman is enjoined to be very careful with his words. This, together with [4]: "the gentleman, when faced with something he does not know, is wont to keep his peace," is surely meant to criticize Zilu's own rebuke to his initial response. It seems that being careful with one's words involves knowing when to remain silent.

If the Master meant to answer Zilu, then the long discourse in [5]–[6] or some part of it must contain a plausible *reason* for the assertion of his thesis in [2]. The most plausible reconstruction appears to be something like the following:

Premise: the state of Wey is in disorder (assumed).
Premise: that names be correct is a necessary condition for order (from [5]).
Premise: we desire to reinstate order (assumed).
Conclusion: we ought to correct the names in Wey (thesis [2]; given suitable background assumptions and plausible rules of practical reasoning).

That the Master should speak of an urgent need *to correct* names already suggests that names are not correct in the state of Wey (whatever that may mean).[21] Perusing again the reconstructed historical background, by then father and son had already come to blows, and worse would follow.[22] The Master's argument thus hints at some kind of connection, causal or otherwise, between the present disorder in the sociopolitical realm and a disorder in the realm of names spelt out as a *necessary* condition: if names are not correct then there will not be order.[23] He accordingly proposes that any attempt to remedy the situation in Wey must begin with a correcting of names. We should note that Zilu does not dispute the implicit assumption that Wey is in disorder even though he could be taken as disputing the Master's diagnosis and prescription. This could very well be the reason why he began the conversation with the Master in the first place—to sound him out as to a possible solution.

But surely more than this straightforward logic is at work in the Master's reply. I think his answer indicates something of his estimate of the kinds of appeals that will move a man like Zilu, and also the extent to which he is willing to engage purely pragmatic considerations in his politics and pedagogy. Note that even the rites end up being instrument rather than end-goal: "when the rites and music do not flourish then punishment will not hit the mark." Given the ritely conception of government in the *Analects* (2.3), one would have thought that even if the Master terminated the series at "the rites and music will not flourish," it would have been sufficient for the argument. But he goes on to add "punishment will not hit the mark," and "the people will not know where to place hand or foot." The subtext here appears to be that if the prospect of the rites and music not flourishing does not quite move a Zilu (cf. 11.26), these surely do. It is thus as if the Master does not expect to convince Zilu by an appeal to any substantive conception of "good society." Rather, he argues for his proposal on grounds of avoiding evil consequences. The bottom line is lowly stated in terms of the people not knowing where to place hand or foot, and not, for instance, that the Way does not prevail in Wey. Perhaps in the Master's estimation, Zilu's political ideal amounts to no more than that people know where to place hand and foot. Is this perhaps why the Master thinks that Zilu is eminently suited to be the man in charge of military taxation even in a large country "of a thousand chariots," but knows not if he is *ren* (5.8)? I am not saying that the Master is not concerned about punishment not hitting the mark, or the common folk not knowing where to place hand or foot; rather, the point is that when compared with "the rites and music flourishing," these do not sound particularly elevated as the ultimate goals of political life conceived along Confucian lines.

Actually, the rhetoric here may be even more complicated than that. By formulating his argument the way he does, one wonders if the Master deliberately has left the senses both of "punishment hitting the mark" and "the people knowing where to place hand or foot" somewhat ambiguous. Elsewhere, it is hinted that sociopolitical order can be achieved either with or without the *li*, though two fundamentally different kinds of *order* result (2.3). In other words, the notions of "punishment hitting the mark" and "the people knowing where to place hand or foot" are ambiguous between a reading which presupposes a ritely standard of what it means for punishment to hit the mark or for the people to know where to place hand or foot; and a reading which makes no such presupposition. Even Mozi 墨子 or Hanfeizi 韓非子, no lovers of the rites, can in principle have their own conceptions of "punishment hitting the mark" and "the people knowing where to place hand or foot" or in short, of "sociopolitical order." As such, the very notion that "if names are not correct . . . then there will be sociopolitical disorder" is open to a non-Confucian reading, the way "if names are not correct . . . then the rites and music will not flourish" is not. From a ritely point of view, so-called order without the *li* is not even order at all, strictly speaking.

So it is not completely true that some indifferent conception of order has as its necessary condition the flourishing of the rites, and beyond that, a correct state of names. Rather, it is order of a certain sort—ritely order; and one wonders if Zilu's commitment to such an understanding of order is less than complete (11.26). By leaving his formulation somewhat ambiguous between the two kinds of order, one is kept guessing as to which the Master is talking about. Is the Master in fact counting on just this confusion in Zilu's own mind between these two notions of "sociopolitical order" in his attempt to first win Zilu's agreement, but also to potentially educate him? But I digress.

What about the conclusion that the Master himself draws in [6]: that "the gentleman with regard to his speech is careless about nothing"? Given that the Master meant to answer Zilu's objection in [3], the final conclusion in [6] must bear some connection with the thesis [2], that it is urgent to correct names. But [6] does not seem to be a restatement of the thesis. Rather, it seems to describe the ideal situation that must obtain in order that names can be correct. That is, it describes what the *junzi* 君子 who fears the consequences mentioned in [5] must *practice* in order that they do not happen.[24] The complete sequence of thought is thus:

Premise: the state of Wey is in disorder (assumed).
Premise: that names be correct is a necessary condition for order (from [5]).
Premise: we desire to reinstate order (assumed).
Conclusion: we ought to correct the names in Wey (thesis [2]; given suitable background assumptions and plausible rules of practical reasoning).
Conclusion 2: the gentleman with regard to his speech ought to be careless about nothing (from [6]; practical implication inferred).

And so the argument ends with the implication that if you, Zilu, are interested, on the one hand, in becoming a *junzi* (cf. 14.42), and on the other hand, in reinstating order in Wey, this is precisely what you (and presumably others in your position as well) must do: be careful with what you say. But what could the Master possibly be talking about by his implying that "names are not correct" in the state of Wey? And consequently, what does he mean by the need to "correct names" in the same state?

The Sense of *Zheng* and *Ming*

In the *Analects*, *zheng* (正) often takes on the (verbal) sense of "to correct" or "rectify" (verbal; cf. 1.14, 9.15, 10.18, 13.13[2], 20.2), which is the sense at work here in the Master's reply. The word can be used adjectivally: "correct," "right," "proper" (cf. 8.4, 10.8, 12, 13.3[5], 14.15), or adverbially: "correctly," "properly," (10.26) or even as "squarely" as in "stand facing squarely the wall" (17.10, also cf. 15.5; 7.34, "precisely"). The usage suggests the notion of setting something to "coincide with an implicit standard."[25] This is explicit in the statement that "the gentleman . . . goes to men who possess the way and *zheng* [himself]" (1.14).[26] It would have been easy for *zheng* to get from the above basic meaning to "morally correct," or "moral rectitude" (cf. 13.6).[27]

There are primarily three senses to *ming* under consideration. The most common usage is (1) "name" (both nominal and verbal). Like the English word, it can refer to the names of a fairly indiscriminate variety of things: "the *ming* of birds, beasts, plants and trees" (17.9),[28] including persons (*MZ* 7B.36; *Zuo*, Yin 7.2). Verbally, it can mean: "to give a name to something" (8.19; *Zuo*, Yin 1.3), or "to call someone or something by his or its name" (ibid., Yin 1.5). Sometimes, the "name" under consideration is not designatory but evaluative, that is, "reputation" (4.5, 9.2, 15.20; cf. *MZ* 6B.6, 7B.11), including a posthumous one (*MZ* 4A.2). To have a "reputation" is literally to "have a *ming*." The *ming* in 8.19 (cf. *MZ* 3A.4)—"[the sage king Yao was] so boundless! The people could not *ming* it"[29]—should be seen as a verbal counterpart to this sense of *ming* as "reputation."[30] The designatory and evaluative uses of *ming* as "name" are united by their close connection with the idea of *something said*, or *the act of speaking*. The remaining two senses of *ming* are: (2) the titles of the feudal lords or ministers, or more broadly a person's place or station in the social order (nominal; *Zuo*, Zhao 32.4; Cheng 2.2); and (3) written words (nominal).[31]

Present opinions on the question "what does it mean to *zhengming*?" fall into a few distinct though predictable groupings.[32] These can be categorized according to how they answer two questions: first, what is the *ming* in *zhengming*? Is it the names we use in speech (sense 1); and if so, whether it refers indiscriminately to the names of all kinds of entities or only to some. Second, what manner of "correcting" is involved in correcting names? Is it a correcting of what people say (i.e., the way they use names), or is it really about their behavior? There are basically three common positions:

Position (A): names are not correct when people *call* things or affairs by the wrong names. In other words, *ming* is taken according to sense (1) above. The thought involved is some variety of what Joseph Needham calls "the determination to call a spade a spade, no matter what powerful influences might be desirous of having it called something else."[33] For instance, the thought might be something like: the prince Zhe of Wey, who usurped his father's throne and as such does not behave as a son should, is incorrectly called a "son." To correct names is thus to correct something spoken. Zhe should not be called "son" whatever he should be called. But how does correcting the way we speak connect with sociopolitical and ritual order? Some understand the possibility of the proposal in terms of the prescriptive power of language.[34] Others, taking the lead of Fingarette, understand the *ming* in terms of the performative force of the naming act.[35]

Position (B): to get around the problem of how correcting something spoken can be a matter of effective political policy, others construe *zhengming* as the Master's circumlocution for correcting behavior, things, and affairs *in terms of* their names. So a son who does not behave as a son should be made to conform to how a son ought to behave, as detailed by a definition of the name "son." In Fung Yu-lan's classic formulation, "the actual must in each case be made to correspond to the name. This theory Confucius called the Rectification of Names . . ."[36] In other words, spades should conform to "spade-ness."[37] Often enough, (A) and (B) are presented together as two sides of the same coin, with no clear distinction being made.[38]

Position (C): yet others, impressed by the consideration that the Master said "to correct *ming*" and not "to correct something else in terms of *ming*" propose that *ming* refers to the sociopolitical roles themselves (sense 2). One way to spell out this idea is to say that to correct *ming* is to correct the behavior of people occupying these sociopolitical roles, relationships, and political hierarchies. So: sons who do not behave as sons ought should be made to conform to how they ought to behave, as detailed by what the social position of sonship demands.[39]

To summarize, (A) formulates *zhengming* as a correcting of what is *spoken*, against (B) and (C), which propose *behavior* as the subject of correction. But both (A) and (B), in contrast with (C), construe *ming* as the entities called "names" we use in language (sense 1). For supporters of (A) and (B), there still remains the issue of the scope of *ming*, that is, are all kinds of names covered, or a more restricted class? On one extreme we have Ma Rong (cited in He Yan), who explains *zhengming* as "to correct the names of the hundred affairs (*zheng bai shi zhi ming* 正白事之名)."[40] Most commentators, probably on account of the influence of the supposed background in Sima Qian, tend to restrict the scope of *ming* to ritual terms, or the names of sociopolitical relationships and hierarchies (*ming fen* 名份).[41]

The Gentleman and His Speech

What sense of *ming* is at work in the Master's reply: to correct *ming*? Note the predominant place of "speech" (*yan* 言) in 13.3[6]: "when names (*ming*) are not correct (*buzheng*) then speech will not accord (*bushun*)"; and again, "hence what the gentleman names (*ming*) surely can be put into speech (*yan*)," and finally and most tellingly, "the gentleman with regard to his speech (*yan*), is careless (*gou*) about nothing." If my earlier analysis of the dialogue is correct, then this last statement is about the sorts of things that must happen in order for names to be correct; in which case the entire issue of names being correct or incorrect or being subject to correction is ultimately cast as a matter about speech (*yan*). The *ming* will be correct, and hence *yan* will accord, if only the gentleman *in what he says* (*yu qi yan* 於其言) *is careless about nothing* (*wu suo gou* 無所苟).

Furthermore, the best way to understand the verbal *ming* in "hence what the gentleman *ming*" (13.3[6]) would be as an act of speech (sense 1), since the other sense to *ming* (sense 2) does not lend itself well to the verbal usage. Assuming that *ming* takes basically the same sense throughout 13.3, then *ming* in 13.3 [4, 5] should likewise be construed in terms of speakable "names" (according to sense 1). But if the practical implication of *zhengming* is finally that the *junzi* is careful with his *yan*, what then is the relationship between *ming* and *yan*? Likewise, what is the relationship between "names incorrect" (*ming bu zheng*) and "speech not in accord" (*yan bu shun*)?

The character *yan* in the *Analects* takes on consistently the sense of "speech" (nominal; 2.13, 4.24). It can be used verbally: "to say" (1.7). It also refers to that which was said or a "saying" (nominal; 2.2, 13.15). The predominant sense is that what is at stake is significant, rather than perfunctory, speech (see e.g., 13.15; also compare 16.13 with 17.9). *Ming*, understood according to sense

(1) above, would be closely connected to *yan*. One might say that every act of *ming* ("naming" or "calling by a name") is itself an act of *yan* ("speaking"), even if not every act of speaking is an act of naming. Likewise, every *ming* ("name"), including a reputative one, is instantiated as a part of *yan* ("speech," "something said"), even if, again, not every piece of speech is properly a name.

The character *shun* can take the sense of "to accord with" or "to follow" (verbal; *Zuo*, Cheng 16.5; Xiang 8.3) and sometimes it is meant more strongly as "to obey" or "to submit" (verbal; ibid. Xiang 10.9, 30.10; cf. also *MZ* 6A.1). It is for the most part synonymous with *cong* 從 (*Zuo*, Ai 2.3; Xuan 12.2) and opposed to *ni* 逆, "to go against" (*MZ* 4A.7). Adjectivally, it means "in accord," with the object of the according often implicit (*Zuo*, Wen 14.9; Ai 6.4),[42] and this is the sense of the *shun* in *yan bu shun*. Both *ming bu zheng* and *yan bu shun* can thus be understood as cases of *ming* and *yan* that fail to coincide or accord with some standard.

Upon the analogy of the relationship between *ming* and *yan*, every case of *ming bu zheng* would be a case of *yan bu shun*, though the reverse need not be the case. This is in line with the claim that "if names are not correct, then speech will not be in accord" (13.3[5]), but not the other way round. On the other hand, that which the gentleman names (*ming zhi* 名之) can surely be put into speech (*bi ke yan* 必可言), since what he *ming* is presumably *zheng*, a necessary condition is fulfilled for his *yan* to be *shun*.[43] Therefore, whatever the *referents* of the "names," it is still in the aspect of there being *names* in the sense of being parts of speech that they are to be "corrected." It is true that for segments [1] to [5] the immediate discourse context leaves the sense of *ming* open. But if segment [6] is to cohere with the rest of the conversation, choices narrow considerably. In other words, the overriding concern of the Master in 13.3 is that people speak in some correct manner, more specifically, that they should use names correctly. In light of the above, interpretations of *zhengming* proposing that people's behavior is the direct subject of correction (i.e., positions B and C) are less plausible.[44]

While I think the above establishes an interpretation of *ming* in the phrase *zhengming* in terms of the *names* used as parts of speech, the precise scopes of both the *ming* and also the speeches, which include *ming*, are still open questions. That is, does *zhengming* cover all kinds of *ming* and *yan* or only some? There is also the issue of whose speaking or use of names the Master is referring to in his policy proposal. From segment [6], it appears that it is the *junzi* whose use of names and whose speaking is under consideration. Who then is the *junzi* in 13.3[6]? Whoever he is, he is surely distinct from the corrector of names that the Master himself would have become, should he take up the offer of a governmental position in Wey. Recall the implicit connection between the Master's rebuke of the disciple's criticism in [4]—"The *junzi* when faced with something he does not know is wont to keep his peace"—and the *junzi* and his speech in [6]. Taking [4] and [6] together, the Master seems to be blaming the disciple for his careless speech, on the one hand, and instructing him, on the other. It thus seems that the Master's criticism of Zilu is itself a consequence of the same considerations that underlie his proposal that names must first be corrected in the state of Wey. In other words, 13.3 very possibly portrays for us a specimen of an act of *zhengming* or more broadly, a correcting of speech, in this case, Zilu's speech.

Two implications can be drawn. (1) The class of people under the purview of what the Master is proposing in calling for *zhengming* includes Zilu, a serving official in Wey. I suggest that the *zhengming* proposal of 13.3 is most likely concerned with the speeches of the political elite. (2) A delimiting of the kinds of names and speeches implicated ought to include Zilu's criticism of the Master in [3]. I suspect that for the moment, our formulation of the matter cannot be very much more precise than that. This is because even if it may be plausible to identify Zilu's words in 13.3[3] as a case of either *ming bu zheng* or *yan bu shun*, one still lacks an account of the precise nature of its "incorrectness" or "lack of accord." Furthermore, one also lacks an account of the precise nature of the series of consequences spelt out in 13.3[5].

Conclusion

By achieving greater clarity concerning the sense of *ming* in the Master's argument—*ming* having the sense of names, the sorts of names that we use in language—we can now state the Master's thesis in 13.3 more explicitly:

T: Some mode of correct speaking and naming on the part of the political elite is a necessary condition for sociopolitical and ritual order. This can be further unpacked:

T.1:   An incorrect mode of speaking and naming is a direct cause of sociopolitical and ritual disorder (further unpacked according to 13.3[5]).

T.2:   The reinstatement of sociopolitical and ritual order begins with the correcting of names, that is, by returning speaking and naming to a correct mode. Furthermore,

T.2.1:   This operation of correcting names is to be carried out "from above" by someone in a position of governance.

This above formulation, in a very real sense, can only be the beginning, rather than the end, of an inquiry concerning the so-called *Analects* doctrine of *zhengming* since it poses more questions even as it resolves others. This is not to say that the above analysis has been fruitless but only that it has revealed new possibilities for further study both centered on the *Analects* and perhaps in other allied ancient texts. As it is, the teaching of 13.3 can be stated simply: there are forms of incorrect naming and speaking that can lead directly to sociopolitical disorder, such that any attempt to reinstate order in the sociopolitical realm must begin with the imposition of order on the linguistic realm. Needless to say, this is not a self-evident claim at all: how is this possible or even plausible? How is it that correct speaking can be a *necessary* condition of social-political order? Or for that matter, how is it that correcting the way people speak can be cast in the role of an urgent *policy*? Is there a need to posit a "belief that language possesses a magical power which has unfailing influence on affairs both human and natural?"[45]

To begin to answer these questions, we will have to step back from 13.3 and its specific teachings (and thus beyond the bounds of this paper). We will need to look more broadly at the larger *Analects* teaching on language and politics within which the specific concerns of 13.3 can find their philosophical setting. That, however, constitutes a separate study.

Notes

This is a slightly revised version of an article that first appeared in *Monumenta Serica* 51 (2003). All unmarked references are to the *Analects* or *Lunyu* 論語, cited by book and section number following the division of the text in the bilingual D. C. Lau, *Confucius: The Analects*, 2nd ed. (Hong Kong: Chinese University Press, 1992). All translations from the Chinese are my own. The *pinyin* method of transliteration for Chinese characters is used throughout, though I have generally preserved the spelling used within citations from secondary works. The one exception being "Wey" for 衛, following Michael Loewe and Edward Shaughnessy, eds., *The Cambridge History of Ancient China: From the Origins of Civilization to 221 B.C.* (Cambridge: Cambridge University Press, 1999), xxv. The *Mencius* or *Mengzi* 孟子 (*MZ*) is cited by book and section number according to Lau's bilingual edition (Hong Kong: Chinese University Press, 1984), and the *Xunzi* 荀子 (*XZ*) by chapter and line number in the edition of the Harvard-Yenching concordance series. I have translated the term *junzi* (literally, "lord's son") as "gentleman." First of all, there is an ambiguity between the sociological and moral dimensions of this term, and I prefer a translation that captures a little of that ambiguity. In addition, though the moral ideal of Confucianism as it is now developing is gender neutral, the ancient sense of the term was not. Neutralizing such a loaded term makes it that much harder for us to remember that the text, while familiar and still inspiring, is also rooted in a perspective that is, in many ways, alien and perhaps even disagreeable to us.

1. See, e.g., John Makeham, *Name and Actuality in Early Chinese Thought* (Albany: State University of New York Press, 1994), 35: "What Confucius meant by the 'correction of names' has traditionally been and still remains a subject of interpretative controversy"; Carine Defoort, *The Pheasant Cap Master/He Guan Zi: A Rhetorical Reading* (Albany:

State University of New York Press, 1997), 168: "few scholars, if any, would question the importance of *zhengming* for Confucius, although there is little agreement about the interpretation of the term." See also Cheng Zhongying 成中英, "Lun Kongzi de zhengming sixiang" 論孔子的正名思想 in *Zhongguo zhexue yu Zhongguo wenhua* 中國 哲學與中國文化 (Taibei: Sanmin shuju, 1981), 74.

2. The force of the Master's reply is explicit in the "must be" *bi* 必. However, the final *hu* 乎, is usually interrogative. This is perhaps why D. C. Lau, alone among the translators, adds that element of uncertainty: "*if* something has to be put first, it is *perhaps*, the rectification of names" (emphasis mine); see Lau, *Analects*, 121. Nevertheless, the particle here seems to be more exclamatory than interrogative. See Wang Li 王力, *Gudai Hanyu* 古代漢語 (Beijing: Zhonghua shuju, 1962), 255; and James Legge, trans., *Confucius: Confucian Analects, The Great Learning, and the Doctrine of the Mean* (New York: Dover 1971), 255n: "乎 may be taken as an exclamation, or as = 'is it not?'"

3. The point is not affected by the fact that most translators take the first line conditionally, i.e., "if the prince of Wey . . . ," as conditionals in classical Chinese can be expressed paratactically; see Edwin Pulleyblank, *Outline of Classical Chinese Grammar* (Vancouver: University of British Columbia Press, 1995), 149; and Wang Li, *Gudai Hanyu*, 414–15. But that the Prince of Wey should make such an offer is not beyond possibility. Passage 7.15 speaks of the Master's unwillingness to assist the same prince, implying that perhaps some kind of offer was made.

4. See the collation in Cheng Shude 程樹德, *Lunyu jishi* 論語集釋 (1943; corr. ed., Beijing: Zhonghua shuju, 1990), 885–96; see also Yang Shuda 楊樹達, *Lunyu shuzheng* 論語疏證 (Shanghai: Shanghai guji chubanshe, 1955), 303–4. This connection between the Sima Qian passage and 13.3 is asserted in John Makeham, "Rectifying Confucius' *Zhengming*," *Papers on Far Eastern History* 38 (1988): 1–24; and *Name*, chap. 2, "Confucius and the Correction of Names," which largely reproduces the earlier paper. The *Shiji* 史記 (*SJ*) will be cited by book and page number in Sima Qian 司馬遷, *Shiji* (1959; repr., Beijing: Zhonghua shuju, 1982). The same interpretation is again offered by Makeham in his recent *Transmitters and Creators: Chinese Commentators and Commentaries on the* Analects (Cambridge, MA: Harvard University Asia Center, 2003), 333–38.

5. Sima Qian of course does not *cite* the text; and it is hard to tell if he even had a copy of the *Analects* to cite from. Nevertheless, the *Shiji* wording differs but little from the received text, and may independently preserve an ancient textual variant. Apart from purely stylistic variations, the main difference consists in the very interesting rewording of the first clause to [6]: 君子為之必可名 for the 君子名之必可言 of the received text. When seen against the succeeding 言之必可行, we have an inverted parallelism between 為/名 and 言/行, instead of a progression 名 → 言 → 行. This may be an indication that Sima Qian read the *zhengming* of 13.3 in terms of some kind of match between speech and conduct more than anything else; but the case cannot be argued at length here.

6. The *Zuozhuan* (*Zuo*) is cited by reign, year, and section number in Yang Bojun 楊伯峻, ed., *Chunqiu zuozhuan yizhu* 春秋左傳譯注 (corr. ed., Beijing: Zhonghua shuju,

1990). The dates follow Qian Mu 錢穆, *Xianqin zhuzi xi'nian* 先秦諸子繫年 (Hong Kong: Dongda tushu gongsi, 1979), 523–24.

7. Nanzi has a rather bad reputation in the tradition (see e.g., 6.28). According to the *Zuozhuan* (Ding 14.8), Kuai Kui was moved to desire her death because he suspected that she was having an affair with one Song Chao 宋朝. But the whole narrative is unclear. For a recent reappraisal, see Siegfried Englert and Roderich Ptak, "Nan-tzu, or Why Heaven Did Not Crush Confucius," *Journal of the American Oriental Society* 106, no. 4 (1986): 679–86.

8. Compare also Makeham's account in *Name*, 36, or *Transmitters*, 334–35.

9. Other passages traditionally ascribed to this time frame include 13.7 (*SJ* 47/1933), and also 7.15, where the Master hints that he is unwilling to serve Zhe. There seems to be a strong tradition from the earliest strata (i.e., in Zheng Xuan 鄭玄 and Huang Kan 皇侃) of *Analects* commentaries in identifying the context of 7.15 within the context of the succession crisis; see Cheng Shude, *Lunyu jishi*, 461. See also Qian Mu, *Xianqin*, 42; Yang Shuda, *Lunyu shuzheng*, 162; Lau, *Analects*, 222–23; Makeham, *Name*, 37 and *Transmitters*, 336n94.

10. See Makeham, *Name*, 38–44 (also *Transmitters*, 333–35). In presenting his interpretation of *zhengming*, Makeham goes as far as to say that "most traditional Chinese glosses" of the concept fall into either one of two groups: "those which follow Sima Qian's interpretation or those which follow Zheng Xuan. The former is distinguished by interpreting *Analects* 13.3 in reference to a very specific historical background, the details of which leave little doubt that the term refers to two roles: father and son" (*Name*, 36). The so-called Zheng Xuan type of interpretation is characterized by reading the *ming* in 13.3 as "referring to the title, rank or station of a broad range of subjects . . ." and even beyond that "to the names of all things generally." Makeham's "so-called Zheng Xuan type of interpretation" is more appropriately ascribed to Ma Rong, who glossed the Master's proposal in 13.3 as "to correct the names of the hundred affairs" (*zheng baishi zhi ming* 正百事之名) (Cheng Shude, *Lunyu jishi*, 890). Zheng Xuan, on the other hand, construes *ming* as "written words"; see below note 32.

11. As far as the use of *ming* in the *Analects* is concerned, 17.9, which contains the phrase "the *ming* of birds, beasts, plants and trees," is too apparent a piece of counter-evidence to ignore. In any case, not even Makeham can escape broadening the sense of *ming* to the more general "station or social role" rather than simply "father and son." But why stop here? What makes this level of generality linguistically more defensible than having the *ming* "refer to a broad range of entities," a usage in any case attested within the *Analects* itself? As will be argued later, there is significant pressure within the passage as it stands for assigning a broad sense to *ming* in 13.3.

12. That is, analogous to the manner in which *jian'ai* 兼愛 does refer to an identifiable body of doctrine in the *Mozi* 墨子. I think we do well to heed Knoblock's warning not to confuse the very nontechnically phrased proposal of the Master with the relative more technical discourse of the later Mohist or School of Names; John Knoblock, ed., trans., *Xunzi: A Translation and Study of the Complete Works* (Stanford: Stanford University Press, 1988–94), 3:114–17.

13. Makeham, *Name*, 35.

14. The numbers in square brackets refer to the *zhangju* divisions; see the earlier full quotation of the passage.

15. Arthur Waley, *The Analects of Confucius* (London: George Allen and Unwin, 1938), 22, and Cheng Zhongying, "Lun Kongzi," 65; David Hall and Roger Ames, *Thinking Through Confucius* (Albany: State University of New York Press, 1987), 269.

16. See Cai Mingtian 蔡明田, "Lun Kongzi renxue zhong de zhengmingsixiang" 論孔子仁學中的正名思想, *Kong-Meng Xuebao* 孔孟學報 48 (1984): 6.

17. See below note 23.

18. I think the considerations raised are sufficient to answer Waley's claim that the lateness of the passage is "naively betrayed" by Zilu's reply (*Analects*, 22). Liu Yameng, on the other hand, thinks that "a sufficiently normative, more pragmatic oriented rival theory of government must have existed at that time in light of which the Confucian priority appeared to be readily criticizable even to those of his less conformist disciples like Zilu"; "Three Issues in the Argumentative Conceptions of Early Chinese Discourse," *Philosophy East and West* 46, no. 1 (Jan. 1996): 36. This seems too heavy-handed: I doubt if we really need to posit any "normative rival theory" just in order to understand Zilu's criticisms of the Master in the *Analects*. Nor, as we shall see shortly, is the Master's reply in 13.3 really all that unpragmatic.

19. Any series *if p then q, if q then r, if r then s . . . if y then z* is logically equivalent to *if p then z*, assuming the validity of the hypothetical syllogism.

20. The word *gou* 苟 here has the sense of "be careless of." As Waley puts it, it is "a word for things done 'after a fashion,' in a hugger-mugger way, but not according to the proper ritual. Such things are said to be fluked." See his *Analects*, 66–67, 248. In all but two instances, *gou* is used in the *Analects* as a particle introducing a hypothetical condition similar to "if" (4.4, 7.31, 12.18, 13.10, 13.13, 17.15; cf. *MZ* 1B.14). It is also used in 13.8, adverbially as describing indifference. The word is often paired or even substituted with *tou* 偷 "steal," "stolen"; and is opposed to *jing* 敬 "serious," "reverent"; see e.g., *XZ* 12/20.

21. If it is only a matter of *preserving* the rectitude of names, some other phrase might be more appropriate, perhaps *shouming* 守名, cf. *XZ* 22/10; see also Xu Fuguan 徐復觀, *Gongsun Longzi jiangshu* 公孫龍子講述 (Taizhong: Sili donghai daxue, 1966), 4.

22. See *SJ* 37/1599–1603. Zhe managed to rule for more than a decade. In year 12 of his reign (480 BCE), Kuai Kui made a successful comeback through the actions of fifth-column elements within Wey itself. On account of the courage and prompt action of Zilu, Zhe managed to escape to Lu 魯. Zilu himself was brutally killed when, against better advice, he confronted Kuai Kui alone and unarmed (*Zuo*, Ai 15.5; *SJ* 37/1599–1601). The fighting between father and son continued, with Zhe successfully returning four years after his exile (ibid., Ai 16.3; 476 BCE), only to be on the run again nine years later (ibid., Ai 25.1 and 26.3). By then, Wey was badly weakened and practically a vassal to the successor states of Jin 晉, i.e., Zhao 趙, Wei 魏, and Han 韓 (*SJ* 37/1603).

23. The Master's main premises are posed in the form of a series of "if not-*x* then not-*y*" (13.3[5]), i.e., *x* is a *necessary* condition for *y*. The Master does not promise that if

names are correct, there will be sociopolitical order. He said that if names are *not* correct, then there will *not* be sociopolitical order. In the words of the Mohist Logical Canon, *x* is a *xiao gu* 小故 "minor reason/cause" of *y*: having this, it will not necessarily be so: lacking this, necessarily it will not be so 有之不必得, 無之必不得; Angus C. Graham, *Later Mohist Logic, Ethics, and Science* (Hong Kong: Chinese University Press, 1978), 2/4/1/1 (A 1). See also Cheng Zhongying, "Lun Kongzi," 65–66.

24. Defoort calls this section a "positive description of the gentleman, which concludes Confucius's only explicit recommendation to *zheng ming* in the *Analects*" (*Pheasant Cap Master*, 170).

25. Graham, *Later Mohist Logic*, 170.

26. 君子 . . . 就有道而正焉. Some objects to which *zheng* applies in the *Analects* include mats (10.12, 18), posture (10.26), attire (20.2; cf. *MZ* 2A.9), facial expression (8.4), and character (13.6, 13, 14.15; cf. *MZ* 4A.4).

27. A word closely related is *zhi* 直, "straight." In the *Analects*, *zhi* is sometimes used as a substantive, "the straight" (2.19, 22, 16.4), or abstractly, "straightness" (13.18, 14.34, 17.8, 17.16), apart from being an adjective (5.24, 8.2, 12.20, 22, 13.18, 15.7). Like *zheng*, *zhi* also has the extended sense of moral straightness, which is in fact the predominant usage in the *Analects*. The *Analects* does not use *zhi* verbally though that is possible: "let me straighten (*zhi*) him" (*MZ* 3A.5). However, *zheng* and *zhi* are not identical, as can be seen from their different opposites: the antonym of *zheng* is *pian* 偏 "slant" (*XZ* 23/37), rather than the *qu* 曲 (ibid. 1/1) or *wang* 枉 (2.19, 18.2, 12.22; *MZ* 3B.1) "crooked" opposed to *zhi*. The two words are etymologically related according to the *Shuowenjiezi* 説文解字; see Xu Shen 徐慎, Duan Yu-cai 段玉財 ed., *Shuowen jiezi zhu* 説文解字注 (Shanghai: Shanghai guji chubanshe, 1981), 2B/1a, 12B/45a.

28. 鳥、獸、草、木之名.

29. 蕩蕩乎，民無能名焉.

30. Interestingly enough, outside of 13.3, the *Analects* uses *ming* as "reputation" three out of five times (4.5, 9.2, 15.20). In the *Mencius*, *ming* is used this way some four out of ten times. There is thus a sense to *ming*, well attested in the ancient usage, that is more than designation or description, but also evaluation. This aspect of *ming* is clearly seen from the phrase *fu ming yi zhi yi* 夫名以制義, found in the *Zuozhuan* (Huan 2.8). The phenomenon of the same lexical form having both senses of "name" and "reputation" is hardly unique to ancient Chinese. It is found in the modern Chinese *ming sheng* 名聲. One of the listed senses to the English "name" is "reputation of a particular kind." It can also be found in Biblical Hebrew (e.g., Genesis 11:4 "let us make for ourselves a name . . ."); Greek (e.g., Mark 6:14 "for the name of him [John the Baptist] became manifest . . ."); and the Latin *nomen*, among others. In other words, one must not make hasty inferences about some special feature of the Chinese world view or theory of language on so slender a piece of linguistic evidence as this.

31. Huang Kan citing Zheng Xuan: "*zhengming*, refers to correcting the written words. The ancients call them *ming*, men of today call them *zi* 字. The *Li ji* says, 'Where there are a hundred *ming* and above, they are written upon bamboo strips.' Confucius,

seeing that the teaching of the times are not workable, desired to correct the mistakes in the (written) words" (in Cheng Shude, *Lunyu jishi*, 890). This is in keeping with the fact that as a commentator, Zheng Xuan tends to emphasize the written word in line with general Han scholastic tendencies: see John Makeham, "The Earliest Extant Commentary on *Lunyu: Lunyu Zhengshi zhu*," *T'oung Pao* 83 (1997): 285–87.

32. See also Bao Zhiming, "Language and world view in ancient China," *Philosophy East and West* 40, no. 2 (Apr 1990): 197–99, and Defoort, *Pheasant Cap Master*, 168–73. My list discounts the interpretation of Zheng Xuan; see previous note.

33. Joseph Needham, ed., *Science and Civilisation in China* (Cambridge: Cambridge University Press, 1956), 2:9–10. See also Herrlee G. Creel, *Confucius, the Man and the Myth* (London: Routledge & Keegan Paul, 1951), 321–22.

34. Chad Hansen, *Language and Logic in Ancient China* (Ann Arbor: University of Michigan Press, 1983), 72–73; Benjamin Schwartz, *The World of Thought in Ancient China* (Cambridge, MA: Belknap Press, 1985), 91–93; Makeham, *Name*, 44–50.

35. Herbert Fingarette, *Confucius: The Secular as Sacred* (New York: Harper and Row, 1972), 15. See also Hall and Ames, *Thinking Through Confucius*, 269–75; Angus C. Graham, *Disputers of the Tao* (La Salle: Open Court, 1989), 23–25; Defoort, *Pheasant Cap Master*, 173.

36. Fung Yu-lan, *A History of Chinese Philosophy*, trans. Derk Bodde (Princeton: Princeton University Press, 1952–53), 1:59.

37. Also Legge, *Confucius*, 263–64; Hsiao Kung-chuan, *A History of Chinese Political Thought*, vol. 1, *From the Beginnings to the Sixth Century A. D.*, trans. F. W. Mote (Princeton: Princeton University Press, 1979), 98–100; P. Reding, *Les fondements philosophiques de la rhétorique chez les sophistes grecs et les sophistes chinois* (New York: Peter Lang, 1985), 251: "There is only one way to correct the name: the one who carries the name must conform to the norm which the name expresses" (translated from the French).

38. Zhang Dai'nian 張岱年, *Zhongguo zhexue dagang* 中國哲學大綱 (Beijing: Zhongguo shehuikexue chuban-she, 1982), 560: "*zhengming* means name and reality corresponding to each other, causing the name to match the reality, the reality to match the name." In a similar fashion, Cheng Zhongying and Cai Mingtian spell out *zhengming* in terms of the injunction that speech and deed must match (*yan xing yi zhi* 言行一致); Cheng Zhongying, "Lun Kongzi," 66, and Cai Mingtian, "Lun Kongzi," 6–8. See also Xu Fuguan, *Gongsun Longzi*, 5, and Hu Shih, *The Development of the Logical Method in Ancient China*, 2nd ed. (New York: Paragon Book Reprint Corp., 1963), 24–27.

39. See Lao Siguang 勞思光, *Zhongguo zhexueshi* 中國哲學史 (Taibei: Sanmin Shuju, 1984), 122–27, and Lin Yuanqi 林遠琪, "Kongzi de zhengmingzhuyi yu zhengzhisixiang" 孔子的正名主義與正名思想, *Kong-Meng Yuekan* 孔孟學刊 18, no. 2 (Oct 1979): 9–18.

40. In Cheng Shude, *Lunyu jishi*, 890.

41. E.g., Zhu Xi 朱熹, *Sishu zhangju jizhu* 四書章句集注 (Beijing: Zhonghua shuju, 1983), 141–42; Graham, *Disputers*, 23–25; Makeham, *Name*, 42–43; and Yang Bojun 楊伯峻, *Lunyu yizhu* 論語譯注 (Beijing: Zhonghua shuju, 1984), 134–35.

42. Especially in the earlier portions of the *Zuozhuan*, *shun* can also take a more specialized usage of "in accordance with the order of seniority" (see, e.g., Yin 5.1; Wen 2.5, 5.5; Zhao 26.8).

43. This seems to be the reason for the extra modal 可 in 故君子名之必可言也，言之必可行也, (rather than, for instance, 故君子名之必言也，言之必行也; cf. 13.20), since correct naming is itself only a necessary but not sufficient condition for such speaking that is in accord.

44. As Hansen remarks: "in this passage [13.3], the rectification of names appears to consist in making names accord (with something). The converse notion of making things or people accord with names is tokened in other passages, but these are not explicitly identified as rectification of names—in fact do not deal directly with names at all"; *Language and Logic*, 73.

45. Bao Zhiming, "Language," 198.

Master and Disciple in the *Analects*

14

Jeffrey L. Richey

Introduction

The eminent historian of religions, Jonathan Z. Smith, once remarked that his career largely has consisted of applying history to the ideas of a few influential theorists who, by and large, tended to ignore history in their own work, in an effort to see whether their theories would bear up under the strain of accommodating such data.[1] This essay undertakes a similar experiment with history and theory. It imposes the burden of early Chinese religious history on the venerable theories of one of Smith's predecessors at the University of Chicago, Joachim Wach (1898–1955). Throughout much of the twentieth century, Wach's views concerning the comparative sociology of religion exercised no small influence, and attracted as much criticism.[2] Like the theorists to whom Smith has alluded, Wach has been criticized for his lack of historicism. When confronted with the historical data represented by the Confucian *Analects* (*Lunyu* 論語),[3] will Wach's theories expand, or explode?

Master–Disciple: Relationship and Dialectic

In 1924, Wach published an article in his native German that later became known as "Master and Disciple: Two Religio-Sociological Studies" when it was translated into English and republished posthumously, first in the *Journal of Religion* and again in an anthology of Wach's essays.[4] In this article, Wach posits an essential difference between two kinds of relationships usually seen as central to the emergence of religious traditions. On the one hand, he describes the teacher-student relationship as "a bond . . . constituted through common interest in the object of study; the student respects the teacher as the possessor and mediator of certain crafts, a body of knowledge or an accomplished skill. . . . It is not the person [of the teacher] who is admired and esteemed, but a certain faculty, a skill, knowledge, or capability."[5] Wach contrasts this teacher-student relationship with the master-disciple relationship, which "is found where the tie is personal—not based primarily on subject matter; the individuality of the master and the disciple consequently gains central significance. . . . [which] for the disciple rests in the master's personality, whose very character and activity are irreplaceable.[6] Wach expresses his sense of the contrast succinctly when he says, "The disciple understands the master; the student understands the teaching."[7] If this sounds like the typological distinction between the priest and the prophet drawn by Max Weber (1864–1920), it is because Wach is not far from Weber on this point:

> The term "priest" may be applied to the functionaries of a regularly organized and permanent enterprise. . . . Another distinguishing quality of the priest . . . is his professional equipment of special knowledge, fixed doctrine, and vocational qualifications, which brings him into contrast with . . . prophets, and other types of religious functionaries who exert their influence by virtue of personal gifts (charisma) made manifest in miracle and revelation.[8]

However, Wach explicitly contrasts the master with the prophet: "More people are dependent on the master than on the prophet, in whose place—according even to his own conviction—another person could have been called just as well."[9]

Finally, Wach claims that the qualitative difference between the teacher's and the master's followers—students and disciples—extends to their conduct in the wake of the teacher's or master's death. Among students left behind by a deceased teacher, he says, "embittered disputes are raised concerning the 'authentic interpretation' of the legacy left by the teacher; a contest concerning a successor sets in."[10] Disciples who survive their master, however, "are brought together through the image which is sacred to each of them."[11] The quality of unique, personal sanctity that first drew the disciples to the master while he was alive later binds them to one another after his death, whereas the community of students loyal only to the teaching quickly degenerates into a squabble over orthodoxy and heterodoxy. A master's disciples form a community; a teacher's students form sectarian groups.

Do Wach's theoretical typologies and scenarios fit the facts as they appear in the *Analects*? If so, how, and if not, why not? Finally, to what extent are Wach's theories useful in helping to uncover master/disciple relationships in the *Analects*?

Whether the *Analects* presents Confucius as a teacher ("the possessor and mediator of certain crafts . . .")[12] or a master ("whose very character and activity are irreplaceable")[13] seems to depend on which passage in the *Analects* one cares to examine. In each passage, the issue of Confucius's identity and status in the *Analects* is itself defined by the prior resolution of another issue: whether and how particular figures are understood by the text (which is to say, its editors and redactors) as masters or disciples.

The presentation of certain disciples as masters indicates how such disciples (and their disciples) envisioned Confucius as master. Conversely, the presentation of other disciples as disciples, or even as students, indicates how other disciples envisioned Confucius as master. This dialectic of master and disciple images is crucial to the development of both the *Analects* as a text and early Confucianism (*rujia* 儒家) as an intellectual and religious tradition in early China. One way to interpret competing presentations of important figures such as Confucius and his disciples in the *Analects* is to see them as reflections of competing spiritual lineages within the pluralistic Confucian traditions of the Warring States (403–221 BCE). To test both this hypothesis and Wach's theories, let us examine references to Confucius and one of his foremost followers, Yan Hui 顏回 (Yen Yuan 顏淵, ca. mid-fifth-century BCE?).

Yan Hui as Student

Several passages in the *Analects* present Yan Hui and Confucius as sharing a bond based on common interest in particular skills or bodies of knowledge—in other words, as student and teacher. Most of these passages are among the least interesting references to Yan Hui in the entire text. Yan Hui is described as excelling in particular areas of Confucius's curriculum. For example, he is said to rank among Confucius's top four students where *dexing* 德行, or the exertion of moral charisma, is concerned (11.3), and frequently is depicted as eagerly, even childishly or simple-mindedly attentive to all that Confucius has to say, sometime to the point of arousing frustration on the master's part (2.9, 9.20, 11.4). In another passage (12.1), Yan Hui humbly inquires about the cardinal Confucian virtue of *ren* 仁 (co-humanity)[14] and, like his fellow student Zhong Gong 仲弓 (Yong 雍) in the following passage, offers what E. Bruce Brooks and A. Taeko Brooks call an "obsequious formula" to Confucius's answer: "Although I am not clever, please allow me to act on what you have said."[15] Finally, in one telling passage (9.11), Yan Hui himself describes how he finds Confucius's teachings on *wen* 文 (culture) and *li* 禮 (ritual) to be both enormously attractive and maddeningly difficult to understand.

In all of these passages, Yan Hui is unswervingly focused on what Confucius has to offer by way of teachings, rather than on Confucius himself. Furthermore, while these episodes generally portray Yan Hui as a capable and hard-working student of Confucius, they do not hint at the intimacy between Confucius and Yan Hui that is documented in other portions of the text; nor do they present Yan Hui as peerless among Confucius's students. If these narratives and sayings preserve an authentic historical memory of Yan Hui, they do so as monuments to his exemplary, but not unique, status. Even his exemplary status seems to rest upon his single-minded pursuit of Confucius's teachings, not necessarily his mastery or embodiment of them. All of these themes, however, emerge in other sequences within the *Analects*.

Yan Hui as Disciple

The beatification of Yan Hui intensifies in other passages, in which a different kind of relationship develops between him and Confucius. In 11.23, Yan Hui's attachment clearly has been transferred from the mere teachings of Confucius to the sacred person of the master: "When the master was surrounded in Kuang, Yan Yuan [= Yan Hui] fell behind. The master said, 'I had given you up for dead,' to which Yan Hui replied, 'If the master is alive, how dare I die?'" Moreover, Confucius's view of Yan Hui seems quantitatively higher here. In 11.19, Confucius says that Yan Hui "indeed is almost there" (*ye qi shu hu* 也其庶乎), evidently because of his *lükong* 婁空 (constant emptiness or poverty), and that he is a *xian* 賢 (worthy) (6.11), no longer just one among several top learners. In 11.8, Yan Hui's father, Yan Lu 顏路 (sometimes regarded as a follower of Confucius in his own right), apparently assumes such profound attachment to Yan Hui on Confucius's part that he asks Confucius to give up his carriage in order to provide an outer coffin for his deceased son. Confucius refuses to grant Yan Lu's request, noting that he did not do this for his own son, which would have entailed a transgression of ritual propriety by Confucius (whose social status demanded that he travel by carriage in the funeral procession). Yet he does not seem to object to Yan Lu's invitation to share the fatherly duty of funeral expenses, which implies that he saw himself as a kind of second father to Yan Hui. Indeed, Wach says that "as a guide of souls, as a door of salvation, [the master] demand[s] the complete devotedness of the disciple, of the 'son.'"[16]

In a cluster of sayings found in books 6 and 11 of the *Analects*, Yan Hui sheds his merely exemplary status and becomes truly unique. He alone is said to have truly "loved learning" (*haoxue* 好學) (6.3, 11.7). Among all of Confucius's disciples, only he consistently demonstrated the moral stamina of his *xin* 心 (heart-mind[17]) through the practice of *ren* (6.7). Moreover, his uniqueness is magnified by his untimely death (6.3, 11.7); not only was he unique, he is irreplaceable. Confucius regards Yan Hui's death as a demoralizing personal loss inflicted by heaven (*tian* 天) (11.9), and defends his extravagant grief for his fallen disciple by asking, "If not for [my] *furen* 夫人 [= man],[18] for whom should I grieve extravagantly?" (11.10). In spite of Confucius's principled objections to a lavish funeral for Yan Hui (on the grounds of ritual propriety), the surviving disciples bury him with unsparing honors, at which point Confucius offers the following soliloquy: "Yan Hui! You treated me as a father, while I have not been able to treat you as a son. This was not my fault" (11.11). Here, master and disciple become father and son, as hinted at in 11.8.

Nonetheless, in these passages, Confucius falls short of calling Yan Hui his equal or his superior. While Yan Hui is no longer Confucius's student, but rather his disciple—making Confucius a master, rather than a teacher—the master-disciple boundary is well defined. Although Confucius grieves for his deceased disciple, his sense of this boundary is not blurred by his sorrow: "What a pity!

I watched him progress, but I never saw him fulfill his potential" (9.21). This qualified exaltation of Yan Hui as disciple preserves Confucius's status as master, and is echoed by other texts. In the *Analects*: "Zhong Ni 仲尼 [= Confucius] cannot be slandered" (19.24) and "The master cannot be equaled" (19.25). And in the text identified with Confucius's foremost early interpreter, Mengzi 孟子 (Mencius, ca. 372–289 BCE): "Ever since humankind came into this world, there has never been one greater than Confucius."[19] In the *Lunyu Jijie* 論語集解 (*Collected Explanations of the Analects*) compiled by He Yan 何宴 (ca. 190–249 CE) et al., there appears this commentary: "[Yan] Hui had almost attained the sage's way."[20] Almost, that is, but not quite.

Yan Hui as Master

Finally, two passages outside of these sayings-clusters in books 6 and 11 make two extraordinary claims about Yan Hui *vis-à-vis* Confucius. In a discourse on prudence and efficacy in holding office, Confucius poses a rhetorical question to Yan Hui: "Is it just you and I who are like this?" (7.11). In another dialogue, with his disciple Zi Gong 子貢, Confucius asserts that neither he nor Zi Gong is equal to Yan Hui (5.9). In the first passage, Yan Hui is established as Confucius's equal; in the second passage, Confucius not only raises Yan Hui above another beloved disciple, but also above himself.

If a figure such as Yan Hui 顏回 is presented as a disciple, then that is one thing. "The disciple will never become a master," says Wach; "the work of the master will not continue, since no one can continue it except he who began it."[21] If such a figure is depicted as a master in his own right—one who continues the work of the former master, which seems impossible for the disciple during the master's lifetime—or even surpasses his master, then "a new master has arisen."[22] In other words, the disciple *qua* disciple serves to perpetuate the cult of the deceased master, while the disciple who assumes the sanctity of the master becomes a master himself, and acquires a cult of his own.

In the third cluster of sayings from the *Analects* discussed above, Yan Hui alternately appears as co-master with Confucius and as Confucius's own master. On the one hand, Yan Hui is described as Confucius's equal, both in explicit terms (7.11) and by implication (6.3, 6.7, 11.7). The *Analects'* enshrinement of Yan Hui as his master's peer is reinforced by later Chinese Buddhist texts, in which Yan Hui and Confucius are understood to be manifestations of various *bodhisattvas*.[23] For example, in the sixth- or seventh-century CE *Qingjing faxing jing* 清淨法行經 (Scripture of the Practice of Pure *Dharma*), Yan Hui is identified as the *bodhisattva* Guangjing 光淨 and regarded as having been sent by Shakyamuni Buddha to convert the Chinese, along with Confucius and Laozi 老子 (also disguised as Chinese sages).[24] In fact, allegations of Yan Hui's parity with Confucius as co-*bodhisattva* persisted through the Tang 唐 dynasty (618–907 CE).[25]

On the other hand, in these passages it is Yan Hui, not Confucius, who is described as irreplaceable (5.9), while a strong personal attachment to Yan Hui is voiced through the mouths and actions of Confucius and other disciples (11.9, 11.10, 11.11). This type of status inversion between Yan Hui and Confucius is paralleled in the fourth-century BCE "Daoist"[26] text *Zhuangzi*, in which Yan Hui first startles Confucius with his display of contemplative powers and then humbles him so much that he exclaims: "It turns out that you are the worthy one [*xianren* 賢人]! I'd like your permission to become your disciple."[27]

Unsurprisingly, later Confucian commentaries on the *Analects* move to counter the heterodox equation of Yan Hui with Confucius and to neutralize any suggestion that Yan Hui outdid his master. In his *Lunyu yishu* 論語義疏 [Elucidation of the meaning of the *Analects*], Huang Kan 皇侃 (488–545 CE) reads *Analects* 5.9 to say that "Confucius conceded that Zi Gong was not as good as Yan Hui," even though a literal reading indicates that Confucius admits that he cannot match Yan Hui.[28] Huang Kan quotes Liu Xin 劉歆 (46 BCE–23 CE) to support his view that the worthy (*xian* 賢 —for example, Yan Hui) is essential to the success of the sage (*shengren* 聖人 —for example, Confucius): "Yan was sub-partner to the sage [*ya shengren zhi ou* 亞聖人之偶]. As such, Yan and Kong [Confucius] were a natural pair, distinguished in form by a jot of *qi* [氣]."[29] Finally, in Huang Kan's own commentary on book eleven of the *Analects*, he says: "The relation between the sage and worthy is like a shadow or an echo."[30]

"Master and Disciple" in Light of the *Analects*

> The figure of the master lives in the heart of the disciples. So long as he dwells in their midst, the image grows and takes on form. Through this image each disciple is able to focus his own experience, which is enriched stroke by stroke from a living center.[31]

Philip J. Ivanhoe reminds us that "before we begin to read a text like the *Analects* we would do well to ask ourselves, Which *Analects* and Whose Confucius are we trying to understand?"[32] We might well ask ourselves, "Which *Analects* and Whose Yan Hui are we trying to understand?" For it is clear that the *Analects* preserves multiple views of Yan Hui (as student, as disciple, and even as master) each of which implies a distinct view of Confucius (as teacher, as master, and even as disciple). Moreover, Wach's theory helps to explain the historical and sociological process by which the *Analects*—and through it, Confucian orthodoxy and heterodoxy—were constructed. To summarize:

1. Presentations of *Yan Hui as student* probably are the results of redaction performed by other disciple-masters or their disciples and are

intended to convey a portrait of the beloved disciple that is compatible with later orthodoxy. For example, it is likely that followers of other key figures, such as Zi Gong, were responsible for such scaled-down images of Yan Hui.

2. Presentations of *Yan Hui as disciple* arguably are the most historically plausible because they seem more moderate and credible than other competing presentations. Views similar to presentations of Yan Hui as student accord well with later orthodoxy.

3. Finally, presentations of *Yan Hui as master*, like similar presentations of Yan Hui as student, probably arise from redactive activity—in this case, the redaction performed by followers of Yan Hui. Unlike the other two modes of presentation outlined here, views of Yan Hui as master are incompatible with later orthodoxy, and for this very reason are embraced by various heterodox texts and traditions such as those of the Zhuangists and the Buddhists.

To the extent that sectarian squabbling produced the discrete sayings-sources and other traditions that furnished the raw material for the *Analects*, Wach would be right to call Confucius a teacher, and his followers, students. To the extent that the memory of their master overshadowed individual concerns and catalyzed a shared experience, Wach would correctly identify Confucius's devotees as disciples with a master. To the extent that "a new master arises" in Yan Hui (or "in the heart of [his] disciples," at any rate), Wach would not err in seeing Yan Hui as a master in his own right. Finally, to the extent that Wach's theory enables us to see the multiple Confucian communities of practice that underlie and shape the historical development of the *Analects*, rather than to reduce the text to some essentialized core, we are wise not to discard the valuable work of a master who died over fifty years ago. After all, what could be more Confucian than to "transmit, rather than to innovate" (*shu er bu zuo* 述而不作)? (7.1).

Notes

The preparation of this essay has benefited from consultations with Jane Geaney, Keith Knapp, Guolong Lai, Edward Slingerland, and Thomas Wilson, as well as audiences at the "Transmission and Innovation in Confucian Traditions" session of the Confucian Traditions Group at the American Academy of Religion Annual Meeting in Toronto, November 2002, the "New Work on an Old Master: Confucius and the *Analects*" conference at the University of Michigan's Center for Chinese Studies in March 2003, and the Society of Fellows in the Humanities at Columbia University in April 2004. I owe these and many other individuals a debt of gratitude for helping to sharpen and clarify my thoughts, and for the opportunity to share my work with them. Moreover, it is an honor to have my work appear in the same volume as that of my teacher, Shun Kwong-loi; I thank him for the invitation to do so.

1. March 15, 2004, personal communication.

2. See Eric J. Sharpe, *Comparative Religion: A History*, 2nd ed. (Chicago: Open Court, 1986), 238–40, 274–76.

3. On the *Lunyu*, see Anne Cheng, "Lun-yu 論語," in *Early Chinese Texts*, ed. Michael Loewe (Berkeley: Society for the Study of Early China and the Institute of East Asian Studies, 1993), 313–23; Roger T. Ames and Henry Rosemont, Jr., trans., *The Analects of Confucius: A Philosophical Translation* (New York: Ballantine Books, 1998), 7–9, 274–75; and Bryan W. Van Norden, introduction to *Confucius and the Analects: New Essays*, ed. Bryan W. Van Norden (Oxford: Oxford University Press, 2002), 3–36.

4. Joachim Wach, "Master and Disciple: Two Religio-Sociological Studies," *Journal of Religion* 42, no. 1 (January 1962): 1–21, and *Essays in the History of Religions*, ed. Joseph M. Kitagawa and Gregory D. Alles (New York: Macmillan, 1988), 1–32. In each case, Susanne Heigel-Wach and Fred Streng translated Wach's German original into English. Further references to this essay are drawn from the 1988 anthologized version. Frederick M. Denny et al. critique this essay in "Joachim Wach's 'Master and Disciple' Revisited: A Contemporary Symposium," *Teaching Theology and Religion* 1, no. 1 (1998): 13–19.

5. Wach, "Master and Disciple," 1.

6. Wach, "Master and Disciple," 2.

7. Ibid.

8. *The Sociology of Religion*, trans. Ephraim Fischoff (Boston: Beacon Press, 1963), 28–29.

9. Wach, "Master and Disciple," 12.

10. Wach, "Master and Disciple," 7.

11. Wach, "Master and Disciple," 8.

12. Wach, "Master and Disciple," 1.

13. Wach, "Master and Disciple," 2.

14. On the translation of *ren* as "co-humanity," see Peter A. Boodberg, "The Semasiology of Some Primary Confucian Concepts," in *Selected Works of Peter A. Boodberg*, ed. Alvin P. Cohen (Berkeley: University of California Press, 1979), 37–38.

15. See Brooks and Brooks, *The Original Analects* (New York: Columbia University Press, 1998), 90.

16. Wach, "Master and Disciple," 28.

17. In ancient China as in many other premodern cultures, the heart was regarded as the seat of cognitive as well as affective activity.

18. Confucius's use of the term *furen* — used to mean both "husband" and "man" generically in ancient Chinese divinatory, historical, and poetic texts — is intriguing. One wonders if Confucius's relationship with Yan Hui was homoerotic in some way, and

furthermore, whether homoeroticism played any part in master-disciple relationships among early Confucians.

19. *Mencius* 2A2.

20. John Makeham, *Transmitters and Creators: Chinese Commentators and Commentaries on the Analects* (Cambridge, MA: Harvard University Asia Center, 2003), 40.

21. Wach, "Master and Disciple," 2–3, 8.

22. Wach, "Master and Disciple," 8.

23. In Mahayana Buddhism, a *bodhisattva* (Sanskrit: "enlightenment-being") is one who vows to help others attain enlightenment, rather than pursuing the Buddha's teaching strictly for his or her own benefit.

24. See Erik Zürcher, *The Buddhist Conquest of China: The Spread and Adaptation of Buddhism in Early Medieval China* (Leiden: E. J. Brill, 1972), 1:313–15. Zürcher tentatively identifies Guangjing with the Indian figure of Vimalaprabha.

25. David McMullen, *State and Scholars in T'ang China* (Cambridge: Cambridge University Press, 1988), 34.

26. In my view, whether texts such as the *Zhuangzi*, which predate the emergence of the term "Daoist" (*daojia* 道家/*daojiao* 道教), should be labeled as such is an open and probably unanswerable question.

27. *Zhuangzi*, chap. 6, *Dazongshi* 大宗師 (The Great Ancestral Teacher), section 7.

28. Makeham, *Transmitters*, 93.

29. Makeham, *Transmitters*, 120. *Qi* is defined in early Chinese texts as the vital energy or fluid that animates the cosmos, including the human body.

30. Ibid.

31. Wach, "Master and Disciple," 29.

32. "Whose Confucius? Which Analects?" in Van Norden, *Confucius and the Analects*, 130.

Confucius:
The Organization
of Chinese Society

15

Ronald Suleski

Who Was Confucius?

Is it possible to understand the Chinese people without knowing something about Confucius and his influence on Chinese society? The ideas of this ancient philosopher might seem relevant neither to those living in the bustling, cosmopolitan Chinese cities of today, nor to residents of the countryside, who are absorbed with the intensive labor of agriculture. Yet the ideas of Confucius have touched virtually every aspect of Chinese civilization and culture and profoundly influenced the Chinese conception of the individual and of human beings.

Different Chinese individuals accept Confucian ideas in varying degrees, and they do not act on them in the same ways. A scholar in Beijing might call an international conference where learned papers examine some particular detailed point about Confucius and his actions. A harried business executive in Shanghai has perhaps read very little about the life of Confucius, though she might be familiar with popular mythology about China's most famous teacher. (Indeed, Confucius is sometimes referred to as the First Teacher, *xianshi* 先師) A peasant in the southern coastal province of Fujian probably can recite very few of the historic specifics about the life and times of Confucius. But it is almost certain that the influence of Confucius can be found somewhere in the lives and actions of every Chinese, if not in the way an individual behaves, then in the way other Chinese treat that individual. As China moves away from the highly politicized decades of the 1960s and '70s when the philosophy of Confucius was officially disparaged, Chinese now, in the beginning of the new millennium, feel free to acknowledge the teachings of this revered sage, which continue to shape the way human beings treat each other in contemporary Chinese society.

Among all the names of Chinese people that a Westerner will ever hear, the name Confucius probably sounds the least like an authentic Chinese name. In fact, it is not a Chinese name. The name "Confucius" was created by Catholic Jesuit scholars from Europe who began visiting China in the late 1500s. During the 1600s, they compiled information about the Chinese people, Chinese history, and culture and sent their reports back to their superiors at the Vatican in Rome. The Catholic priests employed educated Chinese to help them learn the language and literature of China. These Chinese were in effect informants who, in an early example of the practice of anthropological fieldwork, described for the Jesuits the historical mythology, cultural traditions, and social customs of the China of their time. Sooner or later the Chinese informants mentioned the name of a great scholar, teacher, and philosopher known to everyone in the country. The man they described had the family name of Kong, and many people referred to him as Respected Master Kong, in Chinese at the time spoken as *Kongfuzi* 孔夫子. The Jesuit scholars decided that if this Chinese scholar was so well respected, he could be considered equal to the great thinkers of their own Western tradition, philosophers from the classical periods of Greece and Rome such as Socrates (469–399 BC) or Cicero (106–43 BC). The Jesuits wrote in Latin, the medium of communication within the Roman Catholic Church, and among all educated Europeans then. Using a Latin alphabet to both phoneticize and Latinize the name of this influential Chinese scholar, they wrote it as Confucius.[1]

The actual man we call Confucius was named Kong Qiu 孔丘 (551–479 BC); Chinese today refer to him by an abbreviated form of Master Kong (*Kongzi* 孔子). His home was in the eastern portion of north China in the state of Lu 魯, in what today is called the city of Qufu 曲阜 in Shandong province 山東省. In that city one can still find a compound of buildings designated as the ancestral temples of the Kong family and many memorial plaques. Much of the destruction that befell the ancient buildings and artifacts in Qufu during the Cultural Revolution in the 1960s has now been repaired, and Qufu is once again a center for tourists and pilgrims interested in visiting the ancestral home of Confucius.[2]

At the time of Confucius's birth, China was divided into nine or ten competing states. The great house of Zhou 周 that 500 years earlier had ruled over all of north China was in a state of disarray. The rule of the Zhou kings had gradually dissipated as several prominent regional families, each headed by a prince, became the de facto political powerholders in their immediate regions. Each prominent family emphasized their degree of closeness to the royal Zhou household as a mark of their legitimacy. They refrained from adopting the title of King (*wang* 王) but continued to refer to themselves by various princely appellations. The states they ruled competed with each other for political and military gains, and the aristocratic classes engaged in continuous rounds of diplomatic negotiations and political ploys. The princes in each state, though they surrounded themselves with opulence and claimed a sort of "divine right" obtained through the powerful spirits of their ancestors, always faced potential challenges to their legitimacy. Secondary officials appointed by each prince had backing from their own powerful families as well as from groups of fellow aristocrats. The networks formed by the princely families and their allies continuously struggled to protect or expand their political prerogatives. Warfare was not constant, though the threat of warfare always lurked in the background. This historical period is known as the Spring and Autumn period (*chunqiu shiqi* 春秋時期) (722–481 BC), a term that captures the sense of continuous flowering and waning among the various states.[3]

Confucius was born into one of the minor aristocratic families in the state of Lu. The ruler of Lu claimed to be a direct descendent of the old Zhou ruling house, and therefore was able to maintain an aura of special legitimacy. Even though his family was poor, some of Confucius's relatives, including his father, had previously held political or military posts, and Confucius was accepted as a member of the aristocratic class. At that time in China there was a clear division between the common people, who generally remained illiterate and labored with their hands, and the aristocratic elite, who received some formal education and saw themselves as the natural governing class and preservers of a rich traditional culture. One was born into the aristocracy, so even impoverished members of the ruling class such as Confucius and his family were nevertheless considered to be part of this elite group. Since the aristocracy saw itself as the natural governing class quite separate from the common people, they associated with each other with relative ease and freedom as members of the same privileged class. Government ministers of all ranks felt it appropriate to meet with other members of the aristocracy and even to solicit advice on local affairs. Thus even a minor aristocrat who did not hold an official post, such as Confucius during most of his life, was welcomed by the aristocratic rulers of Lu and neighboring states and invited to confer on official matters. In 501 BC when he was fifty-one years old, Confucius was given a fairly high government post. He held the post for a few years, but for most of his life he held no important government office. Confucius never became a rich man. He probably survived through the stipends and gifts given to him by the officials with whom he conferred and from the students he gathered about him, several of whom were sons of well-placed families from Lu and the neighboring states.[4]

How Human Beings Should Live

In his own time Confucius became known throughout the states in north China as a great teacher. He was respected for his detailed knowledge of the ancient rites and ceremonies that played a critical and highly symbolic role in official life. These ceremonies were centuries old and had been sanctified with time. With his reputation as an expert in the origins and proper conduct of the rites, Confucius attracted many students who hoped to achieve high political office. They discussed not only the organization, evolution, and forms of the ancient rites but also whether current governments conducted the ceremonies faithfully and correctly and other political and social issues.

During the many years that he taught and conferred with government officials, Confucius also developed his personal philosophy of life. Based on the few remarks we can attribute to him as recorded by his students, Confucius outlined a number of principles that many Chinese people still follow today. For example, Confucius's view of human beings was basically optimistic: all human beings can improve themselves and their condition in life through diligent effort. In spite of the well-defined class divisions that existed in the society around him, Confucius held that one's social status at birth and inherent intelligence were less important than this basic attitude of perseverance.[5] Formal education was key to helping people rise to social and personal heights. Confucius indicated that education should be open to everyone without discrimination. Later followers emphasized this point even more strongly, and it became a tradition in China for wealthy families to open private academies where their own children and those from the surrounding countryside were taught the basic skills of reading, writing, and memorization. The goal that Confucius set for himself was to become a true gentleman (*junzi* 君子). This word is sometimes translated to mean a superior person or a refined person. As used in the time before Confucius, the term referred to a ruler (*jun* 君), and it indicated that the gentleman always acted as if he were the responsible son (*zi* 子) of a highly placed ruler. (During Confucius's time, rulers were always men.) But Confucius extended the concept to apply to any person who endeavored to always act with propriety and dignity. If the world were filled with gentlemen, Confucius felt, the affairs of public society and personal life would be conducted with politeness, order, and decorum.[6]

Confucius often spoke of the importance of kindness or benevolence (*ren* 仁) as a basic principle to guide human conduct. "Do unto others as you would have them do unto you" (*ji suobuyou, wushi yuren* 己所不欲, 勿施於人) was a reliable rule about how to treat people. Western cultures call this the Golden Rule. Confucius indicated that sometimes the most complex-seeming question could be solved by an application of this simple principle.[7]

Confucius also felt strongly that young people should respect their elders, a concept we in the West call filial piety. The Chinese word for filial piety is *xiao* 孝. In most situations, he reasoned, a younger person receives nurturing and guidance from an elder person who has more experience in life and therefore a broader perspective. Although this respect should extend to everyone who is older, it is most important when dealing with members of one's own family and especially one's parents. Observers have long remarked that the Chinese, and through their influence many of the other peoples of East Asia, show a great deference toward the elders in their society. Old people are given more respect and are extended more courtesies than are younger people. While in practice Chinese society can be as dismissive and cruel toward weaker old people as can any other society, most Chinese will find it nearly impossible to justify such behavior. These basic principles, developed by Confucius and restated numerous times by his followers, have become the core set of values that guide the Chinese people in their own lives today. These values impart a strong sense of the importance of proper behavior, a great respect for education, and a confidence that through dogged persistence and hard work individuals can better themselves.

A Philosophy of Personal Maturity

Towards the end of his life (he died at the age of seventy-three), Confucius summed up his experience. On one level, Confucius spent his life trying to better himself in order to become a true gentleman. This was a goal that many later Chinese scholars shared; they similarly hoped to gain the wide respect of society by displaying their refined manners and erudition. In a more universal sense, though, Confucius was describing the stages by which he grew from a lightly formed youth into personal maturity. The stages of growth he outlined have become the model by which the Chinese people divide the stages of human life and judge the behavior appropriate to each stage. The evolution Confucius described for himself is more or less the process by which most human beings grow into full adulthood, as applicable to our own times as it was to his.

"At fifteen," Confucius said, "I was interested in studying" (*wu, shiyouwu, er zhiyuxue* 吾, 十有五, 而志於學).[8] Confucius begins the summation of his life at age fifteen because he is describing his path to maturity, and maturity was not expected to emerge during childhood. As must have been true during the time of Confucius, today in China childhood is seen as a carefree time unencumbered by broader social responsibility,[9] but also a time to inculcate approved social behaviors and attitudes. Chinese scholars influenced by the teachings of Confucius have produced numerous primers for children about how to treat elders and how to study hard for the good of one's family, country, and personal advancement. By the time they become teenagers, children are expected to assume a quieter demeanor and to act respectfully toward the adults they encounter. In both traditional and contemporary China young teenagers are expected to begin assuming some responsibilities toward their families and toward the larger society. Some begin to learn a trade, many assist their parents with household or farm duties, and most take responsibility for their own younger siblings or neighborhood children. Ideally children continue with their formal schooling, where during the junior-high and high-school years serious study becomes a central feature of their lives. By the time they are fifteen, childhood exuberance and careless irresponsibility are no longer tolerated. Children of that age in Chinese society are expected to be respectful and silent in the presence of adults. By the time he was fifteen, Confucius tells us, he put aside the irresponsibility of childhood and began to assume the responsibilities of a teenager. For him youth was a time to study, learn, and prepare for life beyond his immediate family. His thinking began to turn towards the social role he would play as an adult.

"At thirty," he continues, "I became an adult" (*sanshi er li* 三十而立). This is my translation of a phrase that could mean several things. It certainly indicates that Confucius had gone through some rite of passage, if only in his own mind. Confucius is not talking about sexual maturity, which probably took place around age sixteen or seventeen, or about marriage, because sources say that Confucius married at the age of nineteen. By the time he was thirty, Confucius had been married for thirteen years and had a son aged twelve. Confucius is referring not to outward appearances but to a psychological and emotional maturity that he attained only at the age of thirty. I feel the phrase means that in personal terms Confucius no longer felt like an inexperienced youth. He became an adult.[10] Similarly, contemporary Chinese society expects thirty-year-olds to be on their career or job track. They should contribute as adults in some way to the household of their parents, whether or not they continue to live at home, although many do continue living with their parents.

"At forty, I could not be misled" (*sishi er buhuo* 四十而不惑), Confucius said. By the time he was in his forties, Confucius felt he understood much about the ways of the world. He was fully an adult with over a decade of adult experience. He could form his own opinions based on his own experiences, and was less easily swayed by passing fancies.[11] When Chinese reach their forties, society grants them no dispensation from accepting adult responsibility. Life becomes the serious business (especially for men) of earning money, building a career, and raising a family. Society demands that the outward forms of social responsibility and obligations be faithfully observed by all adults so that society may function smoothly. Any deviation by a man in his forties from the roles of husband, father, and primary wage earner is viewed disapprovingly by Chinese society which, especially when compared to contemporary American society, has a rather intolerant view of those who act outside of their prescribed social roles.

In continuing to describe himself as an adult, Confucius said, "In my fifties, I finally understood human nature" (*wushi, er zhitianming* 五十, 而知天命). This marks the stage during which Confucius achieved full emotional maturity. We might also translate this statement to mean that in his fifties Confucius finally felt he "understood about life." By this time in his life Confucius had seen political fortunes change, just as he had no doubt seen personal tragedies among his acquaintances. He had come to understand the workings of society and the varied behavior of human beings. Though he seems to have remained optimistic about human beings, he was no longer naive about human behavior and had come to accept the vagaries of human existence.[12] If translated more literally, this phrase reads, "At fifty I understood the will of heaven" (*zhi tianming* 知天命). What did the term "heaven" (*tian* 天) mean to Confucius? The word refers to the unknowable forces beyond the control of human beings, perhaps the power of departed ancestors, that in some way swayed the events of mortals. The will (*ming* 命) of heaven (or the command given by heaven) refers to the processes of life and society that were beyond the control of single individuals, a process that we sometimes call fate.

Confucius seems to say that he had come to understand what life was really like, how chance encounters and coincidence often determine events. He no longer felt he could accomplish everything he set his mind to; he was able to accept that much of life was impossible to explain and even less possible to control. At this stage, Confucius reached his mature understanding of adult life. I like to translate this phrase, in a somewhat colloquial manner, to read, "When I was in my fifties, I finally knew which way was up."

By the time he had reached old age (in the days of Confucius few lived into their sixties, so in his seventies he must have been viewed as a truly ancient person), Confucius was able to act in a way that had become very natural and second nature for him, yet was approved of by society. His behavior reflected a lifetime of learning about people and living within society. He was able to act with confidence in his own beliefs and with little anxiety about meeting unreasonable expectations. "At sixty, I knew how to act (I knew what to do)" (*liushi er erxun* 六十而耳順), he says, then continues, "In my seventh decade, my heart knew what was right for me, and I never went to extremes" (*qishi-zhang congxinswoyao, buyuju* 七十章, 從心所欲, 不踰矩). He had become, as many older people do, completely comfortable with himself. He called upon the lessons of his many life experiences as a guide for his daily conduct and he had confidence in the decisions he made. Confucius had achieved the goal of being at peace with himself.[13]

When viewed from this perspective, Confucius expounds a personal philosophy, a plan for how individuals ought to conduct themselves over the course of their lives. Many of the comments that can be justifiably attributed to Confucius deal with these themes. They comprise a guide for how an individual should learn to take on responsibility as part of larger human society, and in the process can grow into a personal maturity that is deeply ingrained and reassuringly self-accepting.[14]

Enter Mencius

About a hundred years after the death of Confucius, a scholar who had never met him became very well known throughout north China as a teacher who could elaborate on the philosophy of the great master. In the course of explaining and expanding on the teachings of Confucius, this scholar emphasized the aspect of Confucius's comments that deal with the importance of the individual's role within society. He shifted emphasis away from the philosophy of personal growth leading to satisfying maturity that Confucius expounded and towards a philosophy based on outward social obligations. In the centuries that have followed, down to the present day, the Chinese have concentrated on seeing the importance of the individual defined primarily by the role he plays as a member of society. They feel that individuals should strive to better themselves in order to be more responsible adults in their family and within society.

The scholar was a man named Meng Ke 孟軻. The Chinese refer to him as Master Meng (*Mengzi* 孟子), though the Jesuits gave him a Latinized name, Mencius (390–305 BC). Mencius is given credit for having elaborated on and for having codified the teachings of Confucius. After his death the students of Mencius collected their notes of his lectures and conversations and published them under the title of *The Works of Mencius* (*Mengzi* 孟子). Whereas *The Analects of Confucius* is a short work composed of fragmentary comments that never explore any one topic at length, *The Works of Mencius* contains much more material, with longer and more detailed discussions.[15]

When Mencius lived China was still politically divided into more than ten competing states ruling the north and central parts of the country. By that time the influence of the Zhou house was greatly weakened, just as the influence of diverse aristocratic families and ministers had proportionately grown within each state. Warfare was endemic and military ploys replaced the diplomatic niceties of earlier decades. Describing the atmosphere of constant military actions and maneuverings for power, this age is known as the period of the Warring States (*zhanguo shiqi* 戰國時期) (403–221 BCE).

Like the great master before him, Mencius was an aristocrat who traveled among the princely states acting as a teacher and advisor to government ministers. He gathered a larger number of students than Confucius did and he has left for posterity a more detailed record of his thinking. Since his interpretation of the thinking of Confucius is so widely accepted by Chinese today, it might be said that his thinking has become more influential than the thinking of Confucius himself. However, among the Chinese people Mencius is considered the most important disciple of Confucius, but never a rival to the great master.

Mencius knew that Confucius had been concerned about filial piety and the obligations of a son toward his parents, and he saw that Confucius often spoke of how people should interact with each other. Mencius structured this thinking about social interactions by postulating that all society is organized around five basic relationships (*wulun* 五倫) and each individual during their lifetime is involved in all five. Four of these relationships are unequal, where one party holds a dominant position, but in each of the five relationships there is an element of reciprocity.

For example, in the relationship of the ruler and subject (*junchen* 君臣), the subject has a duty to obey the ruler. Equally as important, however, the ruler has an obligation to be beneficent and caring toward the subject. In the relationship between father and son (*fuzi* 父子), the son is expected to obey and honor the father, but the father has a responsibility to guide and teach the boy.

In the cases of the relationship between husband and wife (*fufu* 夫婦) and between elder brother and younger brother (*xiongdi* 兄弟), a similar set of mutual obligations and responsibilities is expected. Only in the relationship between friends (*pengyou* 朋友) does a situation of equality occur. Among friends there should be a tight bond of trust and of assistance given whenever needed.

We can expand the way we think about these relationships. For example, the relationship between ruler and subject stands for the relationship between citizen and authority. The relationship between father and son implies the important psychological and emotional relationship between parents and children. The relationship of elder brother and younger brother refers to the relationship between siblings. Further, we might characterize all of these relationships as being between benefactors and beneficiaries. This is a positive way of thinking about the mutual duties and obligations that come along with all human relationships.

In emphasizing the social roles played by individuals, Mencius deflects concern away from the development of the inner person and the goal of personal emotional growth. In his own life Confucius saw the creation of a deeply internalized maturity as the mark of the gentleman, but for Mencius the correct conduct acted out in more visible social roles was perhaps more important because it was the clearest way the individual could express an inner maturity. Confucius, of course, also emphasized the importance of proper outward behavior. His concern was evident in his interest in the ancient rites and ceremonies conducted by government officials. The rites symbolized the orderly workings of human society and the dignified role of the aristocracy as leaders within society. Based on conclusions drawn from the comments of Mencius, though, Chinese society logically concluded that proper outward conduct in social relationships and in public affairs was proof enough that one had become a gentleman.

The standard set by Mencius and adopted by Chinese society at large was to judge a gentleman by the degree to which he practiced correct etiquette (*li* 禮). This was an easier standard to meet than that expounded by Confucius, who had outlined the lifetime of experience that finally brought him complete maturity. It was easier for society to pass judgment on observed behavior than to fathom if an individual's actions were based on an inner sincerity, since public actions were clear for all to see.

Originally the word *li* referred to ceremonies and ritual, but by the time of Mencius it had acquired the meaning, when applied to individuals, of "proper behavior" and "politeness." The equation was that a gentlemen should always observe correct etiquette. It meant that if people interact with each other in a proper way, and in a somewhat predictable way, then social interactions will go smoothly. The concept of proper etiquette identifying the true gentleman was adopted by virtually every section of Chinese society. In practice, the idea called for the exchange of a number of polite phrases to smooth all social interactions. It meant avoiding direct confrontations over differences, sharp debates, and heated discussions in favor of oblique statements. The mark of a civilized conversation became the ability of both parties to be outwardly soft and accommodating, even if in fact a disagreement was taking place. The faster pace of social life in China today has somewhat simplified the exchange of polite phrases, though the practice remains in place. Foreign delegations to China in the 1970s when the government strictly controlled visitors' movements, for example, rarely heard government officials straightforwardly refuse any request. When the visitors would suggest a deviation from the prearranged schedule of activities they were met with the polite phrase, "That would not be convenient" (*bufangbian* 不方便), which was the proper way when applying the teaching of Confucius and Mencius, to say "no."

Confucianism and Chinese Social Relationships

Confucius's interpretation of the interaction of human beings with society became a philosophical school that in the West is called Confucianism. In the broadest terms it includes the thinking of Confucius, Mencius, and many other teachers and scholars. The Chinese call this social and moral philosophy the Teaching of the Scholars (*rujiao* 儒教). When Confucius outlined the stages of his life on his personal path to maturity, he created a pattern of human development that the Chinese view as the most appropriate model for the stages of individual growth. As Mencius elaborated that process in the context of human relationships, he described how the individual should function as a member of human society. As part of social interaction, the Chinese conceive of relationships between people almost always (except for very close friends) as unequal. It seems natural and not unfair that in interpersonal relationships one of the parties will always enjoy a greater degree of power or influence because of authority or age.[16]

Americans tend to favor relationships that have a greater degree of equality, so associations of peers, people similar in age and social standing, predominate. When two individuals clearly have quite different degrees of authority, say the relationship between a boss and the employees in the workplace, Americans try to diffuse the difference in authority by using given names. In China people usually call each other by their surname, and persons clearly of a higher status are called by their titles. In this practice a person who is a section chief in a government office might simply be addressed as Section Chief (*buzhang* 部長). When the communists came to power in 1949, they critiqued the Confucian system of differentiated relationships as a feudalistic preserve of status-based divisions within society. Influenced by European Marxists, the communists decreed that people, both males and females, refer to each other as comrade (*tongzhi* 同志), a term of equality devoid of status distinctions. That practice lasted only a little more than thirty years because it was too foreign to the ways in which Chinese society preferred to organize relationships. Today the word comrade is used in China mainly as an unspecific form of address, to hail someone with whom there is no formal relationship, such as when summoning a waitress or asking a question of a bus driver. The important exception in China these days of people who consciously prefer to use the word comrade are gay lovers. They use it to refer to their partners because it is gender free and denotes equality, and the term seems to express exactly the type of relationship they prefer.

In general usage, people prefer the older, status- or age-specific forms of general address, such as Mister (*xiansheng* 先生) or Miss (*xiaojie* 小姐). A young person surnamed Pei is called young Pei (*xiao Pei* 小裴), while an older person named Li will be addressed as old Li (*lao Li* 老李). To be called old in China is an affectionate mark of respect. Familial terms of endearment are applied freely throughout society. Father's friend is quickly called uncle (*shushu* 叔叔), just as any older woman who is kind might be called auntie (*gugu* 姑姑).

Recognizing that differences in status need not preclude a closeness or mutual respect between people, the Chinese are more willing than Americans to form friendships that cut across lines of age or authority. The Chinese see the bond among themselves, determined by the institution of which they are a part, as more important than the age differences of members within that institution. This allows the Chinese to feel more comfortable relaxing and socializing with their workplace cohorts than Americans like to do. Bosses and their employees, teachers and their students often spend more time enjoying meals together or vacation outings than do Americans, where the differences in authority remain close to the surface, despite everyone calling each other by their first names. The result for the Chinese is a great degree of bonding between people within the same institution, such as the company or the school. Chinese usually feel a much stronger connection to their school or with their company than is true for Americans.

Perhaps the hinge that allows Chinese to feel perfectly comfortable in relationships of inequality is the deeply ingrained concept of filial piety. Although in its most strict sense it means giving great respect toward one's parents or older relatives, Chinese society has extended the idea to mean that in Chinese society all elders are owed respect. This idea of filial piety plays itself out most strongly within the family and in the relationship between parents and children. That in fact is one of the clearest ways it was presented in the discourses of Confucius and Mencius. In ancient times, as is true today, even after an individual has become legally and socially an adult Chinese society expects that person to abide by the wishes of the parents.

Friendship, the only relationship of total equality that the Chinese allow, is a special bond much admired by society. In China same-sex friendships are the only ones accepted by society without suspicion. Friends often become so close that they use kinship terms like elder brother (*xiong* 兄) or younger brother (*di* 弟) when referring to each other. The strongest friendships are between those who have grown up together. Male homosexual relationships form and flourish very easily within Chinese society, as long as they are kept from public view, because society accepts that two males will form close emotional bonds.

Eventually much of Confucian thinking became popularized and simplified, which allowed its precepts to spread easily throughout Chinese society and to be understandable to everyone, educated and uneducated alike. The dialectical musings in some of the earlier Confucian literature about the meaning of a particular virtue were reduced to the shorthand of a single written character for each virtue, instantly recognizable to almost every adult Chinese. To have such powerful written symbols whose meanings were crystal clear to the typical citizen was important in traditional China when literacy rates were often low. Even the untutored could recognize certain written characters, especially those representing the Confucian virtues.

Sometimes called the Five Constants (*wuchang* 無常), these basic virtues are kindness (*ren* 仁), integrity (*yi* 義), proper etiquette (*li* 禮), understanding (*zhi* 智), and reliability (*xin* 信). When these written words appear in a decorative setting, perhaps a single word brushed onto a scroll, the Chinese react more to the powerful Confucian-inspired value it carries than to the dictionary meaning of the word. The written word for each virtue carries its formal meaning of the exact quality it signifies, and equally it carries an affectational meaning of the type of behavior it implies and the personal conduct it calls for. These are guides to conduct and, hopefully, to the underlying emotions that propel action. Each single word conveys its importance as one of the cardinal virtues espoused by Confucian thinkers. Its implications for conduct are so clear that seeing the word is enough for most Chinese.[17]

Philosophical and Religious Elaborations of Confucianism

Down through the centuries Confucian values continued to be the set of principles accepted by the majority of Chinese people about how human life and society should be organized. These basic principles have not changed much over time. Viewed as an intellectual philosophical system, though, Confucianism was far from stagnant, and changes regularly took place as one aspect or another of Confucian thinking was manipulated or redefined in order to achieve various political or philosophical ends.

For example, China had many thinkers who explained the physical world in terms of matter, forces, and action. Their line of interpretation, composed of a metaphysical view of phenomena, was grafted onto Confucian ethical principles, adding a new dimension of intellectual analysis and speculation. The scholar given most credit for this synthesis, Zhu Xi 朱熹 (1130–1200 CE), divided all matter into its fundamental principle (*li* 理, written differently than the *li* 禮 of etiquette) and its physical manifestation (*qi* 氣). This was an exciting attempt to link the universal qualities existent in all objects and actions with the diverse particularistic ways in which they manifested themselves. In Confucian ethical terms this might be expressed by saying that the fundamental principle of human beings is that people are basically good (*shan* 善), as Mencius taught, while the particular way in which people express themselves, perhaps by trying to act as a gentleman as Confucius had taught, is the physical manifestation (*qi* 氣) of their goodness. This way of explaining Confucianism along metaphysical lines is called neo-Confucianism.[18]

Zhu Xi's ideas expanded the ways in which Confucianism could be analyzed and understood, and he became a textbook hero whose ideas continue to be taught in Chinese schools. Ordinary Chinese society though, and the ways that people conducted their daily lives, was only indirectly affected by these more purely philosophical concepts. Intellectual philosophical speculation enlivened the debates of scholars, but did not fundamentally alter the way people applied Confucian values in the course of their own actions. As for the bulk of the people in China, the peasants who had very little formal education, theirs was an inarticulate Confucianism. They understood the basic precepts and followed them whenever possible. They knew the popular symbols (the written characters for Confucian virtues) and reacted to them with appropriate feelings of respect. But they could explain virtually nothing about the philosophical schools that espoused and reinterpreted Confucianism every few hundred years. The intellectual debates of educated scholars by and large did not impact the ordinary Chinese person, while popular Confucian ideas, based on custom and widespread usage, did.

Though the Chinese have never forgotten that Confucius was a human being, he has also been revered and treated like a deity. Tang Taizu 唐太祖, the Tang dynasty Zhenguan Emperor 貞觀皇帝 who reigned 627–650, recognized the force of Confucius as a powerful symbol of ethics, morality, and personal improvement through education, and he issued an edict to build temples honoring Confucius throughout the country. Confucius would be honored as the God of Literature (or the patron of literature—*wendi* 文帝) and the temples were naturally called Temples to the God of Literature (*wenmiao* 文廟). This was done, and in practice the temples became symbolic sites for the temporal authority of the government and for the ethical authority of the ruling elite. The temples often had small schools or study halls built on their grounds where basic classes in literacy were given especially for children who lived in the vicinity. They also took on the function of an unofficial city hall or town square, where government decrees or public notices were read out by local officials and government announcements were posted.[19]

Confucius the man would never have agreed to anyone declaring him a deity. His thinking stressed the importance of real people in the real world and he relegated the role of gods and religious practices to a secondary position.

The aristocrats of Confucius's time still held the beliefs of the earliest Chinese peoples of the Shang 商 (1766–1122 BC), who felt there was a close link between living human beings and the spirits of their departed ancestors. It was easy for the elite of the time to move back and forth between purely secular concerns dealing with government or society and appeals to mystical or supernatural forces. Confucius was willing to acknowledge the existence of those beliefs and he felt no need to argue for or against them. Without himself making a judgment on the validity of religious ideas, Confucius could not see how the deities could either help humans to gain maturity or help society as it struggled for stability.

Today, even though they continue to accord him great respect, the Chinese people no longer consider Confucius a deity, but many of the temples to his honor remain. Some are being turned into museums where the remnants of Confucian ceremonies are conducted for the entertainment of tourists. Many are being refurbished and polished up as destinations for sightseeing groups. To see an ornate religious temple turned into a tourist spot would have delighted Confucius. His attitude towards the supernatural was well expressed in his famous quip, that intelligent humans should "respect the gods and spirits, but keep them at a distance" (*jing guishen, er yuanzhi* 敬鬼神, 而遠之).[20]

Confucianism in the Twentieth Century

As the twentieth century arrived, improved methods of transportation and communication allowed greater numbers of people from Western cultures to visit China. These visitors included Christian missionaries, business executives, students, prostitutes, and tourists, among others, and they tended to congregate in only a few of China's cities, usually those along the ocean coastline. The international treaty ports, so-called because they were opened to foreign trade in the late 1800s through diplomatic treaties, became places where Chinese could see the customs and habits of people who represented a Western way of life. In those days, about fifty or sixty years before the advent of daily television broadcasting in China, the port cities with their foreign enclaves of Western restaurants, churches and business houses acted as China's window on the world.

Chinese were traveling outside of China, too. Most often they went on government grants in order to study abroad. At the turn of the nineteenth century many were visiting Japan, which was then absorbing and imitating the outward forms of Western culture as rapidly as possible. Some of the strongest lessons that Chinese students attending school in Japan learned were actually about the powerful creative forces of Western society and how contemporary societies in Europe and America were constantly challenging their own traditions. The students returned to China eager to begin debates contrasting their newly learned ideas of human relationships with the Confucian-bound society in which they had grown up. The panoply of Western influences coming into China were in general limited to the larger coastal cities, while the vast majority of Chinese in the rest of the country continued about their lives mostly oblivious to the potential challenges posed by the quite different and yet for some strongly inviting Western set of social values.

The debates that sprang up served to show the differences in thinking between the Chinese and Western peoples. By describing each value system almost as opposites of the other and by emphasizing the differences between them, the debaters, both Chinese and Western, were able to form clear distinctions between the two. Presenting the two approaches to social organization as a dichotomy made it more difficult for people to realize that in practice neither the Chinese Confucian nor the Western philosophy of strong individualism was a rigid or inflexible set of beliefs. In practice what emerged from the debates were modifications in how the Chinese people thought about and acted within their own society. The result was a gradual modification of traditionally held Confucian values within Chinese society and a partial accommodation to the influence of Western concepts.

As each of the debates successively surfaced during the twentieth century, some particular aspect of widely accepted Confucian values was selected for special scrutiny and evaluation. For example, in the course of the twentieth century young students objected to the stifling hold of their elders over social conventions, Marxist politicos lambasted as oppressive the class divisions that Confucius took for granted, while Confucian principles were even given credit for Asia's unprecedented economic growth at the end of the twentieth century.

Some of the oldest social constructs adopted by any human society, those of Confucianism, were measured against some of the newest interpretations coming in from abroad, especially the ideas generated by the capitalist societies of western Europe and the United States. The debates that ensued were bound to be hurtful to some and in one way or another upsetting to all those who took part in them because they were not abstract discussions about theoretical possibilities. They were concrete observations about the lives of real, living people and about how deeply ingrained principles urgently needed, many people said, to be changed.

Criticize Lin Biao and Criticize Confucius as Feudalistic Class Oppressors

In 1949 the Chinese Communist Party (CCP) came to power on the Chinese mainland and established the People's Republic of China (PRC). In line with most of the Marxist movements that controlled governments during the twentieth century, official bodies preferred to use the word "people's" (*renmin* 人民)

in their titles. But People's China (*Renmin Zhongguo* 人民中國) did not mean people as individuals, but rather people as the masses, the common folk who comprised the bulk of ordinary citizens. Anything carried out for the benefit of the masses was automatically considered legitimate. The teaching of Confucius could have easily been recast in this mold and used to bolster Marxist control over society because through the centuries Confucianism had become a way of encouraging obedience from citizens toward their government. Actually in the early years of their rule over the PRC, Communist Party leaders were not overly anti-Confucian. Confucius was still perceived as a great teacher and philosopher and school textbooks described his insights in a generally positive manner.[21]

But Chinese intellectuals had been exposed to highly critical reinterpretations of Confucian thought since the early 1900s. When the antiestablishment Marxist scholars joined the fray of reappraising Chinese society, there seemed little chance that Confucian thought could play much of a constructive role in helping to bolster the CCP's hold over the country. Marxism taught that all premodern feudal and capitalist societies were based on class exploitation, with the bourgeoisie (*zichan jieji* 資產階級), the class that held land and wealth and therefore controlled the means of production, oppressing the masses of people who had no material wealth. The masses were defined as the proletariat (*wuchan jieji* 無產階級) or the propertyless classes. The basic goal of Marxism was to destroy the bourgeoisie and allow the proletariat to collectively own and have access to all land and wealth. Confucianism, by specifying distinct hierarchical relationships and describing responsibilities and obligations within the context of those relationships, seemed to Marxists to lack the sweeping vision and the liberating goals of Marxism.

In the early 1970s the ways in which Confucianism reinforced the strong class basis of premodern society became a centerpiece in the politically inspired campaign to Criticize Lin Biao and Criticize Confucius (*pi Lin pi Kong* 批林批孔). The immediate object of political ostracism was Lin Biao 林彪 (1908–1971), a heroic general in the People's Liberation Army who was appointed to the number-two post in China in 1967. Lin used his extensive power to name many of his colleagues to high military posts. His goal was to stem the chaos of the Cultural Revolution then wrecking havoc in China by empowering the military to impose order over society. This became a problem for the supreme national leader Mao Zedong 毛澤東 (1893–1976) and his supporters, who were using the fluid political climate of the Cultural Revolution to restructure the CCP bureaucracy of administrative functionaries. Mao feared Lin's group, since it included the military apparatus centered on the People's Liberation Army (*renmin jeifang jun* 人民解放軍) and could eventually take full control of the country, perhaps even removing Mao and his followers from their positions.

The story of Lin's removal from the political scene is a case of truth being stranger than fiction. Accounts put out by Chinese government officials said that in 1971 Lin was planning a military coup against Mao by plotting to assassinate him, possibly by bombing a train. When the plot was discovered and Lin realized he was about to be arrested, he and his son, another high-ranking military official, hurriedly took off with their immediate families in a military plane headed for the Soviet Union where they could seek asylum. The plane ran out of fuel over Mongolia, crashed, and burned. The documentation of these dramatic events has never been fully convincing. But shortly thereafter Mao began removing Lin's colleagues from their military posts and making his own new appointments within the military command system.

The method of announcing and explaining the details of this series of events to the general public both in China and abroad took the form of the political campaign to Criticize Lin Biao and Criticize Confucius. As part of that campaign the way in which Confucius had accepted and tacitly endorsed the oppressive class divisions of feudal society was held up for critical examination and condemnation. Lin Biao was portrayed as a leader who, like Confucius, outwardly claimed to have the best interests of society at heart while working to keep his own privileged class in power.[22]

The campaign pointed out that Confucian thinking was fundamentally a product of the aristocratic classes of ancient China, who generally ignored and oppressed the common peasant. Confucians proposed strict hierarchical relationships as natural, the criticism went, because they always placed Confucians in a position superior to the common man. Confucius often drew a distinction between the gentleman (*junzi* 君子) and the common man (sometimes called the small person, *xiao ren* 小人), and postulated that the class of gentlemen would rule society with their knowledge while the common men worked at physical labor. Confucians emphasized a respect for proper form and style, with its strong emphasis on etiquette (*li* 禮), as a way to constantly differentiate the bourgeoisie from the proletariat, whose behavior was dismissed by implication as crude and coarse. It was charged that the Confucian ideal of benevolence (*ren* 仁) was idealistic and impossible even for Confucius, who could show benevolence only towards members of his own class.

Turning to a criticism of Confucius the man, the campaign charged that Confucius had been a member of the feudal aristocracy, associating with the conservative bureaucrats of his time who colluded to oppress the common people. His definition of how people at different levels of society ought to act preserved the divide between the privileged elite of society who enjoyed many material possessions and the masses who toiled in near poverty. In spite of saying that education should be open to all, the criticism continued, Confucius himself never took any steps to extend education to the masses because he never had any intention of doing so. He advocated a society of clear male dominance, where women had only the most passive roles to play. He posited a society that was filled with inequality and oppression for the majority of people.

In sum, Confucius was a political swindler (*zhengzhi pianzi* 政治騙子). He was a feudal reactionary thinker who used his ideas of good behavior and benevolent government as a trick to keep masses of people in servitude to the authorities and to the aristocrats. Lin Baio's ideas were linked to those of Confucius by saying that Lin Biao had loudly proclaimed to be on the side of the masses, standing next to Mao on the Tiananmen Gate and waving the little red book of Mao's quotations during the Cultural Revolution, while in fact secretly assembling a network of his own followers who were planning to take control of the masses. Along with all the other aspects of traditional Chinese culture that fell victim to scathing criticism during the Cultural Revolution, Confucian values were illuminated in an overly political light, and they became another part of China's cultural heritage judged as beyond redemption. The political extremists working with Mao Zedong wanted feudal Confucian values completely swept away.[23]

Mao and his group's use of a Confucian analogy to attack his contemporary political rival illustrates the degree to which Confucian terminology and even facts about the life of Confucius were taken to be common knowledge among the people. Mao's followers knew that Confucius and the list of virtues he taught as guides to life were instantly recognizable symbols. Because they retained emotional content, any discussion of them was sure to prompt interest and heated debate. Even after several decades of deemphasizing Confucian values within the People's Republic, Mao's campaign showed how universally understood within China Confucian teachings remained.[24]

After several decades of exposure to Marxist ideology, by the time of the political campaign against Lin Biao many Chinese had become convinced that there was some truth in the Marxist's harsh critique of Confucian thought. They had come to believe that moderating rigid class divisions was desirable and were suspicious of all strongly class-based societies. They were keenly aware that the common people were powerless in the face of established authority and that powerless people were easily exploited. In the best humanistic tradition they wanted to believe, as most people do, that human beings could work as equals toward a common good. Marxism, in its most idealized form, seemed to be exactly the opposite of degenerate Confucianism, and many loudly condemned Confucian thinking. (Note that under the rigid control of the communist authorities at the time, most people, and especially the intellectuals, had little choice but to follow the official anti-Confucian line in some form or another. This does not mean they supported Confucianism, because the antifeudal arguments seemed to make good sense, but rather that the debate about Confucianism was highly orchestrated and can hardly be called an open debate.)

In the hurly-burly of China today where the goal for many is to secure their own future by making money, what exactly constitutes the common good is in need of redefinition. As China lurches toward a market-based economy and masses of people move about the country looking for work, some feel nostalgia for the old days of Marxist ideological dominance. Then at least the goals of society were clearly defined. Then society had a collective purpose and its energies were constructively channeled toward clearly defined targets with a purposefulness that today neither Confucianism, and certainly no longer Marxism, seem able to provide. The past, with its more clear delineations of ebbs and flows derived from hindsight, can come to seem preferable to the always-fluid present.

Do Asian Values Equal Confucianism and Economic Growth?

As the twentieth century was drawing to a close, Confucian concepts about social organization once again became the centerpiece of an active debate. The spirited public discourse, carried on in large part through the international media, became known as a debate over Asian Values. The Chinese government and Chinese people living within the PRC were not major participants in the debate, even though it was their heritage and their social values under consideration. Instead, it was Chinese living outside of China, often in other parts of Asia, who championed Asian Values and carried the discussion forward.

The proponents of the Asian Values concept were determined to explain to the international community how such amazing economic growth had taken place in the Asian economies from the 1970s through to the 1990s. On a route from Tokyo to Seoul, through Hong Kong, down to Singapore, Bangkok and Jakarta, symbols of urban wealth such as cell phones, designer fashions, and trendy bistros were common sights.[25]

In many ways the most encouraging phenomenon to emerge from those years of rapid economic growth was the rise of an internationalized class of Asian urban professionals (the Asian equivalent of American yuppies). The members of this class were usually employed in the fields of banking, finance, or cross-border trade, or the businesses that catered to them such as public relations, consulting, and accounting firms; high-tech industries and software-related fields were in this category. The comfortable salaries and high status they enjoyed stimulated the growth of restaurants, hotels, and retailers of luxury items. Automobile dealerships and travel agencies sprang up like mushrooms in most of the Asian capital cities. Whether they had grown up speaking Korean or Mandarin, Cantonese, Malay or Thai, it was surely English they shared as the common language among them. English enjoyed unparalleled strength as the medium of international commerce, and as the linguistic vehicle by which America's dynamic culture was spreading across the world. Often young men, but increasingly including young women as well, were college graduates who could use English well. It's not that much of the vocabulary of the new technologies were in English, because any of the native Asian languages could absorb foreign words for technology, but that English was associated with the idea of a fast-paced, transnational, jet-setting lifestyle, a style that equaled money and sophistication.

These young people were the trend-setters who supported the sophisticated urban culture in Asian countries. Their jobs were high pressure and required massive amounts of energy and time; it helped that most of the yuppie professionals were young, often not yet married, and they had ample energy to spend on the job. Working late into the night or on weekends was not uncommon. It seemed necessary in some industries, since just as the financial markets in Asia were closing in the late Tokyo afternoon, those in London were already in full swing, waiting for the giant New York Stock Exchange to begin morning trading. In the internationalized marketplace, the work clock never stopped ticking. The younger people, for whom all of this was fresh and new, reveled in the constant waves of work activity.

The emergence of this professional class was very encouraging to those Americans who promote the benefits of pluralistic and open societies because these new Asian yuppies seemed to carry a positive and progressive set of liberal American-like values. Although these young people lived in a number of different Asian cultures, their forward-looking ideas were similar. They were tolerant of cultural differences and eager for new ideas. Radiating out from the influences of their sound professional training and their often-daily contacts with the world outside of Asia, they relied on the unencumbered flow of information and, through satellite television or cable news, kept abreast of international events. They were accepting of change and cultural variances, to the point of eagerly welcoming influences from abroad. Seemingly not bound together against outsiders by their own divisive nationalistic or religious ideologies, they were a sophisticated group, comfortable with new ideas of cultural pluralism.

They were proud to be Asians, but also saw themselves as citizens of the world. They were members of a new world class of international professionals whose values were liberal, tolerant, and transnational. They shared as many similarities with their colleagues in the United States or western Europe as they did with their fellow Asians. They were the heralds of a truly integrated global economy, many commentators observed, whose power would raise the standard of living for all of the people of Asia.

As far as many Asian political leaders saw things, however, the phenomenal economic growth experienced in Asia had been made possible by the sound Confucian-based value system that formed the underpinnings of Asian societies. These leaders were older than the young professionals just emerging as a new social class. Unlike the new urban professionals who were born into a world of television and jet travel, the older Asian leaders were the product of an earlier, more socially conservative time and they clearly remembered the atmosphere of Asia during World War II and the pre-economic boom values of a slower-paced region. The lead advocate of traditional Confucian values was Lee Kuan Yew

李光耀 (b. 1923), the man who governed the city-state of Singapore as Prime Minister from 1959 to 1990.

Lee had taken Singapore from an island of slow-moving poverty with its almost inconsequential landmass and molded it into an oasis of social stability with a high standard of living for its people. The liberal and active young Lee grew gradually into a dominant and somewhat intolerant, if benevolent, ruler. He was a paternalistic leader in the Confucian mold. He would do anything to improve the lot of his people, but he would not abide strident criticism of his power. After thirty-one years as Prime Minister, he officially retired and in 1991 took the title Senior Minister, in which post he continued to be the single most powerful figure in Singapore.

The British-educated Lee worked for years to create a positive climate for Confucian values in Singapore and to shape its society, a multiethnic mix of Indian and Malay dominated by a majority of Chinese residents, along Confucian lines. Since the Confucian set of values he was endorsing had influenced almost all the cultures of Asia in some way, he said these were in fact Asian Values, shared equally by the Malay and Thai peoples of Southeast Asia, along with the East Asian Chinese, Koreans, and Japanese.[26]

With Singapore's economy going strong in the 1980s, it seemed clear to Lee that traditional Confucian thinking had not only been a sound value system for premodern society, but also was proving to foster rapid economic growth in the new postmodern environment. He said that Confucian-influenced Asian Values had allowed the nations of Asia to achieve rapid, unprecedented economic and material growth while retaining a strong sense of cultural cohesion. By the late 1980s most of Asia had transformed itself from a group of third-world developing nations into economic powerhouses almost overnight, without having gone through the severe class conflicts or economic panics that had been a feature of all of the Western industrialized nations. Yet in spite of rapid change, Asian societies remained stable and well organized. His analysis was correct, as long as one ignored the case of the PRC and spoke generally of the post–World War II decades. That was the framework in Lee's mind, since it was his personal experiences he was taking as a frame of reference.[27]

Asian Values meant an emphasis on the family as the basic unit of society. This was a key factor in preserving social cohesion, inhibiting selfish, individualistic, or extremely disruptive actions. Because of the set of values that determine their actions, Lee said, Asians always act in the best interests of their family; they tend to see themselves in relation to larger society and they display a concern with the reactions of society to their individual actions.[28] When the Asian set of values was exercised in the workplace, according to this argument, Asians proved to be better workers then individualistic Americans or western Europeans. Asians were willing to work hard and conscientiously because they felt obligations toward their family to provide a steady income and not bring disgrace to their elders. Seeing themselves as members of the broader society, they were willing to work for lower wages and avoid labor disputes such as strikes; that is to say, they were willing to sacrifice personal rewards as long as they were convinced they were helping the advancement of society. They felt strong bonds to the company they worked for and so paid attention to the quality of their work. Asian managers, in the best Confucian tradition, felt an almost parental obligation toward their employees, granting lifetime employment and displaying a great reluctance to fire anyone. Certainly the cases of South Korea, Hong Kong, Singapore, and post–World War II Japan, where workers had indeed accepted substandard wages in order to collectively build a better economy, underscored his point.[29]

At the national level, Lee felt the secret to economic success was that in each of the Asian nations the political, social, and economic energies of the people had been carefully shepherded by a strong, paternalistic, and beneficent leader. It was true that none of the newly rising nations of Asia had a pluralistic democratic tradition or an open society where conflicting opinions or open debates were encouraged or respected. These were the conditions that many western Europeans and Americans felt were necessary for the evolution of consumer capitalism, yet each of the economically expanding Asian nations instead had a highly controlling political and economic elite, and in many cases a single autocratic ruler, a version of Lee Kuan Yew, who determined the limits of dissent.[30]

It suited Lee Kuan Yew quite well to define the important role of the Asian leader as he did, because he was defining himself and taking credit for having led Singapore into economic prosperity. Although South Korea had the autocratic President Park Chung Hee 朴正熙 (1917–1979) and in Japan a cabal of political power-holders aligned to the Liberal Democratic Party maintained a steady grip on the leadership, none of the other Asian nations had a single leader to guide the economy. This analysis must exclude the PRC under Mao Zedong and the Democratic People's Republic of Korea (DPRK) of North Korea under Kim Il Song 金日成 (1912–1994) since, although both were strong and autocratic leaders, neither man was trying to build the type of capitalistic economic growth that prompted Lee's analysis.

Undeterred by these qualifications to his argument, Lee Kuan Yew saw himself as a paternalistic, caring leader who was in some sense the head of an extended clan, in this case the clan being the entire city-state of Singapore. Just like the ideal father of traditional Confucian China, he knew what was best for his nation and he worked sincerely to being it about. He would be strict when necessary, but even his punishments, he felt, were administered in the best interests of the recipient. He did not welcome any critical evaluation of his performance, because it was the role of the children, and equally of citizens, to obey the father, or the ruler. The ruler would guide them toward their own best interests. Sustained public criticism of his official policies seemed to be the one sure way of arousing Lee's anger. It was as if his children were sassing him back during an argument, a breakdown of the virtue of obedience that no Confucian father could tolerate.

All of the bonds and responsibilities so lovingly described by the advocates of Asian Values were clearly derived from the Confucian worldview. In order to make the argument seem stronger, stark contrasts were drawn with an equally simplified explanation of what were called Western Values. According to this definition, Western Values promote the formation of a strong individual. The Western individual always acts with her own interests at heart. In the workplace, the Western worker is interested in claiming all of the vacation time due to her. Whereas Asian workers make a show of only reluctantly taking short vacations so as not to disrupt the work of their company, in the West workers plan for blocks of vacation time that are as long as possible, then they proudly announce how they and their families will have an adventure of leisure that has nothing to do with their company. Western workers keep photos of family members on their desks, illustrating the importance they place on bonds beyond the workplace. Asian workers keep family photos out of their workplace and ask family members not to call them at the company in order to give their full loyalty and attention to the company during working hours.[31]

The Economics of Economic Growth

From the point of view of Western economists, the process by which several poor Asian nations transformed themselves into economic powerhouses in the 1970s and 1980s had more to do with manufacturing costs and financial flows than with any traditional Asian social philosophy. The determining factors, American economists felt, were the drives of Western companies to lower the production costs of their goods by having them manufactured in countries with a lower standard of living where lower wages were paid to workers. This practice was termed global sourcing. From the 1960s on, the nations of Asia, with stable societies and workers whose incomes were a fraction of what Americans had to be paid, were ideal for this purpose. Japan was the first to catapult itself into the ranks of a leading international economy, with a take-off that began in the late 1950s. By the end of the 1970s Japanese automobiles and electronic products dominated the markets in all of the advanced industrialized nations. At the end of the twentieth century Japan's economy was ranked as the second largest in the world, following only that of the United States.[32]

I saw the process take place in Korea, which entered the competition for growth in the 1970s and achieved its affluence by the end of the 1980s. Korea benefited from the wealth of the Japanese economy, whose workers by the 1980s had priced themselves out of competition because of rising wages. American manufacturers, still seeking low-cost offshore producers, turned to the highly literate, disciplined workforce of South Korea. In rapid succession Korean companies won American contracts to produce sports equipment, running shoes, and clothing with designer labels. Initially the South Koreans continued to live frugally, working hard for low wages and encouraged by a government that kept a tight lid on social movements of any kind. South Korean political leaders reacted with a no-nonsense show of force to repress any attempt by workers to agitate for higher wages. The government asked the workers (in effect, they ordered the workers) to sacrifice personal income growth for the sake of the national economy, to continue working for low wages so that high levels of employment and manufacture could be sustained, thus raising the wealth of the entire country.[33]

At first the newly manufactured clothing, sportswear, and watches destined for export to Japan, Europe, and the United States were priced well beyond the ability of most Koreans to purchase. Soon, however, during my visits to Korea I saw inexpensive imitations of these export products, called knockoffs, offered for sale in the local markets in Seoul and other South Korean cities. Unauthorized copies of high-priced clothing and jewelry, from Rolex watches to Polo shirts, were essentially pirated products that looked exactly like the genuine article but sold domestically at very low prices. By being able to enjoy the same products in the same styles and colors as more affluent consumers in Japan and the West, and at prices they could afford, Koreans developed an awareness of international brand names, of the trends in fashions and accessories.

Before long Korean companies were turning out technologically sophisticated high-value-added products like good-quality televisions, VCRs, and cassette recorders for the export market. In America and Europe such products gave strong competition to Japanese companies because the Korean products were available in comparable quality but at lower prices. Within Korea, domestic models of these same electronic products were created for the home market. From automobiles, to computers and the latest software, each advance in manufacturing resulted in greater profits for Korean companies in all their export markets, while at the same time slightly lower-priced but similar goods of the same high quality were put on sale within Korea.[34]

Eventually the wages and benefits given to South Korean workers began to rise along with the material wealth of the entire country. American manufacturers found the cost of manufacturing in Korea rising, so they turned successively to other Asian nations with a lower standard of living in order to continue producing goods at the lowest possible cost. In those nations the same process was repeated: goods produced for export gradually found their way into the local markets, and the local workers began to find their wages rising to levels where they could afford the better-quality products. The underlying stimulus for this entire process was American companies seeking lower costs through offshore production. In each Asian country the companies that were able to win the bulk of American contracts grew very rich, forming themselves into large corporations or building on a corporate base formed earlier already in place. In South Korea a number of mammoth conglomerates (*chaebol* 財閥) such as Samsung, Hyundai, and Lucky Goldstar (LG) became powerful world-class businesses.[35]

South Korea's success was followed by economic growth in Taiwan, Thailand, Malaysia, and Indonesia, with the Philippine economy benefiting as well. Economists dubbed these exploding economies the New Tigers of Asia. There were so many of them rising so rapidly with unquestioned strength that the only real problem was how many countries to include in the new category. Were there only four New Tigers (South Korea, Taiwan, Thailand, Malaysia), or were there nine (the original four expanded to include Hong Kong, Singapore, Indonesia, Vietnam, and the Philippines)? With high employment, rising Gross Domestic Product (GDP), and an expanding professional urban class leading the way in consumer spending, it was an embarrassment of riches for Asia. Pundits in both Asia and America in the early 1990s freely said that the twenty-first century would be the Asia-Pacific Century and that growth in economic expansion and productivity would shift away from the Western industrialized democracies to the nations of Asia.

Hong Kong and Singapore were also part of this process. They had some manufacturing, but achieved their prominence through an exponential growth in financial services. Using online computers, satellite communications, and open fax and telephone lines, they were wired up to the global economy. With their lightly regulated financial sectors, they became meccas for the inward and outward flows of capital that was fueling the Asian Miracle.[36]

An Asian Financial Crisis Ends the Century

In 1997 the economies of the New Tigers suddenly collapsed, ushering in the Asian financial crisis that dominated every conversation about Asia for the next two years. The problem was caused by the abrupt flight of foreign capital out of Asia. The American and west European banks that spawned Asia's economic boom became the cause of its rapid and unexpected demise.

In one country after another, Western banks asked for repayment of the large loans they had extended to Asian banks. The Asian banks had in turn made loans to corporations, medium-sized companies, and wealthy individuals within their own countries. Faced with the unexpected need to return their loans, most companies and individuals, and even the larger corporations, could not quickly come up with the money for repayment. The governments of each New Tiger intervened as best they could, but the amounts involved were in total more than even the governments could easily finance. The domino effect once predicted by American strategists during the Vietnam War—that the nations of southeast Asia (unless protected by American military power) could fall to totalitarian Communism in an unstoppable chain reaction—was replaced in the 1990s by the chain reaction of Asian economic collapses caused by banks in the United States and western Europe.

Many economists consider the term "financial crisis" inaccurate. Instead, they prefer to call it a liquidity crisis, since the Western banks wanted their cash returned, but the cash had been lent out by the banks and was tied up in real estate and various other projects, so it could not quickly be turned back into cash and repaid. Not even a healthy bank, which always has much of his assets out on loan, can survive such a giant "run on the bank." The problem began in Thailand, rocked Malaysia, then dramatically spread to South Korea. Soon the Indonesian economy, exacerbated by its own internal political disputes, was in chaos. Japan, already mired in a recession that had started around 1991, was unable to be of assistance, and soon the economies of Hong Kong and Singapore were feeling the effects of the economic depression.[37]

In each Asian nation the "real" economy of manufacture, distribution, and consumption was still strong. People had jobs and they were (initially, at least) willing to spend. Companies wanted to continue hiring and retail outlets remained well stocked. The problem was not caused by the real economy, which remained in place as the crisis began, but rather by problems with the financial economy. When money began to leave as the banks called in their loans in order to repay the Western lenders, jobs were lost, consumer spending plummeted, and the real economy fell into a depression.

All of the new economies of Asia were caught in a similar trap when their real economies (the manufacturing sector) were unable to get the funds they needed to survive because of the collapse of their financial economies (the banking sector). Before the crisis both parts seemed inextricably bound, but the crisis revealed that the financial sector and the influx of funds from Western democracies had been an engine driving economic growth forward.[38]

The flight of capital out of Asia was precipitated by a crisis of confidence among Western bankers and financial institutions. They feared the money they sent into Asia had been lent to companies and individuals who probably could not pay it back. To justify calling in their loans, Western bankers and economists argued that Asian economies had become overextended and pointed to the dark side of Confucian-based values. The criticisms leveled against each Asian economy were so cutting and appeared so well-founded that the proponents of Asian Values, those who had cited them as the reason for Asia's economic growth, found themselves in undignified retreat. Western economists argued that financial deals in Asia were made through the secretive collusion of well-placed individuals. In each Asian nation, paternalistic elites who held top power became friends with wealthy individuals and chiefs of the major corporations. When this cabal needed funds, the autocratic government suggested to managers of local banks that they make the loans. Banks, acting on unofficial government orders, dared not investigate the financial situation of the corporations or individuals. A lack of due diligence (investigation of a client's financial standing before committing to a loan or investment of money, accompanied by thorough audits) did not prevent the banks from extending loans to favored corporations.[39]

Confucianism, Western critics pointed out, encouraged national leaders to act as the head of a large clan or family, protecting the clan (which usually meant the leader and the government) from outside scrutiny of its activities. Since it was the Asian way to conduct business in private, closed-door meetings, Asian societies lacked any well-developed civil society of public interest groups or citizens who might hold the government accountable for its actions. Moreover, Confucian values discouraged criticism of the motives or sincerity of the top elite, who were assumed to be acting as virtuous Confucian gentlemen.

Closed relationships were in accordance with the teachings of Mencius: the head of each family, the father, should act unilaterally for the best interests of his family. Confucian teachings held that the father should be respected, obeyed, and not questioned. In calling for respectful obedience, Confucius and Mencius (though they did not have the concept at the time) were working against the idea of transparency in public dealings. Western economists said transparency meant that all public transactions should be predictable, fair to all parties involved, and completely documented. Theoretically, when transactions are carried out in an open manner, they will tend to be rational (since they can be challenged and must be defensible), and those involved can be held accountable for their actions. Asian economies dismissed the need for transparency and worked against it by placing a higher value on the strength of personal contacts and the trustworthiness of the parties immediately involved.

An emphasis on personal trust and a distrust of transparency created a weak system of financial controls in Asia. Accounting standards and auditing procedures varied with each country and always seemed, at least to Western-trained accountants, to lack thoroughness. Due diligence was regularly overlooked. Companies that could not account for the use of their funds, or individuals who had little likelihood of repaying a loan, could still receive money as long as their personal relationships with banking or government officials were in order.

The political system in Asia was in itself fairly typical of how power politics are conducted in many nations of the world, where an autocratic leader does not tolerate criticism and does not hold himself accountable to the public. Asian leaders spent many of the decades following World War II limiting the degree to which criticism of their power could be made public. Lee Kuan Yew may have felt himself to be sincere, but he limited freedom of expression in Singapore no less than autocratic leaders in Latin America, the Arab world, or Africa. When South Korean leaders called for workers to accept lower wages and a lower standard of living in order to achieve economic growth for all (as they did in the 1970s and early '80s), the leaders were employing the tactics of capitalist managers trying to maximize profits by keeping wages low. By this line of reasoning the personal fortunes of Korea's corporate chiefs were rising in part because the worker's wages were held down.

With an autocratic head of state stifling the freedom of inquiry or expression in each nation, individuals or public interest groups that called for greater accountability by corporations or officials found it difficult to be heard. The problems that precipitated the flight of capital in 1997 did not appear overnight. They were well-known conditions and had been informally discussed within Asia for many years, especially by Western executives. But keep in mind that those same Western business leaders and bankers had continued to do business with their Asian counterparts. As long as the growing economy presented opportunities for financial gain, no one had seemed in a hurry to alter the system of decision-making networks. After the panic started, though, Western economists criticized the private decision-making meetings held behind closed doors as symptomatic of the worst of Asian Values. Such collusive practices were called crony capitalism. According to Western observers, when the questionable lending decisions fostered by crony capitalism brought down the Asian economies, they ipso facto brought about the collapse of the argument in favor of Asian Values.

What of the emerging class of internationalized urban professionals in Asia? They were hit hard by the Asian financial crisis of the late 1990s. The prestigious corporations that employed them tottered to the brink of bankruptcy, while a host of smaller companies closed their doors. College graduates entering the job market after 1998 could not find professional jobs because most companies curtailed or ceased recruiting new employees. With the close of the twentieth century Asia's young professionals were struggling hard to survive. Whether or not they survive as a new class and a new force in twenty-first-century Asia will depend on how the economies of each Asian nation recover from the Asian financial crisis in the long term.

Despite the deep gloom brought on by the financial crises, soon after the new millennium began, the Asian economies rebounded. To be sure, there were fewer jobs, lower wages and a giant sense of insecurity among those who wanted middle-class status, but in terms of production, capital flows, and global trade, all of the major Asian economies performed well. Even Japan finally emerged from its long recession.

Pundits asked, If the closed and secretive connections fostered by Asian Values had caused the crisis in the first place, why were Asian societies, having undergone virtually no major cultural change, now rather quickly coming back to financial life? Perhaps the problems lay not in indigenous Asian Values, but rather in the faulty or dangerous fiscal management that had been foisted on Asia by the global economic managers. According to these observers, global money mangers wanting to take advantage of strong Asian currencies and high interest rates forced Asian banks to borrow money, and then caused the crises when they suddenly called in their foreign loans. The causes of the Asian financial crisis continue to be debated, the reemergence of strong Asian economies continues, but the emerging professional class in Asia remains insecure about its future.[40]

Within China, which managed to avoid the worst of the financial crisis and whose economy continued to expand, the class of young urban professionals continues to grow. New construction and cell phones are now a common sight in urban settings. Will China have the most vital Asian economy in the coming decades?

Understanding the Chinese Individual in Today's World

Probably the most insightful way to understand Chinese society and the individuals who compose it today is to look through the lens of Confucian values. The Chinese have discussed and debated those ideas for so long that they have permeated all the structures of Chinese society and they influence, to a greater or lesser degree, the ways in which society functions. The relative importance given to any social organization in Chinese society is determined by Confucianism, as are the limits of acceptable or unacceptable behavior each institution is allowed. Confucian thinking has also defined the individual who exists within Chinese society. One does not see oneself as a free agent struggling for fulfilling expression, but rather as a part of some larger social grouping, which in the majority of cases is the family into which one is born or raised. It seems only natural to the Chinese, indeed it is virtually imperative, that they consider decisions first from the perspective of their family and the effects their decision will have on parents and relatives.

For many, many Chinese, the Confucianism they adhere to is an inarticulate Confucianism. They cannot define it in clear detail. They know the most popularly accepted phrases and symbols of Confucian thought, but little more than that. Still, the values that have been taught for centuries based on Confucian thinking, for example, the primacy of the family and the need to avoid disgracing one's parents and ancestors, are values that determine how they interpret their own motivations and the actions of those around them.

While surrounded by the material objects of the real world and in the midst of the fluid actions of everyday life, it is easy to think that Confucian values are absent. Somehow glass and steel, digitalized electronic devices and the instantaneous currency flows of globalized financial markets seem to negate the ancient philosophical discourses of Confucius and his ideas. But these are in fact only the latest material objects to appear in human society. At most they call for some degree of reexamination and perhaps some adaptation of Confucian thinking, but in and of themselves they do not pose a great challenge to the

Confucian worldview. Do not be misled by thinking that the modern world has no place for Confucianism. Instead, when dealing with Chinese always look for the strand of Confucian values in their actions and you will always find that it is present.[41]

Notes

1. One scholar claims the term *kongfuzi* (孔夫子 Confucius) was rarely spoken in China and was only occasionally written, though it was a term of high respect. See Lionel Jensen, *Manufacturing Confucianism: Chinese Traditions and Universal Civilization* (Durham, NC: Duke University Press, 1997), 7, 81–92. An examination of the Jesuits and their close association with the Mandarin-speaking elite of China from their earliest days in China is in Jonathan Spence, *The Memory Palace of Matteo Ricci* (New York: Viking Penguin, 1984).

2. For a brief, readable, and human account of Confucius in English see John Wills, Jr., *Mountain of Fame: Portraits in Chinese History* (Princeton, NJ: Princeton University Press, 1994), 11–32.

3. The name is taken from the *Spring and Autumn Annals* (*Chunqiu* 春秋), a historical work compiled in ancient times that covers some of the events of this period.

4. Some of the students may have been relatives of Confucius. See E. Bruce Brooks and A. Taeko Brooks, *The Original Analects* (New York: Columbia University Press, 1998), 11.

5. The interpretation that Confucius's philosophy put forward an optimistic view of human nature was made by one of the first American scholars to write a full-length biography of Confucius. See H. G. Creel, *Confucius: The Man and the Myth* (New York: John Day Company, 1949), 132–33. The Confucians themselves, however, had long historical debates about the basic nature of human beings: was it good (*shan* 善) or bad (*e* 惡)? Different Confucian scholars came to different conclusions. For a brief summary of these positions see *Zhongguo ruxue zidian* 中國儒學字典 [Dictionary of Chinese Confucianism] (Shenyang: Liaoning renmin chubanshe, 1988), 533–34. Confucius himself felt that he was merely transmitting ancient values and was not a creator of new ones.

6. *Junzi* is a term that also has many English translations, among these are: "proper man," "superior man," "complete man," "wise and virtuous man," in addition to "gentleman." For comments on these various translations see Mary Cheadle, *Ezra Pound's Confucian Translations* (Ann Arbor: University of Michigan Press, 1997), 121–23. Females were expected to have the virtues of compassion, modesty, and forbearance.

7. For a useful overview of the life of Confucius and his philosophy and the place of humanness (*ren*) see John Berthrong, *Transformations of the Confucian Way* (Boulder, CO: Westview Press, 1998), 15–22. In describing the meaning of the word reciprocity (*shu* 恕), Confucius stated the Golden Rule as, "What you do not want done to yourself, do not do to others" (*jisuo buyu, wushi yuren* 己所不欲, 勿施於人). See James Legge,

The Chinese Classics (1893; repr., Hong Kong: Hong Kong University Press, 1960), 1:301. Because he phrased this in negative terms, some people call this the Silver Rule. Modern day spoken Chinese still often phrases positive ideas by stating them in terms of two negatives, just as Confucius did so many centuries ago.

8. I prefer direct English translations that show the relevance of what Confucius was saying to contemporary life, but many other translations make use of poetic language. For example: "At fifteen, I set my heart on learning," William Theodore De Bary, "Constructive Engagement with Asian Values," *Harvard Asia Quarterly* 2, no. 2 (Winter 1998): 10. De Bary is using respected scholar D. C. Lau's translation; see D. C. Lau, *Confucius: The Analects* (Hong Kong: Chinese University Press, 1983), 11. "At fifteen, I had my mind bent on learning," Legge, *Chinese Classics* 1:146. "At fifteen I thought only of study," James Ware, *The Best of Confucius* (Garden City: Halcyon House, 1950), 23. "At fifteen I began to devote myself to learning," Cheng Lin, *The Four Books: Confucian Classics* (Shanghai: World Publishers, 1948), 8. "At fifteen I set my mind upon wisdom," William Soothall, *The Analects of Confucius* (published by the author in China, 1910), 149. "At fifteen I began to be seriously interested in study," Lin Yutang, *The Wisdom of Confucius* (New York: Modern Library, 1938), 160. Ezra Pound's especially poetic translation gives this passage as "At fifteen I wanted to learn," "The Analects of Confucius," *Huron Review* 3, no. 1 (Spring 1950): 13. For interesting comments on Ezra Pound and on his relationship to Chinese studies see Jonathan Spence, *The Chan's Great Continent* (New York: W.W. Norton, 1998), 168–74. T. R. Reid assesses translators and their abilities in *Confucius Lives Next Door: What Living in the East Teaches Us about Living in the West* (New York: Random House, 1999), 118–24. For a lively biography of Confucius that draws on passages taken from many of the established classical Chinese sources, see Jin Jingfang 進景芳 et al., *Kongzi xinzhuan* 孔子新傳 [A new biography of Confucius] (Changsha: Hunan chubanshe, 1991), 28–103.

9. Present-day Western scholars argue that childhood is a relatively new concept. This was not the case in China, where the concept of childhood has a long tradition. See Hsuing Bing-chen (Xiong Bingjen 熊秉真), *Tongnian yiwang: Zhongguo xunzi de lishi* 童年憶往:中國孩子的歷史 [Recalling childhood: The history of children and grandchildren in China] (Taipei: Maitian chuban, 2000). The English-language version is *A Tender Voyage: Children and Childhood in Late Imperial China* (Stanford, CA: Stanford University Press, 2005). Comments on the pampered and sophisticated life of many urban Chinese kids today are in Jun Jing, ed., *Feeding China's Little Emperors: Food, Children, and Social Change* (Stanford: Stanford University Press, 2000). Examples of how East Asian cultures indulge their young children can be found in James Watson, ed., *Golden Arches East: McDonalds in East Asia* (Stanford, CA: Stanford University Press, 1997).

10. Confucius turned thirty in the year 518 BCE. Some popular versions of the expression *sanshi er li* 三十而立 interpret the phrase "to stand up" (*er li* 而立) as "to establish one's will" (*er lizhi* 而立志). This interpretation is taken by a Chinese scholar who gives the translation as "At thirty, I had formed my character," Lin, *Four Books*, 8, and also by Lin Yutang, *Wisdom of Confucius*, 160. Other versions are: "At thirty, I was established

(stood on my own feet)," De Bary, "Constructive Engagement," 10; "At thirty, I stood firm," Legge, *Chinese Classics*, 1:146; "At thirty I took my stand," Lau, *Confucius*, 11. A translation that in my estimation captures the meaning better is "[A]t thirty I began playing my role," Ware, *Best of Confucius*, 23. The phrase *lizhi*, meaning to grow strong or to acquire determination, was used by Mencius (and not by Confucius) in reference to a weak man growing determined. See James Legge, *Chinese Classics,* vol. 2, *The Works of Mencius* (Hong Kong: Hong Kong University Press, 1960), 489, where the translation is given as "the weak acquire determination." A translation "the weakling's purpose stands" is in Leonard Lyall, *Mencius* (New York: Longmans, Green & Co., 1932), 229. In the process of popularizing Confucianism, the words of Confucius in this case apparently became confused with those of Mencius.

11. This is also translated as: "At forty I had no perplexities," De Bary "Constructive Engagement," 10, and the same in Lin Yutang, *Wisdom of Confucius*, 160; "At forty, I had no doubts," Legge, *Chinese Classics*, 1:146; "At forty I came to be free from doubts," Lau, *Confucius*, 11, and similar in Soothall, *Analects of Confucius*, 149; A good contemporary translation is, "[A]t forty I was sure of myself," Ware, *Best of Confucius*, 23. Pound links the two stages by saying, "At thirty I had a foundation; at forty, a certitude," Pound, "Analects," 13.

12. Since I consider this a crucial statement by Confucius, it is particularly interesting to look at the many ways it has been translated: "At fifty I learned what Heaven commanded of me," De Bary, "Constructive Engagement," 10; "At fifty, I knew the decrees of Heaven," Legge, *Chinese Classics*, 1:146; "At fifty I understood the Decree of Heaven," Lau, *Confucius*, 11; "At fifty I knew the Will of Heaven," Lin Yutang, *Wisdom of Confucius*, 160. My own sense of the meaning of this phrase for modern Americans is closely captured in "[A]t fifty I was conscious of my position in the universe," Ware, *Best of Confucius*, 23.

13. "By sixty my ear had become attuned to it. At seventy I could follow my heart's desire without transgressing," De Bary "Constructive Engagement," 10; "At sixty my ear was docile," Soothall, *Analects of Confucius*, 151; "At sixty nothing that I heard disturbed me," Lin Yutang, *Wisdom of Confucius*, 160; "At sixty, my ear was an obedient organ [for the reception of truth]. At seventy, I could follow what my heart desired, without transgressing what was right," Legge, *Chinese Classics*, 1:146; "At sixty my ear was attuned, at seventy I followed my heart's desire without overstepping the line," Lau, *Confucius*, 11; "At sixty I had become receptive to the truth, at seventy I could follow my heart's desire without trespassing the moral laws," Lin, *Four Books*, 8. Ware translates these passages as, "[A]t sixty I was no longer argumentative; and now at seventy I can follow my heart's desire without violating custom," *Best of Confucius*, 23. Ezra Pound links the last stages of Confucius's life by translating the passages as, "At fifty, knew the orders of Heaven; at sixty, was ready to follow them. At seventy could follow my own heart's desire without overstepping the T-square." Pound, "Analects," 13. ("Overstepping the T-square" seems to be a dated phrase that I have never heard used in conversation.)

14. Thousands of books exist in all of the East Asian languages that popularize Confucian teachings in terms of a personal philosophy. For one example, from Taiwan,

see Li Xu 李旭, *Kongzi de rensheng zhexue* 孔子的人生哲學 [Confucius's human philosophy] (Taipei: Yangji wenhua shiyeh fufen yuxian gongsi, 1994). An example from Hong Kong, is Wang Xingkang 王興康, *Lun Yu: Renzhe di jiaohai* 論語：仁者的教海 (The Analects: The benevolent person's guide) (Hong Kong: Zhonghwa shuzhu, 1996). Many scholars feel that Confucius and his followers had a deep understanding of the human psyche. For a good introduction, see Frederick Mote, *Intellectual Foundations of China*, 2nd ed. (New York: McGraw-Hill, 1989), esp. p. 42.

15. For an account of Mencius's elaborations on the basic teaching of Confucius see Yang Guorong 楊國榮, *Mengzi pingzhuan; zuoxiang neijing zhi jing* 孟子評傳：走向內經之境 [Critical biography of Mencius: Toward understanding the inner classic] (Nanning: Guangxi jiaoyu chubanshe, 1994). A detailed though concise review of the works of Mencius appears in D. C. Lau, introduction to *Mencius*, vol. 1 (Hong Kong: Chinese University Press, 1984). The names of Confucius and Mencius have been linked throughout Chinese history, to the point of often being treated as a single word, *kongmeng*. For one example see *KongMeng tuge* 孔孟圖歌 [Confucius and Mencius in pictures and poems] (1904; repr., Beijing: Zhongguo shudian, 1996). The two names remained linked in the highly politicized debates of the Chinese Communists in the 1970s. See *Lin Biao yu KongMeng zhi dao* 林彪與孔孟之道 [Lin Biao and the way of Confucius and Mencius] (Hong Kong: Sanlian shudian, 1974).

16. A brief discussion of being comfortable with unequal relationships is by William Theodore De Bary, *Confucianism: The Dynamics of Tradition*, ed. Irene Eber (New York: Macmillan, 1986), 118–20. Reciprocity in human relationships as between benefactors and beneficiaries is suggested in Henry Rosemont, Jr., "Classical Confucian and Contemporary Feminist Perspectives on the Self," in *Culture and Self: Philosophical and Religious Perspectives, East and West*, ed. Douglas Allen (Boulder, CO: Westview, 1997), 74.

17. An outline of the Five Constants is in *Zhongguo ruxue zidian*, 588. The character *yi* is often rendered as righteousness, while the word *ren* can be translated as benevolence, human-heartedness, goodness, love, altruism, or humanity. See Lau, *Mencius*, xiii. The power of words and of language, especially in its written form, seems especially potent for the Chinese; Language can influence behavior and shape reality. These ideas are developed in Chad Hansen, *Language and Logic in Ancient China* (Ann Arbor: University of Michigan Press, 1983). For a creative and persuasive commentary and translation of many value terms used in Confucianism, I recommend Roger Ames and David Hall, *Focusing on the Familiar: A Translation and Philosophical Interpretation of the Zhongyong* (Honolulu: University of Hawai'i Press, 2001).

18. Neo-Confucianism is an English-language term to describe early Confucian thought as modified by other philosophical concepts. In Chinese, neo-Confucianism would be called *daoxue* 道學 (study of the way) or *lixue* 理學 (study of principles). Zhu Xi became so influential because of the exclusive use of his interpretations in the Chinese civil service examinations that were used from the 1200s until 1905.

19. Temples to honor Confucius had been around in China for several centuries by the time of the Tang dynasty (618–905) edict. He had also been revered as the God of Literature as early as the Wei dynasty (220–264). For a summary of this background

see Zhang Dainian 張岱年, ed., *Kongzi da zidian* 孔子大辭典 [Dictionary of Confucius] (Shanghai: Shanghai zishu chubanshe, 1993), 41–43. A brief comment on Confucius as a deity is in Raymond Dawson, *Confucius* (New York: Hill and Wang, 1981), 84–85.

20. This phrase is translated by Legge as "While respecting spiritual beings, keep aloof from them," see Legge, *Chinese Classics*, 1:191; A different translation is in Lau, *Confucius*, 53. The Analects contain another phrase on this topic: "The subjects on which the Master did not talk were extraordinary things, feats of strength, disorder, and the gods" (*zibuyu, guai, li, luan, shen* 子不語, 怪, 力, 亂, 神). Some translations of this phrase can be found in Legge, *Chinese Classics*, 1:201; Lau, *Confucius*, 61. Confucius's ambivalence toward the spirits (usually written in early Chinese as *guishen* 鬼神) is also stated in *Zhongguo ruxue zidian*, 771–72. This phrase is also translated using the word "spirit" in Michael A. Fuller, *An Introduction to Literary Chinese* (Cambridge, MA: Harvard University Asia Center, 1999), 20 (where the two characters of the word are reversed as *shengui* 神鬼).

21. Even when the first communes were organized in 1958, Communist Party cadre took the family as the basic social unit around which collective activities would be organized. See the article by Martin Whyte in *The Chinese: Adapting the Past, Building the Future*, ed. Robert Dernberger et al. (Ann Arbor: Center for Chinese Studies, University of Michigan, 1986), 334–35. The generally positive view of Confucius presented in China's schools in the 1950s is well illustrated in *Zhongguo lishi (gaoji zhongxue keben)* [Chinese history—Higher-middle school text] (Beijing: Renmin jiaoyu chubanshe, 1957), 1:44–45. In a similar vein, a book published in 1956 described Confucius as a person who upheld the feudal class system but nevertheless was useful in the dissemination of ancient scholarship. See *Zhongguo lishi gaiyao* 中國歷史概要 [Outline of Chinese history] (Beijing: Renmin chubanshe, 1956), 8. A further example of the levelheaded analysis of Confucius in the years before the anti-Lin campaign can be found in Fan Wenlan 范文瀾, *Zhongguo tongshi* 中國通史 [History of China], (1942; repr., Beijing: Renmin chubanshe, 1978), 1:159.

22. The campaign ran from 1973 to 1979. Both the political power struggle and the ideologically driven historical debate about Confucianism are set forth in Wu Tien-Wei, *Lin Biao and the Gang of Four* (Carbondale: Southern Illinois University Press, 1983). The politicized debates are illustrated in *Pi Lin pi Kong wenxuan* 批林批孔文選 [Collection of materials on "Criticize Lin Criticize Confucius"] (Beijing: Renmin jiaoyu chubanshe, 1974). An "official" account of the Lin Biao affair as it impacted Mao was published in 2003, see *Mao Zedong zhuan* 毛澤東傳 [Biography of Mao Zedong], edited by the Materials Research Section of the Central Committee of the Communist Party of China (Beijing: Zhong'an wenxian chubanshe, 2003), 2:1556–604.

23. Criticism of Confucius and Lin Biao are set forth in Wu Tien-Wei, *Lin Biao and the Gang of Four*, 27–29. The term "political swindler" was one of the standard criticisms used against those in disfavor during the Cultural Revolution. See *Wenhua dageming cidian* 文化大革命辭典 [Terminology of the Cultural Revolution] (Hong Kong: Xiang-

long chubanshe, 1993), 74. For the tribulations of Confucius's descendents during the campaign, see Jun Jing, *The Temple of Memories: History, Power and Morality in a Chinese Village* (Stanford, CA: Stanford University Press, 1996).

24. Many of the materials published by the Communist authorities in order to carry forward criticism of Confucius in fact explained his teaching with little class-based criticism. Examples are *Pi Lin pi Kong: ciyu jieshi xuanbian* 批林批孔：詞語解釋選編 [Criticize Lin Criticize Confucius: A collection of terminology explained] (n.p.: Guangxi renmin chubanshe, 1974) and *Ping fa ping ru: ciyu jianshi* 評法評儒：詞語簡史 [Evaluate the Legalists, evaluate the Confucians: Terminology simply explained] (Beijing: Shanwu yinshuguan, 1975). The scholar Paul Ropp has said that the pi Lin pi Kong campaign was so ludicrous that it helped to kill off faith in Mao at the end of the Cultural Revolution. There had been so many heroes turned into villains by 1974 that most people sensed the absurdity of official propaganda. The Maoist extremism of the Cultural Revolution left people without much of anything secure. In a way it made China ripe for a revival of interest in Confucianism. In a world where people were constantly rewarded for attacking each other, the only supports left were the bonds of family. Private communication to the author, August 1999.

25. Within Asia, newly emerging professionals were a subset of the growing middle class, which only began to clearly emerge in Asian societies in the 1980s. For a description of this phenomenon in Korea, Taiwan, Hong Kong, and Singapore, see Hsin-huang Michael Hsiao, ed., *Discovery of the Middle Classes in East Asia* (Taipei: Institute of Ethnography, Academia Sinica, 1993), esp. 6–18. Tokyo Disneyland, with its over-the-top wonders, became a favorite destination of young professionals. See Aviad Raz, *Riding the Black Ship: Japan and Tokyo Disneyland* (Cambridge, MA: Harvard University Asia Center, 1999), 179–80. New Internet technology has linked all young people in Asia to a degree that has never before happened in history. One Chinese scholar, still struggling with things he learned when a student, tries to link globalism and the World Wide Web with Marxism in Bao Zonghao 鮑宗豪, *Quanqiuhua yu dangdai shehui* 全球化與當代社會 [Globalism and contemporary society] (Shanghai: Shanghai sanlian shudian, 2002).

26. Lee's claim that he was describing pan-Asian values was bolstered by the strong support his ideas received from Dr. Mahathir bin Mohammed (b. 1925), the Islamic leader of Malaysia who became prime minister in 1981. The confrontational Mahathir regularly took up the cudgel against Western Values, which he considered inferior to the values of Asian peoples. He finally stepped down as prime minister in October 2003.

27. For a strident yet typical exposition of Lee's view on this subject see *Lee Kuan Yew on the Chinese Community in Singapore* (Singapore: Singapore Federation of Chinese Clan Associations and Singapore Chinese Chamber of Commerce and Industry, 1991). Lee's views contrasting American civilization with Confucian-based values appear in Freed Zakaria, "Culture is Destiny, A Conversation with Lee Kuan Yew," *Foreign Affairs* 13, no. 2 (Mar/Apr 1994):109–26.

28. Francis Fukuyama, "The Primacy of Culture," *Journal of Democracy* 6, no. 1

(1995): 7–14, relates Confucian subordination of the individual to the family to the soft authoritarianism of Lee Kuan Yew.

29. Daniel Bell et al., eds., *Towards Illiberal Democracy in Pacific Asia* (New York: St. Martin's, 1995), 24–26, comments on social stability and sacrifice for the sake of the family.

30. Randall Peerenboom discusses Confucian justification for limiting dissent in *Confucianism and Human Rights*, ed. Wm Theodore De Bary and Tu Weiming (New York: Columbia University Press, 1998); see esp. 236–37.

31. Proponents of Confucian morality as the key to business success in Asia were perhaps thinking of the "merchant-house Confucianism" described by Rozman. See Gilbert Rozman, ed., *Confucian Heritage and Its Modern Adaptation* (Princeton, NJ: Princeton University Press, 1991), 166. Some scholars claim that in Confucian thinking individual existence, or personhood, can only be conferred by the family or by society. See Henry Rosemont's discussion in *Human Rights and the World's Religions*, ed. Leroy Rouner (Notre Dame, IN: University of Notre Dame Press, 1988), esp. 177.

32. Japan's bubble economy of the 1980s burst, and it fell into a prolonged recession that lasted the entire decade of the 1990s and into the start of the new millennia. This economic crisis and Japan's refusal to dismantle trade barriers are addressed in Lonney Carlile and Mark Tilton, eds., *Is Japan Really Changing its Ways? Regulatory Reform and the Japanese Economy* (Washington, D.C.: Brookings Institution Press, 1998). Also see Ronald Suleski, "Japan after the Bubble Burst: Traditional Values Inhibit Quick Comeback," *Journal of the International Institute, University of Michigan* 6, no. 3 (Spring/Summer 1999).

33. This period of exponential economic growth is described in Mark Clifford, *Troubled Tiger: Businessmen, Bureaucrats, and Generals in South Korea* (Armonk, NY: M. E. Sharpe, 1994), see esp. 236–52. Clark's account of these years and of the growth of *chaebol* in the post–Korean War period concentrates on policy failures. Rapid economic expansion in Hong Kong, Singapore, South Korea, and Taiwan is discussed in Eun Mee Kim, ed., *The Four Asian Tigers: Economic Development and the Global Political Economy* (San Diego: Academic Press, 1998).

34. The rapidly improving standard of living in South Korea was made visible by conspicuous consumption. See Denise Potrzeba Lett, *In Pursuit of Status: The Making of South Korea's "New" Urban Middle Class* (Cambridge, MA: Harvard University Asia Center, 1998).

35. A description of the twelve leading *chaebol* in South Korea as of the early 1990s is found in Paku Ton-sun (Pak Tong-soon 朴東筍), *Kankoku zaibatsu no riidatachi* 韓国財閥のリーダーたち [Leaders of the Korean *chaebol*] (Tokyo: Toyo keizai shinposha, 1992). Comments on the *chaebol* after the Asian financial crisis of 1997 are in Gilbert Rozman, "Can Confucianism Survive in an Age of Universalism and Globalization?" *Pacific Affairs* 76, no. 1 (Spring 2002): 11–37.

36. In the euphoria of the times, American businesses complained that Asian markets were closed to them. Others countered that American businesses needed to exert more

effort to increase trade with Asian markets. An example of the latter is Erland Heginbotham, *Asia's Rising Economic Tide: Unique Opportunities for the U.S.* (Washington, D.C.: National Planning Association, 1993). After the Asian financial crisis of 1997, urgings such as these were no longer common.

37. The effects of easy money followed by the rapid withdrawal of funds by foreign banks are analyzed in Steven Radlet and Jeffery Sachs, *The Onset of the East Asian Financial Crisis*, Working Paper Series (Cambridge, MA: National Bureau of Economic Research, 1998). While Asian economies were in their growth phase, most of the large Asian banks lacked large-scale strategic plans and were not key decision makers in the massive transfers of funds and credits to conglomerates. In many ways the Asian banks resembled nothing more than pawnshops that lent out money to help capitalists finance themselves. This analogy, along with an acknowledgement of Confucian values' influence, is in Karl Fields, *Enterprise and the State in Korea and Taiwan* (Ithaca, NY: Cornell University Press, 1995).

38. For comments on how the flight of capital affected the economies of Indonesia, Thailand, South Korea, Malaysia, the Philippines, Singapore, Hong Kong, Taiwan, and Japan, see Ross McLeod and Ross Garnaut, *East Asia in Crisis: From Being a Miracle to Needing One?* (London: Routledge, 1998).

39. Some of the issues surrounding crony capitalism are outlined in Morris Goldstein, *The Asian Financial Crisis: Causes, Cures and Systemic Implications* (Washington, D.C.: Institute for International Economics, 1998), 12. The author points out that the region's biggest weakness was its failure to move beyond its informal and personal ways of doing business and its authoritarian manner of governing. Also see Jim Rohwer, *Asia Rising: Why America Will Prosper As Asia's Economies Boom* (New York: Touchstone, 1995). Rohwer predicted a slowdown in Asian economic growth around the year 2000, but not for the reasons that precipitated the Asian financial crisis in 1997 and 1998.

40. Banking studies that appeared immediately after the crash of the Asian financial markets emphasized its financial rather than its social aspects, but newly emerging middle classes all over Asia were seriously affected. Though concentrating on the banking aspects of the crisis, social problems are discussed in *East Asia: The Road to Recovery* (Washington, D.C.: The World Bank, 1998), 73–98. For some thoughtful comments on the confluence of Asian values and Western values, see Tu Weiming, "Implications of the Rise of 'Confucian' East Asia," *Daedalus* 129, no. 1 (Winter 2000): 195–218. For Confucius as a role model for present-day Chinese entrepreneurs, see Kam Louie, "Sage, Teacher, Businessman: Confucius as a Model Male," in *Chinese Political Culture (1989–1999)*, ed. Shiping Hua (Armonk, NY: M. E. Sharpe, 2001). A review of the state of the South Korean economy following its rebound from the Asian financial crisis is in *Korea's Economy 2002* (Washington, D.C.: Korea Economic Institute, 2002). Also see David Coe and Se-Jik Kim, eds., *Korean Crisis and Recovery* (Washington, D.C.: International Monetary Fund, 2002).

41. In 2004 the PRC government set up its first Confucius Institute (*kongzi xueyuan* 孔子學院), officially for the purpose of teaching Chinese language and culture abroad.

Officially it is under the China National Office for Teaching Chinese as a Foreign Language. Many institutes have now been established in Asian and European nations and in the United States, where they have been organized within universities. This seems to be an exercise in strategic branding for the PRC, an effort to encourage tourism and foreign investment, and to build a positive image abroad about China's role on the international stage.

Contributors

ROGER T. AMES is Professor of Philosophy at the University of Hawai'i at Manoa and editor of *Philosophy East and West*. His recent publications include translations of Chinese classics: *Sun-tzu: The Art of Warfare* (1993); *Sun Pin: The Art of Warfare* (1996) and *Yuan Dao: Tracing Dao to its Source* (1997; both with D. C. Lau); the *Analects of Confucius: A Philosophical Translation* (with H. Rosemont) (1998); *Focusing the Familiar: A Translation and Philosophical Interpretation of the Zhongyong* (2001) and *Daodejing: Making This Life Significant; A Philosophical Translation of the Daodejing* (with D. L. Hall; 2003). He has also authored many interpretative studies of Chinese philosophy and culture: *Thinking Through Confucius* (1987), *Anticipating China: Thinking Through the Narratives of Chinese and Western Culture* (1995), and *Thinking From the Han: Self, Truth, and Transcendence in Chinese and Western Culture* (1997; all with D. L. Hall). Recently he has undertaken several projects that entail the intersection of contemporary issues and cultural understanding. His *Democracy of the Dead: Dewey, Confucius, and the Hope for Democracy in China* (with D. L. Hall; 1999) is a product of this effort.

JAMES BEHUNIAK, JR., is Assistant Professor in the Department of Philosophy at Colby College in Maine. His graduate study was undertaken at the University of Hawai'i where he received his PhD in comparative philosophy. He has been a Visiting Research Scholar at Beijing University, and is the author of *Mencius on Becoming Human* (2005) as well as co-editor with Roger T. Ames of *Mengzi de Renxing Guandian* (*The Mencian Conception of Human Nature*). He has authored several articles on Chinese and comparative philosophy in such journals as *Philosophy East and West*, *Journal of Chinese Philosophy*, and *Asian Philosophy*.

MARY I. BOCKOVER earned her BA in human development from St. Mary's College of Maryland, where Henry Rosemont, Jr., was her teacher, and a PhD in philosophy from the University of California at Santa Barbara, where Herbert Fingarette was her teacher. She is currently Professor of Philosophy at Humboldt State University in California, and her scholarship is mainly in the area of comparative philosophy. Professor Bockover is editor of *Rules, Rituals, and Responsibility: Essays Dedicated to Herbert Fingarette* (Open Court, 1991). She has also authored articles and book chapters such as "The Internet East and West: A Moral Appraisal" in *Reason and Insight* (2002), "Ethics, Relativism, and the

Self" in *Culture and Self: Philosophical and Religious Perspectives* (1997), "The Concept of Emotion Revisited: A Critical Synthesis of Western and Confucian Thought" in *Emotions: East and West* (1995), and "The Internet in China: A Confucian Critique" in *Religion East and West*, Spring 2002. She is honored to now have her work included in this volume that also has articles by her teacher-mentors, Henry Rosemont, Jr., and Herbert Fingarette.

HERBERT FINGARETTE is Professor Emeritus of Philosophy at the University of California, Santa Barbara. Over his career, Professor Fingarette has authored many works in such fields as law, ethics, philosophical psychology, and psychiatry. In 1972 he wrote the landmark work titled *Confucius: The Secular as Sacred*. The book prompted many scholars and students to return to Confucius's seminal text, the *Analects*, for insight and inspiration. Henry Rosemont, Jr., said of the book that it "is one of the most significant philosophical books on the subject to be published in a long time." In the words of A. C. Graham, "*Confucius* has revitalized all our thinking about the sage [and] opens up new prospects of understanding and learning from Confucius." Herrlee G. Creel reported that "In the fifty years in which I have been studying Confucius, I cannot recall that I have found the work of another scholar more stimulating."

PHILIP J. IVANHOE received his PhD from Stanford University. His primary research interests are Chinese religious and ethical thought. Among his publications are: *The Sense of Antirationalism: Zhuangzi and Kierkegaard's Religious Thought*, co-author with Karen L. Carr (2000), *Ethics in the Confucian Tradition: The Thought of Mencius and Wang Yang-ming* (2002), *The Laozi or Daodejing* (2002), *Readings in Classical Chinese Philosophy*, co-edited with Bryan W. Van Norden (2006), and *Working Virtue: Virtue Ethics and Contemporary Moral Problems*, co-edited with Rebecca Walker (2007). Among his forthcoming publications is the anthology *Taking Confucian Ethics Seriously: Contemporary Theories and Applications*, co-edited with Yu Kam-por and Julia Tao (2008).

DAVID JONES is the director of the Center for the Development of Asian Studies in Atlanta and Professor of Philosophy in the University System of Georgia. He is the former president of the Southeast Regional of the Association of Asian Studies. His publications are mostly in the areas of Chinese and Greek philosophy. His current book projects include *The Fractal Self: Intimacy and Emergence in the Universe* (with John L. Culliney), which is born from two papers published in *Zygon: Journal of Religion and Science*. His other edited volumes are *Asian Texts — Asian Contexts: Encountering the Philosophies and Religions of Asia* (with Ellen Klein), *Buddha Nature and Animality* (2007), and *Feast of Logos* (with Jason Wirth and Michael Schwartz). He is the founding editor of *East-West Connections: Review of Asian Studies*. He received his PhD in comparative philosophy from the University of Hawai'i at Manoa and was the East-West Center's "Distinguished Alumnus" in 2004.

HUI-CHIEH LOY is Assistant Professor of Philosophy at the National University of Singapore. He received his PhD from the University of California, Berkeley (2006) with a dissertation studying the moral philosophy of the *Mozi* "Core Chapters." While his research centers on early Chinese thought, he has a continuing interest in ancient Greek, early modern, and contemporary political philosophy. He has published articles in the *International Philosophical Quarterly, Journal of Chinese Philosophy, Monumenta Serica, Philosophy East and West,* and *Oriens Extremus,* and co-edited a collection of essays entitled *Historical Perspectives on East Asian Science, Technology, and Medicine* (2002) with Alan K. L. Chan and Gregory K. Clancey.

AMY OLBERDING works on Chinese philosophy. She is Assistant Professor in the Department of Philosophy at the University of Oklahoma. She earned her PhD in philosophy from University of Hawai'i. Her research interests include philosophical approaches to human mortality, the ethics of the domestic sphere, and philosophical constructions of self and society, particularly as these appear in early Chinese philosophy. Her work has appeared in *Philosophy East and West, Ancient Philosophy, Philosophy and Literature, Dao,* and *International Philosophical Quarterly.* She has also directed a National Endowment for the Humanities grant project concerning East Asian traditions.

PEIMIN NI is Professor of Philosophy at Grand Valley State University in Michigan. He was born in China and his PhD is from the University of Connecticut. Ni's recent publications include *On Confucius, On Reid,* and a co-authored book *Wandering: Brush and Pen in Philosophical Reflection.* He is a former President of the Association of Chinese Philosophers in America, and the current editor-in-chief of the ACPA book series on Chinese and Comparative Philosophy.

JEFFREY L. RICHEY is Associate Professor of Religion in the Asian Studies Program at Berea College in Berea, Kentucky. He earned his PhD in the cultural and historical study of religions at the Graduate Theological Union through its cooperative program with the University of California, Berkeley. He is the editor of (as well as a contributor to) *Teaching Confucianism* (Oxford University Press, 2007), and has published a wide variety of articles on early Chinese thought. He serves as the Chinese philosophy area editor for the *Internet Encyclopedia of Philosophy* (http://www.iep.utm.edu/), and is the founder of the Bluegrass Ancient Studies Seminar (BASS), an annual colloquium dedicated to the comparative study of antiquity.

HENRY ROSEMONT, JR., was George B. and Willma Reeves Distinguished Professor of the Liberal Arts when he retired from St. Mary's College of Maryland in 2001. He also taught at Fudan University in Shanghai for four years beginning in 1982, and continues as Senior Consulting Professor there. A past president of the Society for Asian and Comparative Philosophy, he has lectured widely in the U.S. and in over twenty countries overseas. His publications include *The Analects of Confucius* (with Roger T. Ames), *A Chinese Mirror, Rationality and Religious Experience*, *Leibniz: Writings on China* (with D. J. Cook), and *Explorations in Early Chinese Cosmology*. He is currently Distinguished Visiting Professor of East Asian & Religious Studies at Brown University.

KWONG-LOI SHUN holds degrees from Oxford University, University of Hong Kong, University of London, and a PhD from Stanford University. Prior to taking his current position as Chair Professor of Philosophy at the Chinese University of Hong Kong, he held various positions including: Vice President and Professor of Philosophy and East Asian Studies at the University of Toronto, Dean of the Undergraduate Division in the College of Letters and Science and Professor of Philosophy at the University of California at Berkeley, and Visiting Professor at the National University of Singapore. In his work he focuses on contemporary ethics and on Chinese philosophy. He has published the books *Mencius and Early Chinese Thought* (1997) and *Confucian Ethics: A Comparative Study of Self, Autonomy, and Community*, co-edited with David B. Wong (2004). In addition, he has published numerous articles in leading journals and book chapters, especially on both early and late Confucian thought and on moral psychology.

EDWARD SLINGERLAND is Associate Professor of Asian Studies and Canada Research Chair in Chinese Thought and Embodied Cognition at the University of British Columbia. He received a PhD in Religious Studies from Stanford University. His research specialties and teaching interests include Warring States Chinese thought, cognitive linguistics and conceptual metaphor theory, evolutionary psychology, cognitive science and behavioral neuroscience, methodologies for comparative religion and philosophy, virtue ethics, and the classical Chinese language. His book *Effortless Action: Wu-wei as Conceptual Metaphor and Spiritual Ideal in Early China* (2003) won the American Academy of Religion's award for the Best First Book in the History of Religions. He has also published *Confucius: The Essential Analects* (2003). He is currently working on a book entitled *Embodying Culture: Taking the Humanities beyond Dualism*.

RONALD SULESKI received his PhD degree in modern Chinese history from the University of Michigan. He taught for several years at the University of Texas at Arlington. He moved to Japan in 1979 to take up a one-year Japan Foundation fellowship, which began his eighteen-year stay in Tokyo. During those years he worked as the managing director/president of the Asia offices of American and British publishers. He also served from 1987 to 1994 as president of the Asiatic Society of Japan. He returned to the United States in 1997, and after serving at the Harvard-Yenching Institute, is currently Assistant Director of the Fairbank Center for Chinese Studies at Harvard University. Among his publications is a book on the Japanese language, *Affective Expressions in Japanese* (1982), a translation from the Chinese, *The Red Spears* (1985), and *The Modernization of Manchuria: An Annotated Bibliography* (1994). He also published *Civil Government in Warlord China: Tradition, Modernization and Manchuria* (2002). His most recent book is *The Fairbank Center for East Asian Research at Harvard University: A Fifty Year History, 1955–2005* (2005).

Sor-hoon Tan holds degrees from Oxford University and the University of Hawai'i, and teaches philosophy at the National University of Singapore. She has published works on Pragmatism, Chinese philosophy and cross-cultural philosophy in the *Journal of Speculative Philosophy*, *International Philosophical Quarterly*, *Philosophy East and West*, and the *Journal of Chinese Philosophy*. She has also contributed major and minor entries to *The Encyclopedia of Confucianism*, ed. Xinzhong Yao. She is author of *Confucian Democracy: A Deweyan Reconstruction*.

Index